I enjoy watching TV and listening to radio while I work.
If the TV show is too interesting, my eyes end up glued
to the screen, and my work grinds to a halt. But if the radio
program piques my interest, I find myself unable to leave
my desk, which means the work goes swimmingly.
So, for a number of reasons, I love radio.

—Toyotarou, 2019

Toyotarou

Toyotarou created the manga adaptation for the *Dragon Ball Z*
anime's 2015 film, *Dragon Ball Z: Resurrection F*. He is also the
author of the spin-off series *Dragon Ball Heroes: Victory Mission*,
which debuted in *V-Jump* in Japan in November 2012.

Akira Toriyama

Renowned worldwide for his playful, innovative storytelling and
humorous, distinctive art style, Akira Toriyama burst onto the manga
scene in 1980 with the wildly popular *Dr. Slump*. His hit series *Dragon Ball*
(published in the U.S. as *Dragon Ball* and *Dragon Ball Z*) ran from 1984
to 1995 in Shueisha's *Weekly Shonen Jump* magazine. He is also known
for his design work on video games such as *Dragon Quest*, *Chrono Trigger*,
Tobal No. 1 and *Blue Dragon*. His recent manga works include *COWA!*, *Kajika*,
Sand Land, *Neko Majin*, *Jaco the Galactic Patrolman* and a children's book,
Toccio the Angel. He lives with his family in Japan.

DRAGON BALL SUPER 10

SHONEN JUMP Manga Edition

STORY BY **Akira Toriyama**
ART BY **Toyotarou**

TRANSLATION **Caleb Cook**
LETTERING **James Gaubatz**
TOUCH UP AND LETTERING **Brandon Bovia**
DESIGN **Joy Zhang**
EDITOR **Marlene First**

DRAGON BALL SUPER © 2015 BY BIRD STUDIO, Toyotarou
All rights reserved. First published in Japan in 2015 by SHUEISHA Inc., Tokyo.
English translation rights arranged by SHUEISHA Inc.

The stories, characters and incidents mentioned
in this publication are entirely fictional.

Printed in the U.S.A.

Published by VIZ Media, LLC
P.O. Box 77010
San Francisco, CA 94107

10 9 8 7 6 5 4 3 2 1
First printing, September 2020

viz.com

shonenjump.com

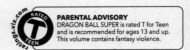

PARENTAL ADVISORY
DRAGON BALL SUPER is rated T for Teen
and is recommended for ages 13 and up.
This volume contains fantasy violence.

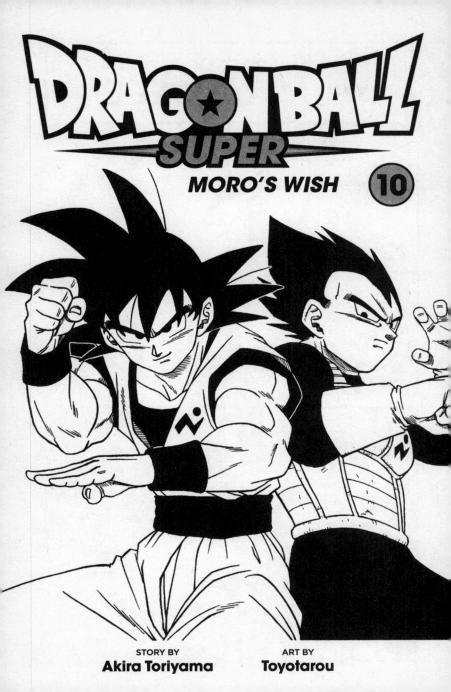

DRAGON BALL SUPER

MORO'S WISH   **10**

STORY BY
Akira Toriyama

ART BY
Toyotarou

CAST OF CHARACTERS

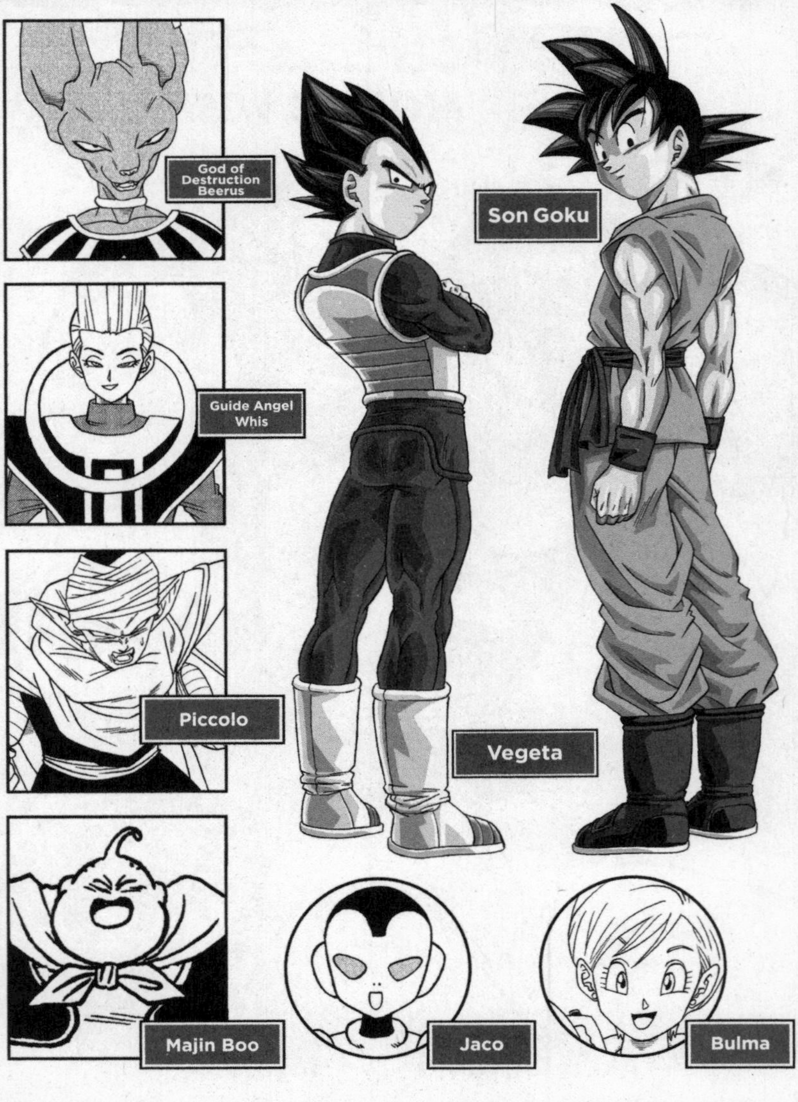
God of Destruction Beerus
Son Goku
Guide Angel Whis
Piccolo
Vegeta
Majin Boo
Jaco
Bulma

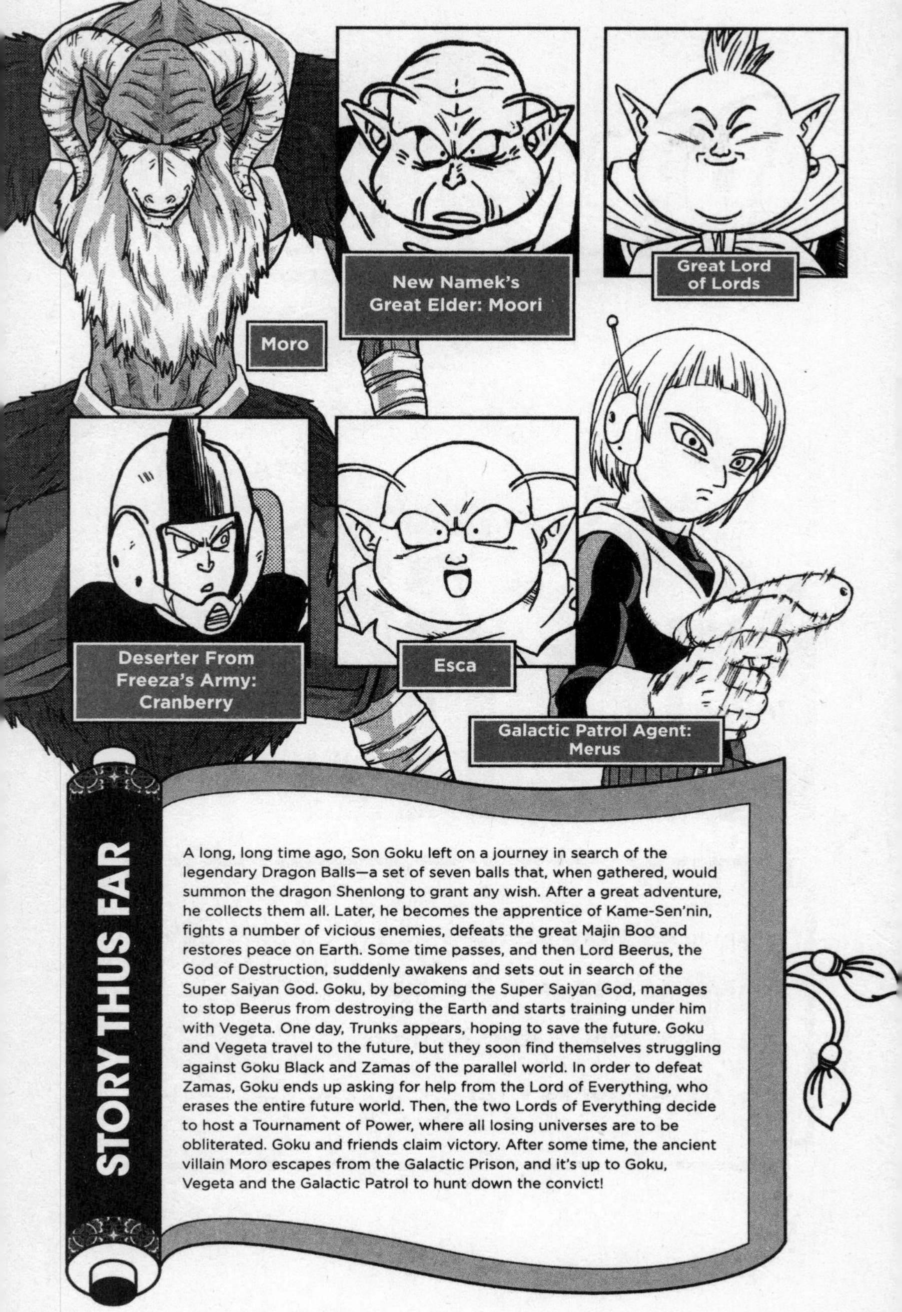
Great Lord of Lords
New Namek's Great Elder: Moori
Moro
Esca
Deserter From Freeza's Army: Cranberry
Galactic Patrol Agent: Merus

STORY THUS FAR

A long, long time ago, Son Goku left on a journey in search of the legendary Dragon Balls—a set of seven balls that, when gathered, would summon the dragon Shenlong to grant any wish. After a great adventure, he collects them all. Later, he becomes the apprentice of Kame-Sen'nin, fights a number of vicious enemies, defeats the great Majin Boo and restores peace on Earth. Some time passes, and then Lord Beerus, the God of Destruction, suddenly awakens and sets out in search of the Super Saiyan God. Goku, by becoming the Super Saiyan God, manages to stop Beerus from destroying the Earth and starts training under him with Vegeta. One day, Trunks appears, hoping to save the future. Goku and Vegeta travel to the future, but they soon find themselves struggling against Goku Black and Zamas of the parallel world. In order to defeat Zamas, Goku ends up asking for help from the Lord of Everything, who erases the entire future world. Then, the two Lords of Everything decide to host a Tournament of Power, where all losing universes are to be obliterated. Goku and friends claim victory. After some time, the ancient villain Moro escapes from the Galactic Prison, and it's up to Goku, Vegeta and the Galactic Patrol to hunt down the convict!

10
DRAGON BALL
SUPER

TABLE **OF** **CON-TENTS**

DRAGON BALL SUPER

CHAPTER 45: MORO'S MAGIC

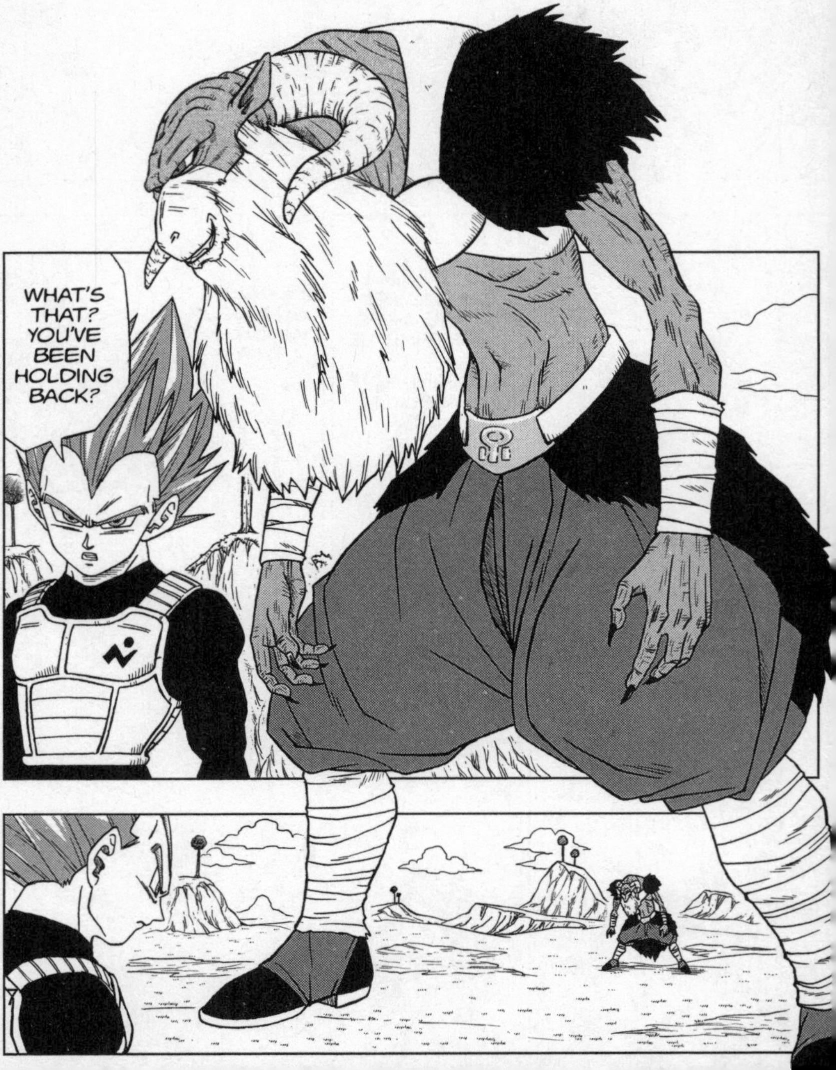
WHAT'S THAT? YOU'VE BEEN HOLDING BACK?

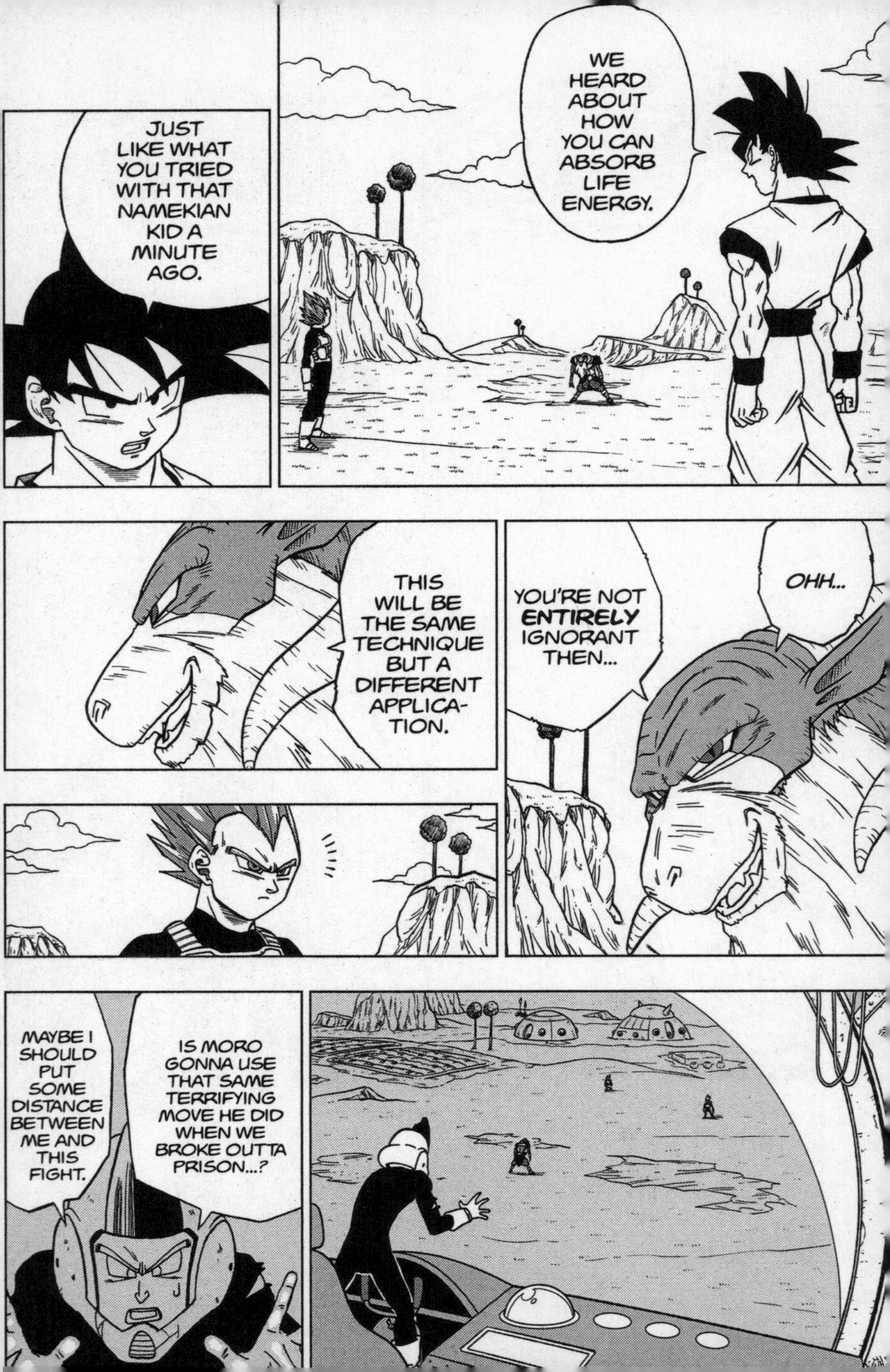
WE HEARD ABOUT HOW YOU CAN ABSORB LIFE ENERGY.
JUST LIKE WHAT YOU TRIED WITH THAT NAMEKIAN KID A MINUTE AGO.
OHH...
YOU'RE NOT **ENTIRELY** IGNORANT THEN...
THIS WILL BE THE SAME TECHNIQUE BUT A DIFFERENT APPLICATION.
IS MORO GONNA USE THAT SAME TERRIFYING MOVE HE DID WHEN WE BROKE OUTTA PRISON...?
MAYBE I SHOULD PUT SOME DISTANCE BETWEEN ME AND THIS FIGHT.

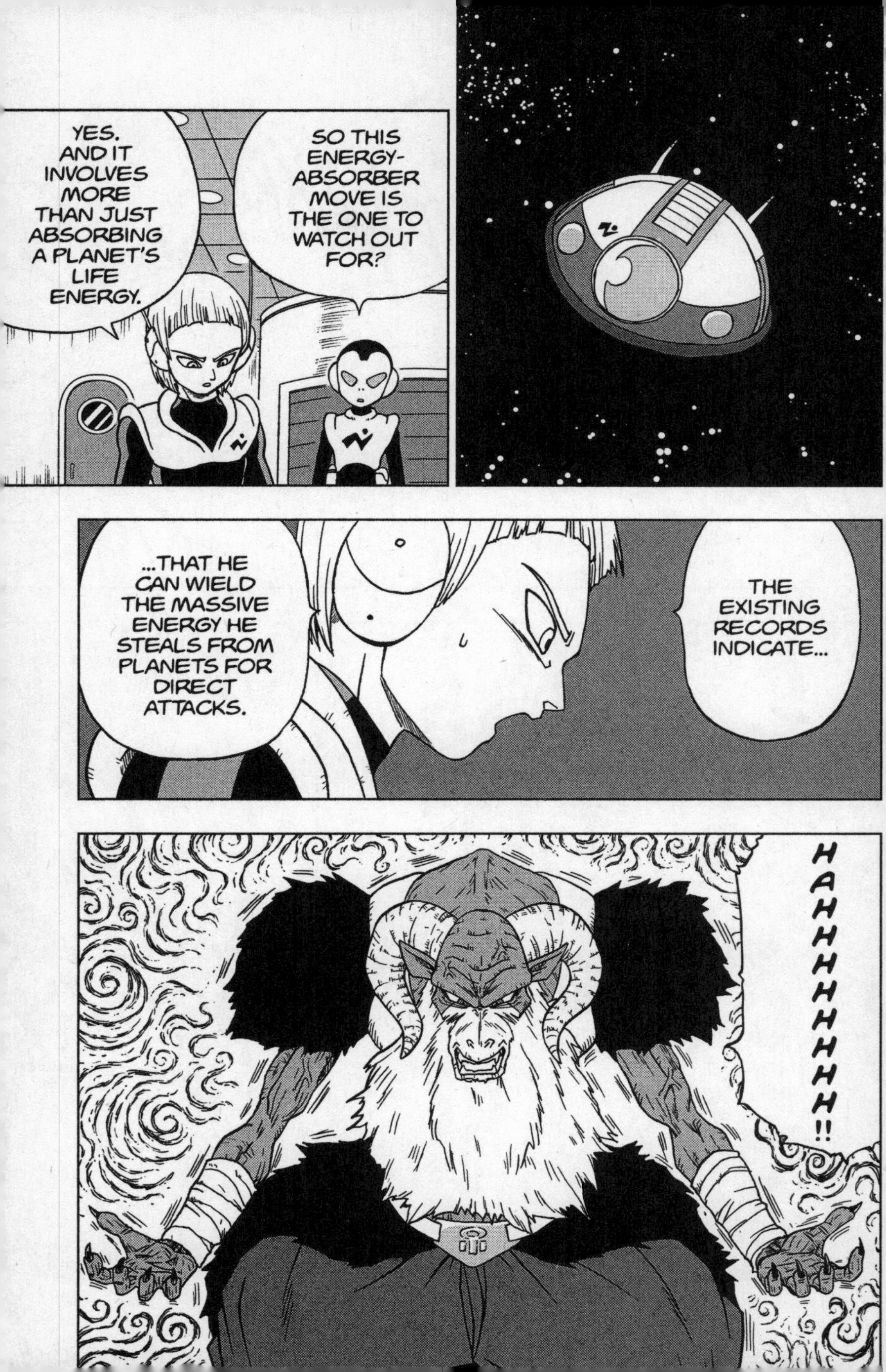
SO THIS ENERGY-ABSORBER MOVE IS THE ONE TO WATCH OUT FOR?
YES. AND IT INVOLVES MORE THAN JUST ABSORBING A PLANET'S LIFE ENERGY.
THE EXISTING RECORDS INDICATE...
...THAT HE CAN WIELD THE MASSIVE ENERGY HE STEALS FROM PLANETS FOR DIRECT ATTACKS.
HAHHHHHHHH!!

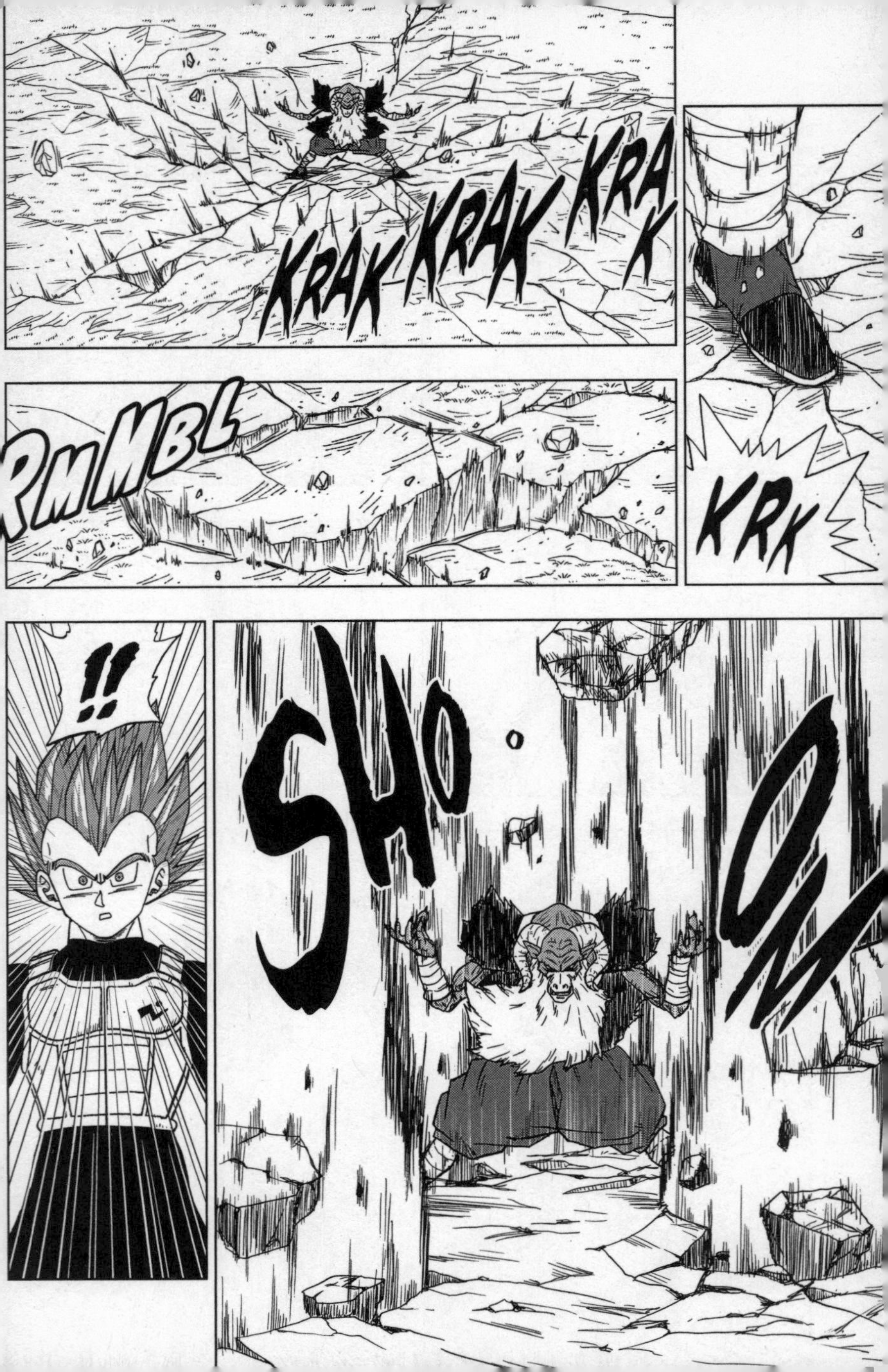
KRK
KRAK KRAK KRAK
RMMBL
SHOOM
!!

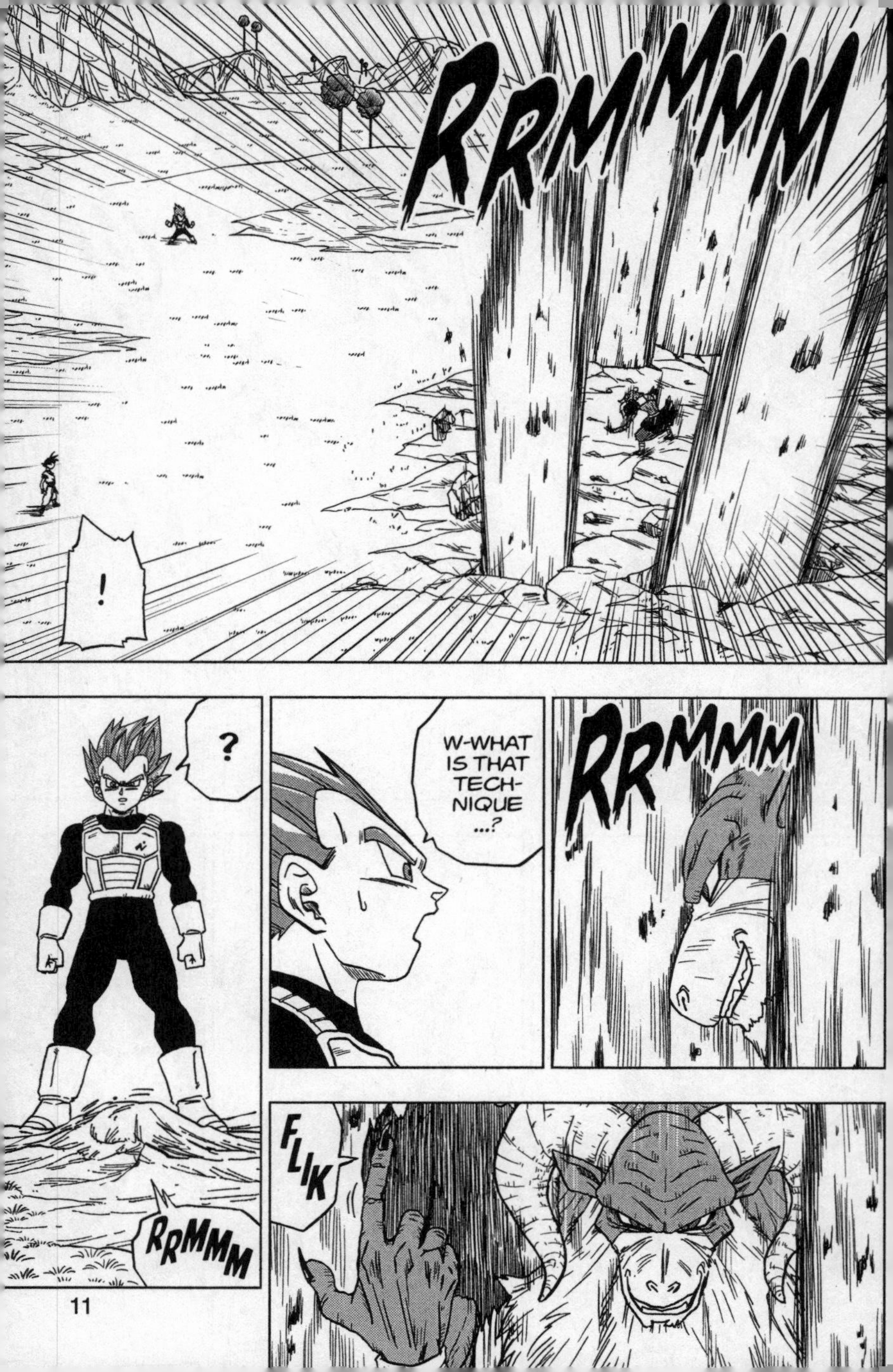
RRMMMM
!
RRMMM
W-WHAT IS THAT TECHNIQUE ...?
FLIK
?
RRMMM

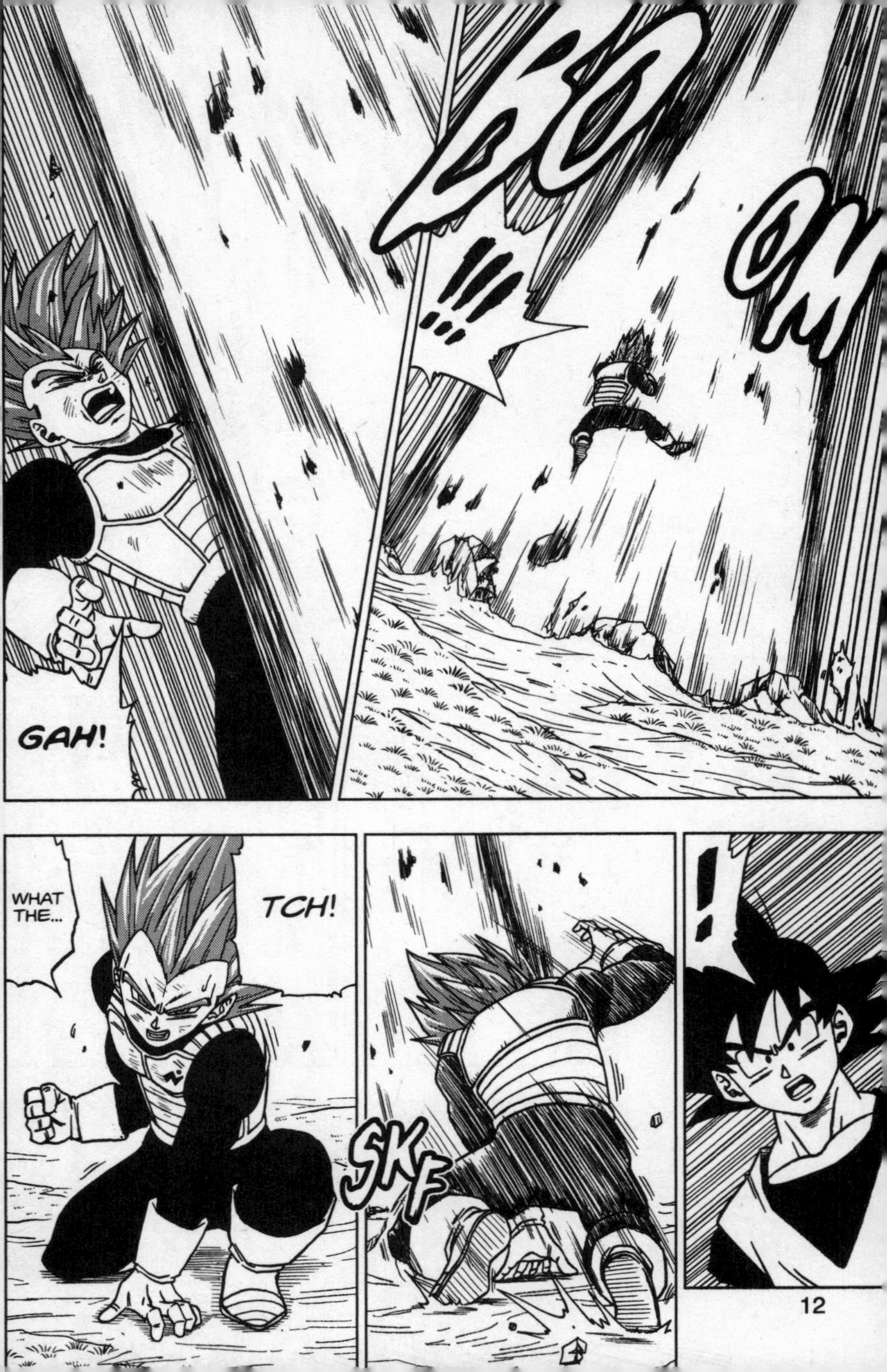
!!!
GAH!
!
SKF
WHAT THE...
TCH!

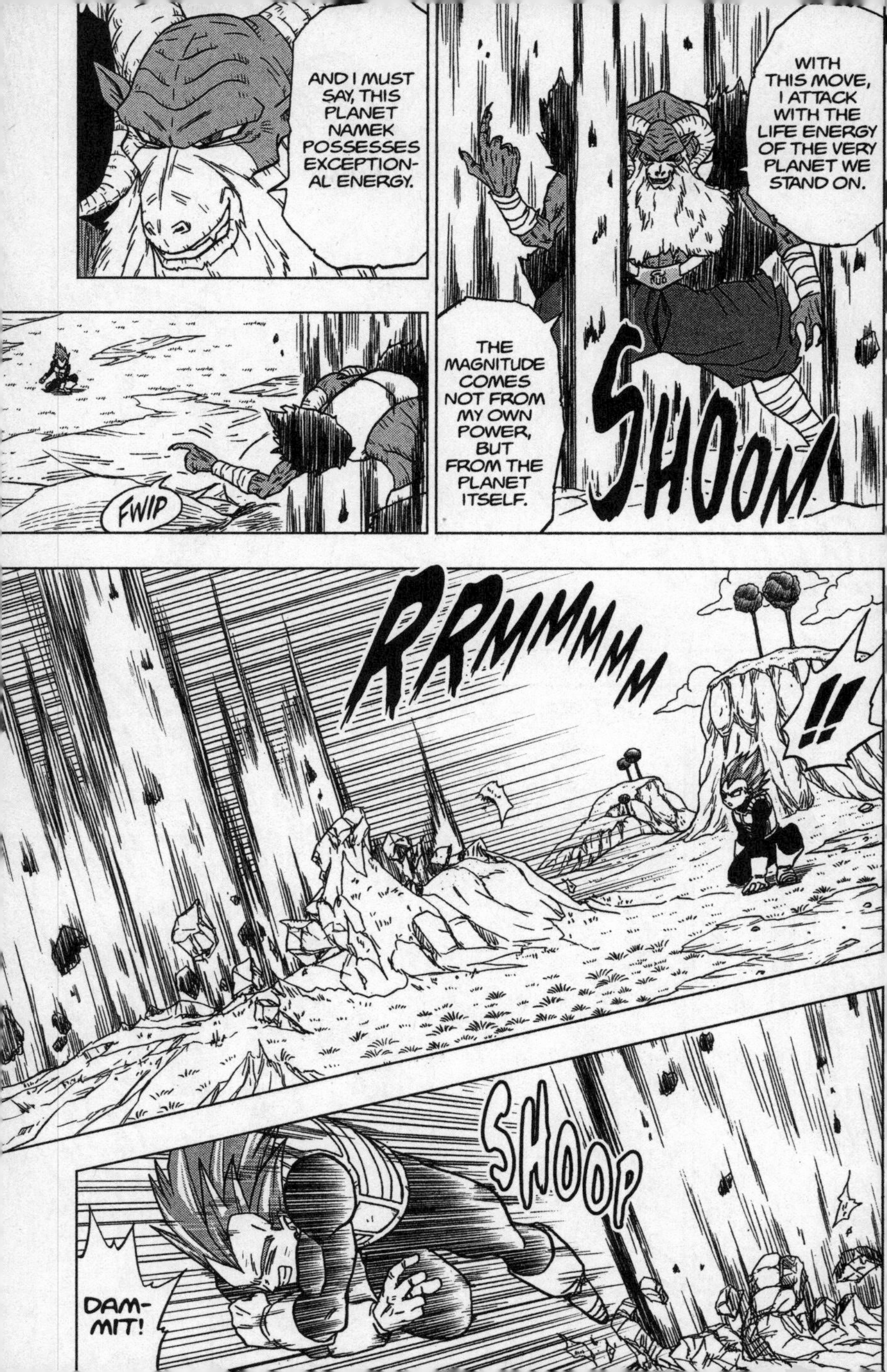
WITH THIS MOVE, I ATTACK WITH THE LIFE ENERGY OF THE VERY PLANET WE STAND ON.
THE MAGNITUDE COMES NOT FROM MY OWN POWER, BUT FROM THE PLANET ITSELF.
SHOOM
AND I MUST SAY, THIS PLANET NAMEK POSSESSES EXCEPTION-AL ENERGY.
FWIP
RRMMMMMM
!!
SHOOP
DAM-MIT!

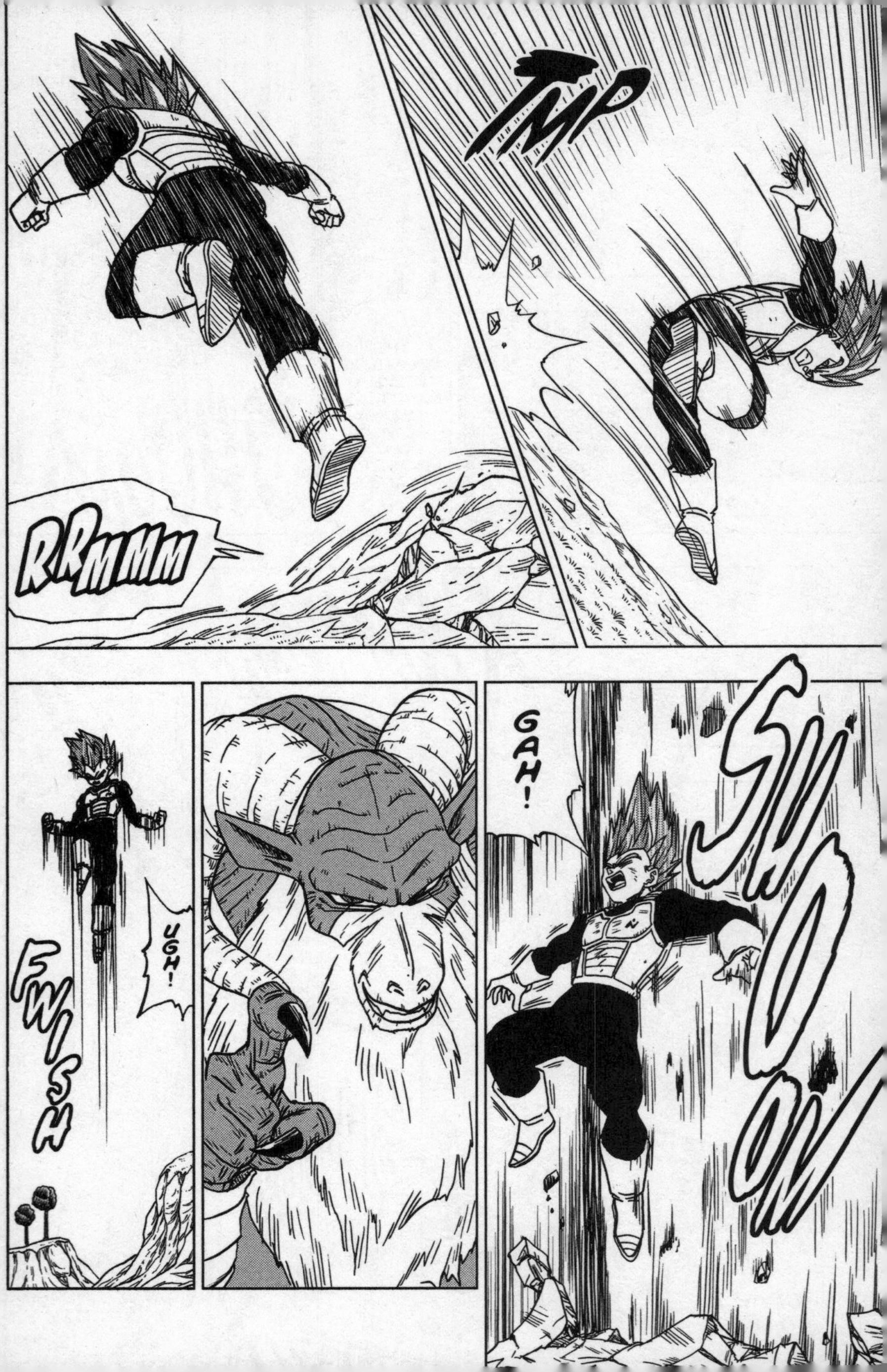
TMP
RRMMMM
GAH!
SHOOM
UGH!
FWISH

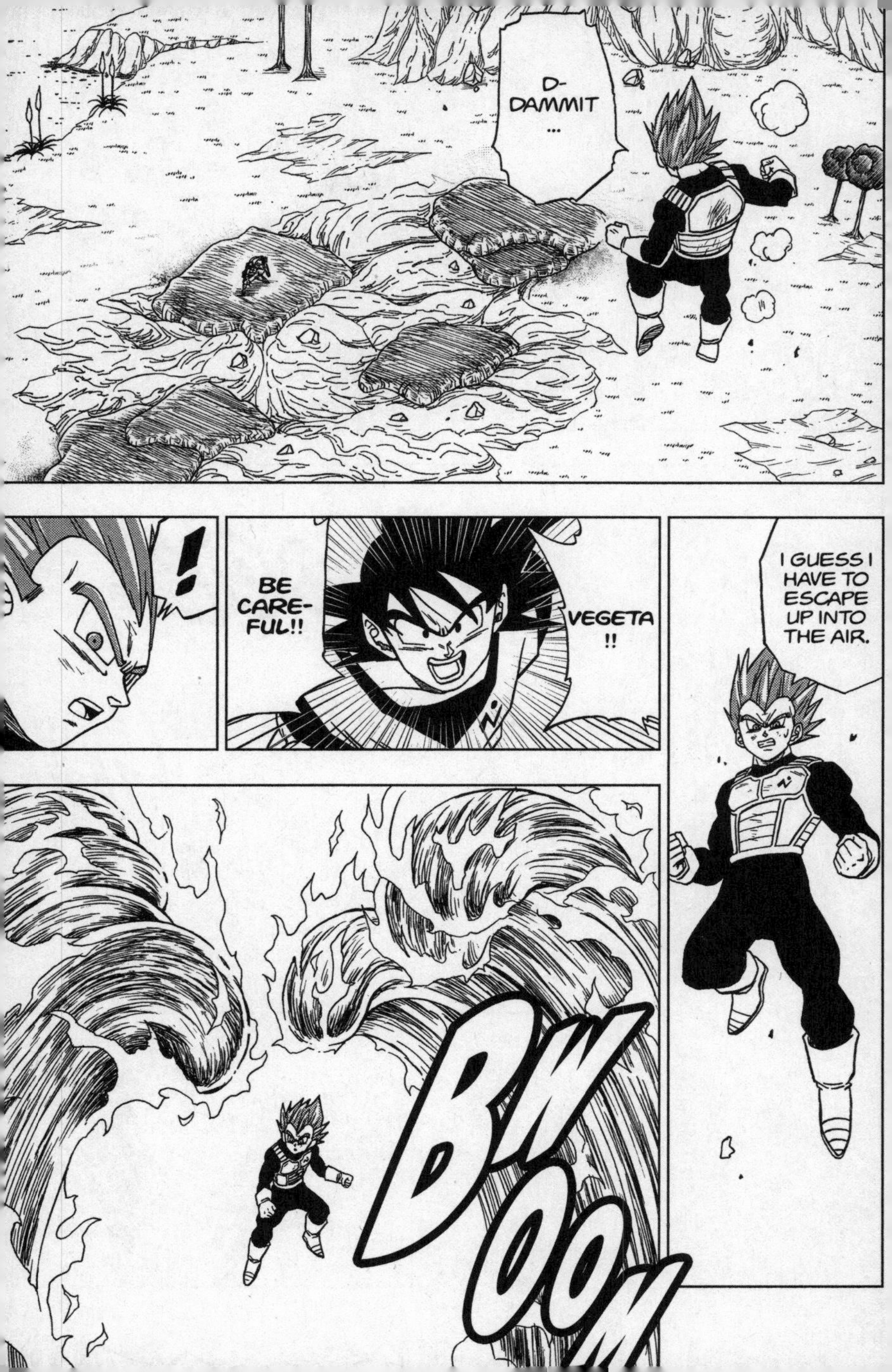
D-DAMMIT ...
I GUESS I HAVE TO ESCAPE UP INTO THE AIR.
VEGETA !!
BE CARE-FUL!!
!
BWOOOM

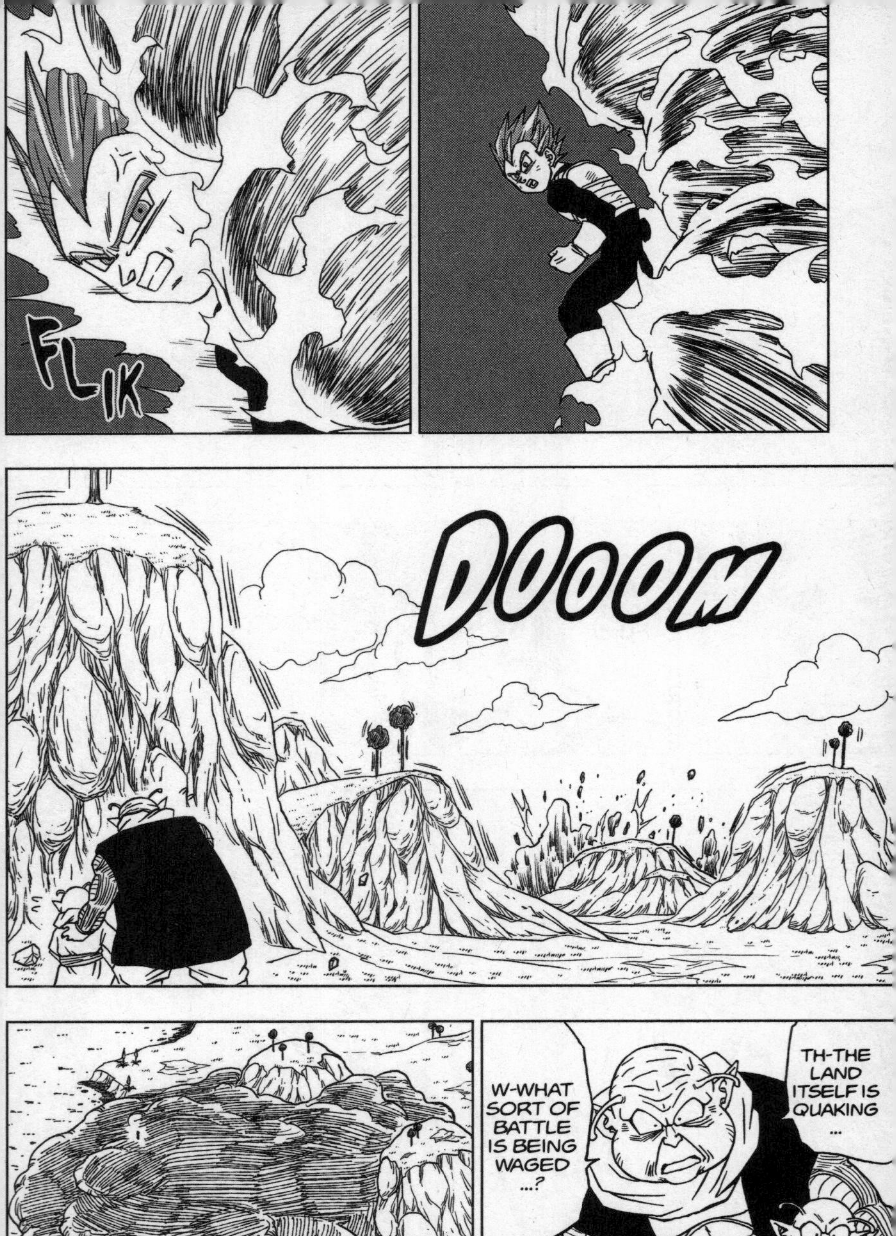
FLIK
DOOOM
TH-THE LAND ITSELF IS QUAKING ...
W-WHAT SORT OF BATTLE IS BEING WAGED ...?

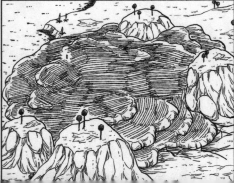

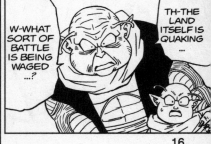

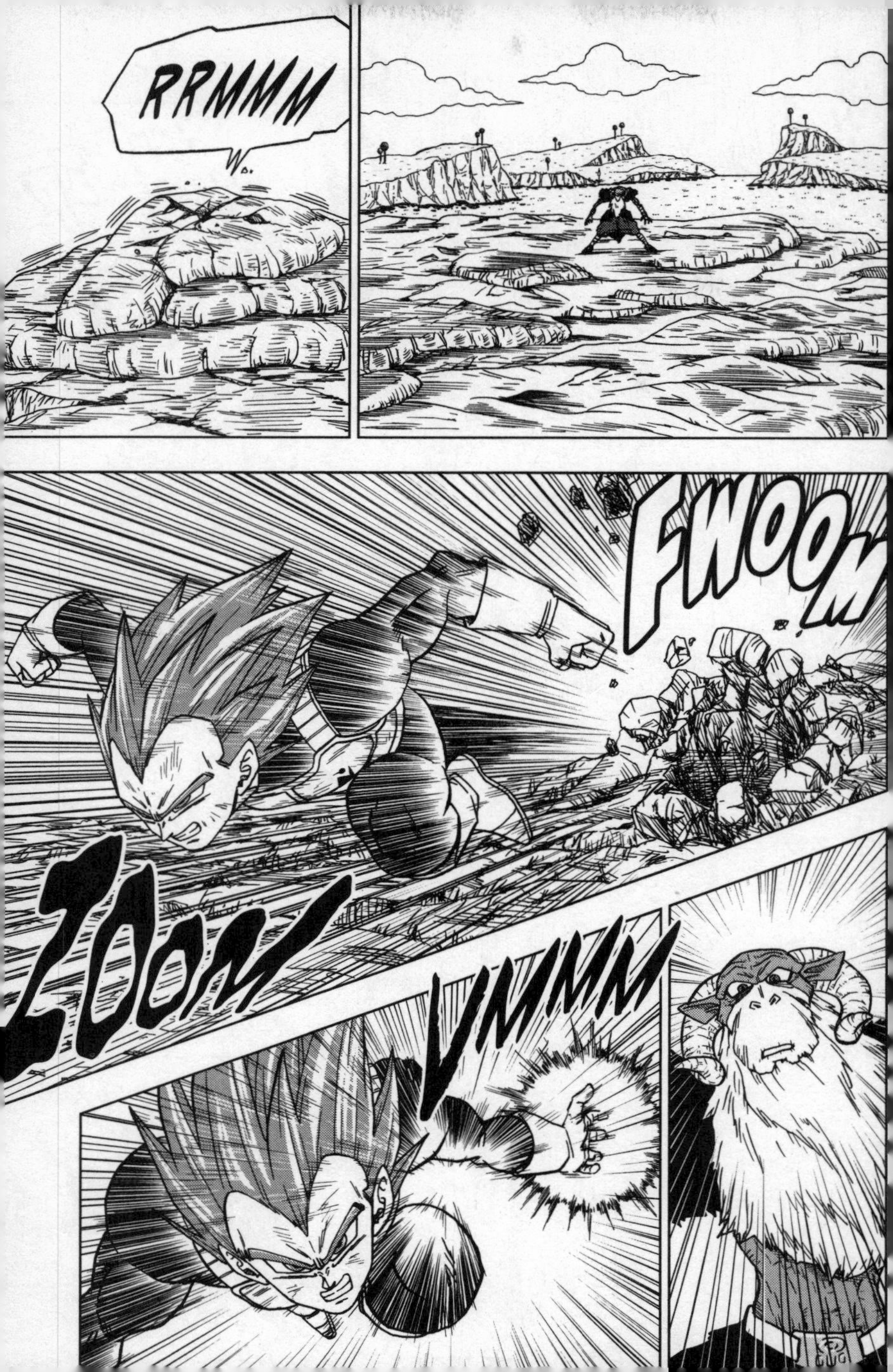
RRMMMM
FWOOM
ZOOM
VMMMM

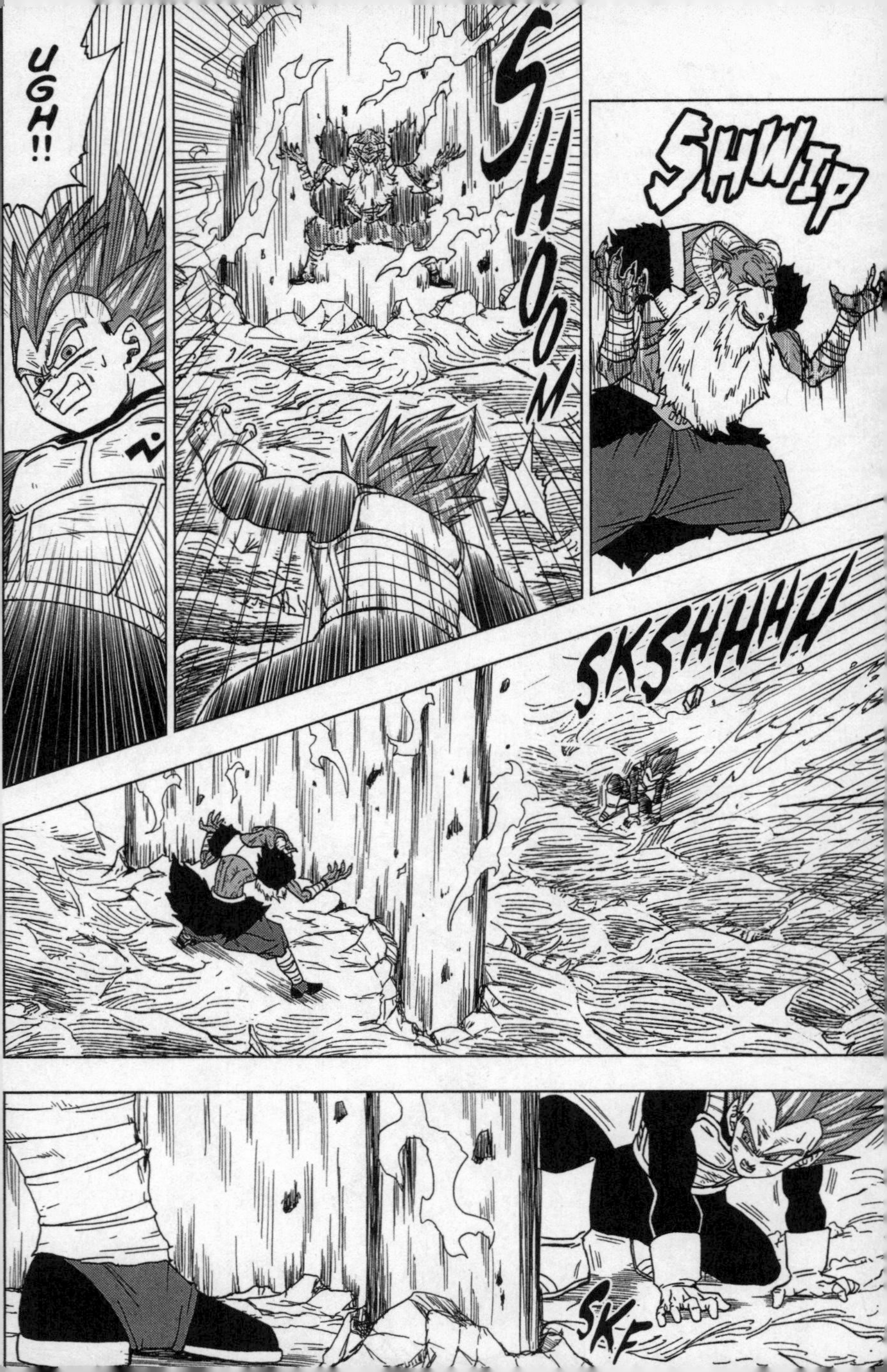
SHWIP
SHOOM
UGH!!
SKSHHHH
SKF

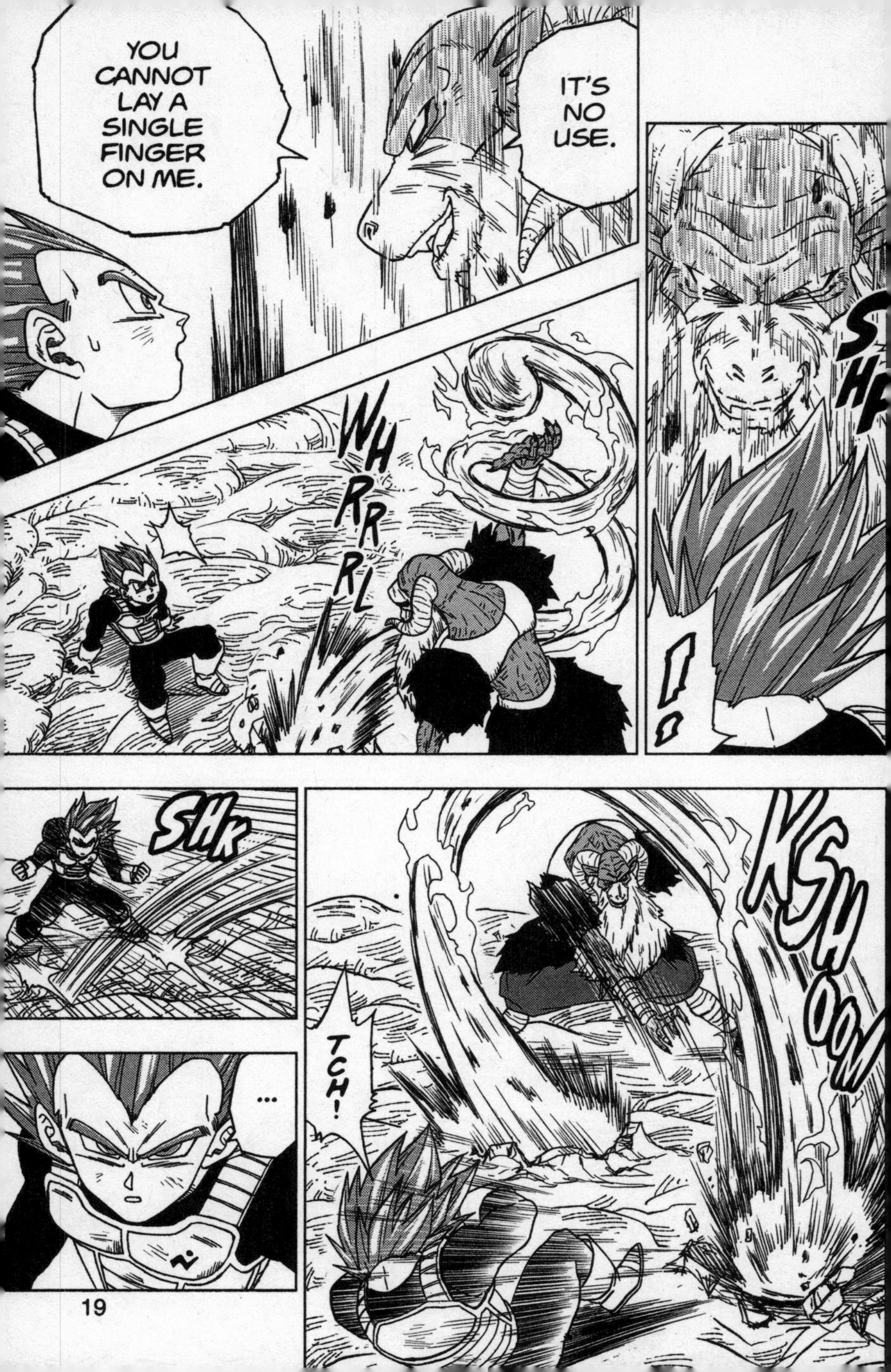

IT'S NO USE.
YOU CANNOT LAY A SINGLE FINGER ON ME.
WHRRRL
SHP
!!
KSHOOM
TCH!
SHK
...

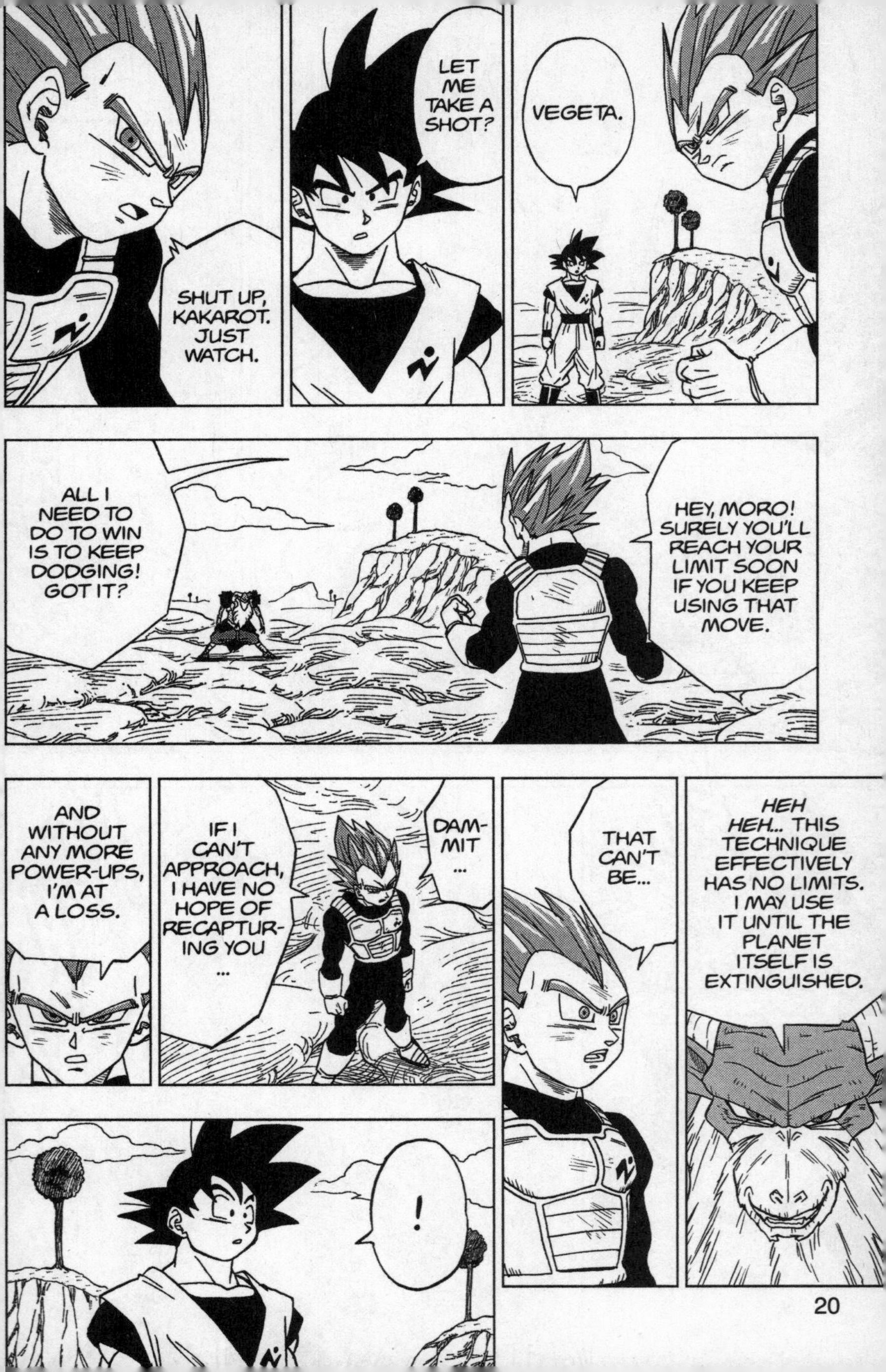
VEGETA.
LET ME TAKE A SHOT?
SHUT UP, KAKAROT. JUST WATCH.
HEY, MORO! SURELY YOU'LL REACH YOUR LIMIT SOON IF YOU KEEP USING THAT MOVE.
ALL I NEED TO DO TO WIN IS TO KEEP DODGING! GOT IT?
HEH HEH... THIS TECHNIQUE EFFECTIVELY HAS NO LIMITS. I MAY USE IT UNTIL THE PLANET ITSELF IS EXTINGUISHED.
THAT CAN'T BE...
DAMMIT...
IF I CAN'T APPROACH, I HAVE NO HOPE OF RECAPTURING YOU...
AND WITHOUT ANY MORE POWER-UPS, I'M AT A LOSS.
!

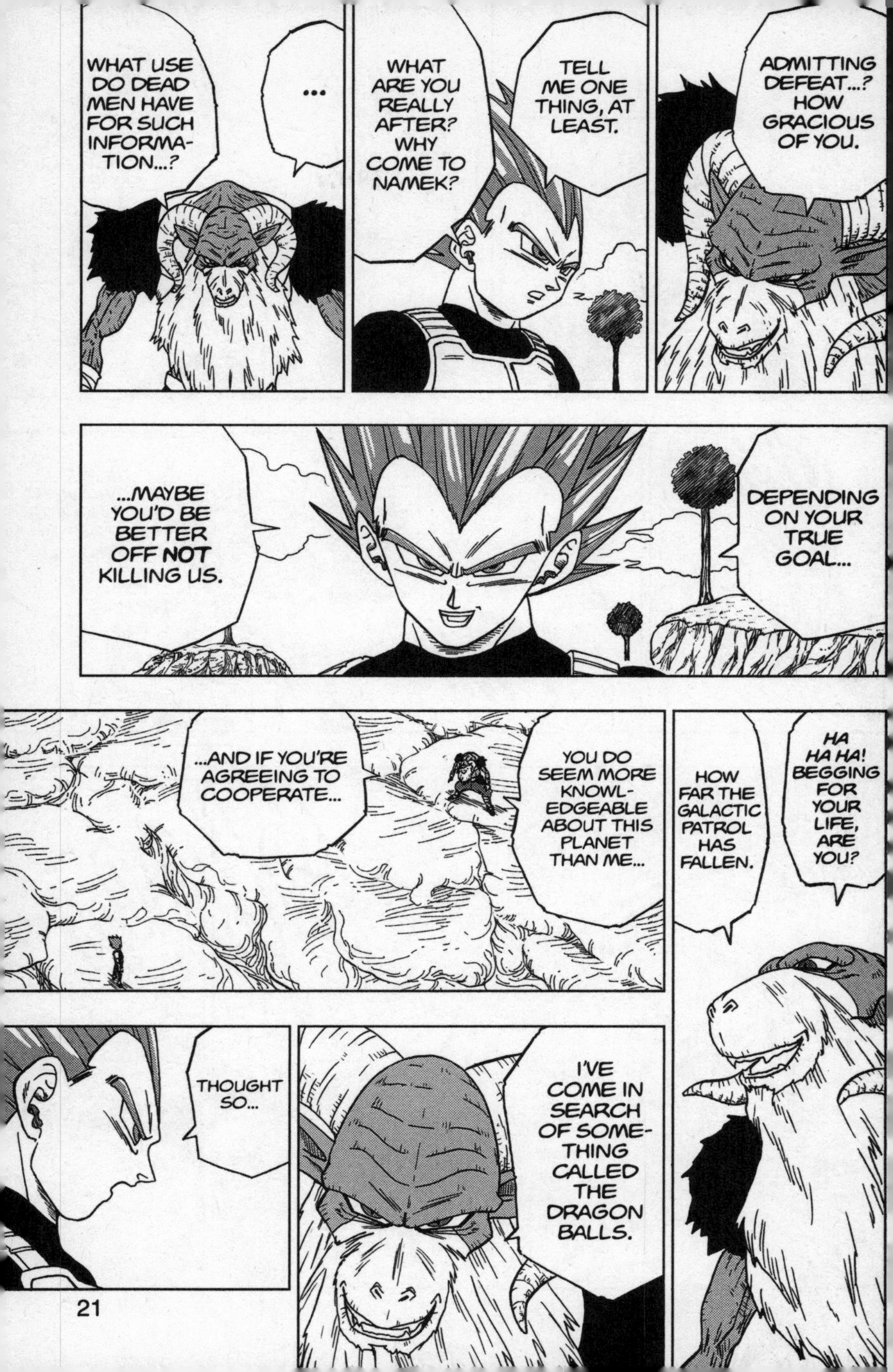
ADMITTING DEFEAT...? HOW GRACIOUS OF YOU.
TELL ME ONE THING, AT LEAST.
WHAT ARE YOU REALLY AFTER? WHY COME TO NAMEK?
...
WHAT USE DO DEAD MEN HAVE FOR SUCH INFORMATION...?
DEPENDING ON YOUR TRUE GOAL...
...MAYBE YOU'D BE BETTER OFF **NOT** KILLING US.
HA HA HA! BEGGING FOR YOUR LIFE, ARE YOU?
HOW FAR THE GALACTIC PATROL HAS FALLEN.
YOU DO SEEM MORE KNOWLEDGEABLE ABOUT THIS PLANET THAN ME...
...AND IF YOU'RE AGREEING TO COOPERATE...
I'VE COME IN SEARCH OF SOMETHING CALLED THE DRAGON BALLS.
THOUGHT SO...

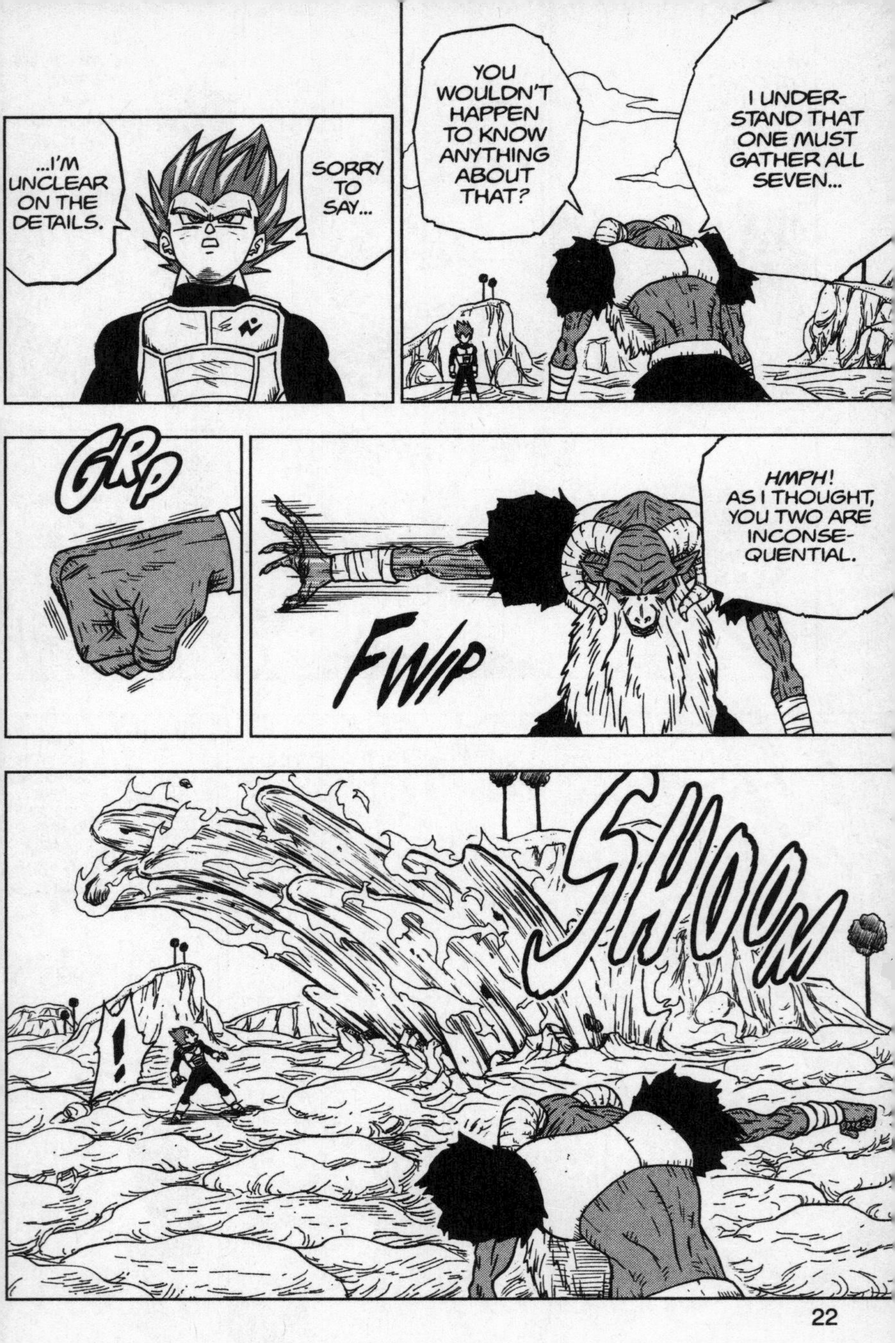
I UNDERSTAND THAT ONE MUST GATHER ALL SEVEN...
YOU WOULDN'T HAPPEN TO KNOW ANYTHING ABOUT THAT?
SORRY TO SAY...
...I'M UNCLEAR ON THE DETAILS.
HMPH! AS I THOUGHT, YOU TWO ARE INCONSEQUENTIAL.
FWIP
GRP
SHOOM
!

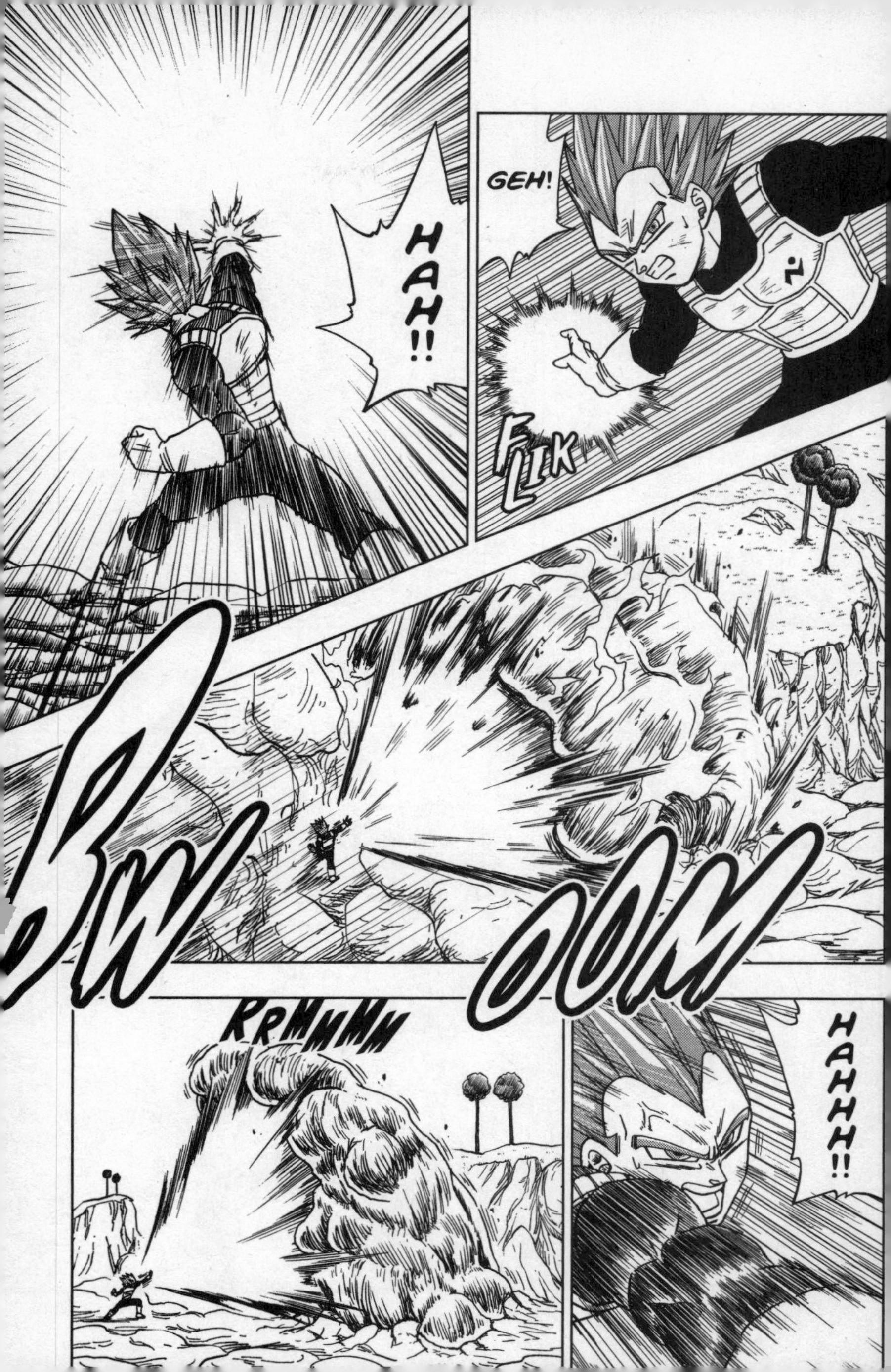
GEH!
FLIK
HAH!!
BWOOM
HAHHH!!
RRMMMMM

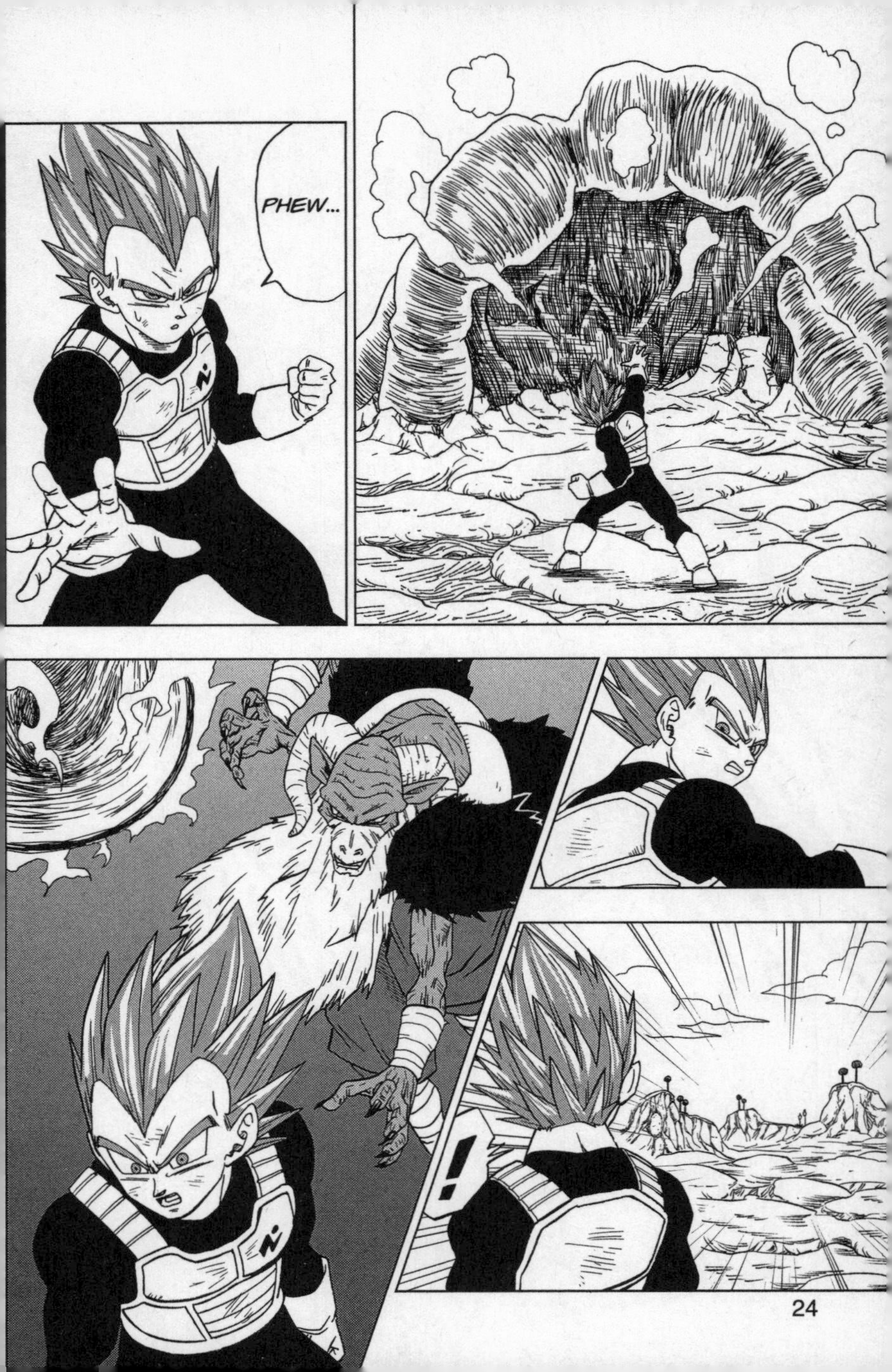
PHEW...
!

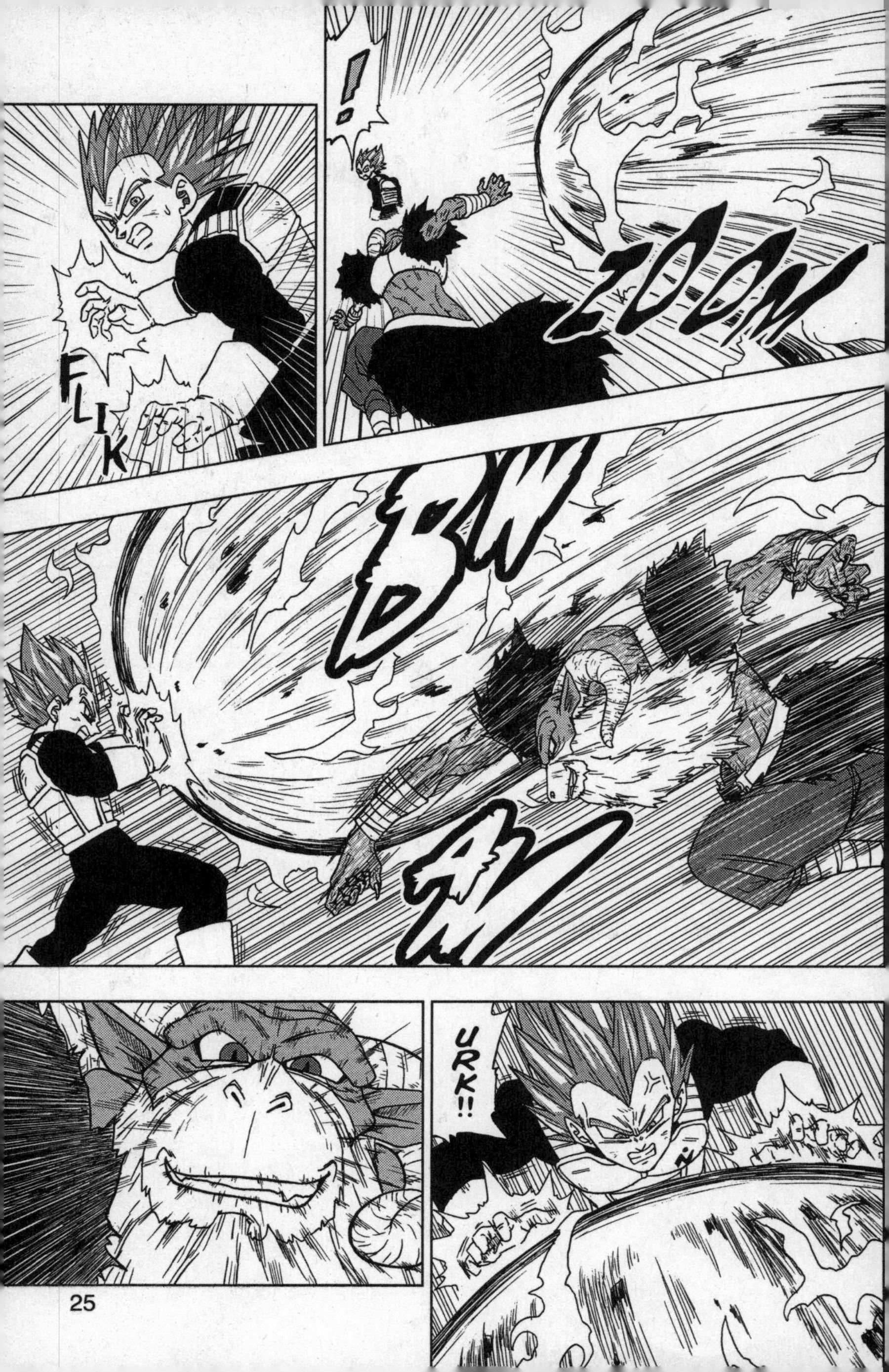
!
ZOOM
FLIK
BWAM
URK!!

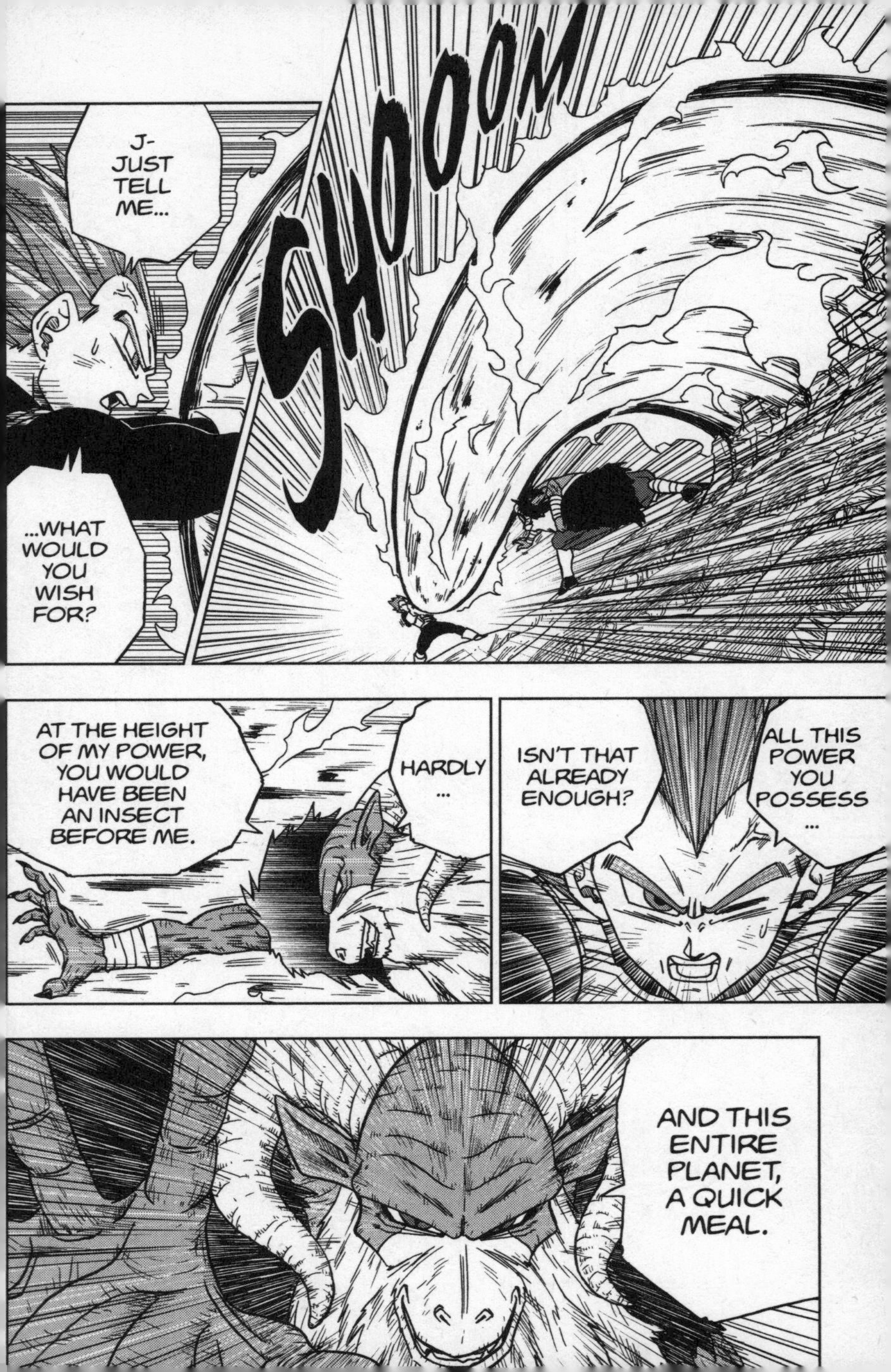
SHOOOM
J- JUST TELL ME...
...WHAT WOULD YOU WISH FOR?
ALL THIS POWER YOU POSSESS ...
ISN'T THAT ALREADY ENOUGH?
HARDLY ...
AT THE HEIGHT OF MY POWER, YOU WOULD HAVE BEEN AN INSECT BEFORE ME.
AND THIS ENTIRE PLANET, A QUICK MEAL.

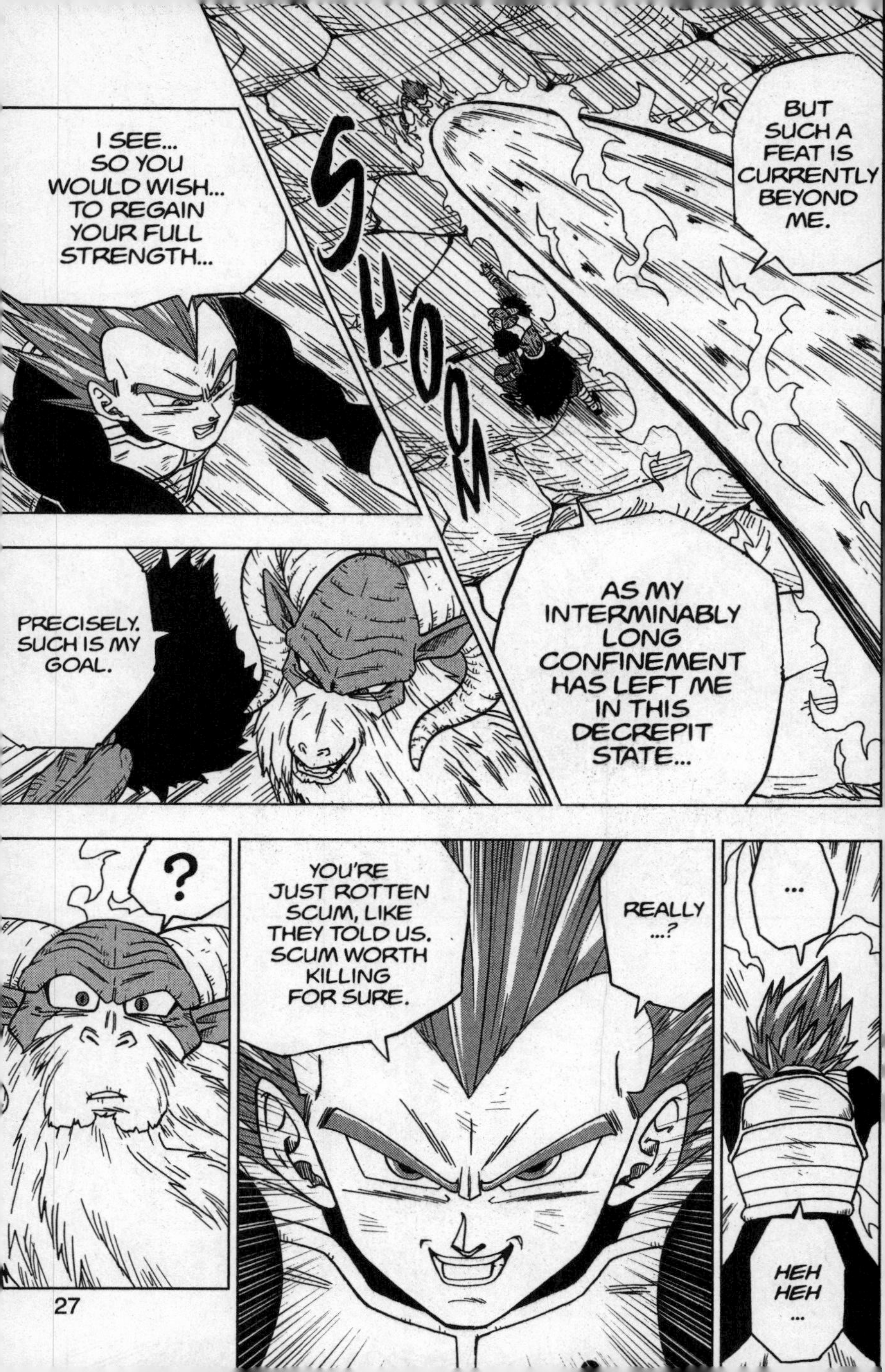
BUT SUCH A FEAT IS CURRENTLY BEYOND ME.
SHOOM
AS MY INTERMINABLY LONG CONFINEMENT HAS LEFT ME IN THIS DECREPIT STATE...
I SEE... SO YOU WOULD WISH... TO REGAIN YOUR FULL STRENGTH...
PRECISELY. SUCH IS MY GOAL.
...
HEH HEH ...
REALLY ...?
YOU'RE JUST ROTTEN SCUM, LIKE THEY TOLD US. SCUM WORTH KILLING FOR SURE.
?

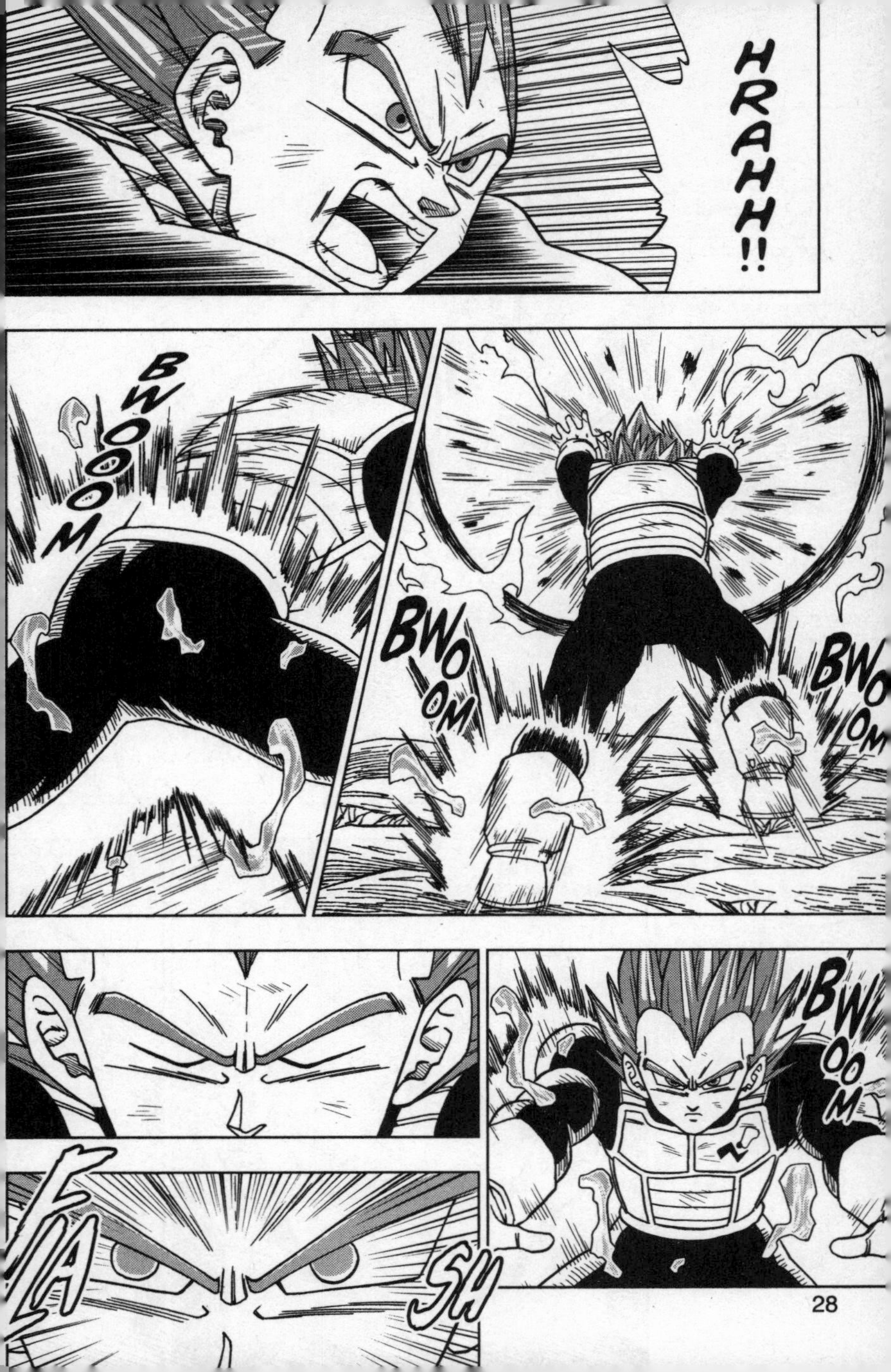
HRAHH!!
BWOOM
BWOOM
BWOOOOM
BWOOOM
FLASH

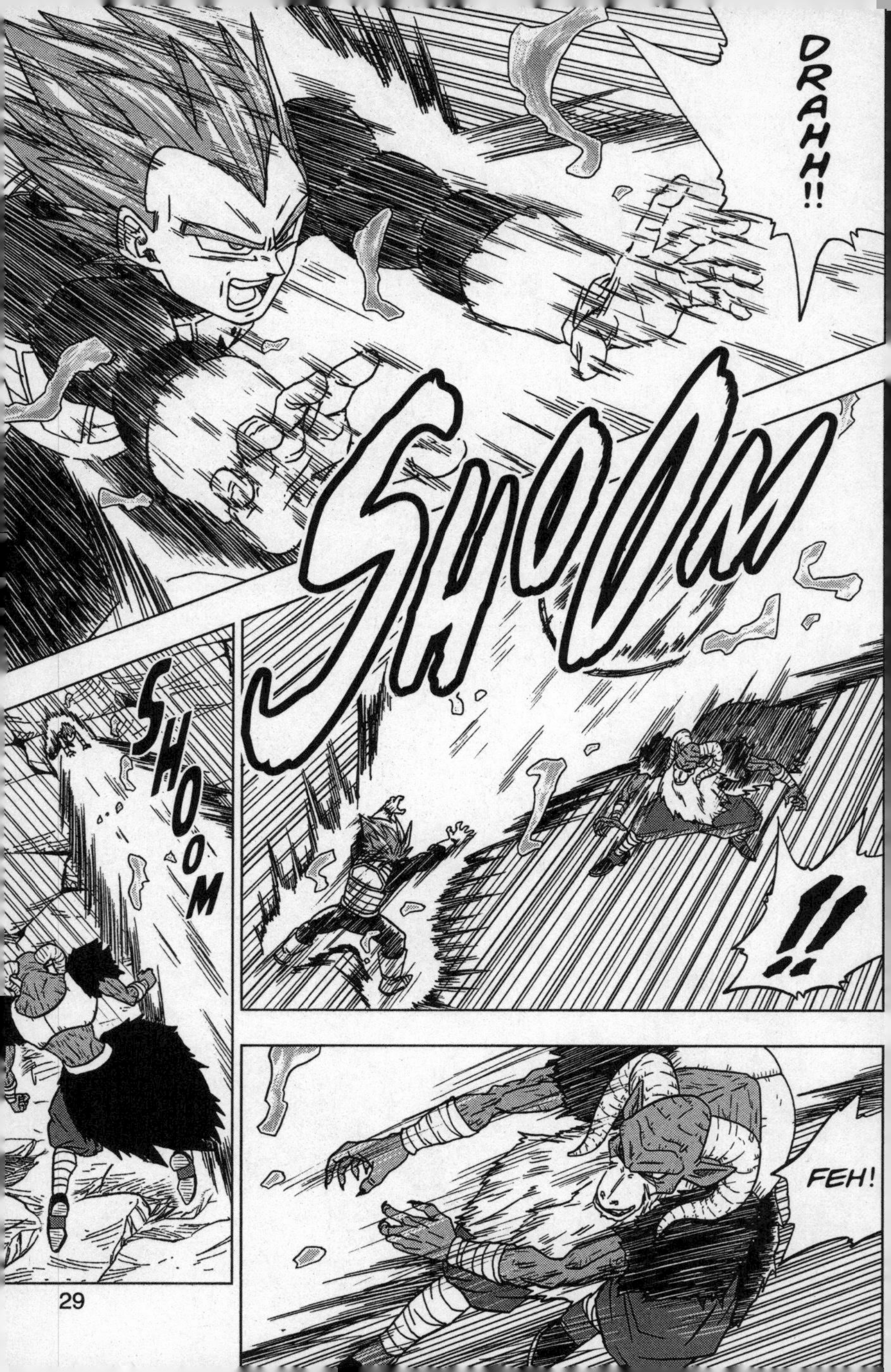
DRAHH!!
!!
SHOOM
FEH!

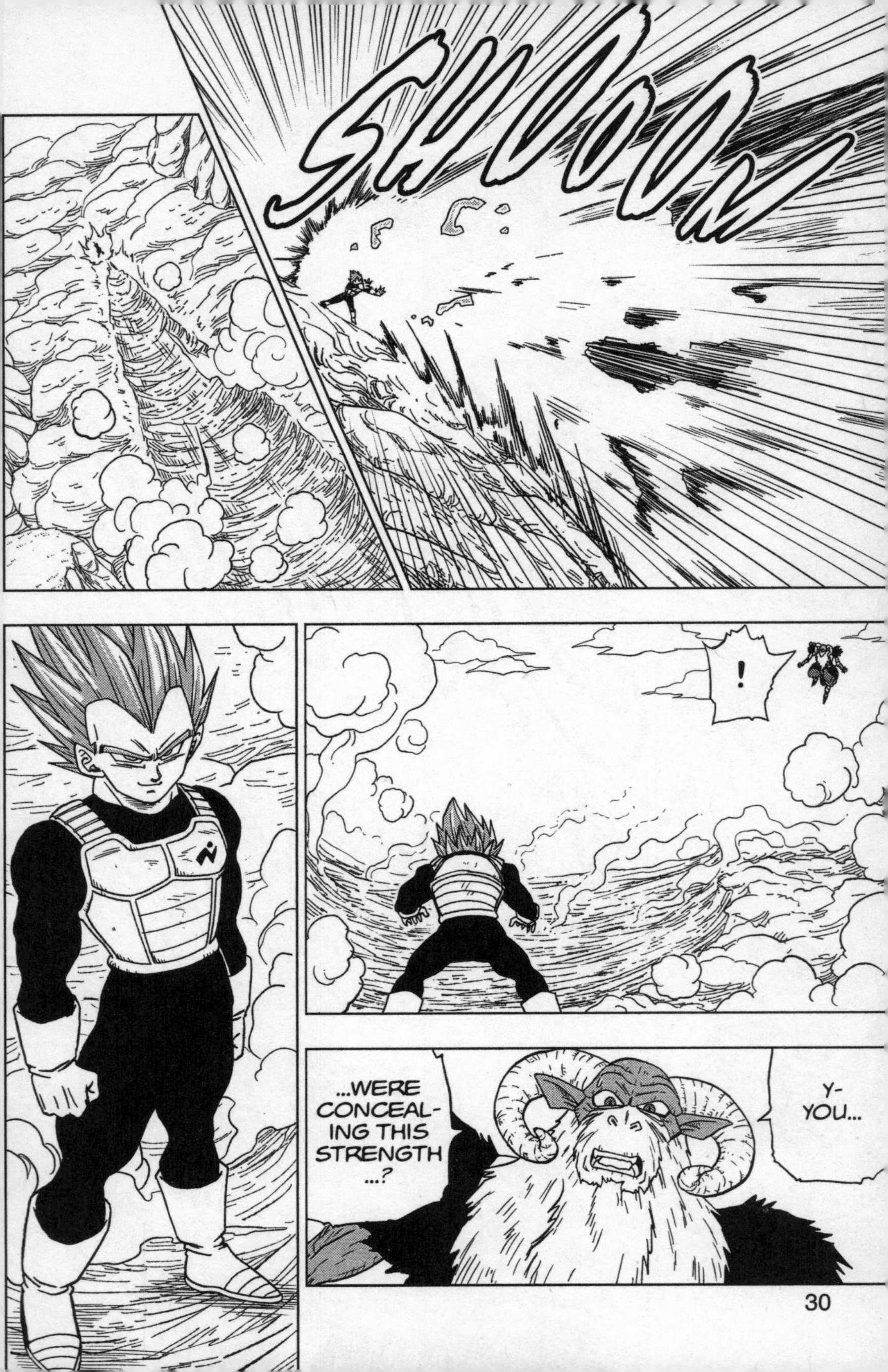
SHUOOOM
!
Y-YOU...
...WERE CONCEALING THIS STRENGTH...?

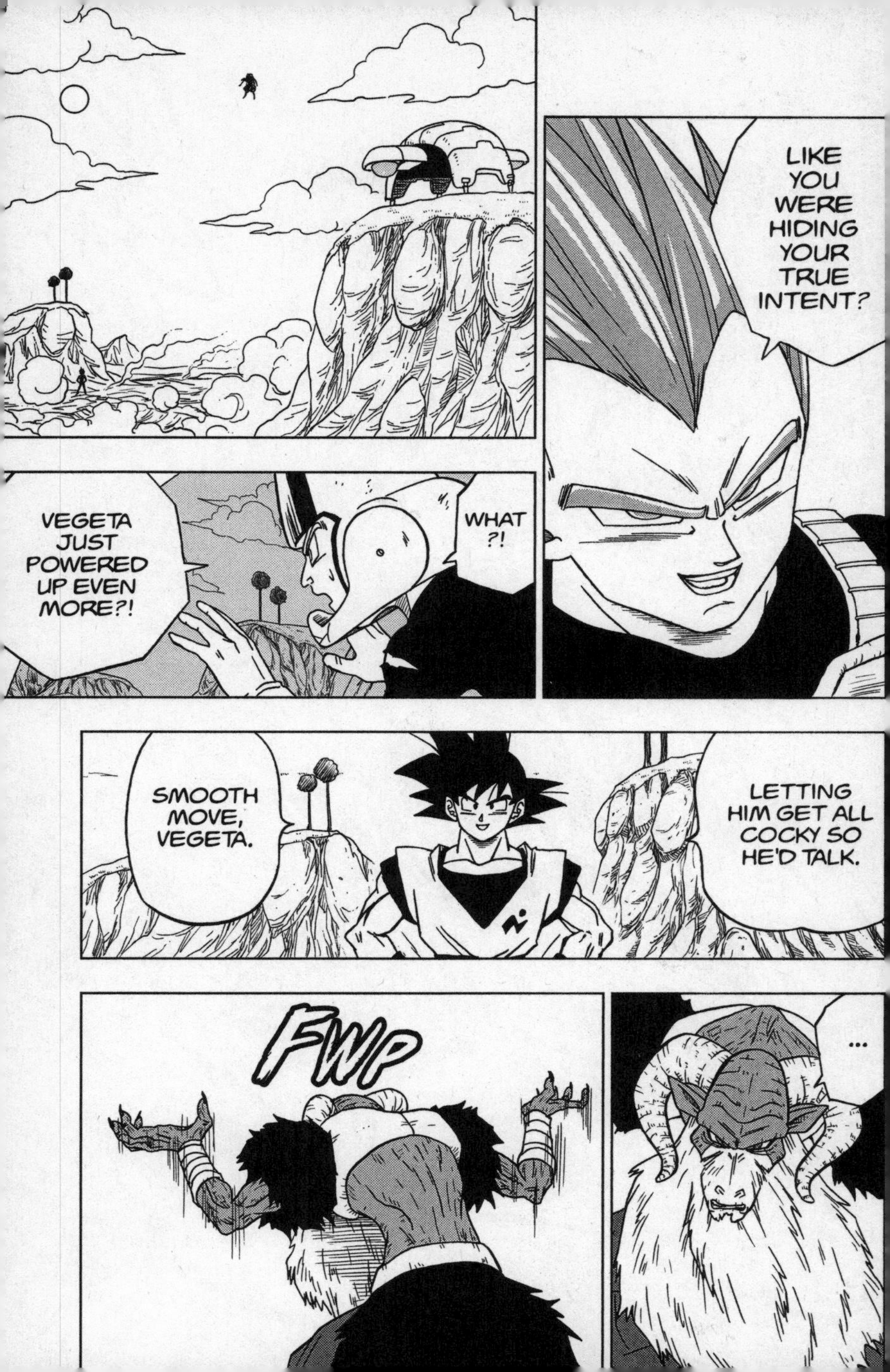
LIKE YOU WERE HIDING YOUR TRUE INTENT?
WHAT ?!
VEGETA JUST POWERED UP EVEN MORE?!
SMOOTH MOVE, VEGETA.
LETTING HIM GET ALL COCKY SO HE'D TALK.
...
FWP

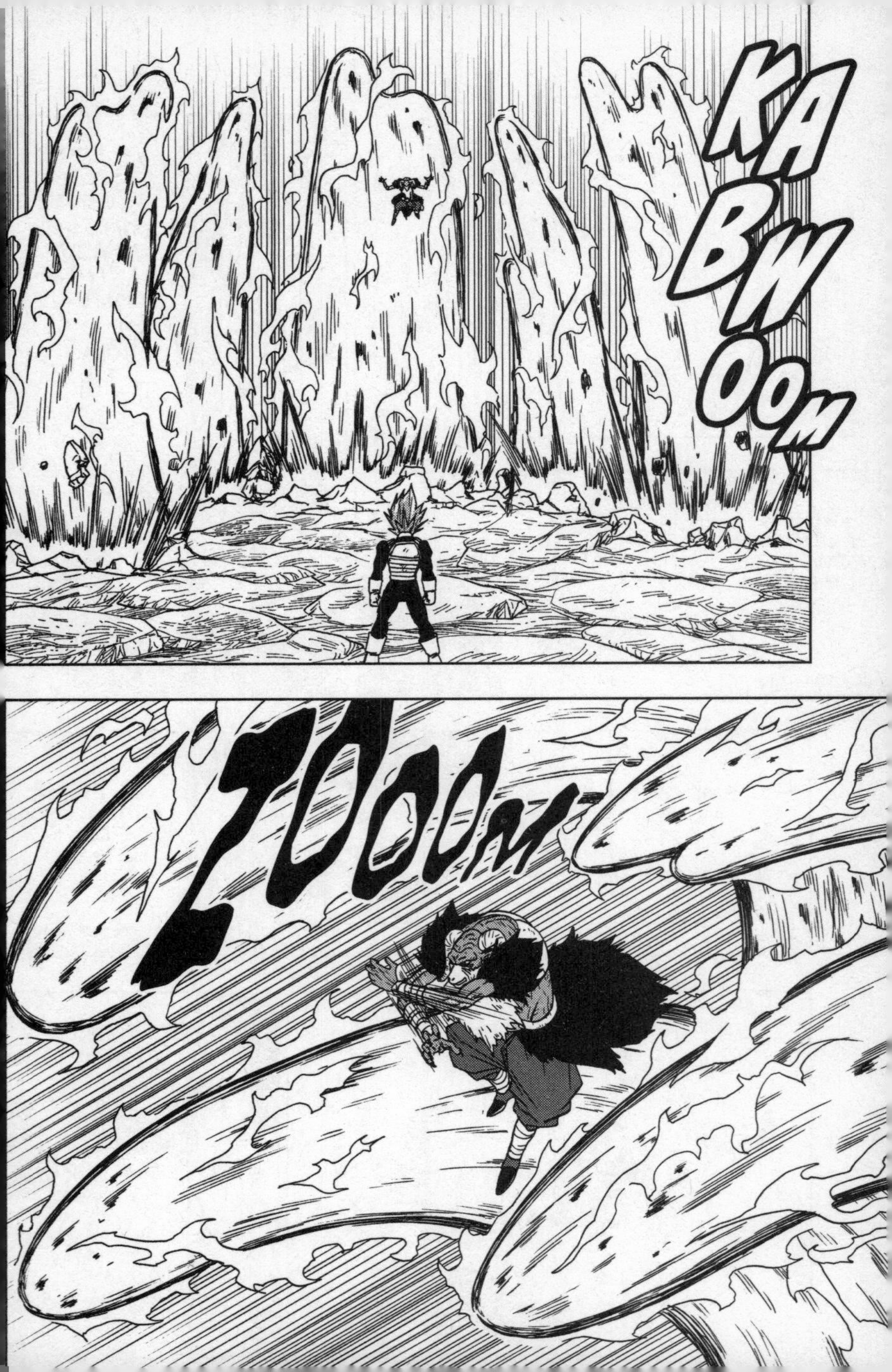
KA BWOOM
ZOOM

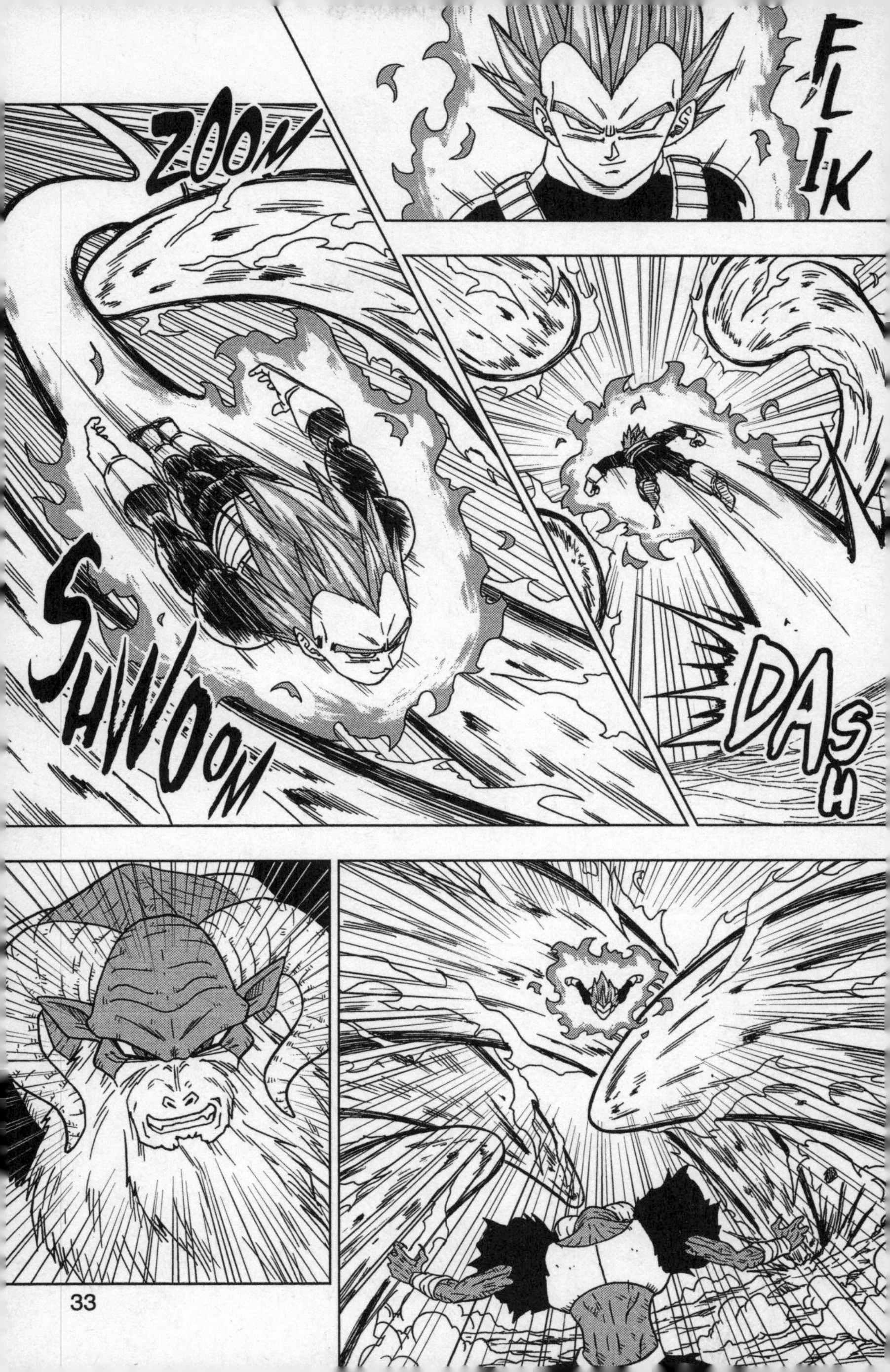
FLIK
DASH
ZOOM
SHWOOM

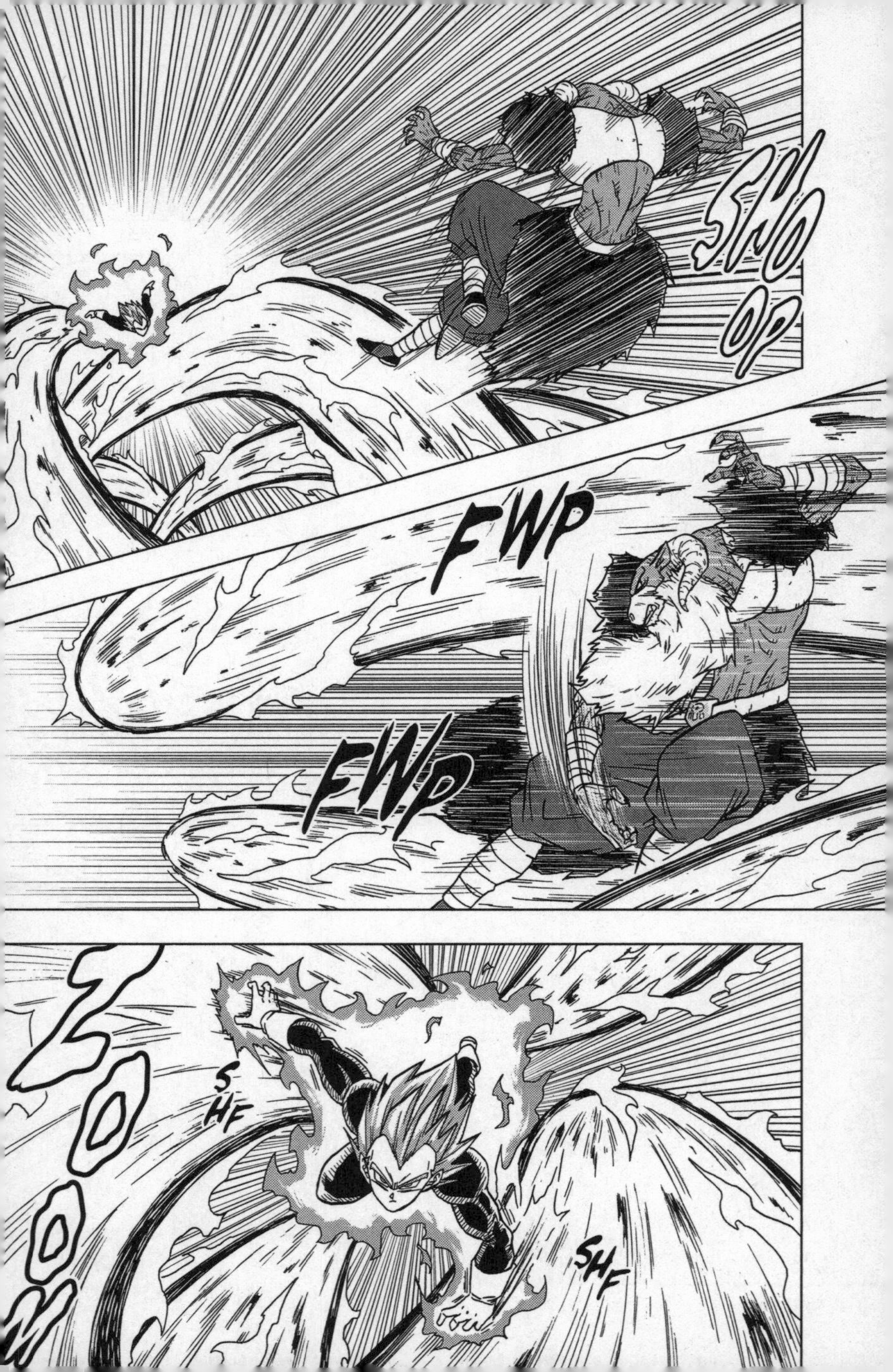

SHOOP
FWP
FWP
ZOOOM
SHF
SHF

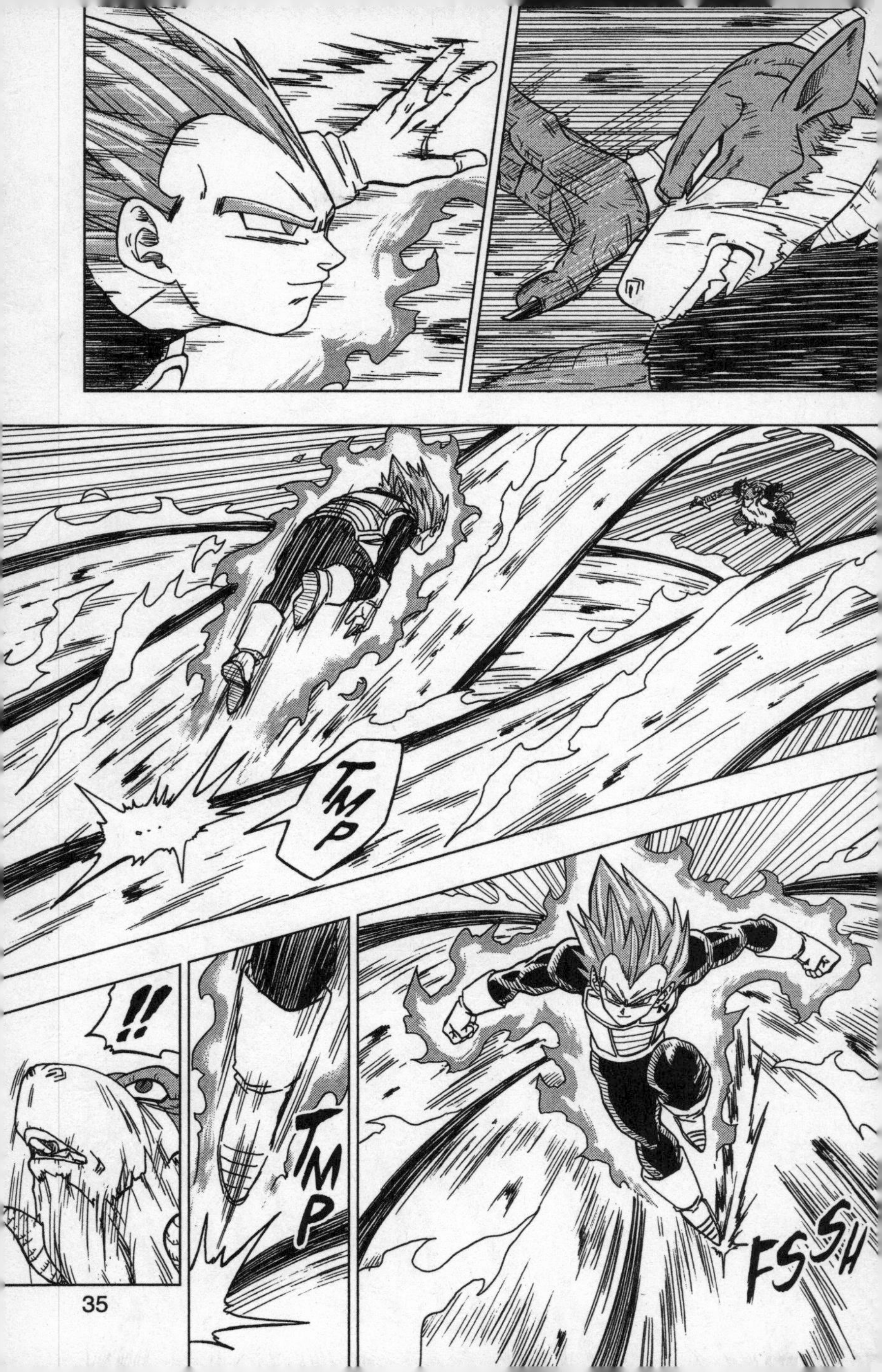
TMP
...
FSSH
TMP
!!

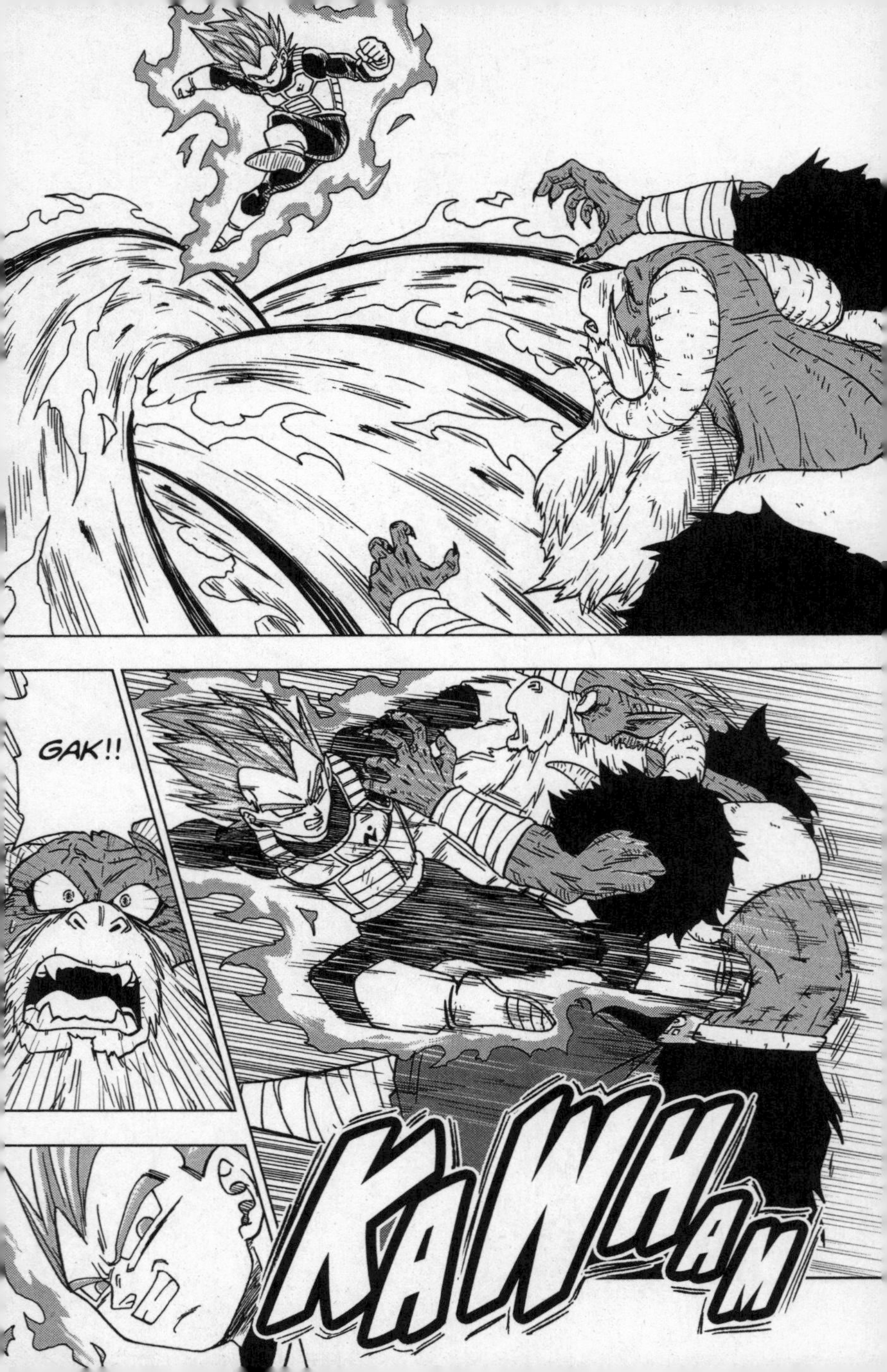
GAK!!
KA WHAM

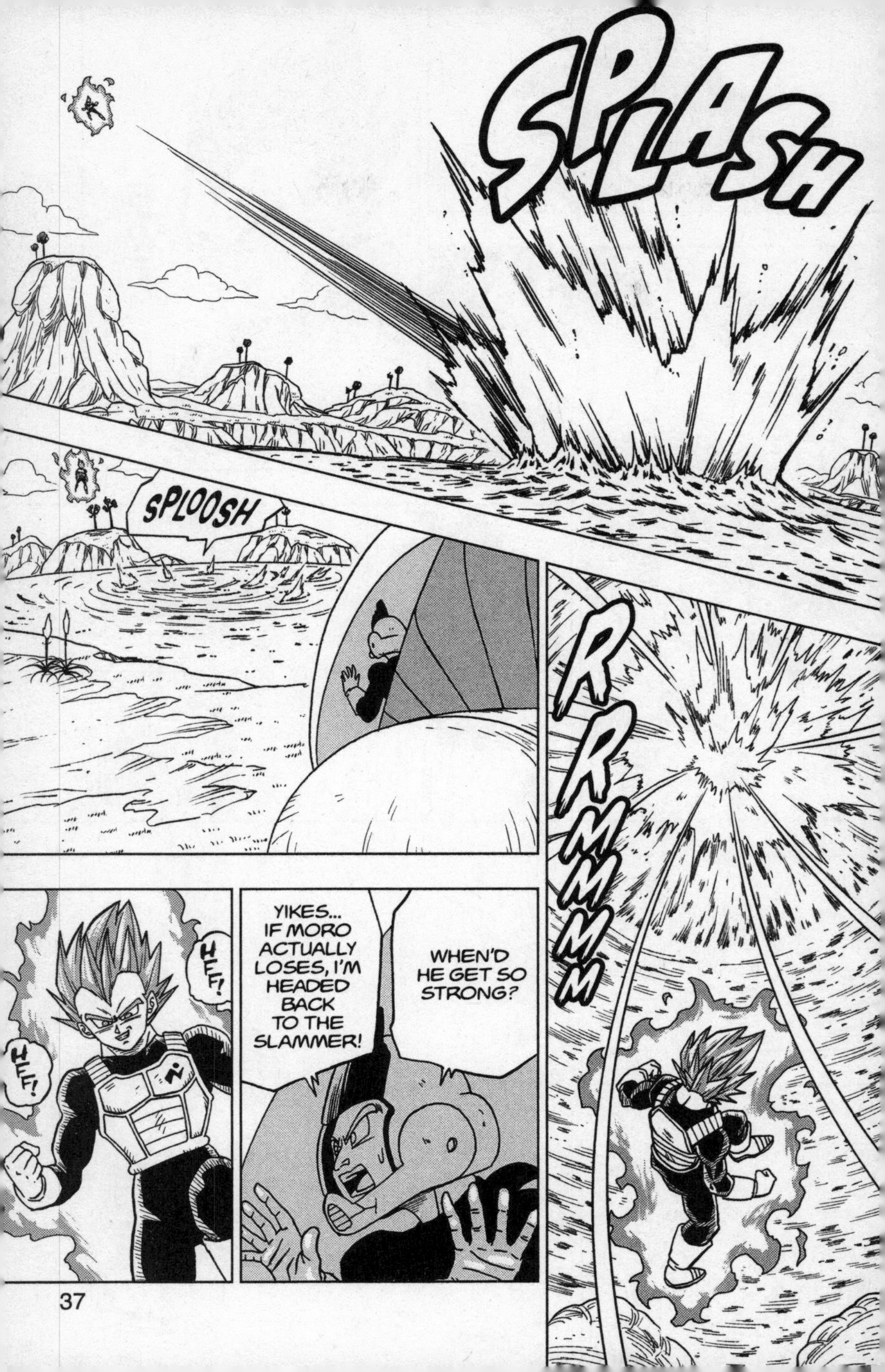
SPLASH
RRRMMMMM
SPLOOSH
WHEN'D HE GET SO STRONG?
YIKES... IF MORO ACTUALLY LOSES, I'M HEADED BACK TO THE SLAMMER!
HEF!
HEF!

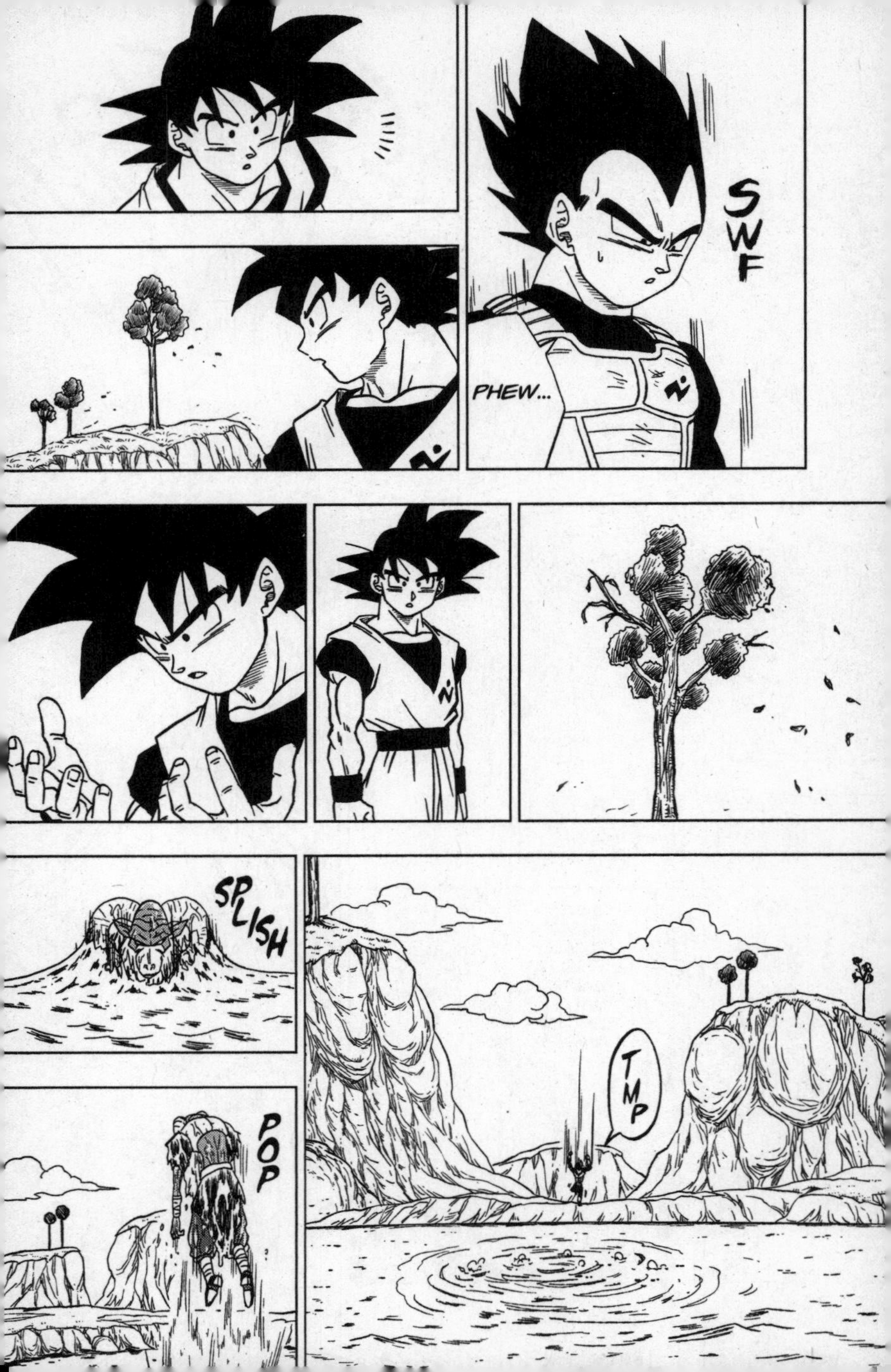
SWF
PHEW...
TMP
SPLISH
POP

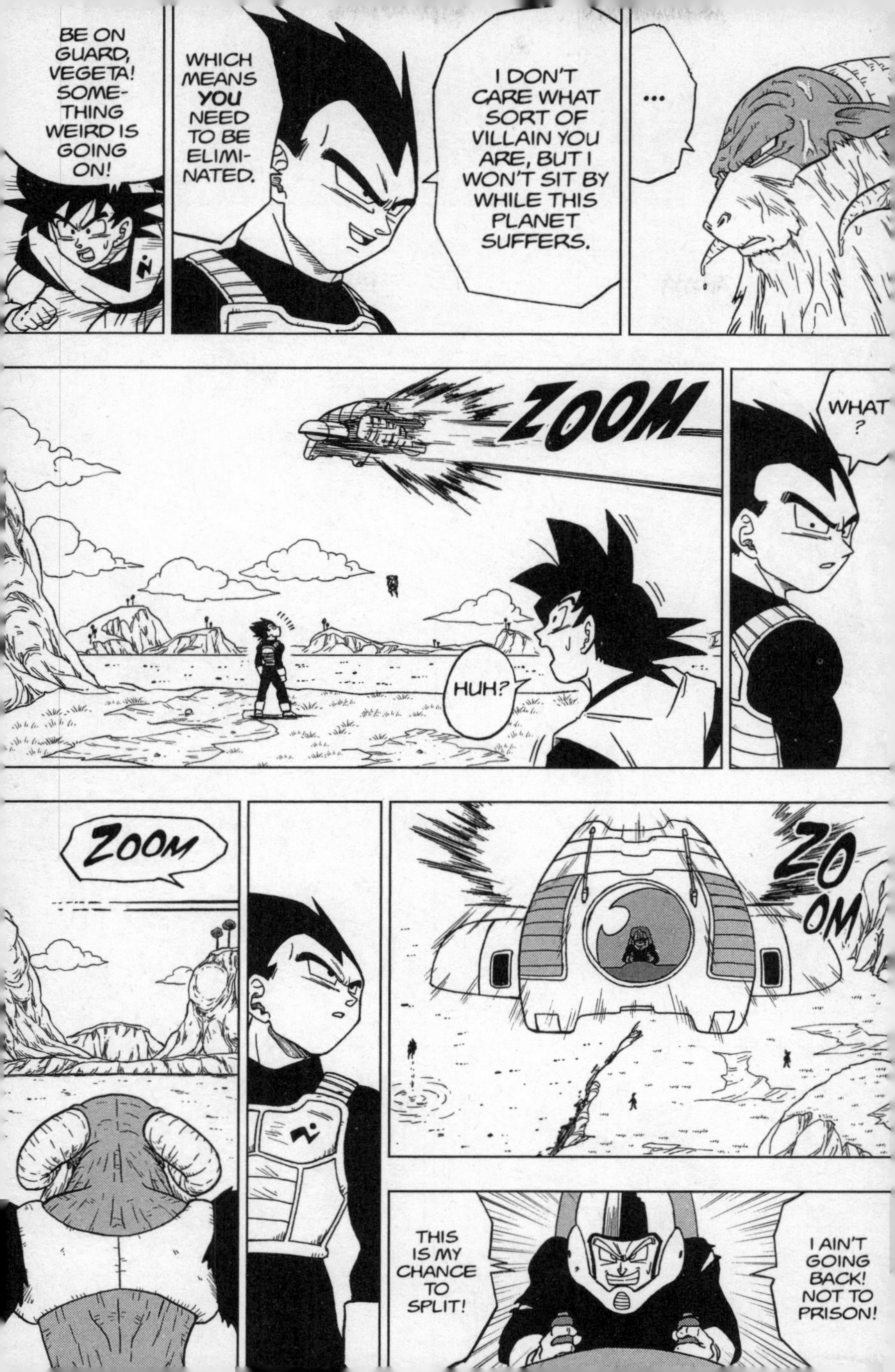
...
I DON'T CARE WHAT SORT OF VILLAIN YOU ARE, BUT I WON'T SIT BY WHILE THIS PLANET SUFFERS.
WHICH MEANS **YOU** NEED TO BE ELIMINATED.
BE ON GUARD, VEGETA! SOMETHING WEIRD IS GOING ON!
WHAT?
ZOOM
HUH?
ZOOM
ZOOM
I AIN'T GOING BACK! NOT TO PRISON!
THIS IS MY CHANCE TO SPLIT!

PEW PEW PEW

DAMMIT!

GAH!

BWAH!

BBOOOMM BBOOOMM BBOOOMM

FWISH

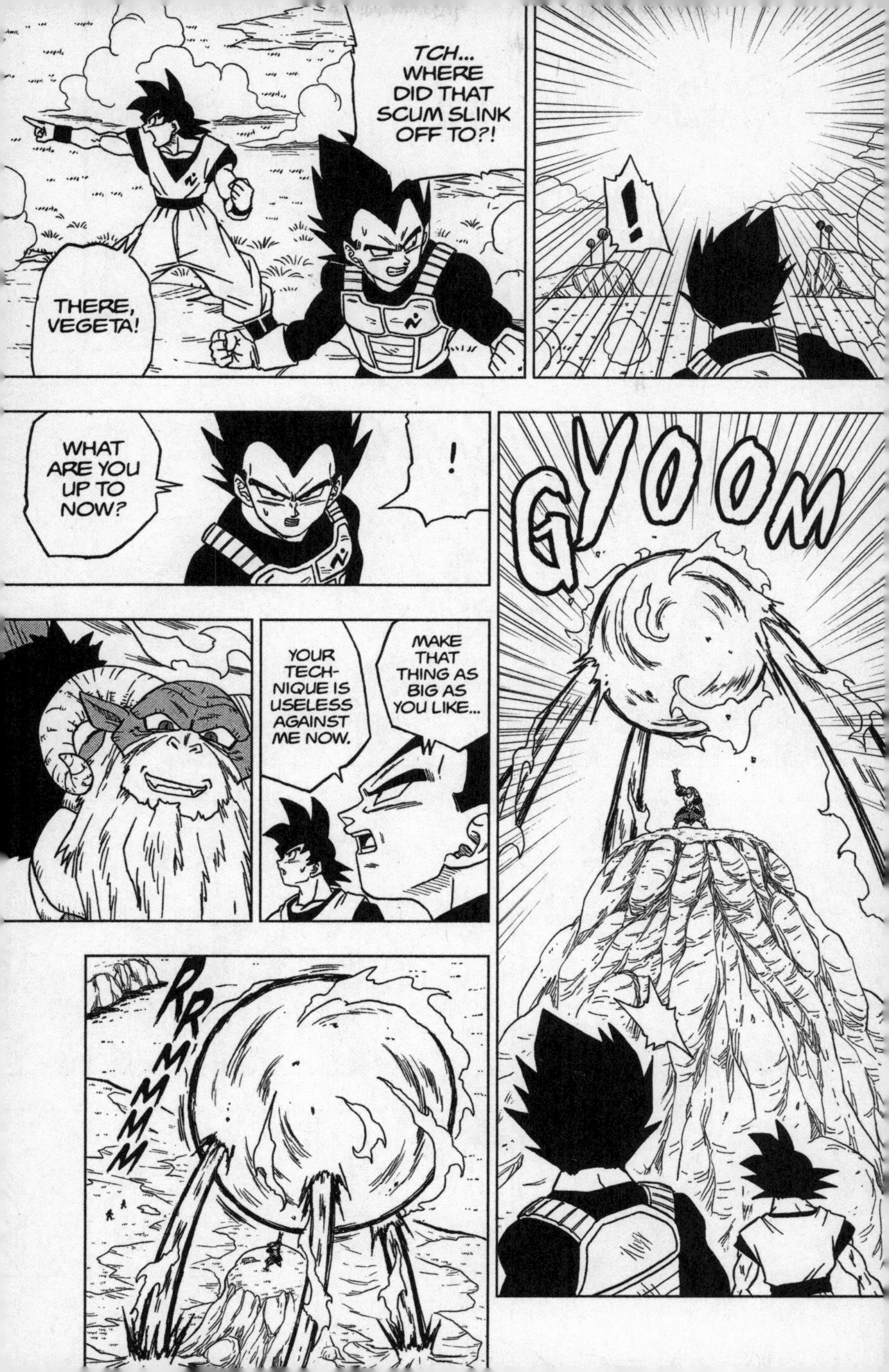
!
TCH... WHERE DID THAT SCUM SLINK OFF TO?!
THERE, VEGETA!
GYOOM
!
WHAT ARE YOU UP TO NOW?
MAKE THAT THING AS BIG AS YOU LIKE...
YOUR TECH-NIQUE IS USELESS AGAINST ME NOW.
RRMMMMM

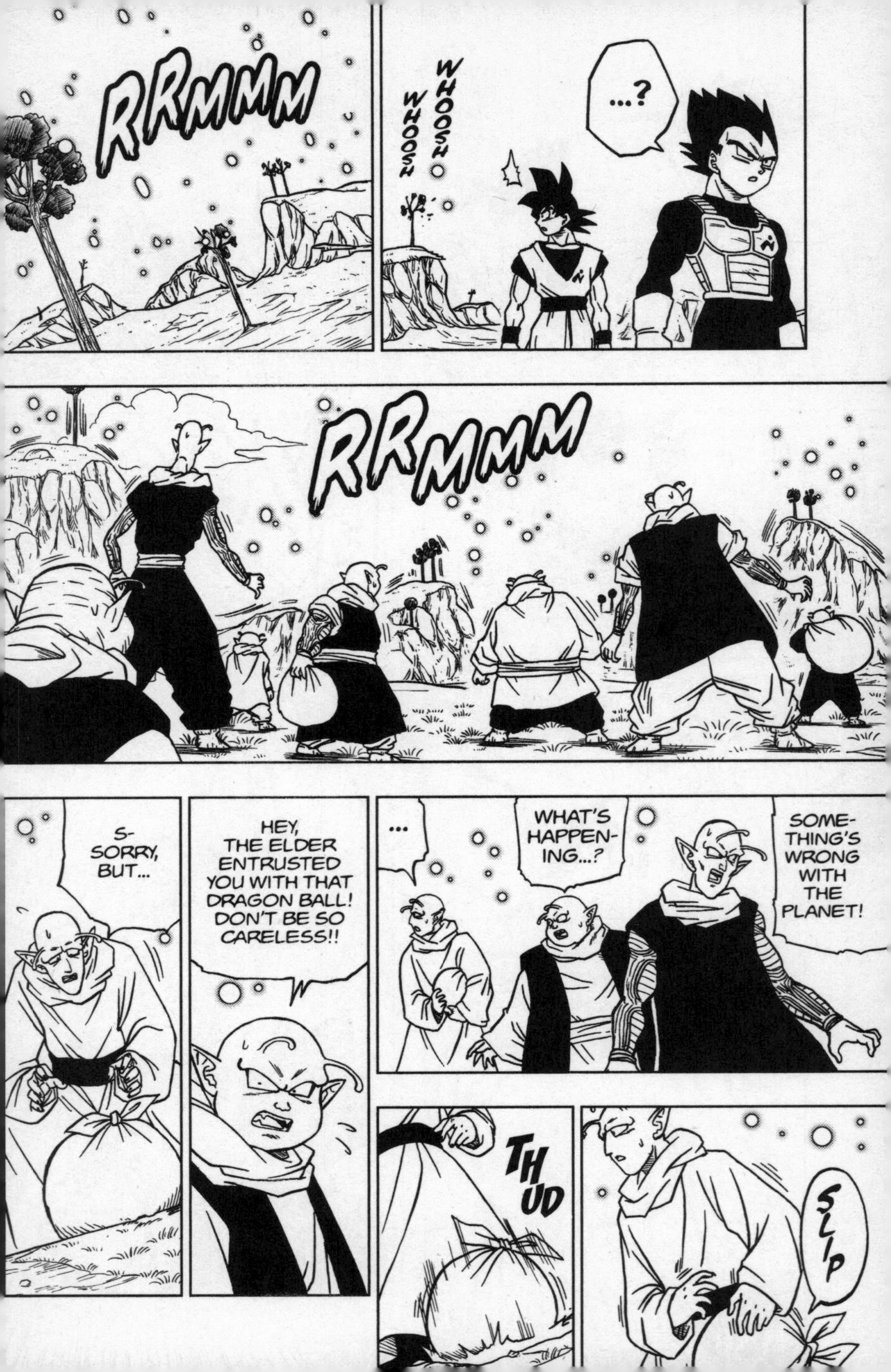
...?
WHOOSH
WHOOSH
RRMMMM
RRMMMM
SOME-THING'S WRONG WITH THE PLANET!
WHAT'S HAPPEN-ING...?
...
SLIP
THUD
HEY, THE ELDER ENTRUSTED YOU WITH THAT DRAGON BALL! DON'T BE SO CARELESS!!
S-SORRY, BUT...

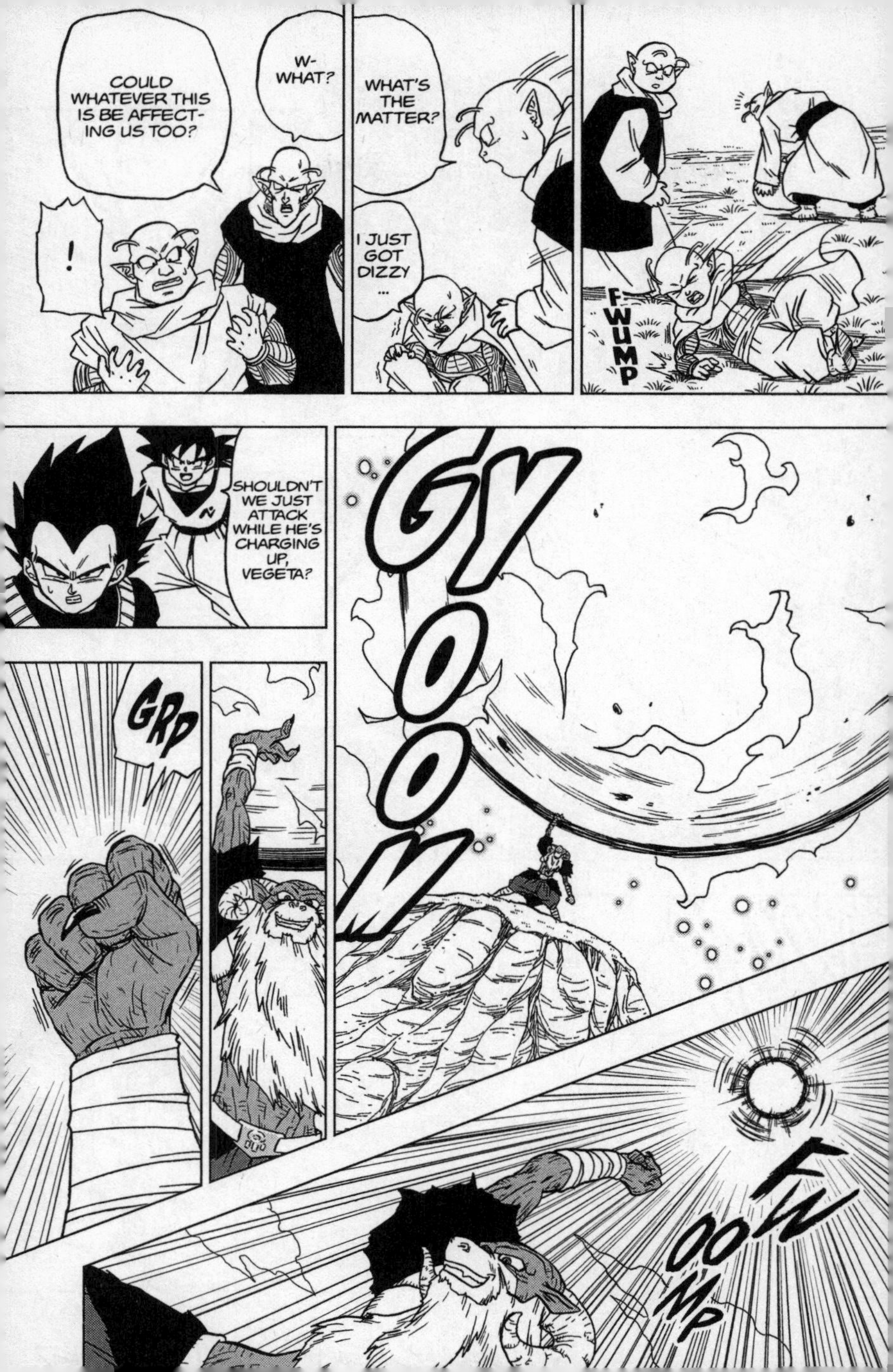
FWUMP
WHAT'S THE MATTER?
I JUST GOT DIZZY ...
W-WHAT?
COULD WHATEVER THIS IS BE AFFECTING US TOO?
!
GYOOON
SHOULDN'T WE JUST ATTACK WHILE HE'S CHARGING UP, VEGETA?
GRP
FWOOMP

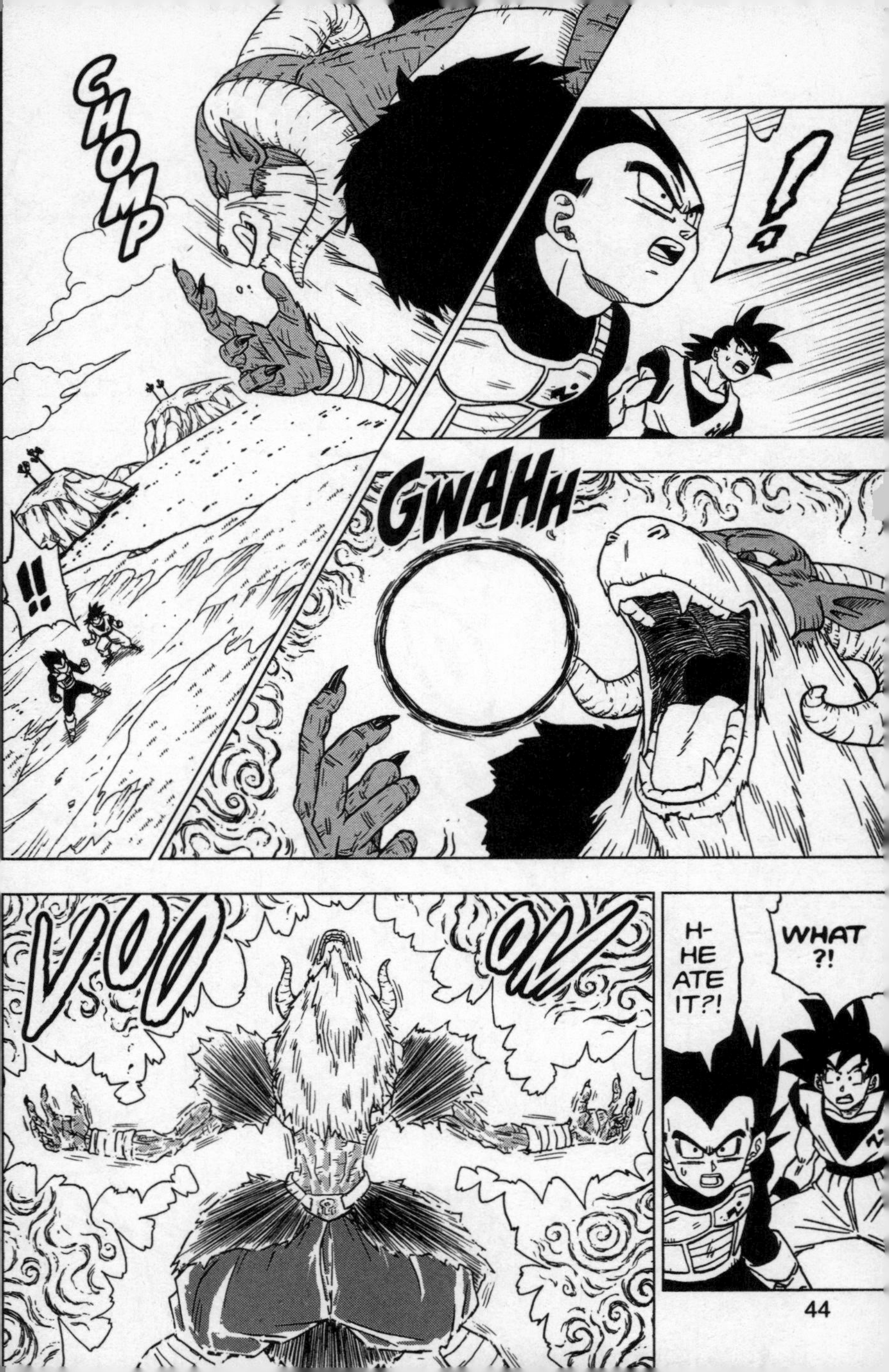
!
GWAHH
CHOMP
!!
WHAT ?!
H- HE ATE IT?!
VOOOV

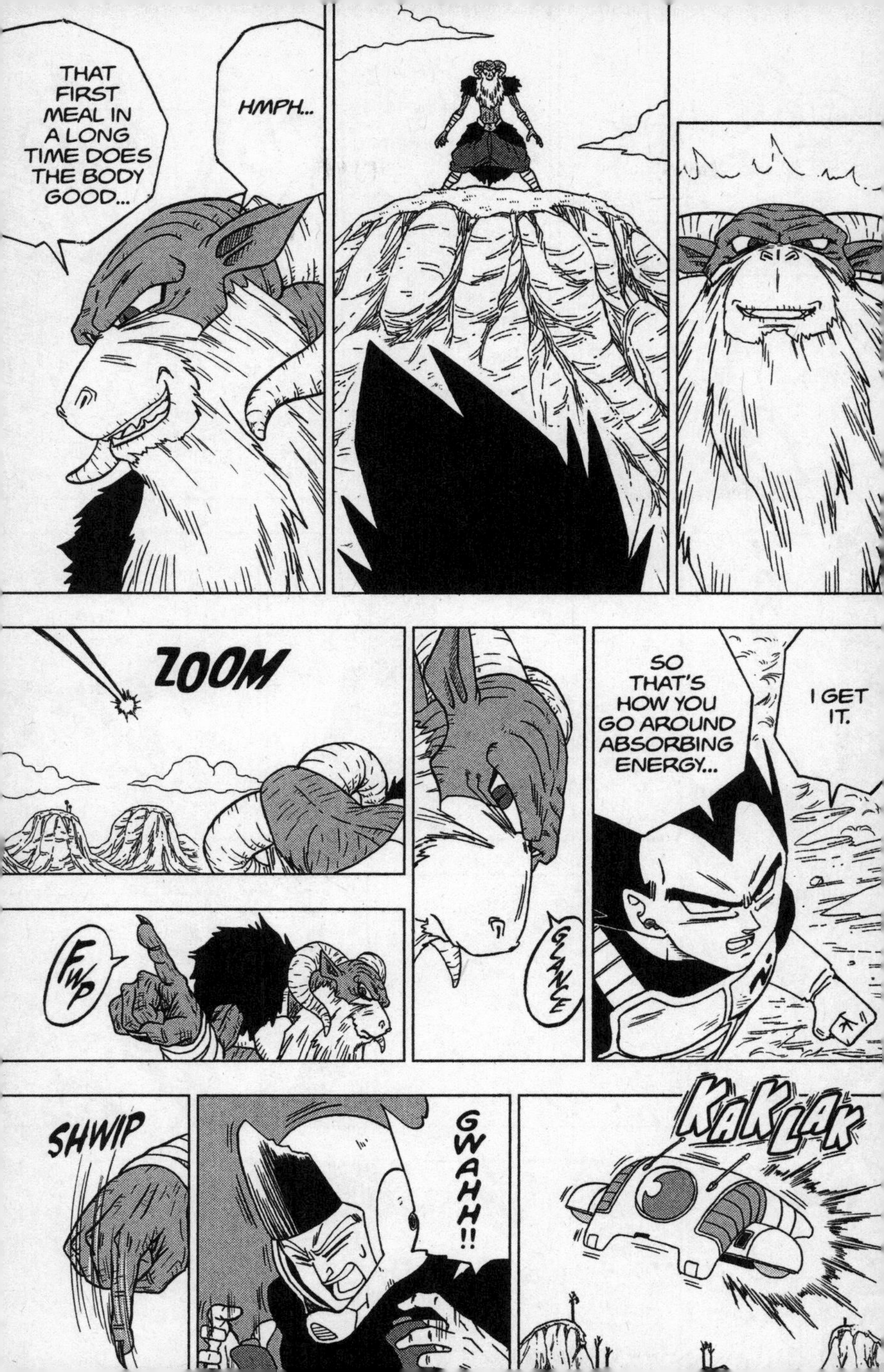
HMPH...
THAT FIRST MEAL IN A LONG TIME DOES THE BODY GOOD...
I GET IT.
SO THAT'S HOW YOU GO AROUND ABSORBING ENERGY...
GLANCE
ZOOM
FWP
KAKLAK
GWAHH!!
SHWIP

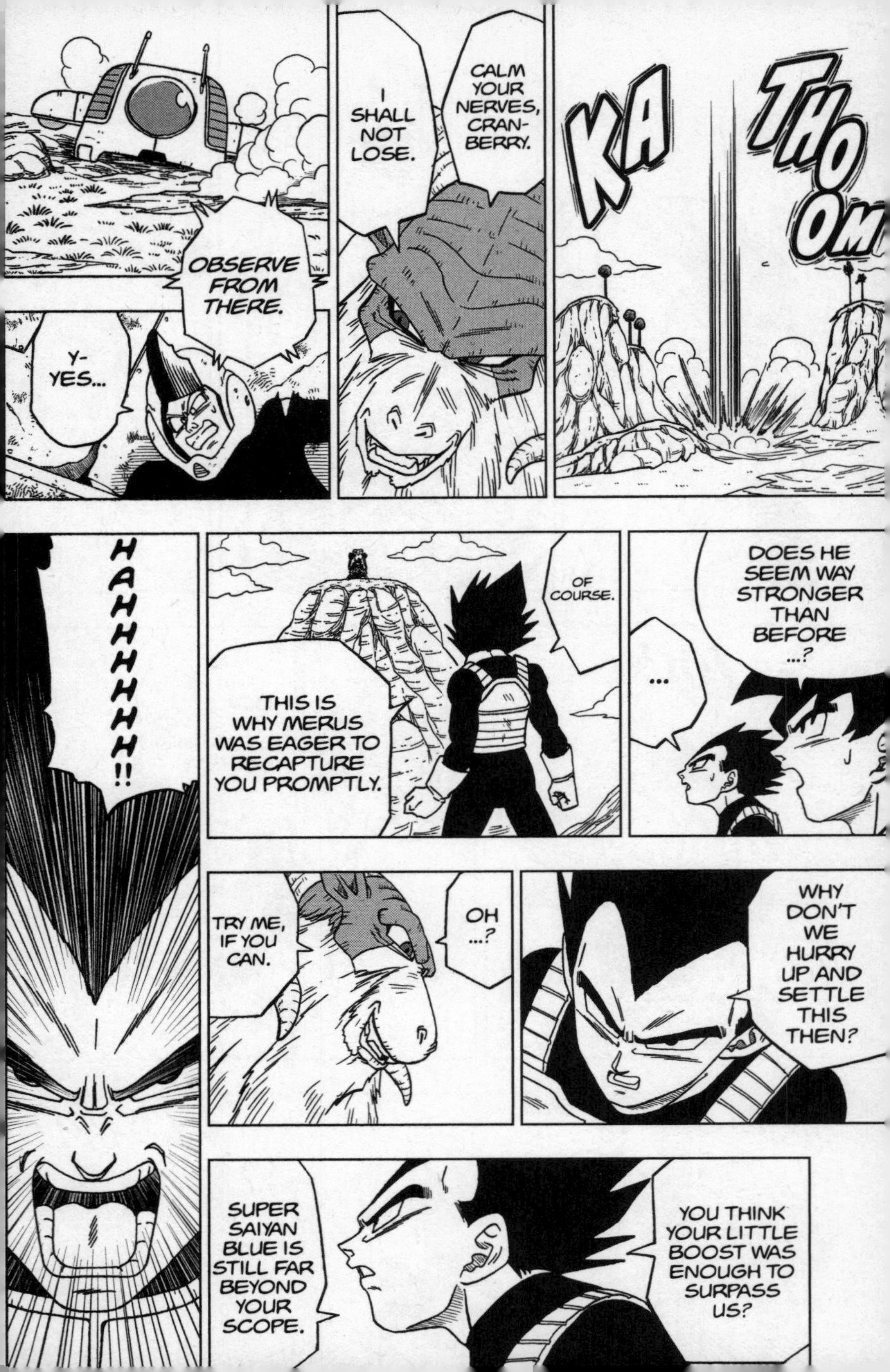
KA THOOM
CALM YOUR NERVES, CRANBERRY.
I SHALL NOT LOSE.
OBSERVE FROM THERE.
Y-YES...
DOES HE SEEM WAY STRONGER THAN BEFORE...?
...
OF COURSE.
THIS IS WHY MERUS WAS EAGER TO RECAPTURE YOU PROMPTLY.
WHY DON'T WE HURRY UP AND SETTLE THIS THEN?
OH...?
TRY ME, IF YOU CAN.
YOU THINK YOUR LITTLE BOOST WAS ENOUGH TO SURPASS US?
SUPER SAIYAN BLUE IS STILL FAR BEYOND YOUR SCOPE.
HAHHHHHH!!

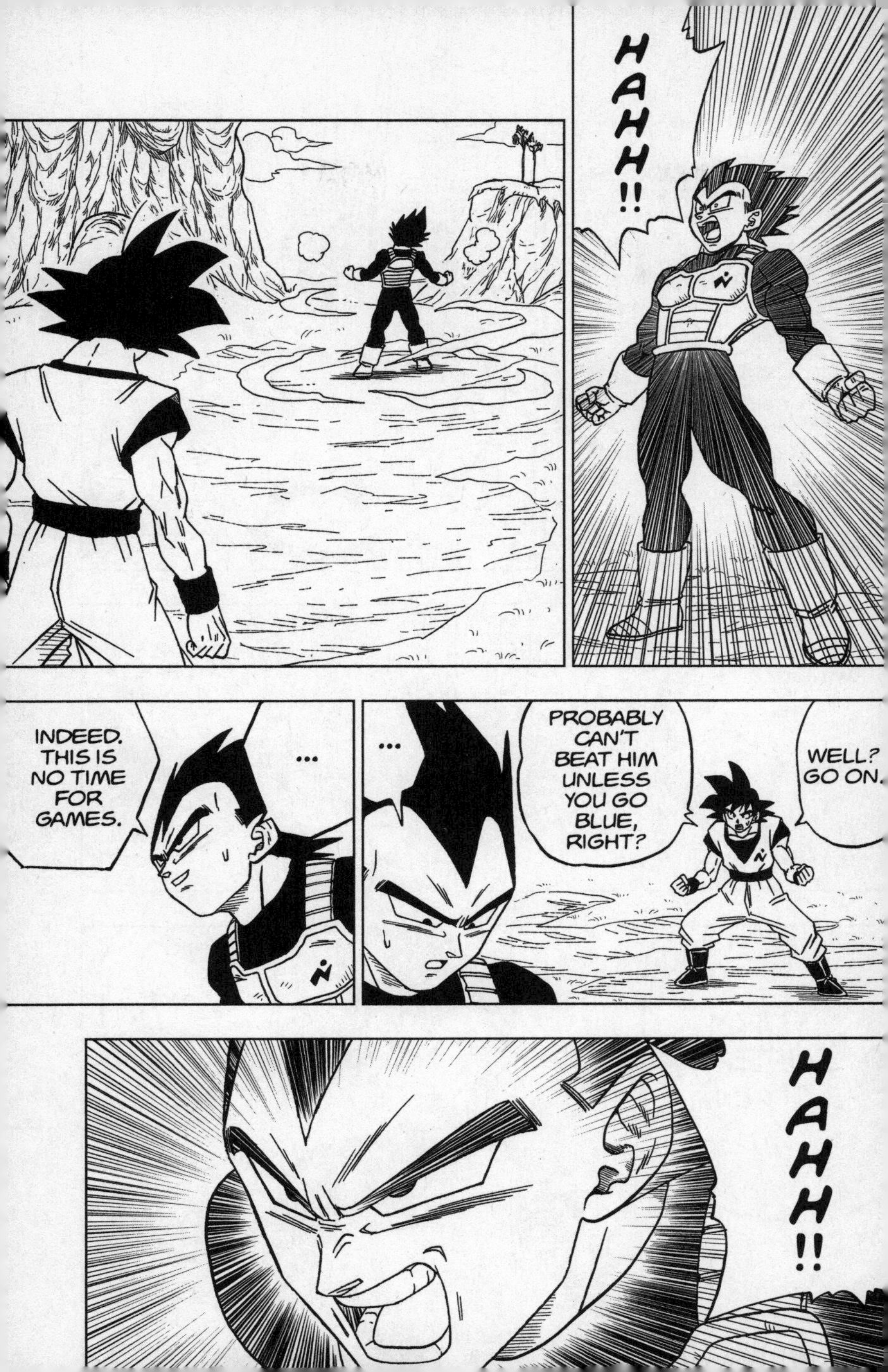
HAHHH!!
WELL? GO ON.
PROBABLY CAN'T BEAT HIM UNLESS YOU GO BLUE, RIGHT?
...
...
INDEED. THIS IS NO TIME FOR GAMES.
HAHHH!!

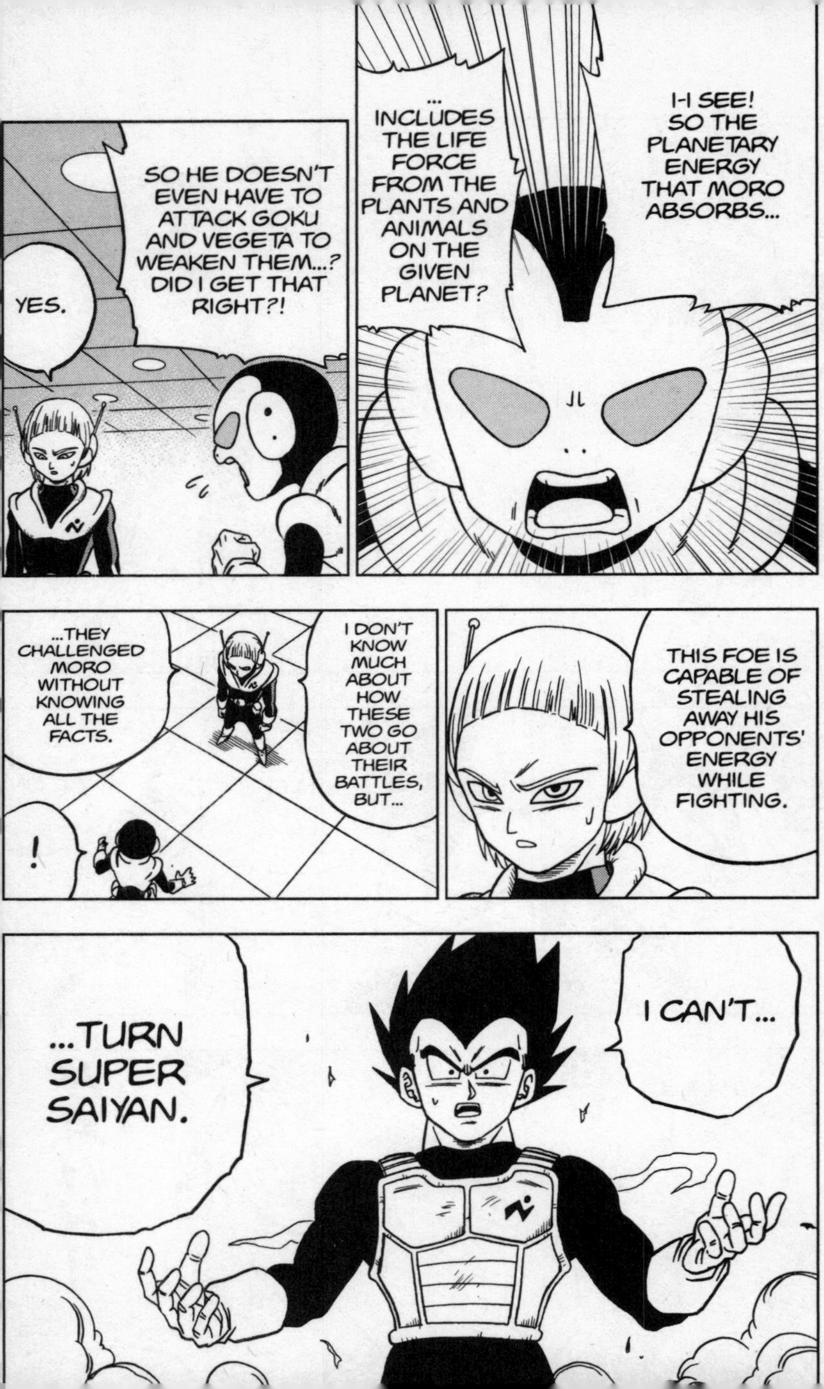
I-I SEE! SO THE PLANETARY ENERGY THAT MORO ABSORBS...
... INCLUDES THE LIFE FORCE FROM THE PLANTS AND ANIMALS ON THE GIVEN PLANET?
SO HE DOESN'T EVEN HAVE TO ATTACK GOKU AND VEGETA TO WEAKEN THEM...? DID I GET THAT RIGHT?!
YES.
THIS FOE IS CAPABLE OF STEALING AWAY HIS OPPONENTS' ENERGY WHILE FIGHTING.
I DON'T KNOW MUCH ABOUT HOW THESE TWO GO ABOUT THEIR BATTLES, BUT...
...THEY CHALLENGED MORO WITHOUT KNOWING ALL THE FACTS.
!
I CAN'T...
...TURN SUPER SAIYAN.

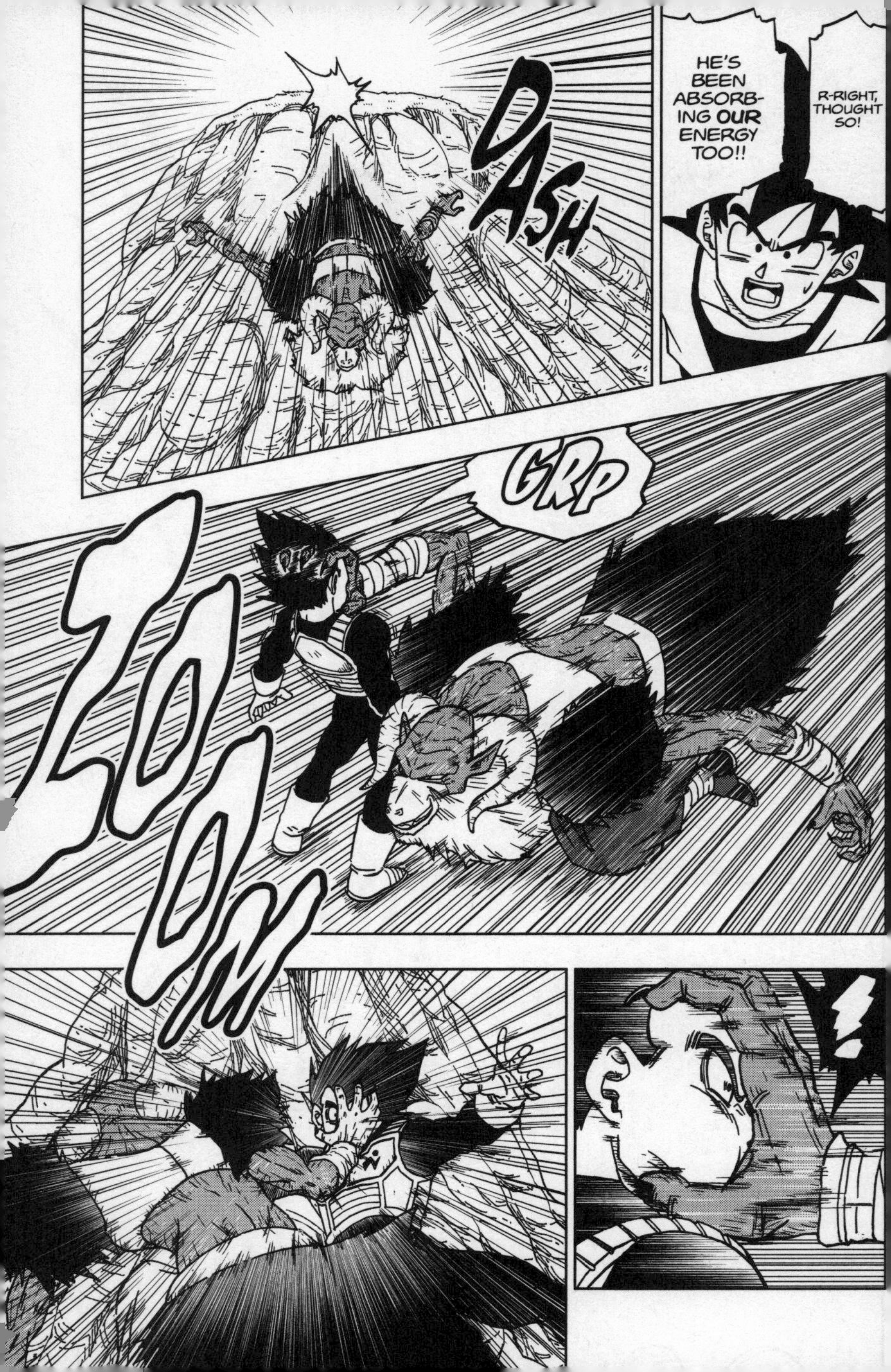
R-RIGHT, THOUGHT SO!
HE'S BEEN ABSORBING **OUR** ENERGY TOO!!
DASH
GRP
ZOOM

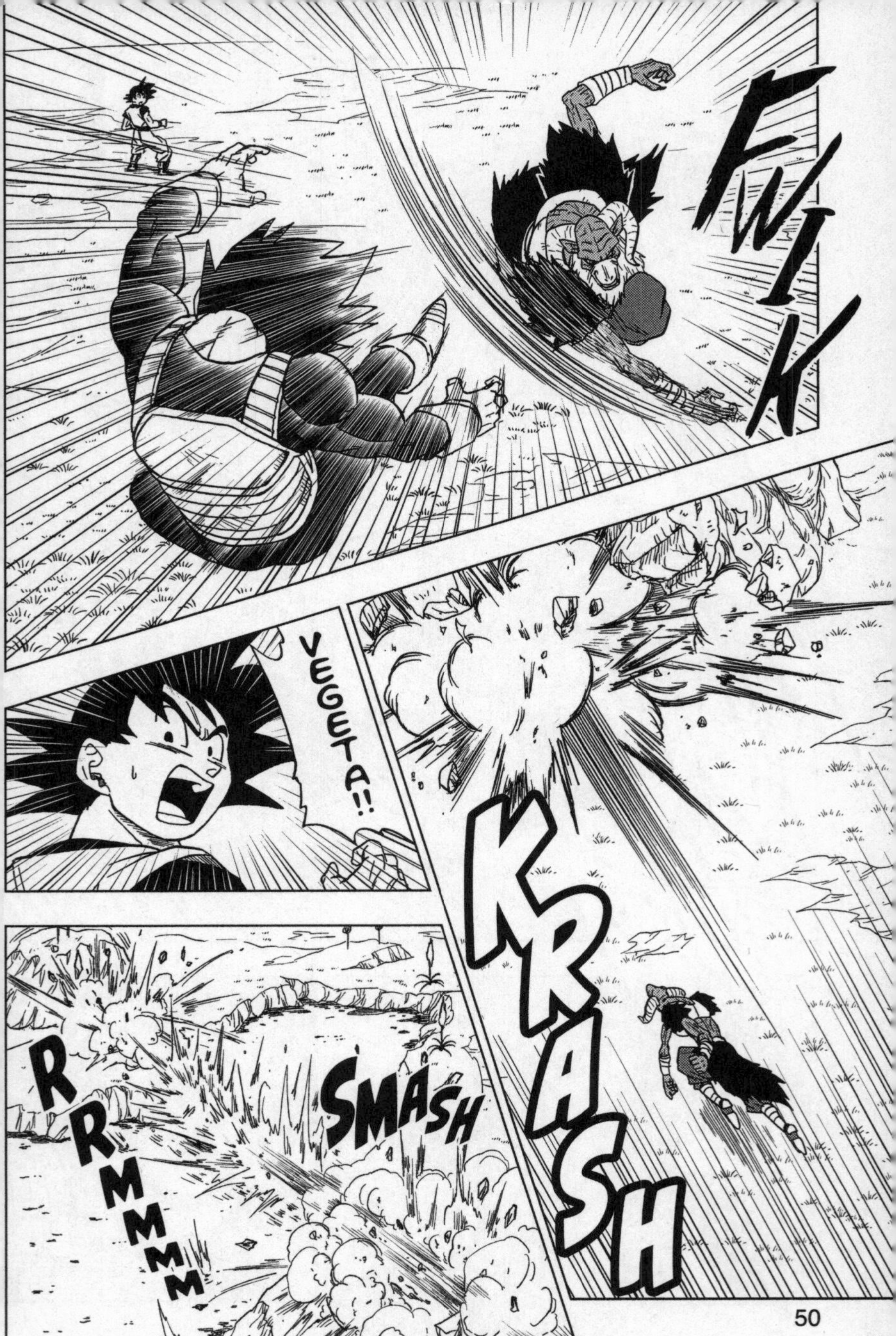
FWIK
KRASH
VEGETA!!
SMASH
RRMMMM

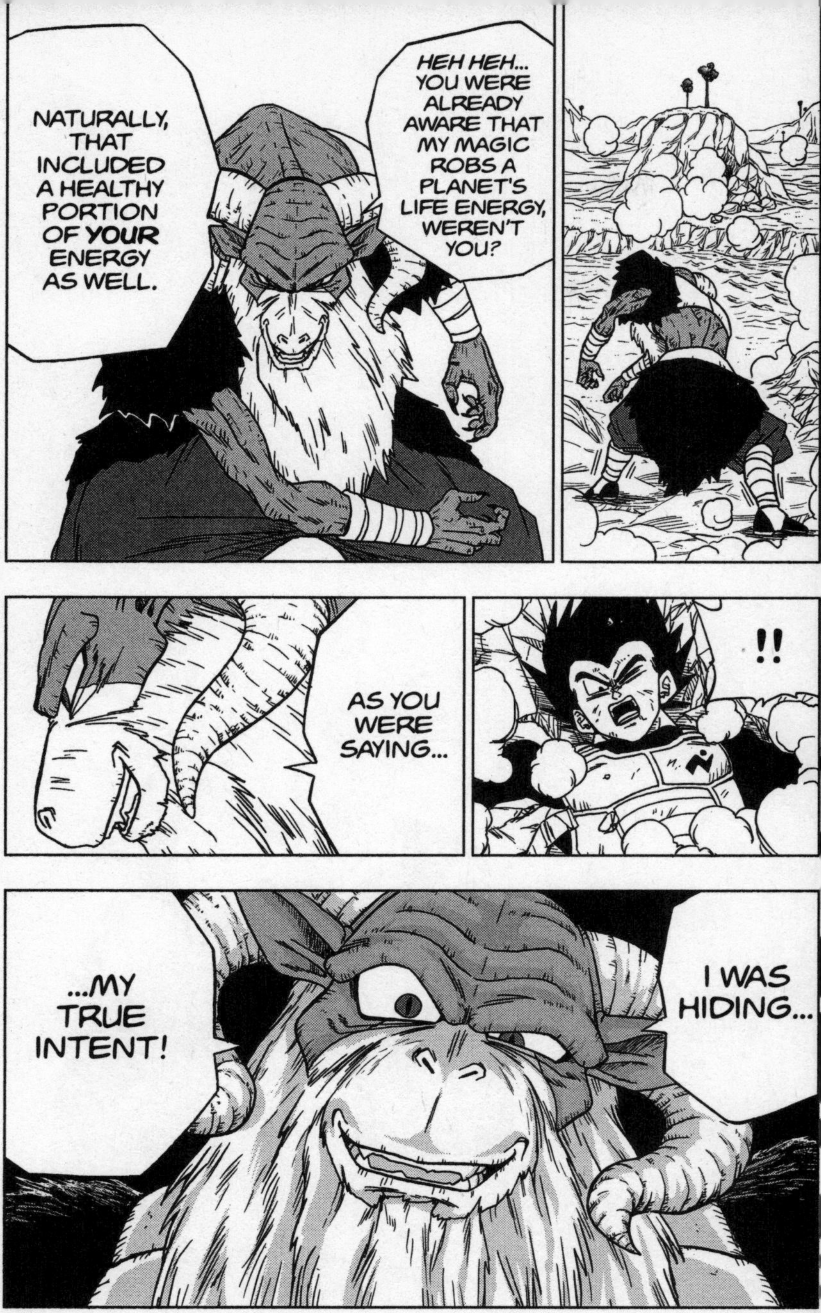
HEH HEH... YOU WERE ALREADY AWARE THAT MY MAGIC ROBS A PLANET'S LIFE ENERGY, WEREN'T YOU?
NATURALLY, THAT INCLUDED A HEALTHY PORTION OF **YOUR** ENERGY AS WELL.
!!
AS YOU WERE SAYING...
I WAS HIDING...
...MY TRUE INTENT!

DRAGON BALL SUPER

CHAPTER 46: NAMEK IN DECLINE

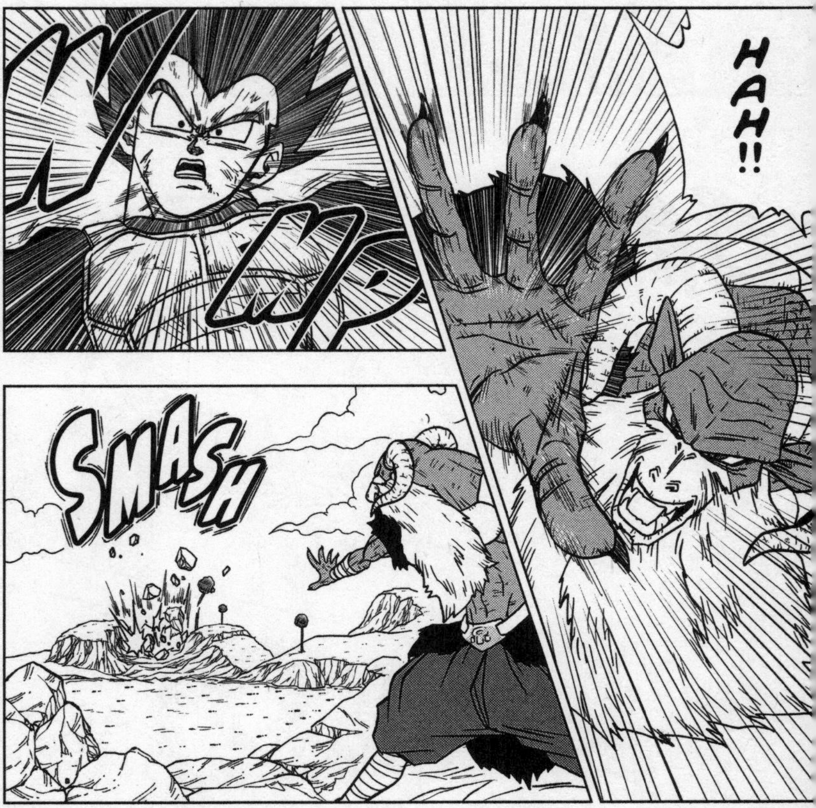
HAH!!
SMASH

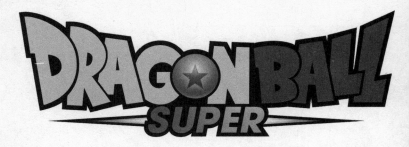

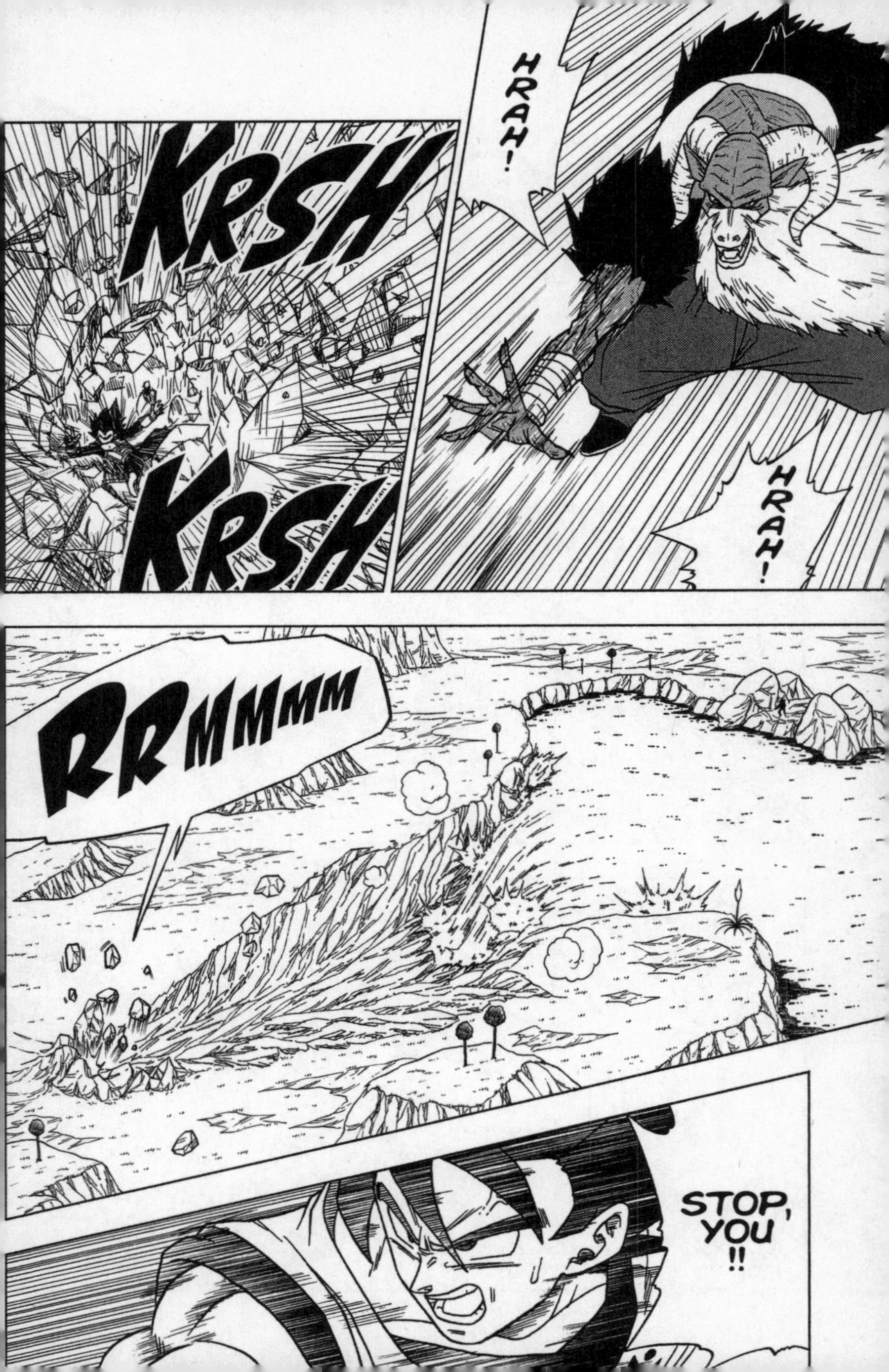
HRAH!
HRAH!
KRSH
KRSH
RRMMMM
STOP, YOU!!

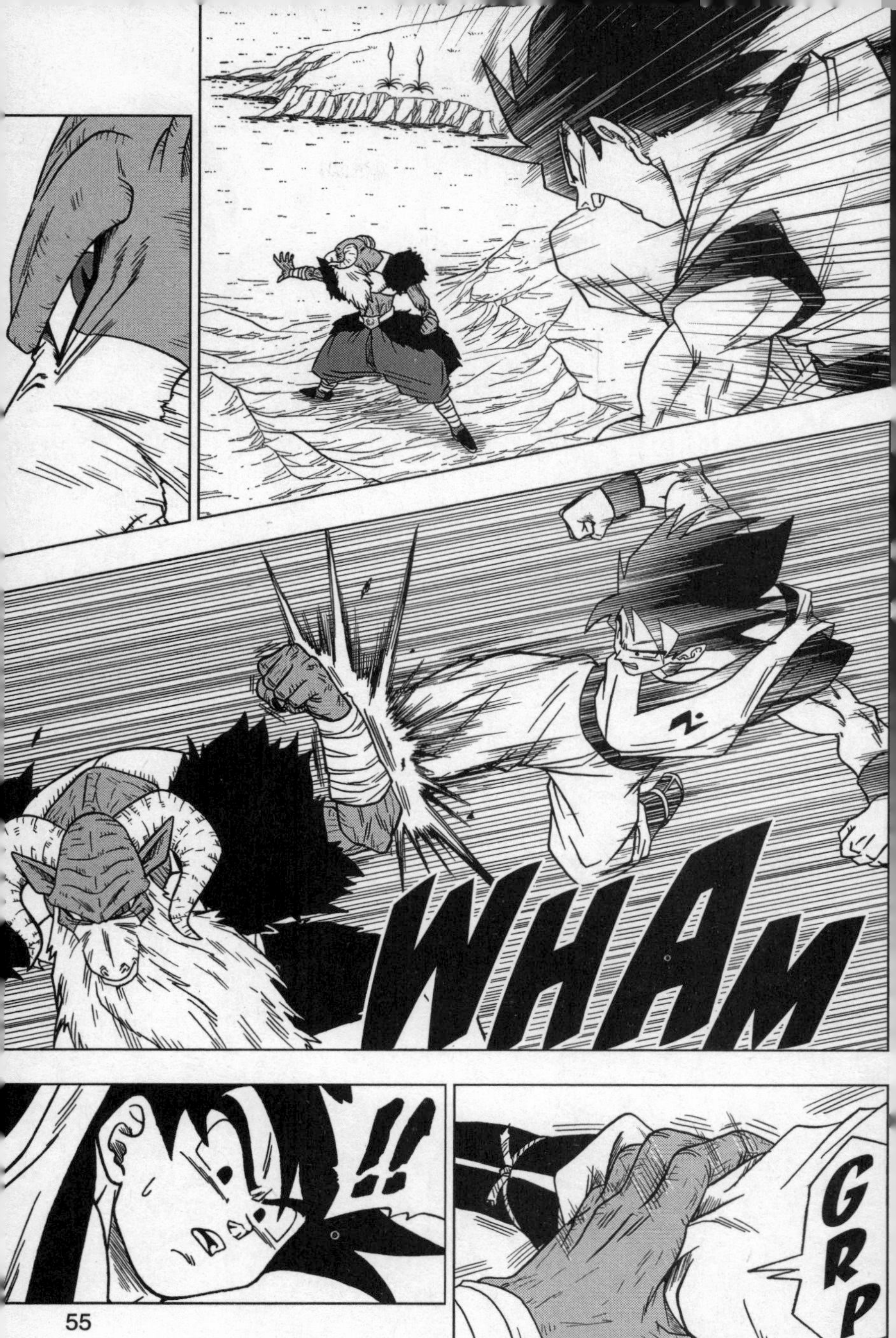
WHAM
GRP
!!

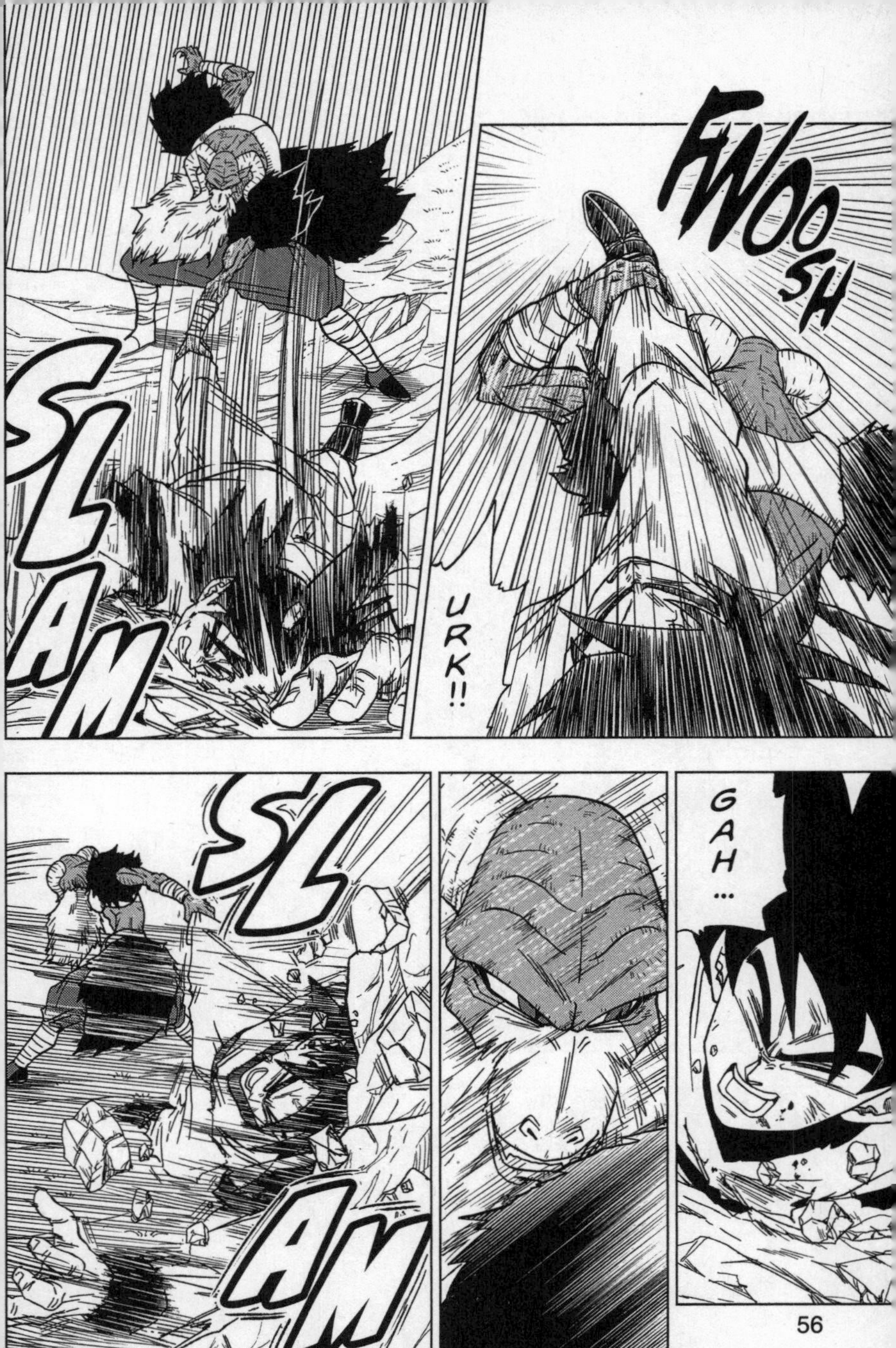
FWOOSH
URK!!
SLAM
GAH...
SLAM

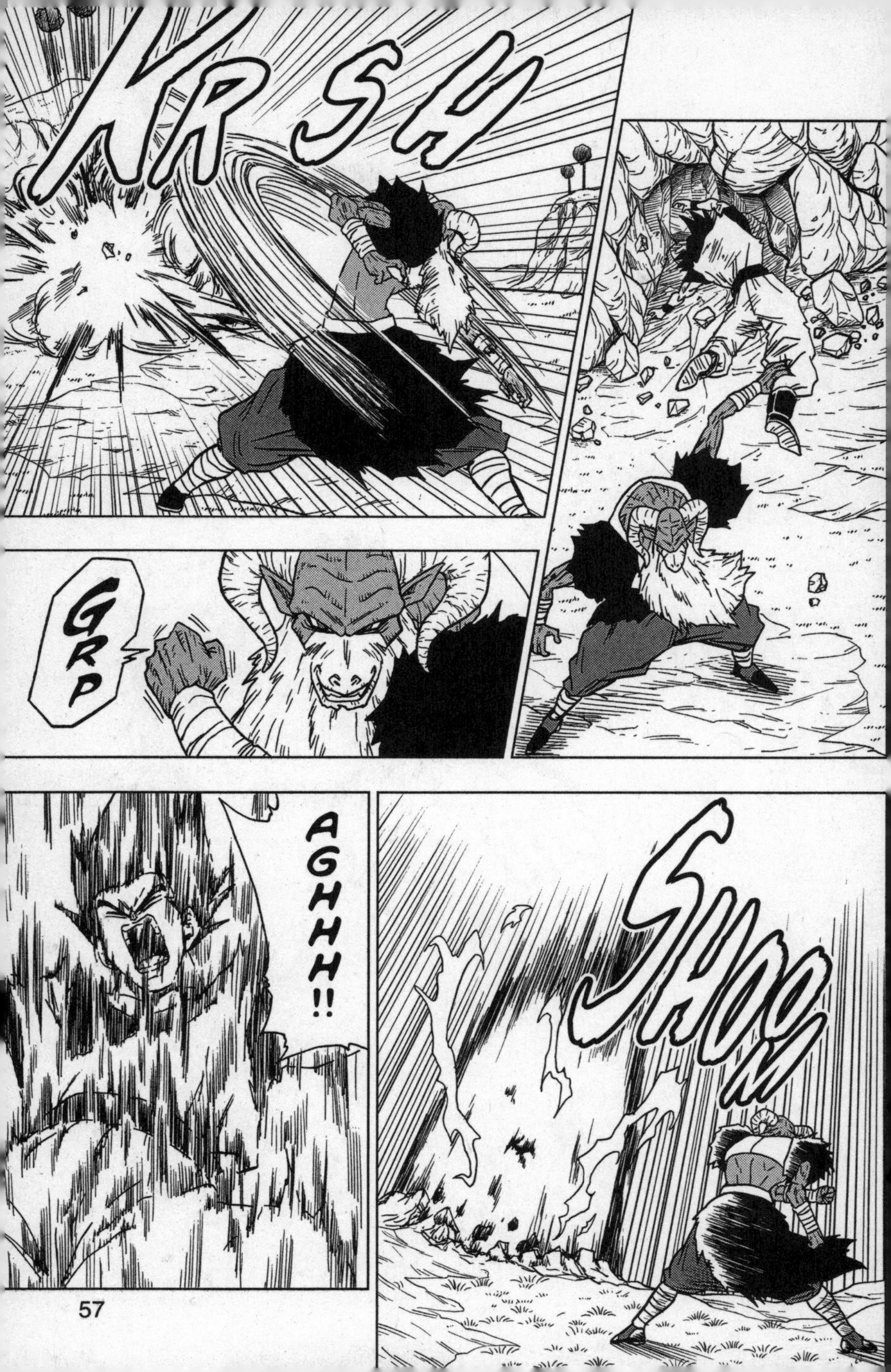
KRSH
GRP
SHOOM
AGHHH!!

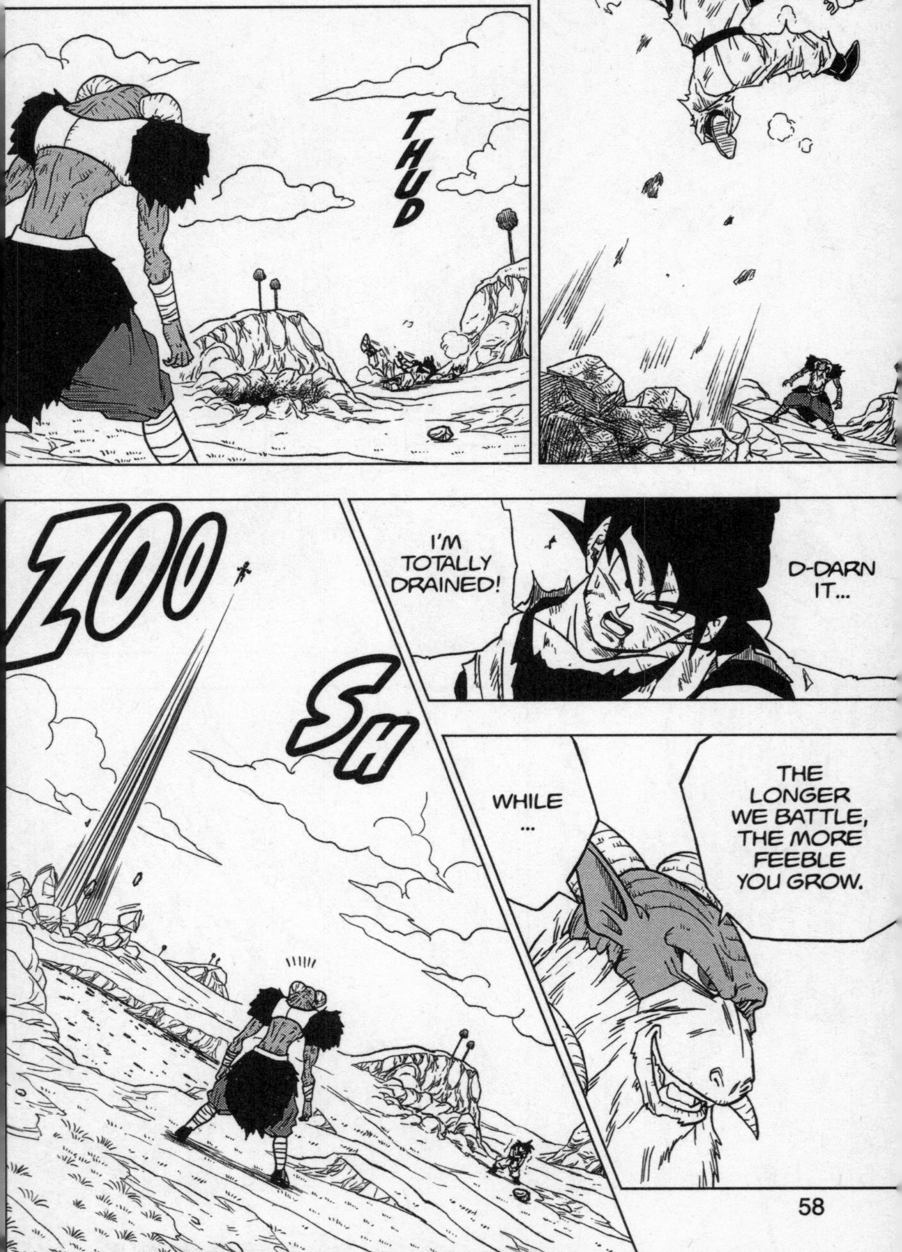
THUD
D-DARN IT...
I'M TOTALLY DRAINED!
THE LONGER WE BATTLE, THE MORE FEEBLE YOU GROW.
WHILE ...
ZOO
SH

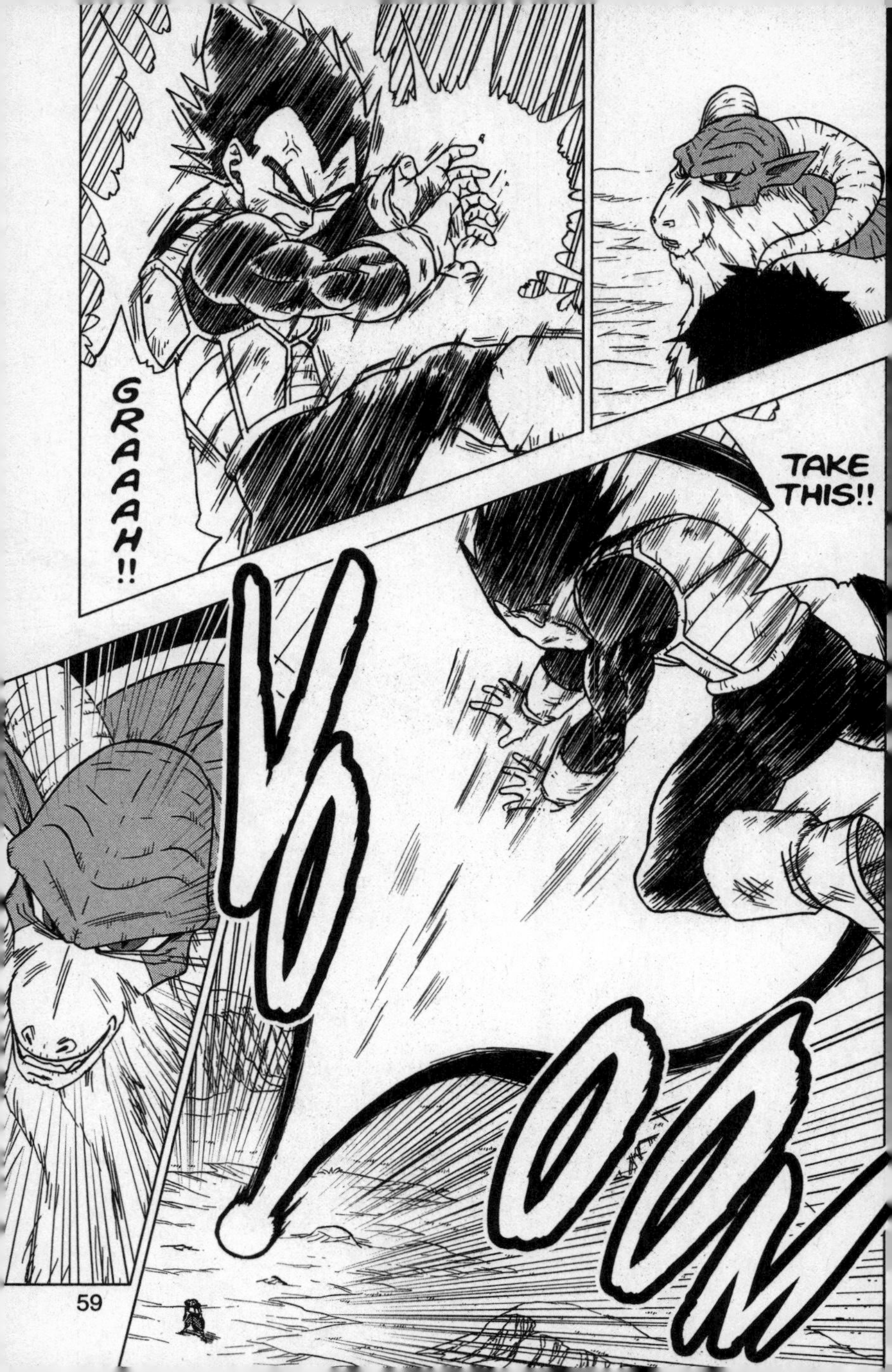
GRAAAH!!
TAKE THIS!!

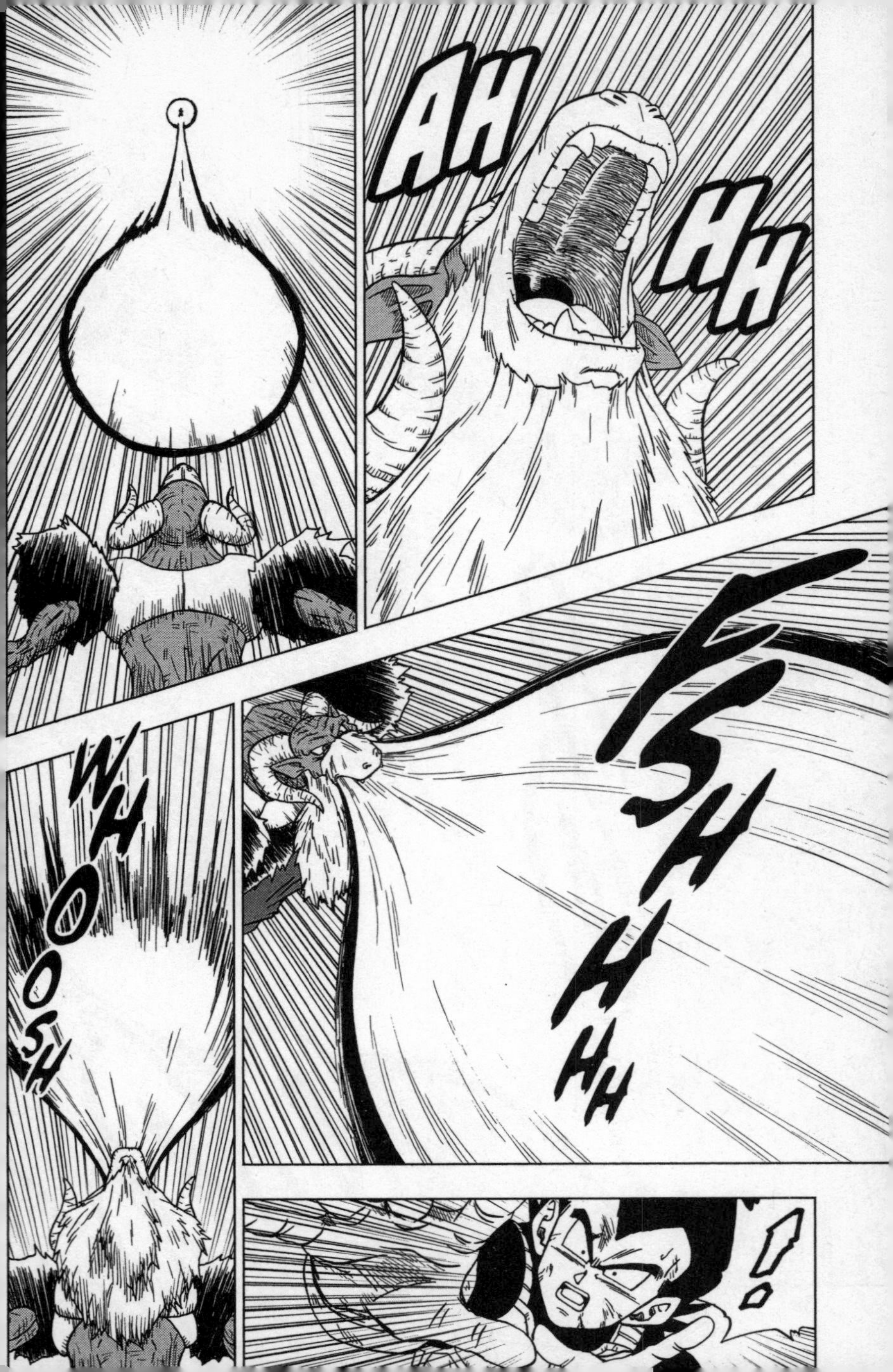
AHHHH
FSHHHHHH
WHOOOSH
!

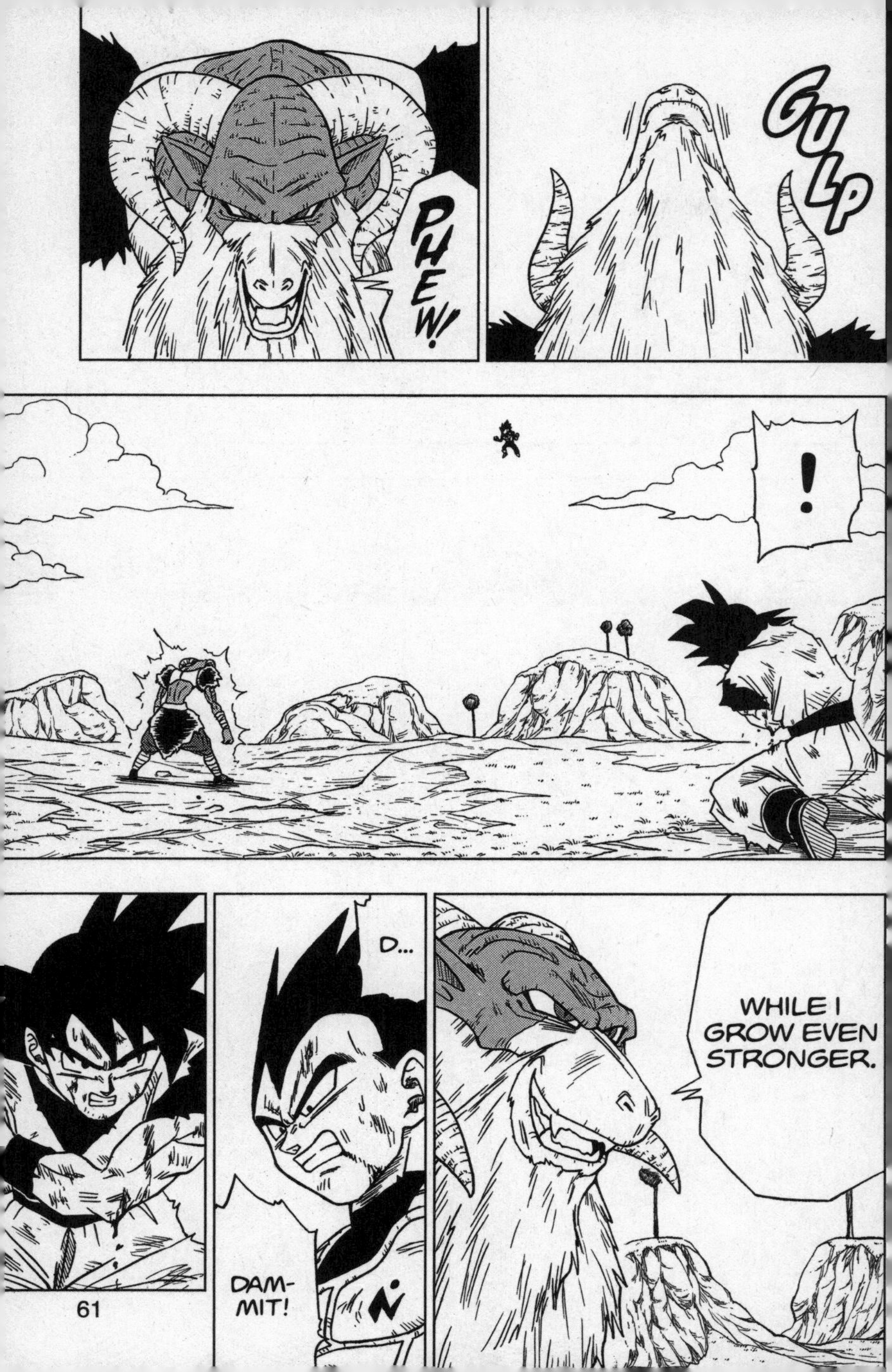
GULP
PHEW!
!
WHILE I GROW EVEN STRONGER.
D...
DAM-MIT!

YAWWWN
...

SO BORED...

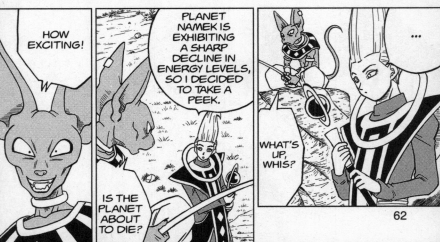

HOW EXCITING!

PLANET NAMEK IS EXHIBITING A SHARP DECLINE IN ENERGY LEVELS, SO I DECIDED TO TAKE A PEEK.

IS THE PLANET ABOUT TO DIE?

WHAT'S UP, WHIS?

...

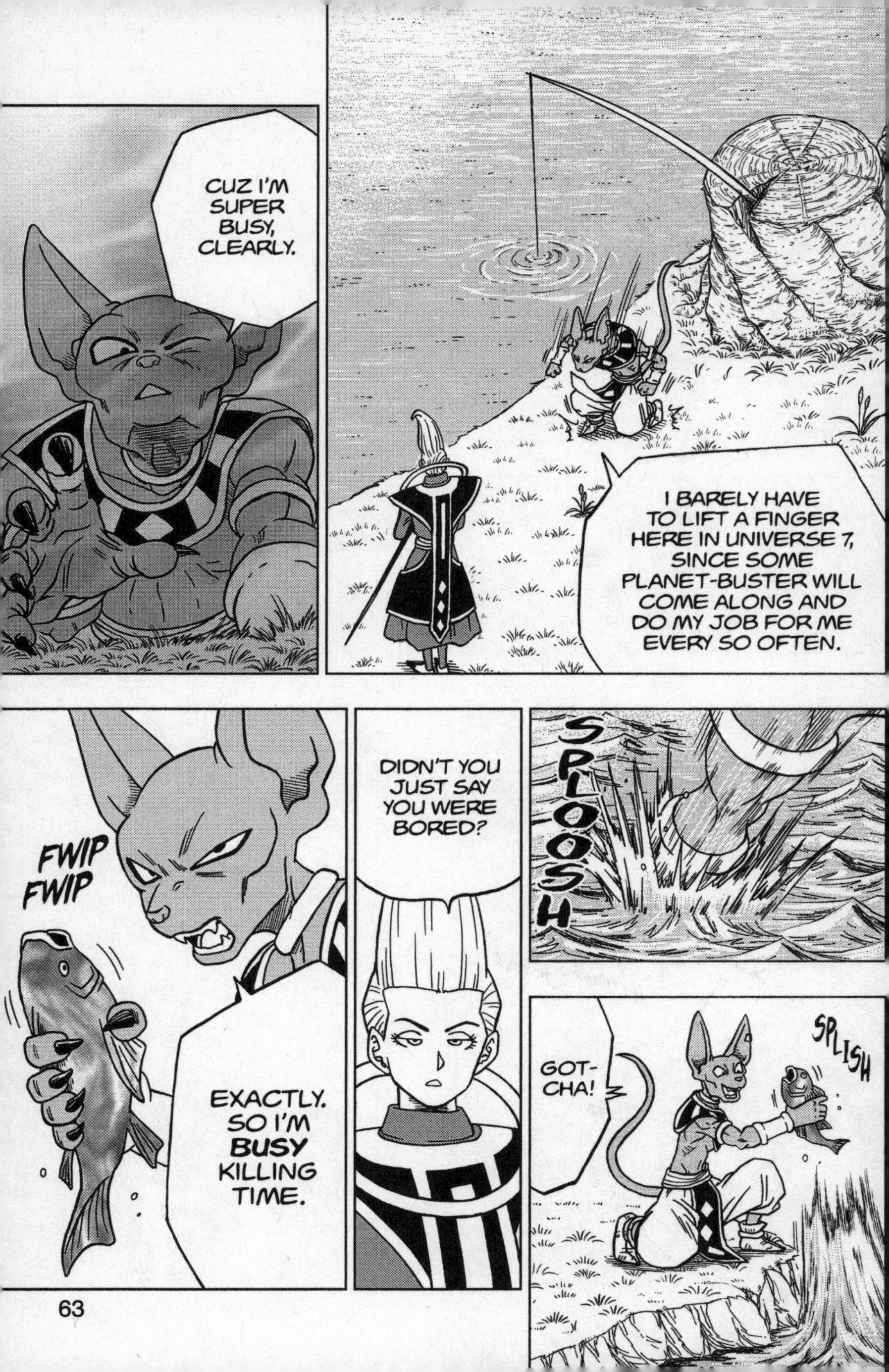
I BARELY HAVE TO LIFT A FINGER HERE IN UNIVERSE 7, SINCE SOME PLANET-BUSTER WILL COME ALONG AND DO MY JOB FOR ME EVERY SO OFTEN.
CUZ I'M SUPER BUSY, CLEARLY.
SPLOOSH
GOT-CHA!
SPLISH
DIDN'T YOU JUST SAY YOU WERE BORED?
FWIP FWIP
EXACTLY. SO I'M **BUSY** KILLING TIME.

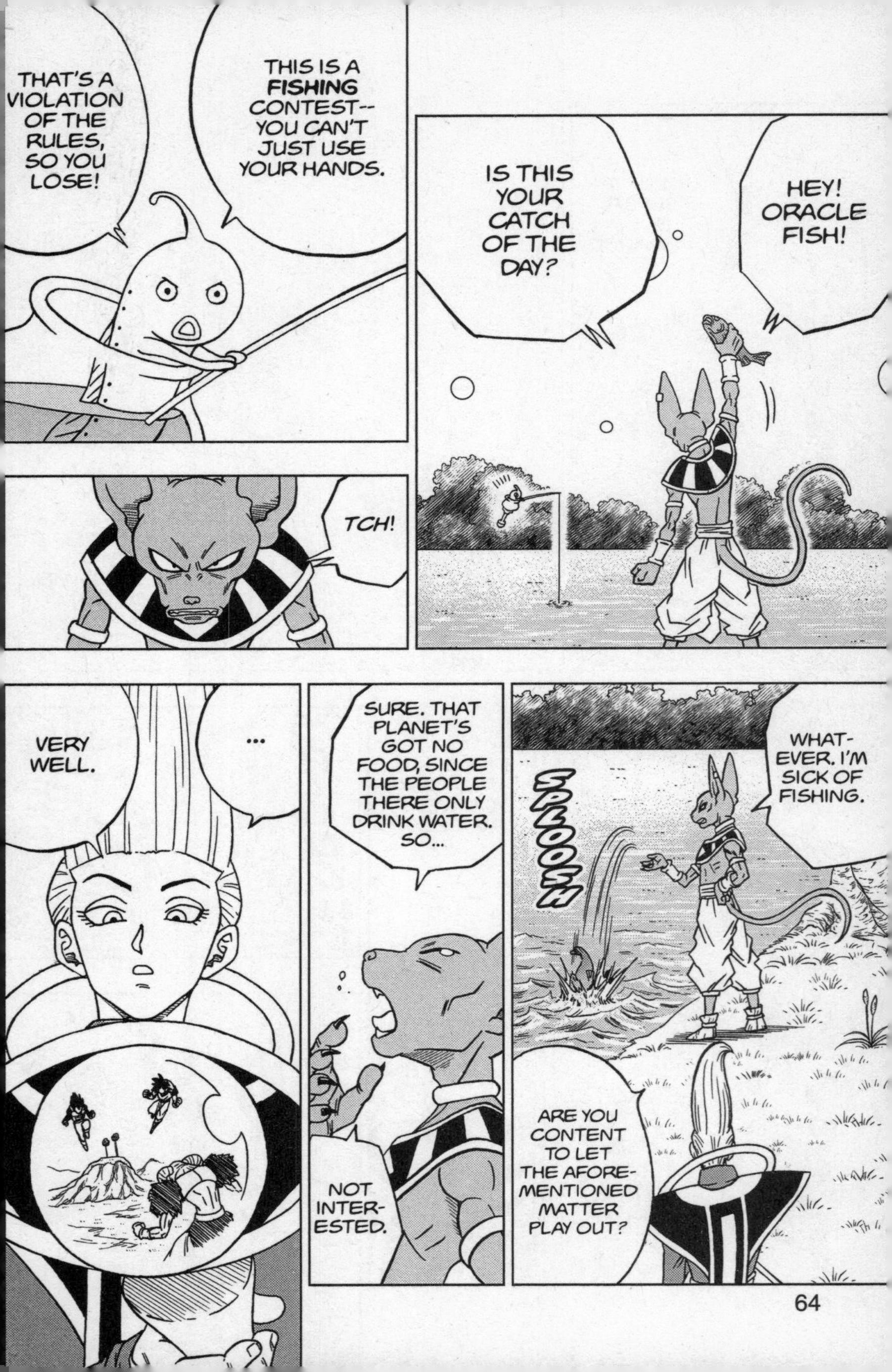
HEY! ORACLE FISH!
IS THIS YOUR CATCH OF THE DAY?
THIS IS A **FISHING** CONTEST-- YOU CAN'T JUST USE YOUR HANDS.
THAT'S A VIOLATION OF THE RULES, SO YOU LOSE!
TCH!
WHATEVER. I'M SICK OF FISHING.
SPLOOSH
ARE YOU CONTENT TO LET THE AFOREMENTIONED MATTER PLAY OUT?
SURE. THAT PLANET'S GOT NO FOOD, SINCE THE PEOPLE THERE ONLY DRINK WATER. SO...
NOT INTERESTED.
...
VERY WELL.

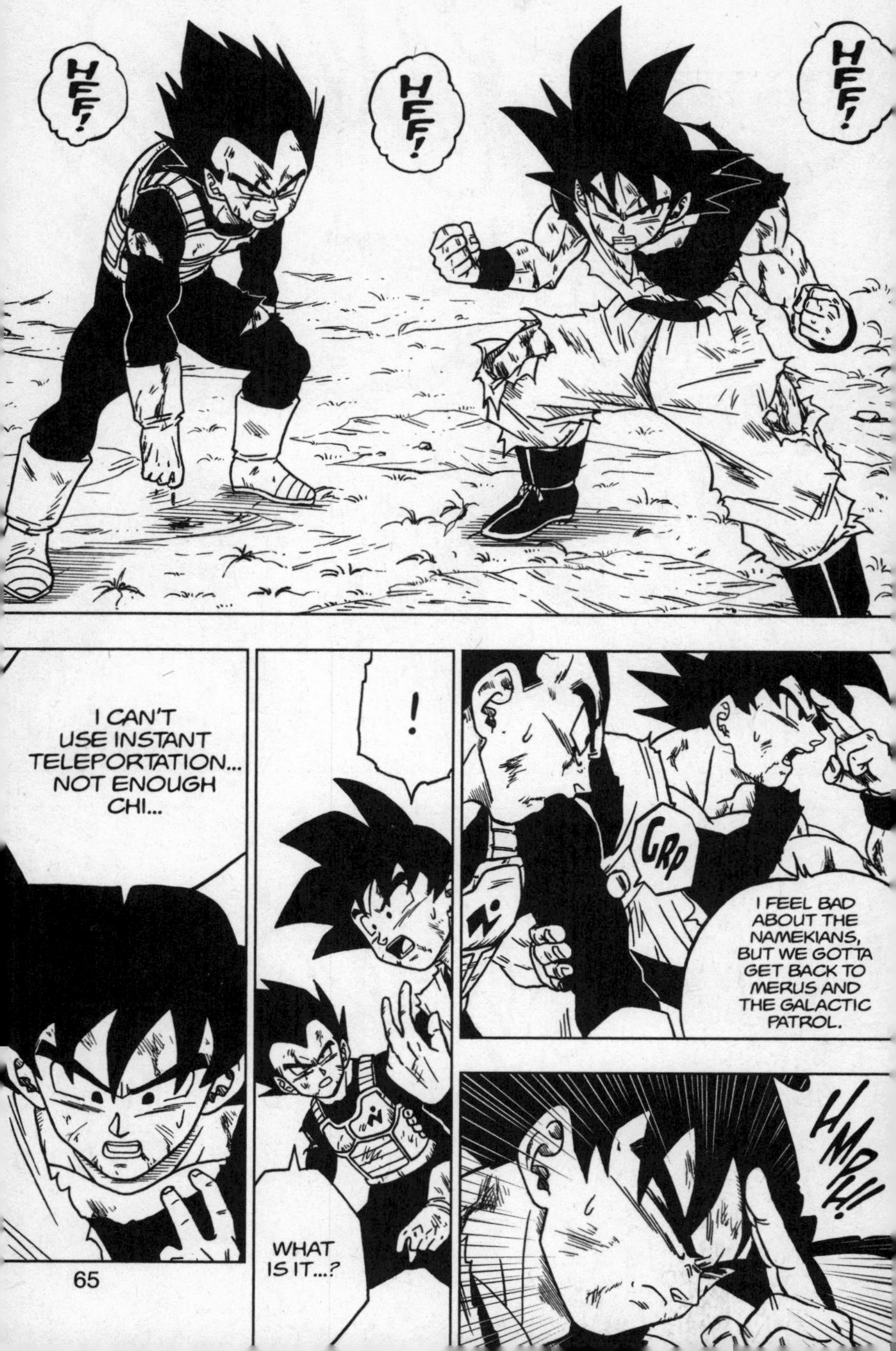
HEF!
HEF!
HEF!
GRP
I FEEL BAD ABOUT THE NAMEKIANS, BUT WE GOTTA GET BACK TO MERUS AND THE GALACTIC PATROL.
HMPH!!
!
WHAT IS IT...?
I CAN'T USE INSTANT TELEPORTATION... NOT ENOUGH CHI...

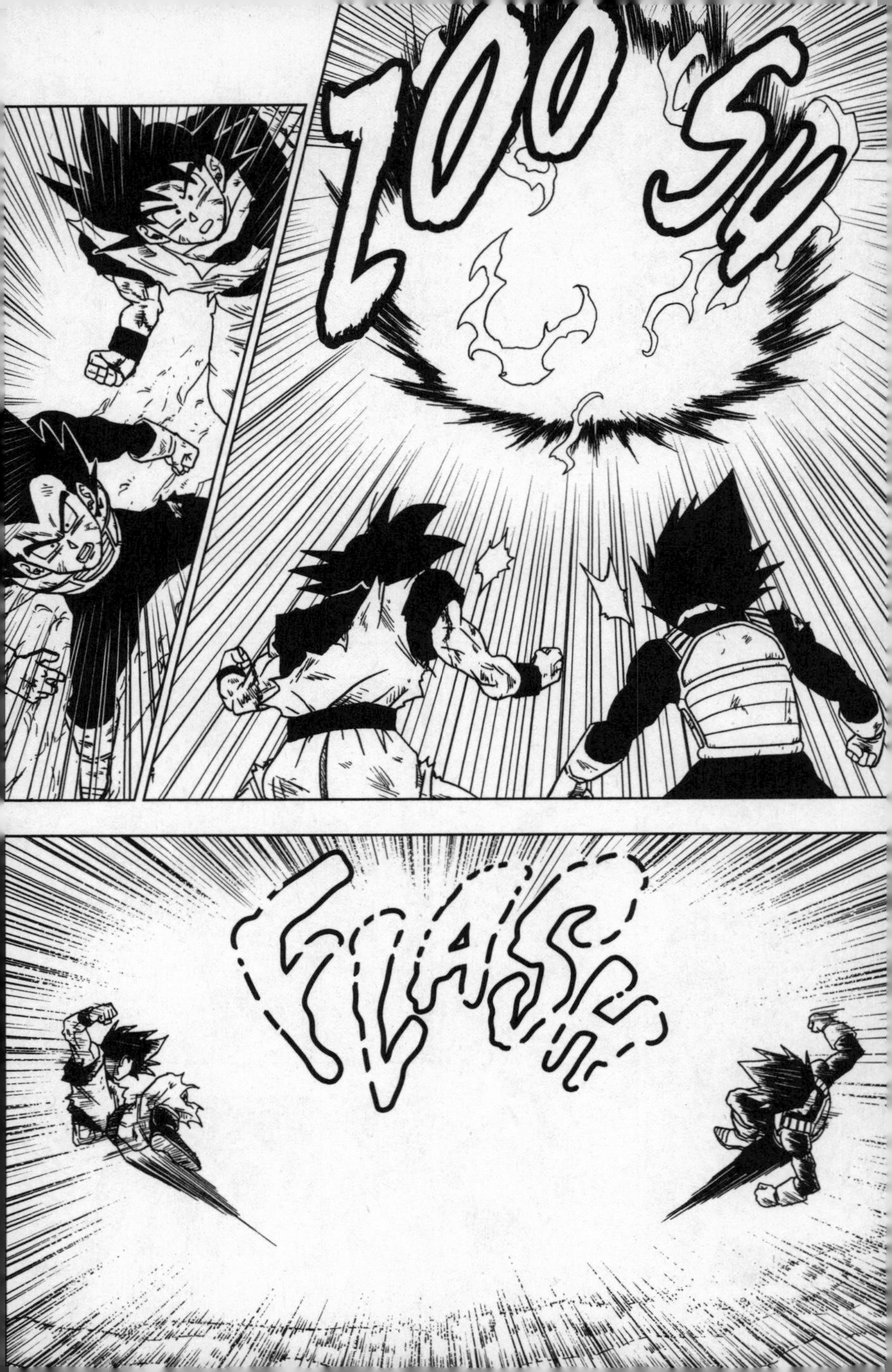
ZOOSH
FLASH

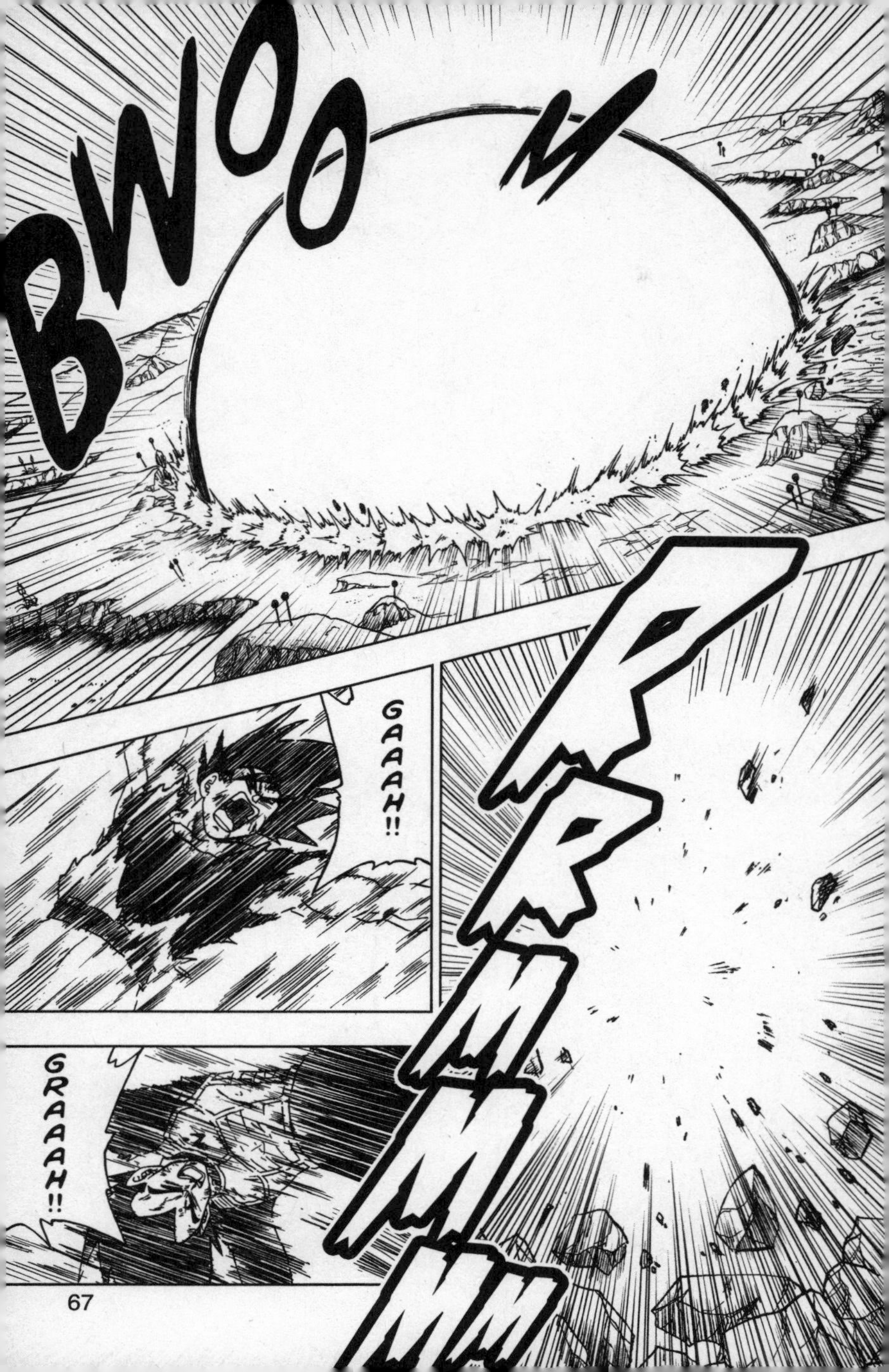
BWOOM
PRMMM
GAAAAH!!
GRAAAAH!!

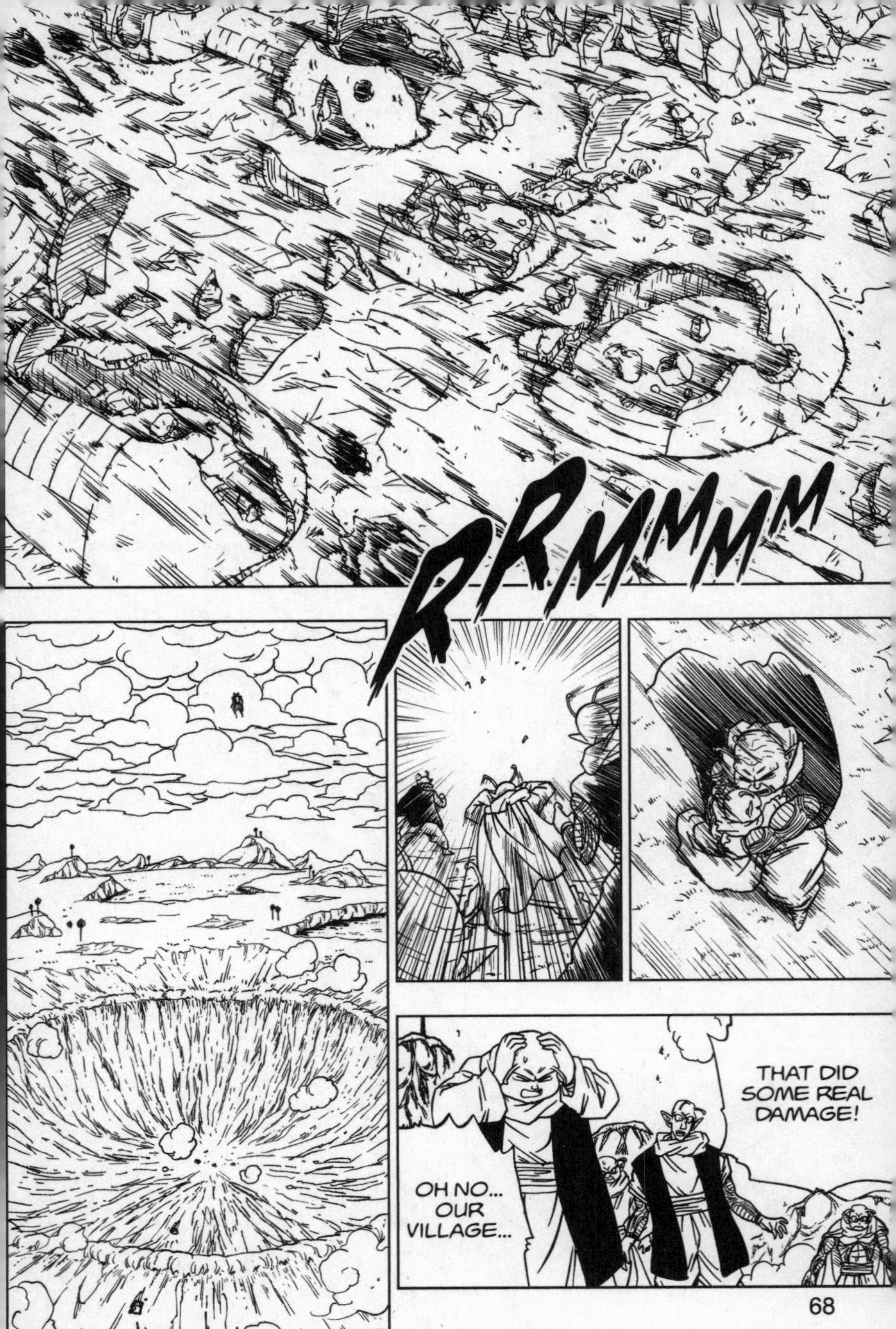
RRMMMM
THAT DID SOME REAL DAMAGE!
OH NO... OUR VILLAGE...

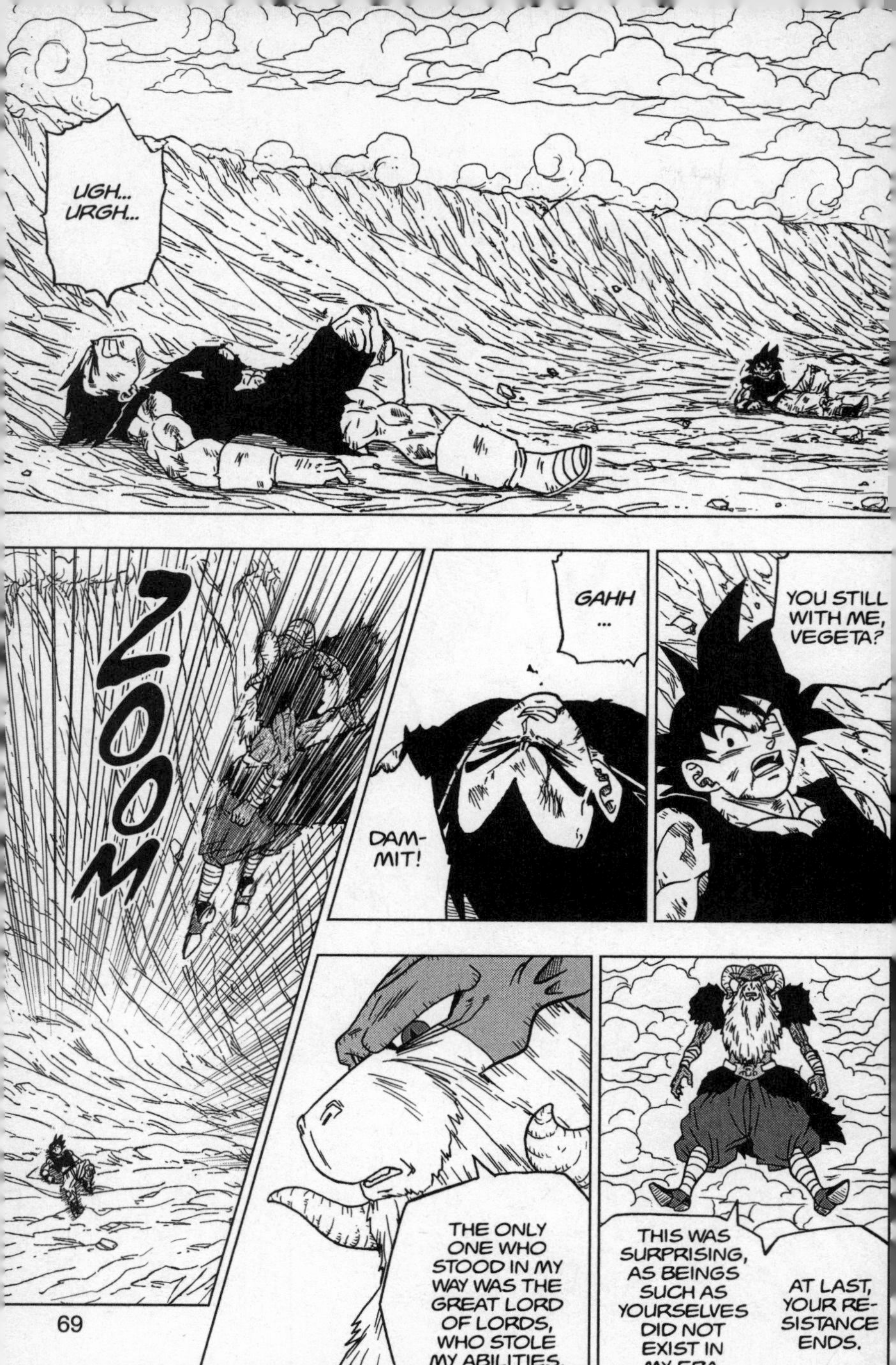

UGH... URGH...
YOU STILL WITH ME, VEGETA?
GAHH ...
DAM-MIT!
AT LAST, YOUR RE-SISTANCE ENDS.
THIS WAS SURPRISING, AS BEINGS SUCH AS YOURSELVES DID NOT EXIST IN MY ERA.
THE ONLY ONE WHO STOOD IN MY WAY WAS THE GREAT LORD OF LORDS, WHO STOLE MY ABILITIES.
ZOOM

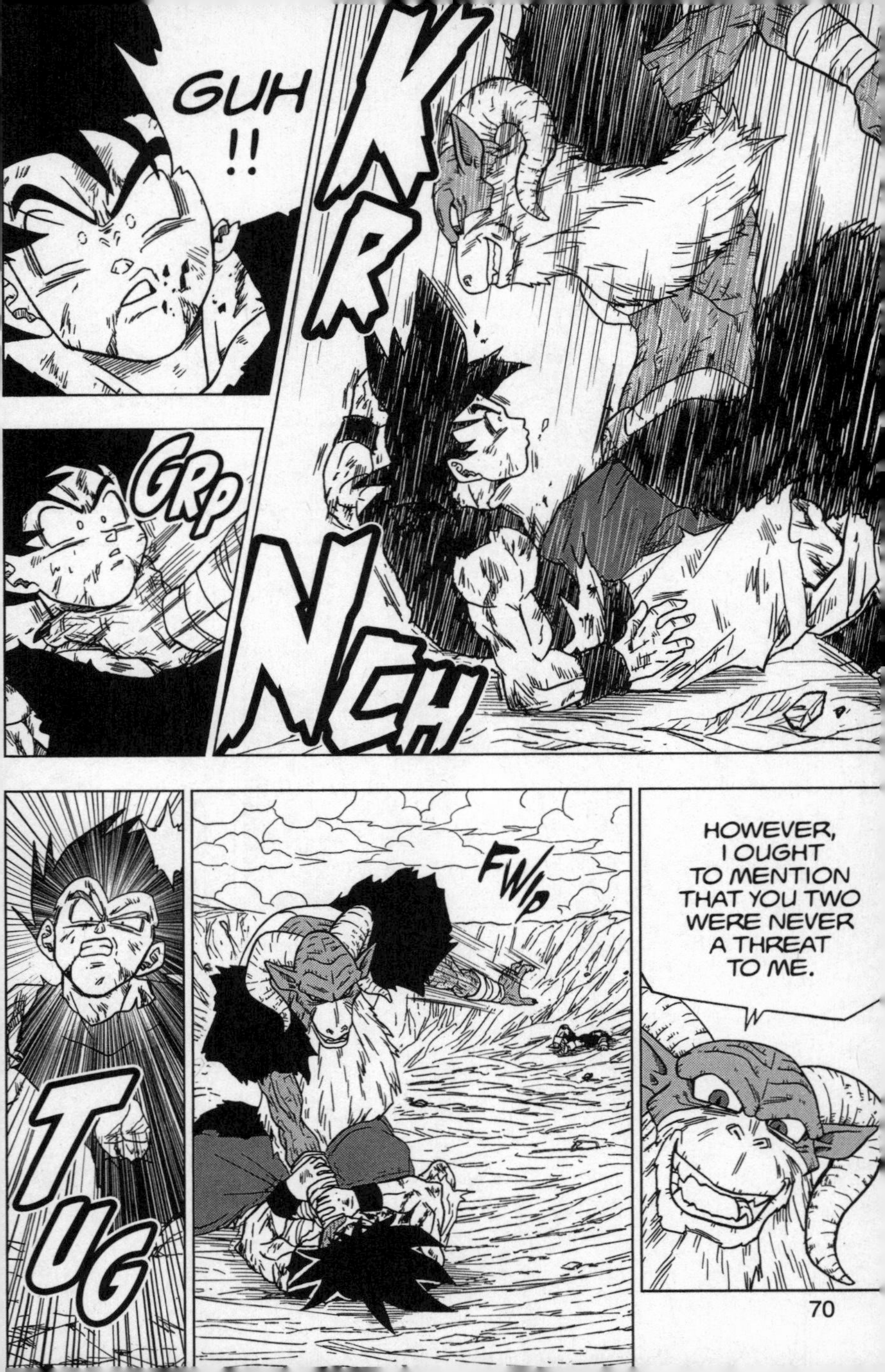
KRNCH
GUH !!
GRP
HOWEVER, I OUGHT TO MENTION THAT YOU TWO WERE NEVER A THREAT TO ME.
FWIP
TUG

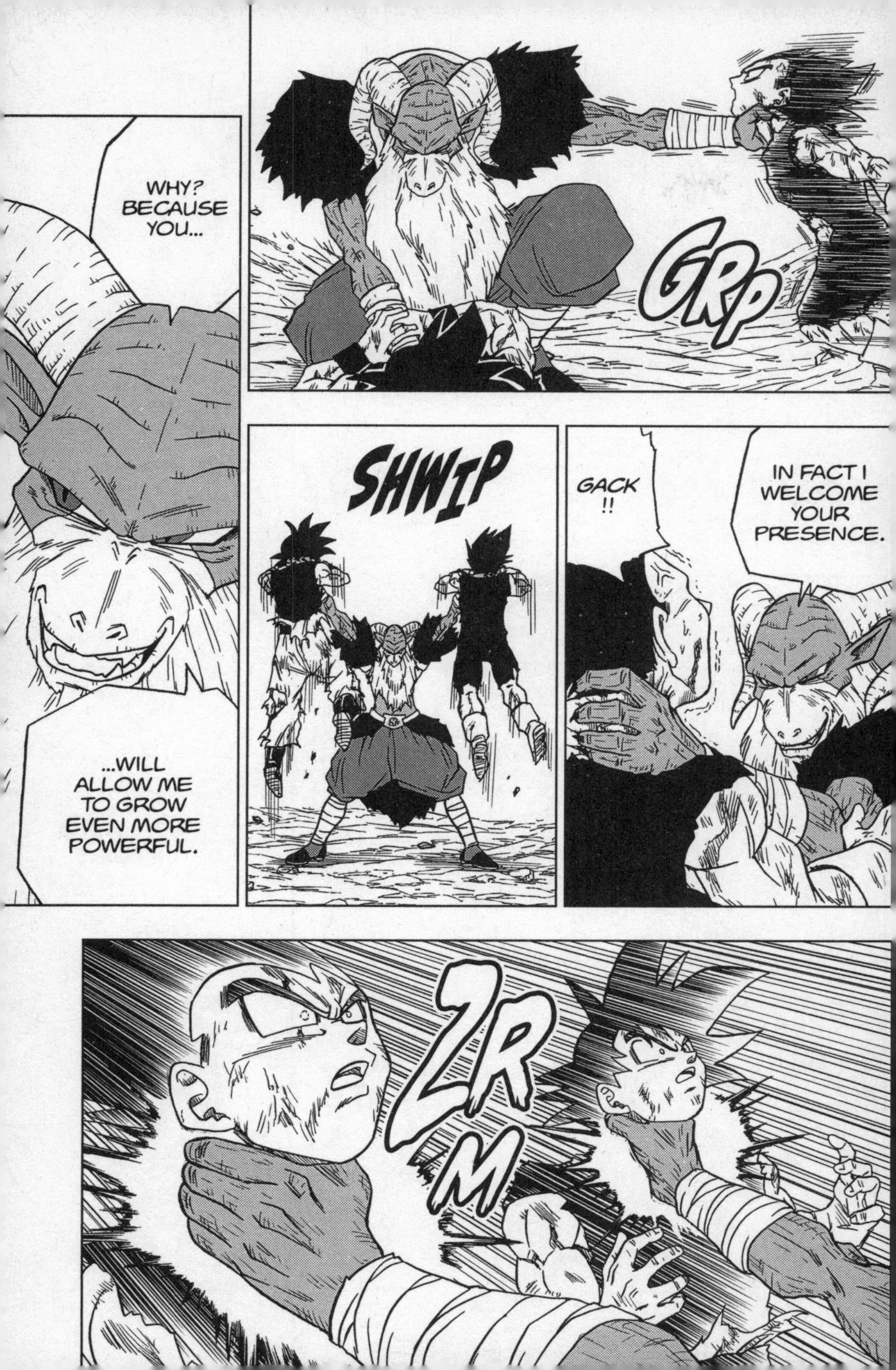
GRP
IN FACT I WELCOME YOUR PRESENCE.
GACK !!
SHWIP
WHY? BECAUSE YOU...
...WILL ALLOW ME TO GROW EVEN MORE POWERFUL.
ZRM

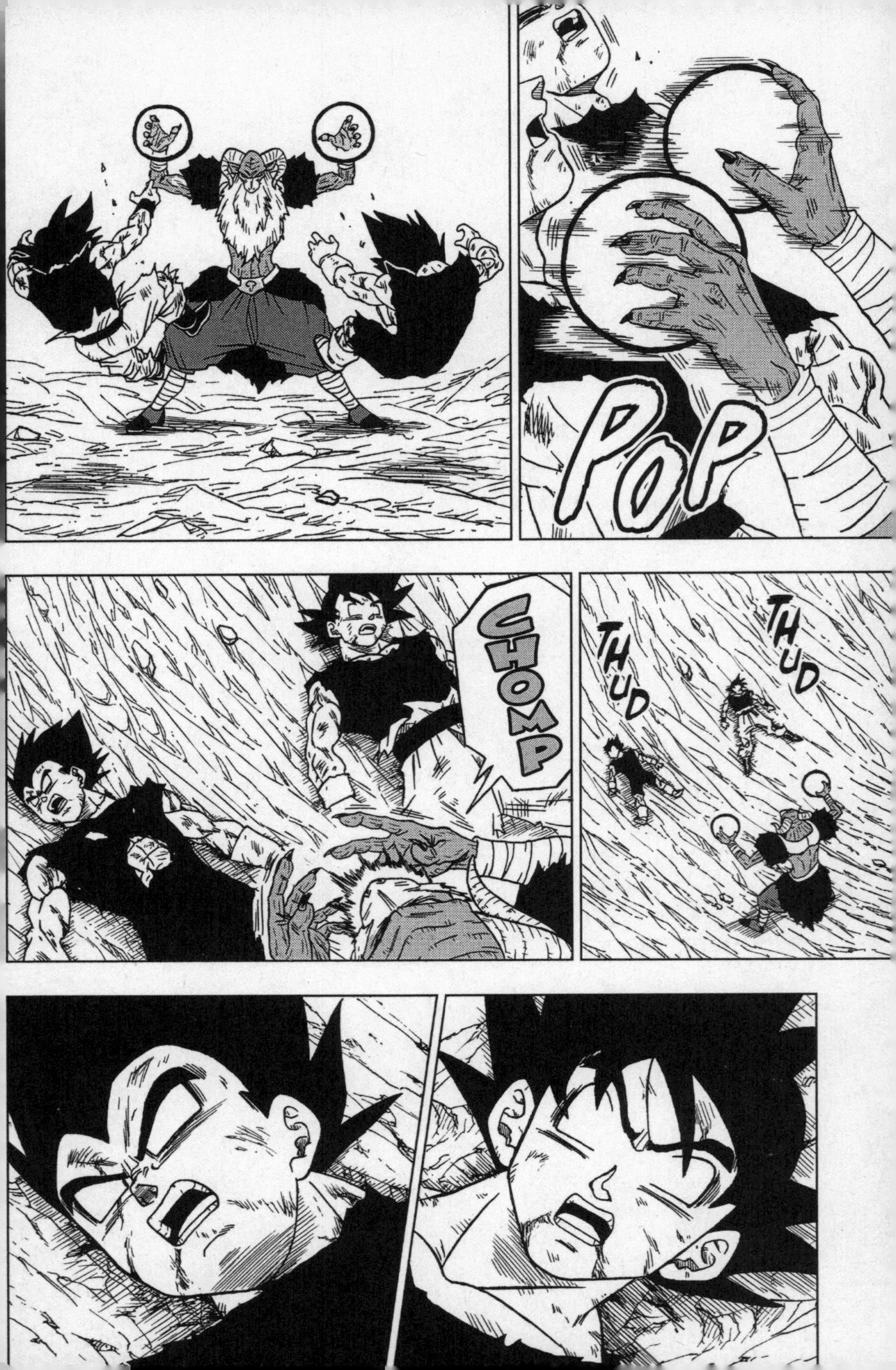
POP
THUD
THUD
CHOMP

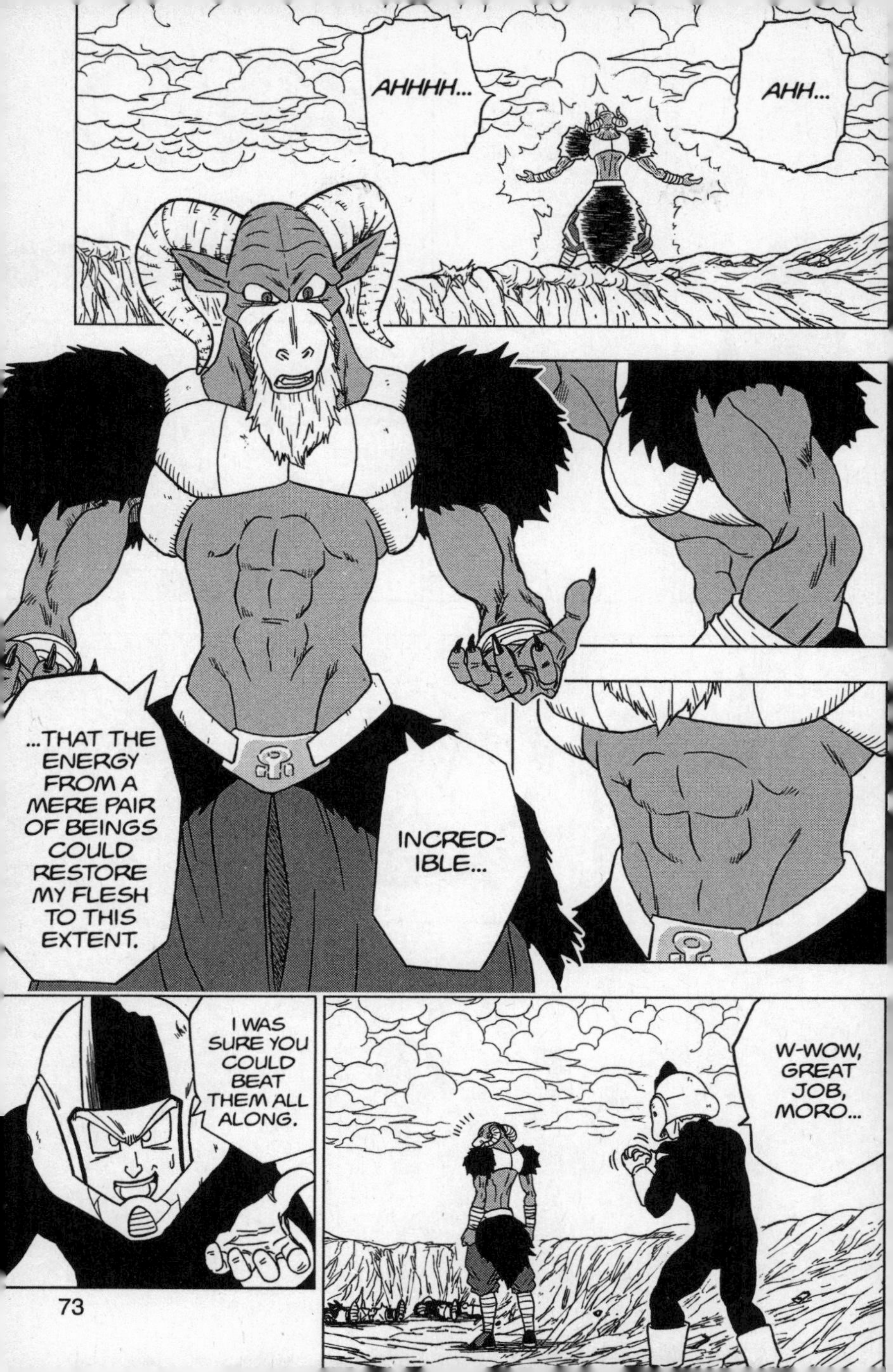
AHH...
AHHHH...
INCRED-IBLE...
...THAT THE ENERGY FROM A MERE PAIR OF BEINGS COULD RESTORE MY FLESH TO THIS EXTENT.
W-WOW, GREAT JOB, MORO...
I WAS SURE YOU COULD BEAT THEM ALL ALONG.

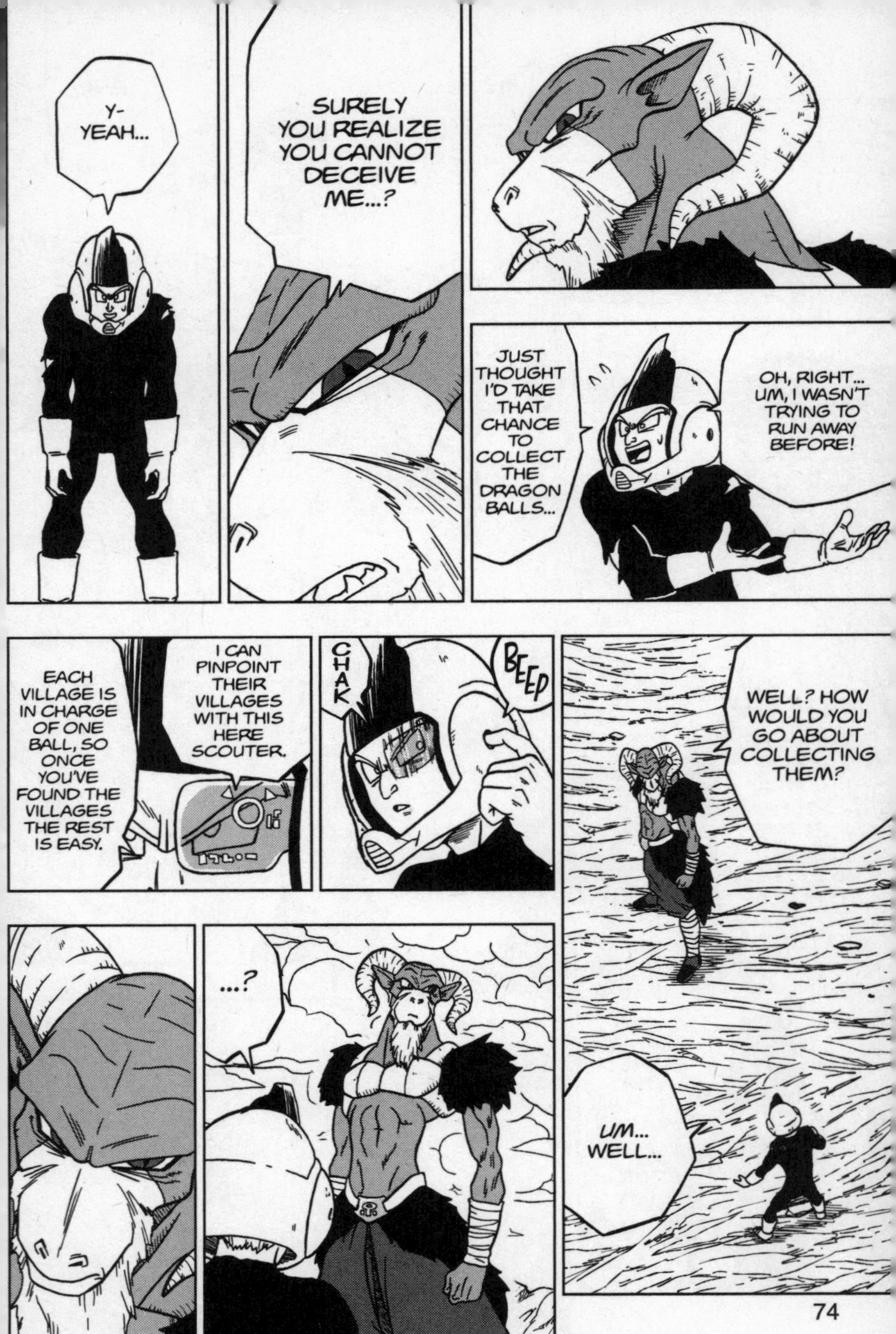
OH, RIGHT... UM, I WASN'T TRYING TO RUN AWAY BEFORE!
JUST THOUGHT I'D TAKE THAT CHANCE TO COLLECT THE DRAGON BALLS...
SURELY YOU REALIZE YOU CANNOT DECEIVE ME...?
Y- YEAH...
WELL? HOW WOULD YOU GO ABOUT COLLECTING THEM?
UM... WELL...
BEEP
CHAK
I CAN PINPOINT THEIR VILLAGES WITH THIS HERE SCOUTER.
EACH VILLAGE IS IN CHARGE OF ONE BALL, SO ONCE YOU'VE FOUND THE VILLAGES THE REST IS EASY.
...?

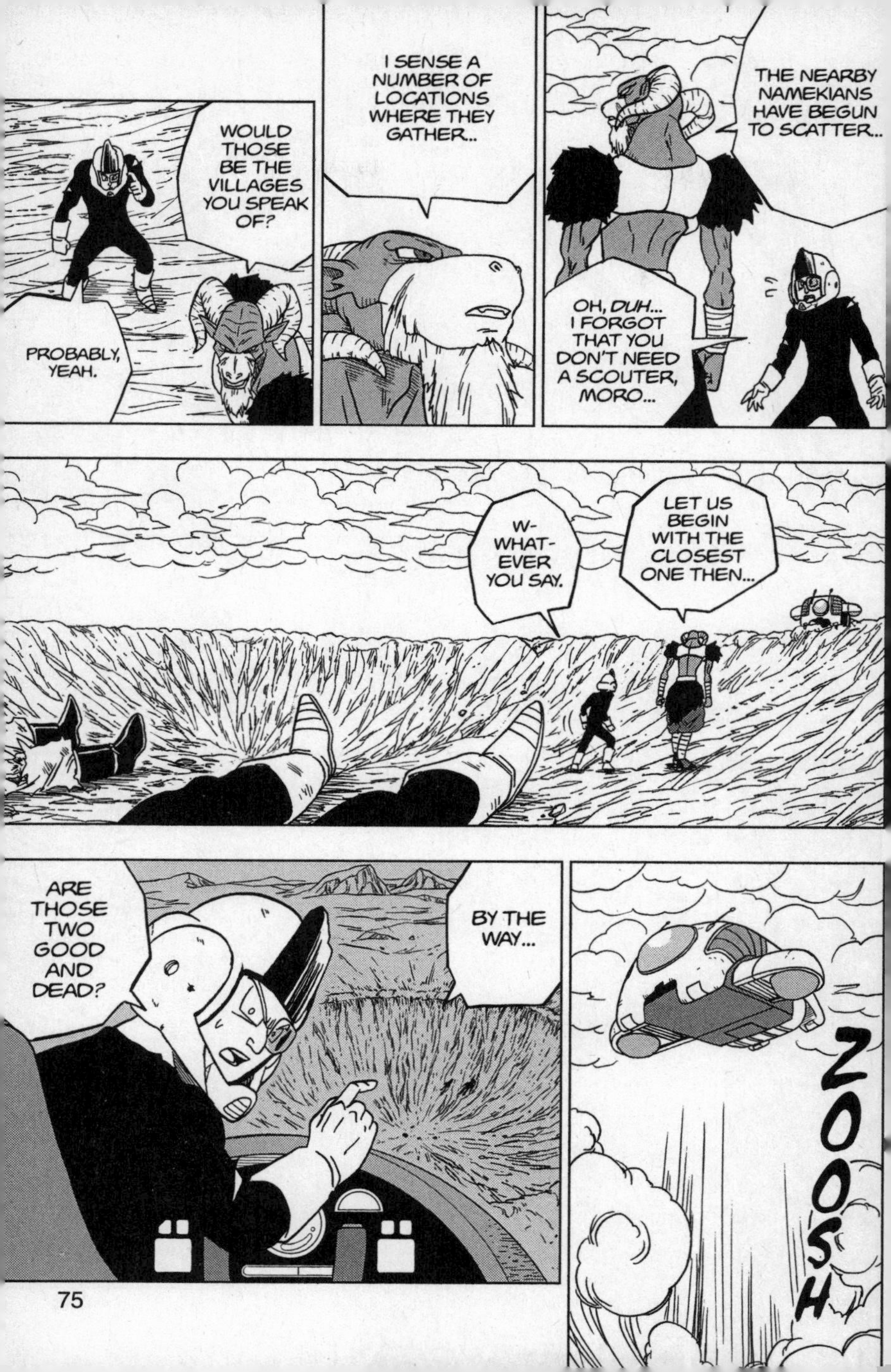
THE NEARBY NAMEKIANS HAVE BEGUN TO SCATTER...
OH, *DUH*... I FORGOT THAT YOU DON'T NEED A SCOUTER, MORO...
I SENSE A NUMBER OF LOCATIONS WHERE THEY GATHER...
WOULD THOSE BE THE VILLAGES YOU SPEAK OF?
PROBABLY, YEAH.
LET US BEGIN WITH THE CLOSEST ONE THEN...
W-WHATEVER YOU SAY.
ZOOOSH
BY THE WAY...
ARE THOSE TWO GOOD AND DEAD?

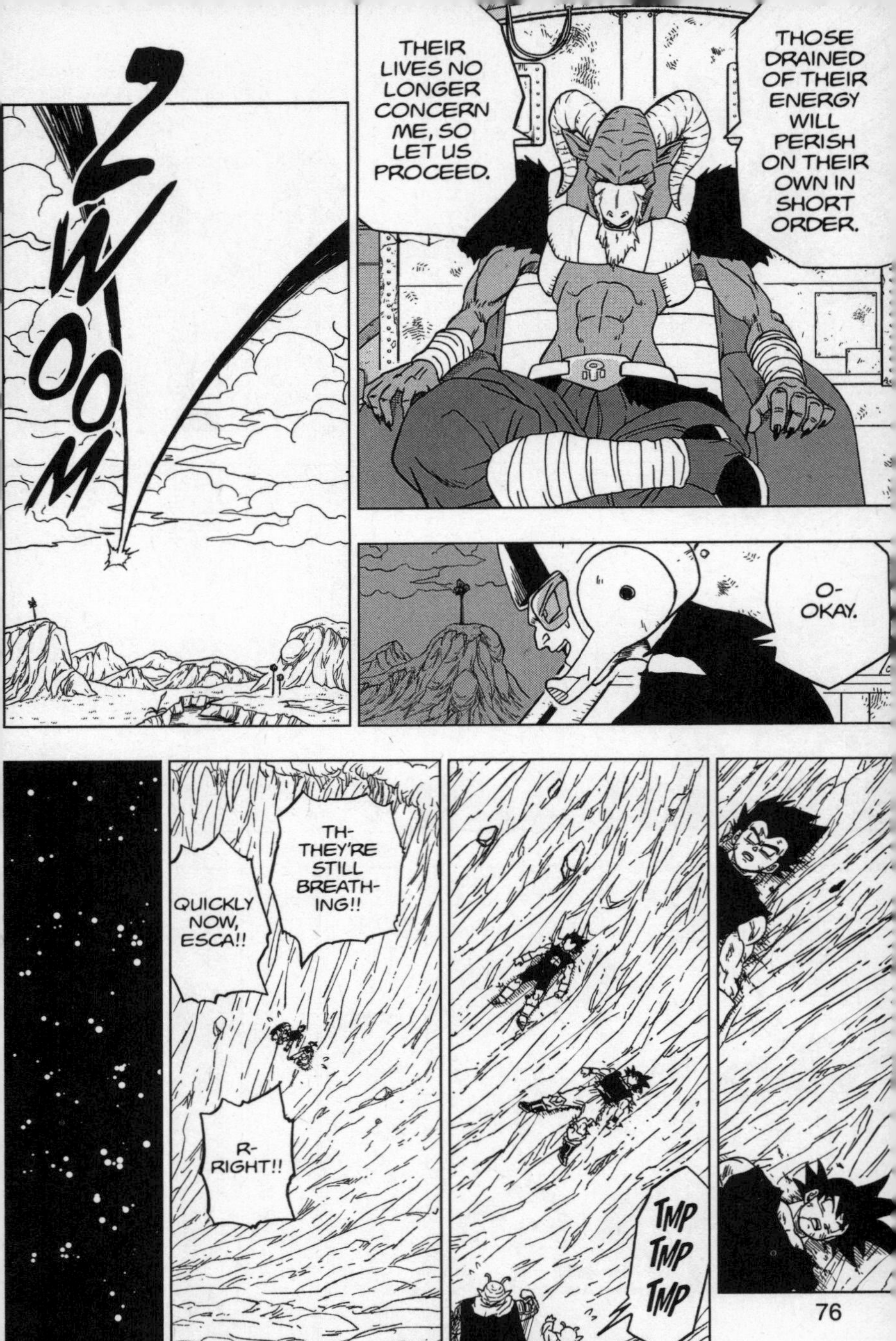

THOSE DRAINED OF THEIR ENERGY WILL PERISH ON THEIR OWN IN SHORT ORDER.
THEIR LIVES NO LONGER CONCERN ME, SO LET US PROCEED.
O-OKAY.
ZWOOM
TMP TMP TMP
TH-THEY'RE STILL BREATHING!!
QUICKLY NOW, ESCA!!
R-RIGHT!!

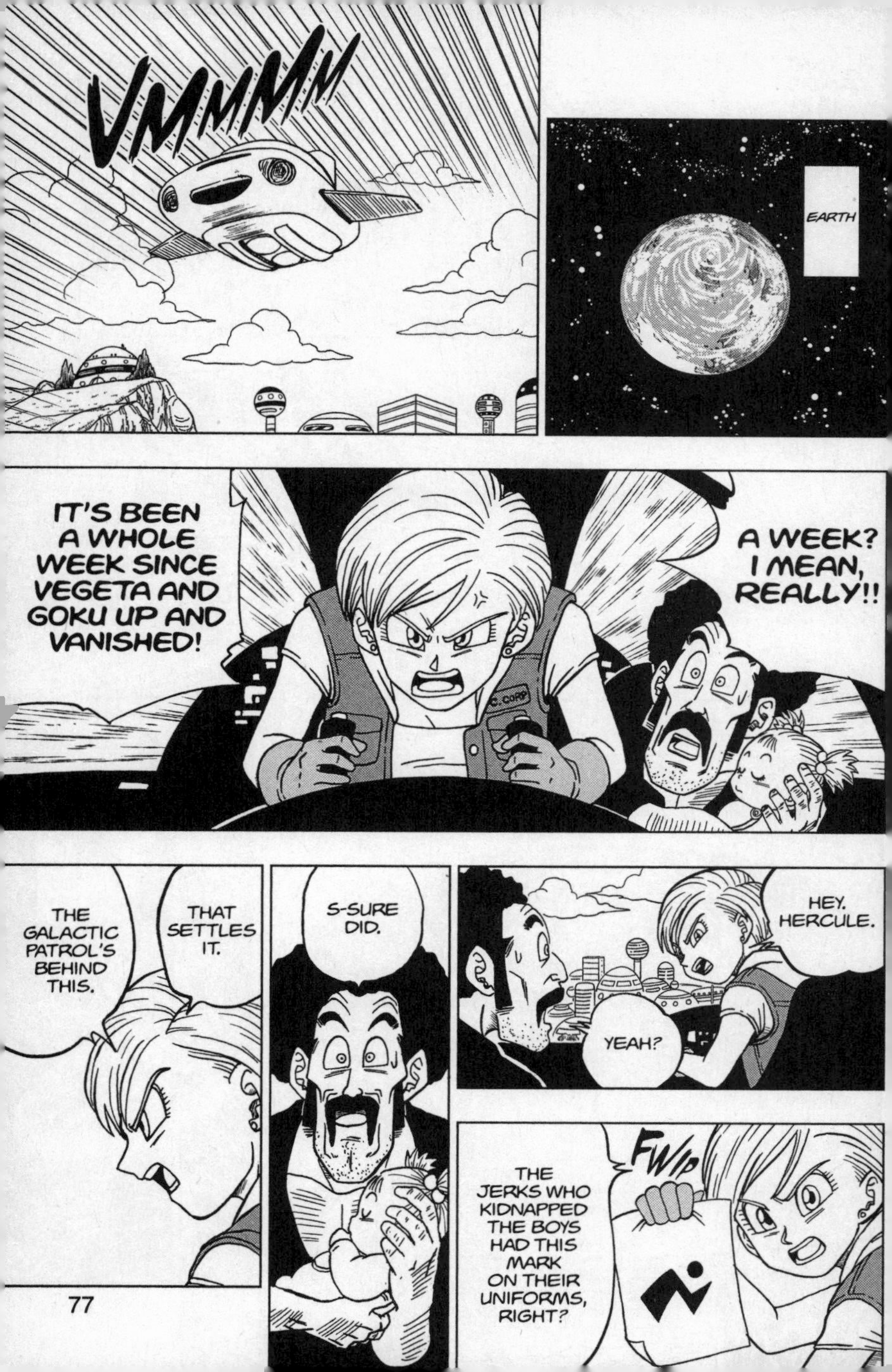
EARTH
VMMMM
IT'S BEEN A WHOLE WEEK SINCE VEGETA AND GOKU UP AND VANISHED!
A WEEK? I MEAN, REALLY!!
HEY. HERCULE.
YEAH?
FWIP
THE JERKS WHO KIDNAPPED THE BOYS HAD THIS MARK ON THEIR UNIFORMS, RIGHT?
S-SURE DID.
THAT SETTLES IT.
THE GALACTIC PATROL'S BEHIND THIS.

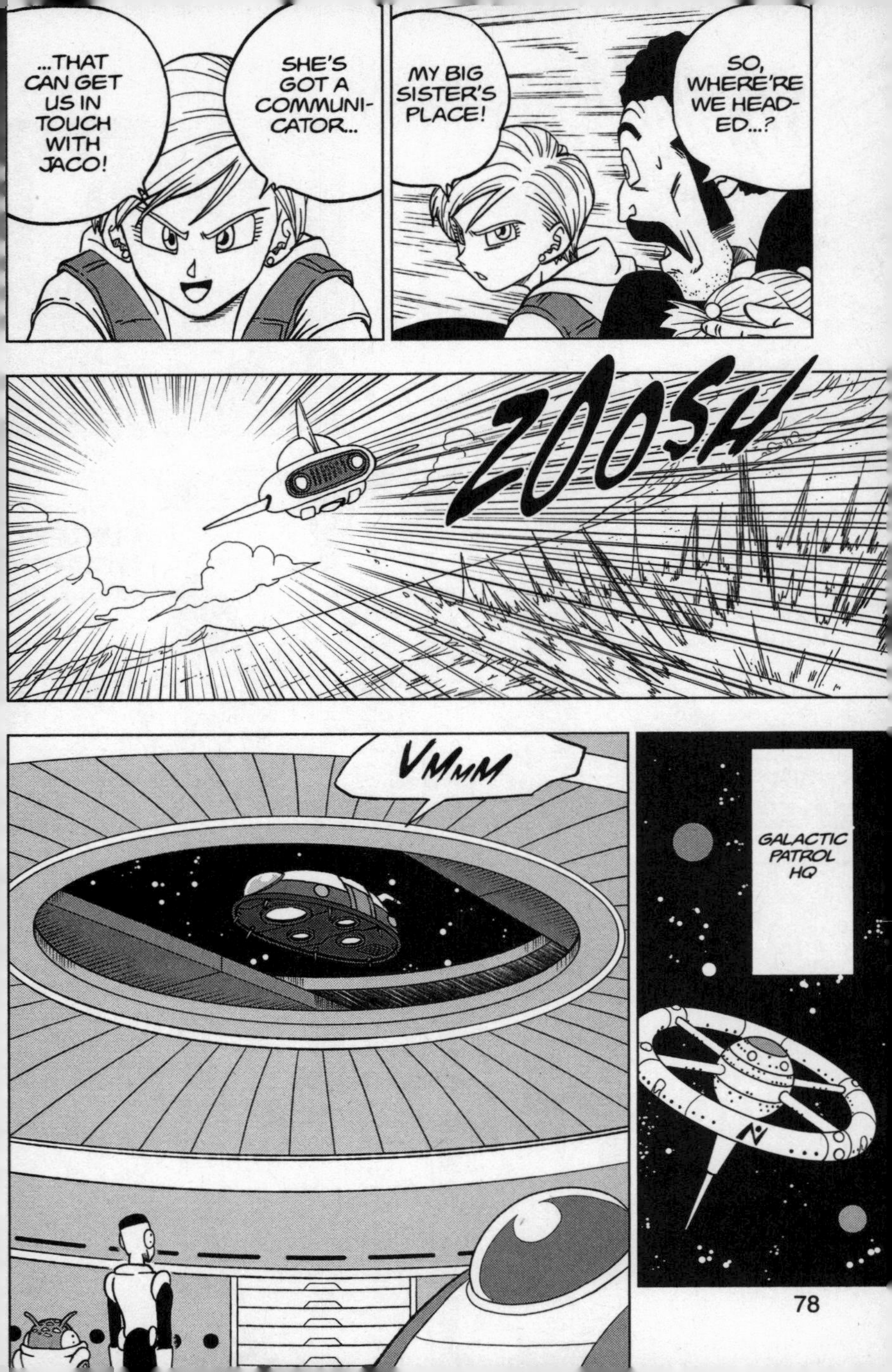
SO, WHERE'RE WE HEAD-ED...?
MY BIG SISTER'S PLACE!
SHE'S GOT A COMMUNI-CATOR...
...THAT CAN GET US IN TOUCH WITH JACO!
ZOOSH
GALACTIC PATROL HQ
VMMM

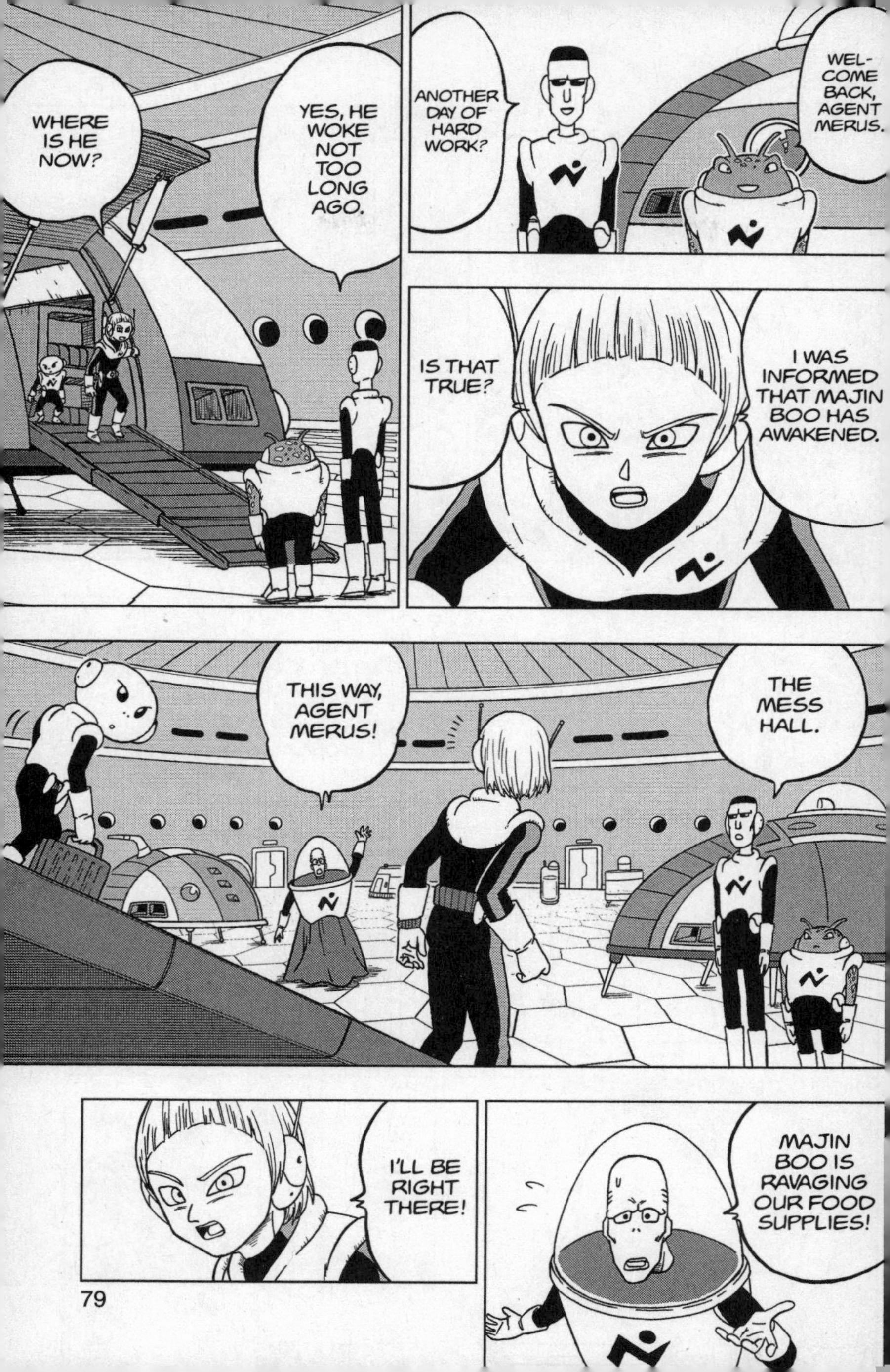
WEL-COME BACK, AGENT MERUS.
ANOTHER DAY OF HARD WORK?
I WAS INFORMED THAT MAJIN BOO HAS AWAKENED.
IS THAT TRUE?
YES, HE WOKE NOT TOO LONG AGO.
WHERE IS HE NOW?
THE MESS HALL.
THIS WAY, AGENT MERUS!
MAJIN BOO IS RAVAGING OUR FOOD SUPPLIES!
I'LL BE RIGHT THERE!

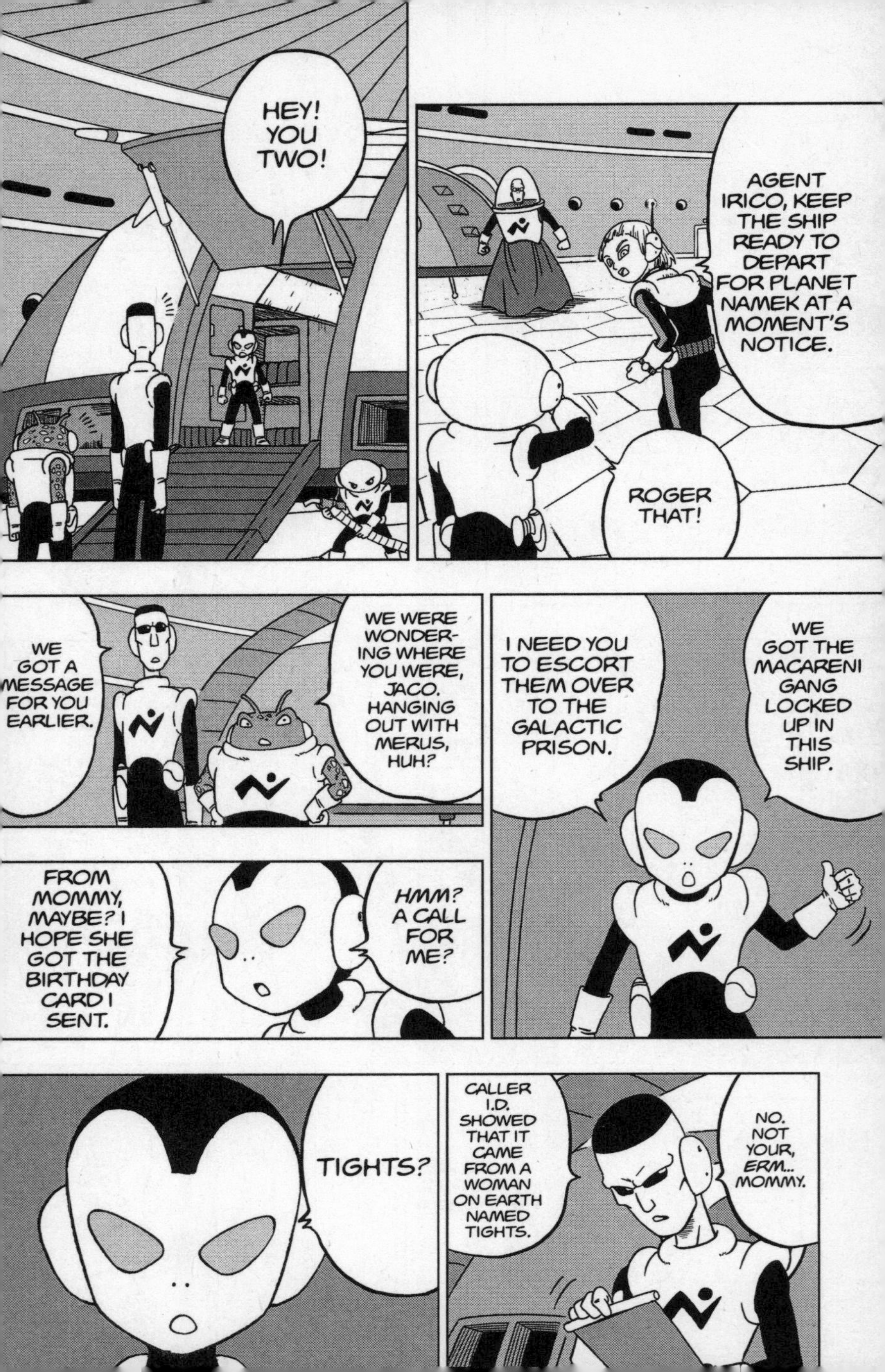
AGENT IRICO, KEEP THE SHIP READY TO DEPART FOR PLANET NAMEK AT A MOMENT'S NOTICE.
ROGER THAT!
HEY! YOU TWO!
WE GOT THE MACARENI GANG LOCKED UP IN THIS SHIP.
I NEED YOU TO ESCORT THEM OVER TO THE GALACTIC PRISON.
WE WERE WONDER-ING WHERE YOU WERE, JACO. HANGING OUT WITH MERUS, HUH?
WE GOT A MESSAGE FOR YOU EARLIER.
HMM? A CALL FOR ME?
FROM MOMMY, MAYBE? I HOPE SHE GOT THE BIRTHDAY CARD I SENT.
NO. NOT YOUR, ERM... MOMMY.
CALLER I.D. SHOWED THAT IT CAME FROM A WOMAN ON EARTH NAMED TIGHTS.
TIGHTS?

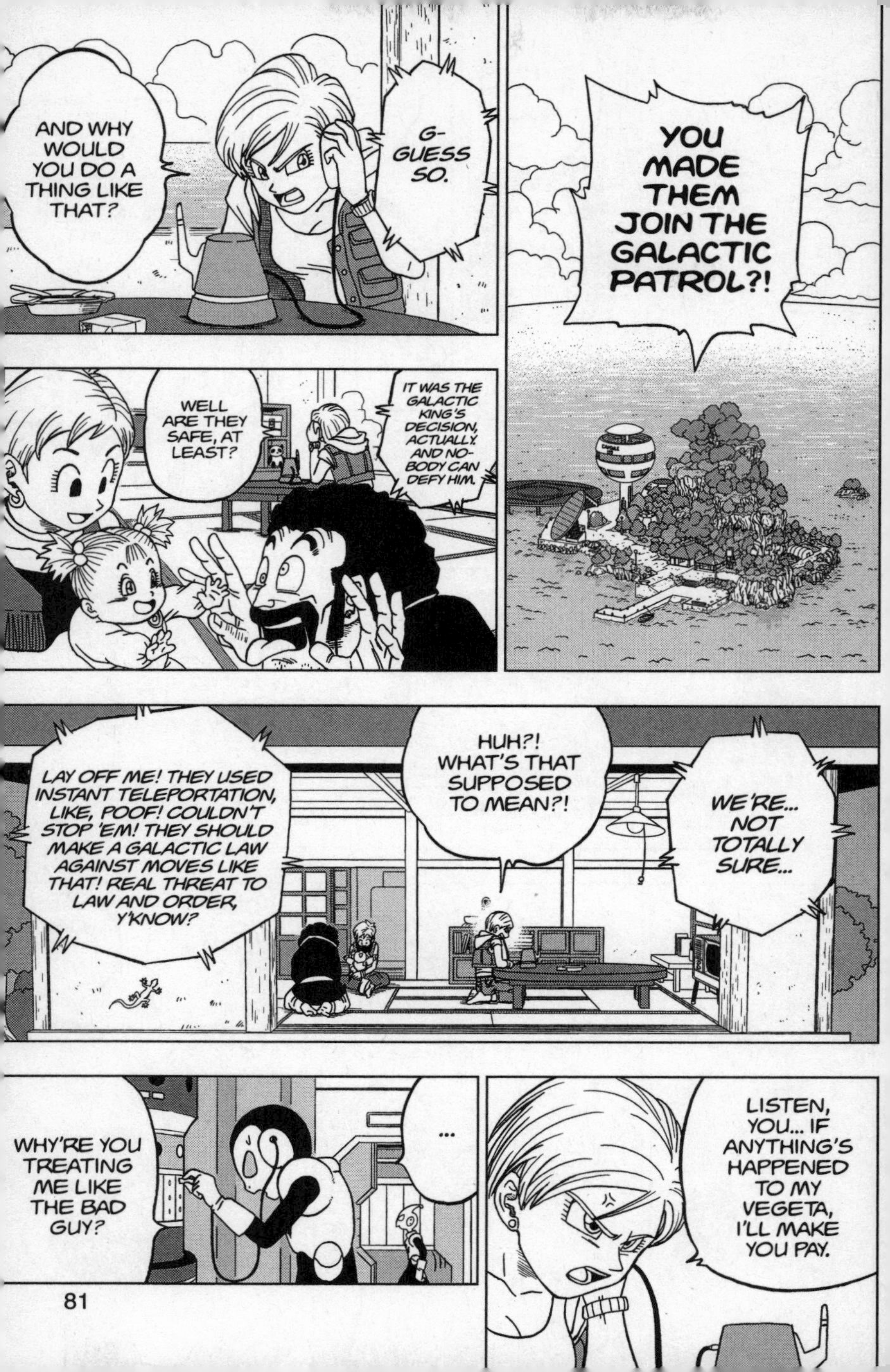

YOU MADE THEM JOIN THE GALACTIC PATROL?!
G-GUESS SO.
AND WHY WOULD YOU DO A THING LIKE THAT?
IT WAS THE GALACTIC KING'S DECISION, ACTUALLY. AND NOBODY CAN DEFY HIM.
WELL ARE THEY SAFE, AT LEAST?
WE'RE... NOT TOTALLY SURE...
HUH?! WHAT'S THAT SUPPOSED TO MEAN?!
LAY OFF ME! THEY USED INSTANT TELEPORTATION, LIKE, POOF! COULDN'T STOP 'EM! THEY SHOULD MAKE A GALACTIC LAW AGAINST MOVES LIKE THAT! REAL THREAT TO LAW AND ORDER, Y'KNOW?
LISTEN, YOU... IF ANYTHING'S HAPPENED TO MY VEGETA, I'LL MAKE YOU PAY.
...
WHY'RE YOU TREATING ME LIKE THE BAD GUY?

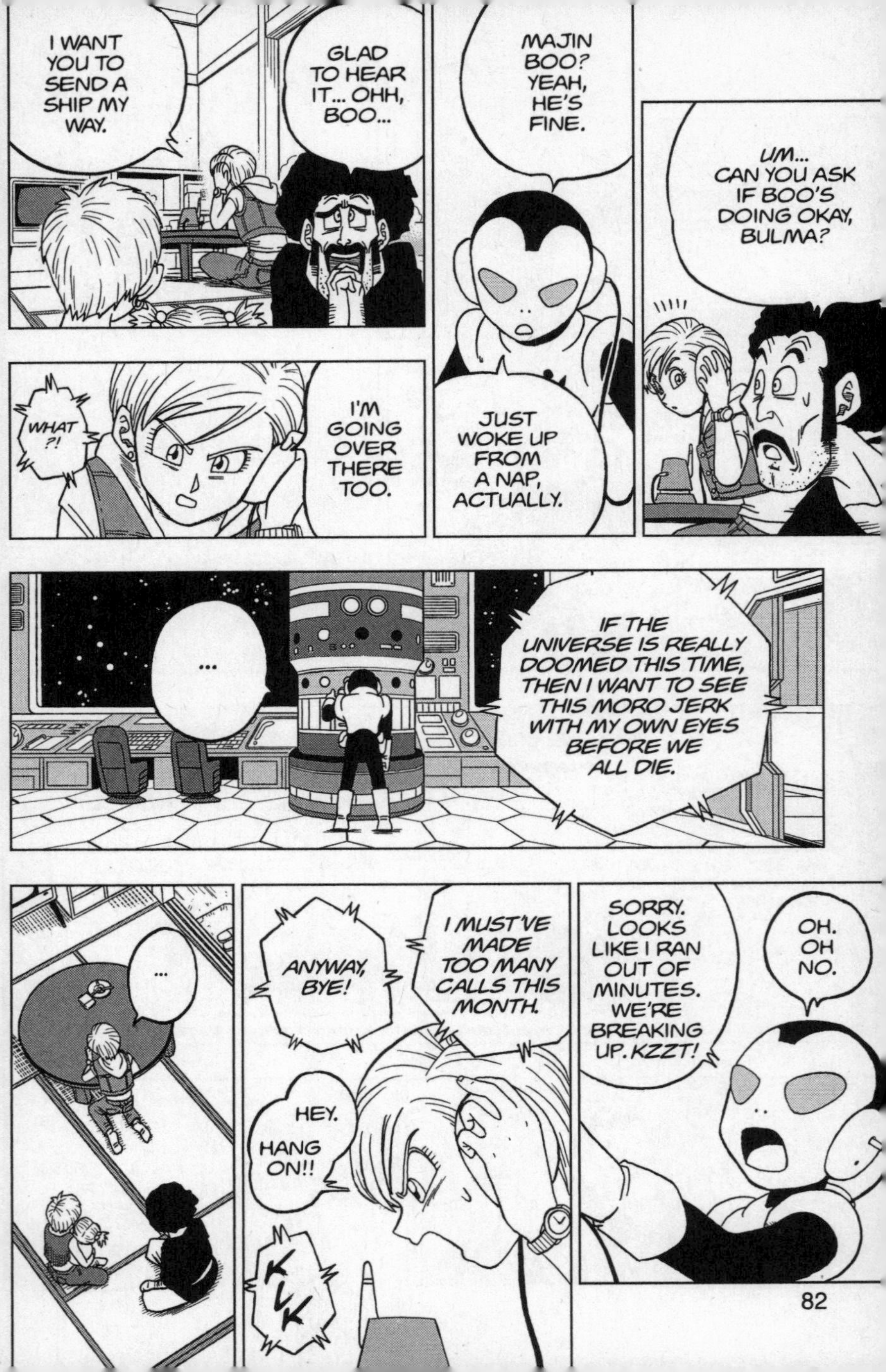
UM... CAN YOU ASK IF BOO'S DOING OKAY, BULMA?
MAJIN BOO? YEAH, HE'S FINE.
JUST WOKE UP FROM A NAP, ACTUALLY.
GLAD TO HEAR IT... OHH, BOO...
I WANT YOU TO SEND A SHIP MY WAY.
I'M GOING OVER THERE TOO.
WHAT?!
IF THE UNIVERSE IS REALLY DOOMED THIS TIME, THEN I WANT TO SEE THIS MORO JERK WITH MY OWN EYES BEFORE WE ALL DIE.
...
OH. OH NO.
SORRY. LOOKS LIKE I RAN OUT OF MINUTES. WE'RE BREAKING UP. KZZT!
I MUST'VE MADE TOO MANY CALLS THIS MONTH.
ANYWAY, BYE!
HEY. HANG ON!!
KLIK
...

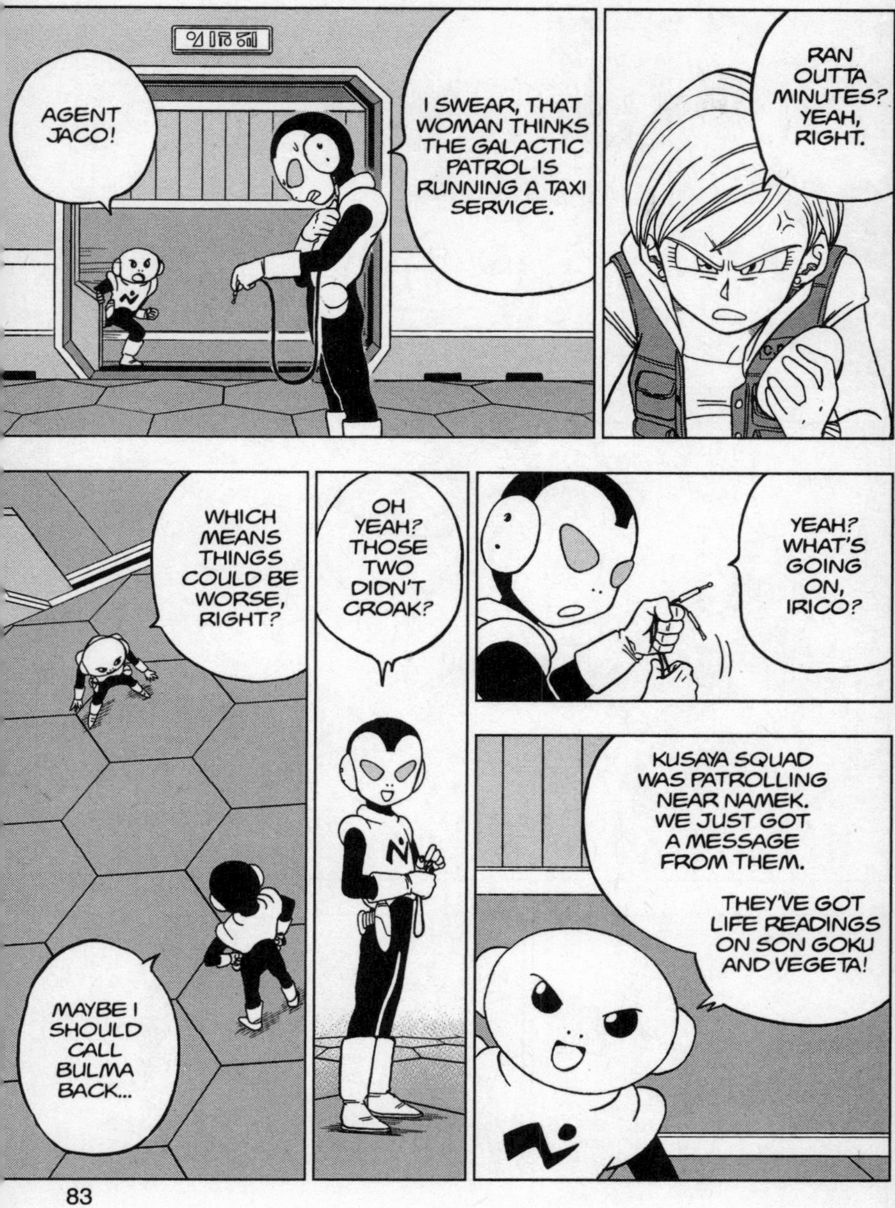
RAN OUTTA MINUTES? YEAH, RIGHT.
I SWEAR, THAT WOMAN THINKS THE GALACTIC PATROL IS RUNNING A TAXI SERVICE.
AGENT JACO!
YEAH? WHAT'S GOING ON, IRICO?
KUSAYA SQUAD WAS PATROLLING NEAR NAMEK. WE JUST GOT A MESSAGE FROM THEM.
THEY'VE GOT LIFE READINGS ON SON GOKU AND VEGETA!
OH YEAH? THOSE TWO DIDN'T CROAK?
WHICH MEANS THINGS COULD BE WORSE, RIGHT?
MAYBE I SHOULD CALL BULMA BACK...

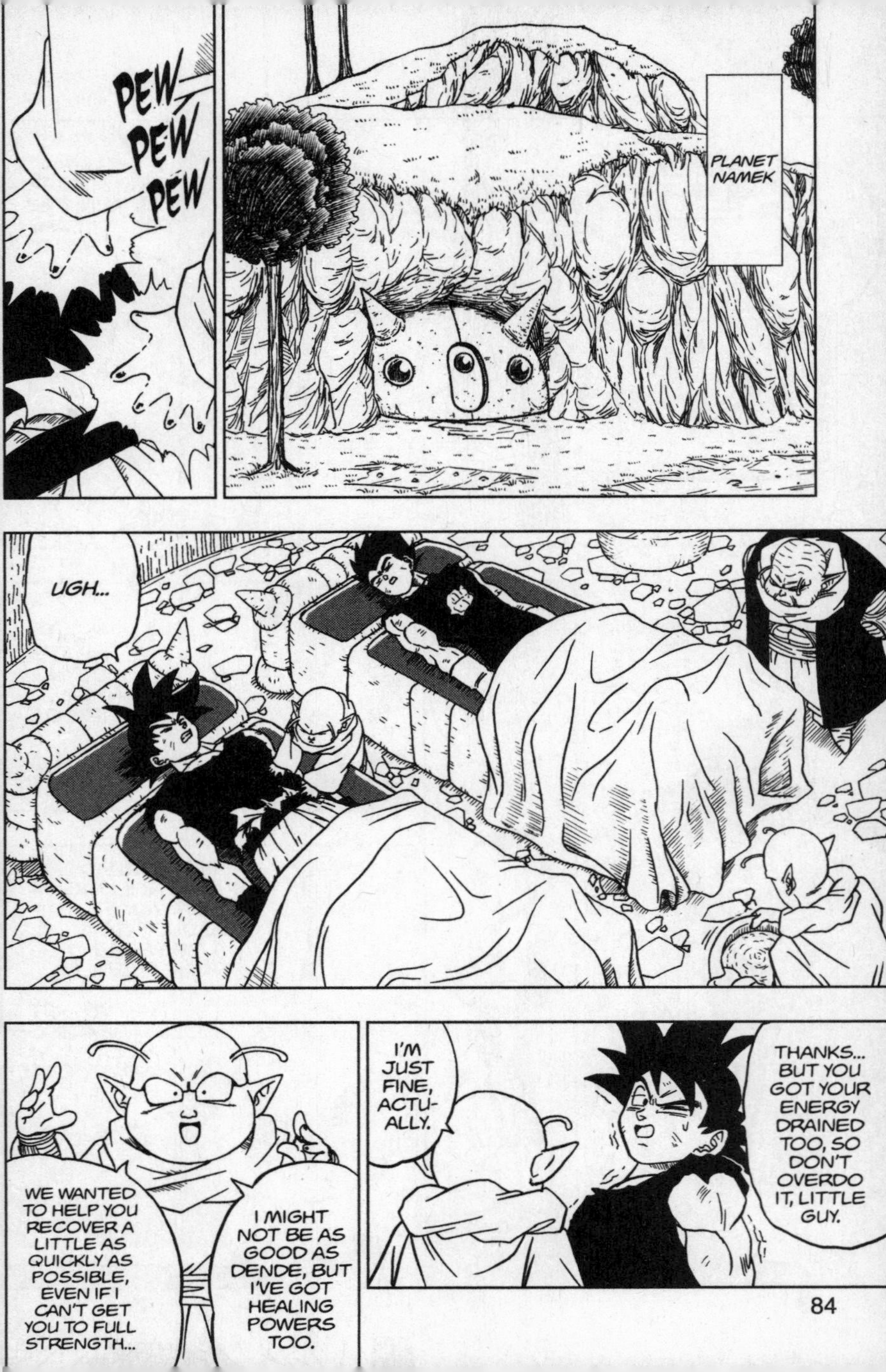
PLANET NAMEK
PEW PEW PEW
UGH...
THANKS... BUT YOU GOT YOUR ENERGY DRAINED TOO, SO DON'T OVERDO IT, LITTLE GUY.
I'M JUST FINE, ACTU-ALLY.
I MIGHT NOT BE AS GOOD AS DENDE, BUT I'VE GOT HEALING POWERS TOO.
WE WANTED TO HELP YOU RECOVER A LITTLE AS QUICKLY AS POSSIBLE, EVEN IF I CAN'T GET YOU TO FULL STRENGTH...

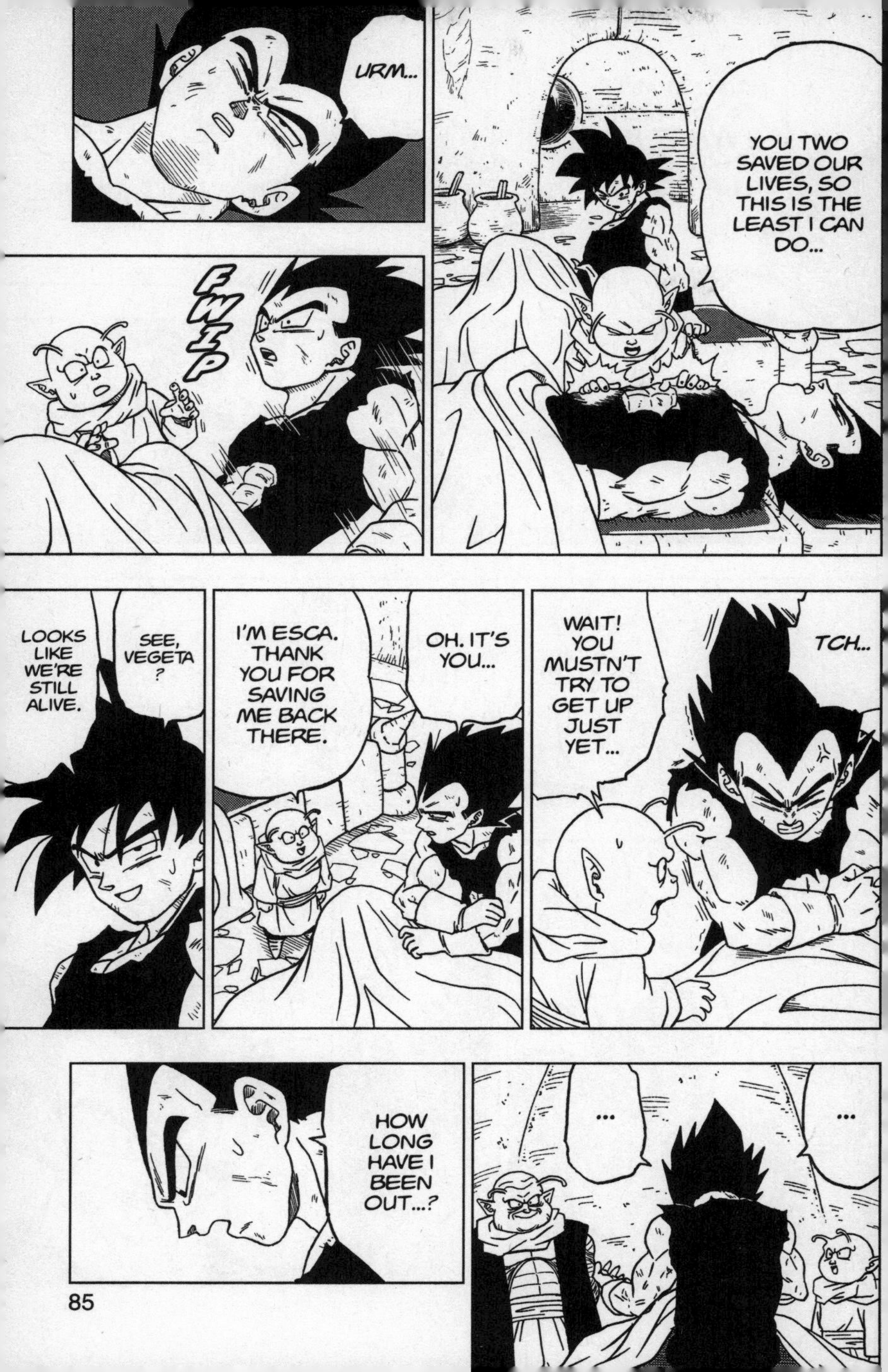
YOU TWO SAVED OUR LIVES, SO THIS IS THE LEAST I CAN DO...
URM...
FWIP
TCH...
WAIT! YOU MUSTN'T TRY TO GET UP JUST YET...
OH. IT'S YOU...
I'M ESCA. THANK YOU FOR SAVING ME BACK THERE.
SEE, VEGETA?
LOOKS LIKE WE'RE STILL ALIVE.
...
...
HOW LONG HAVE I BEEN OUT...?

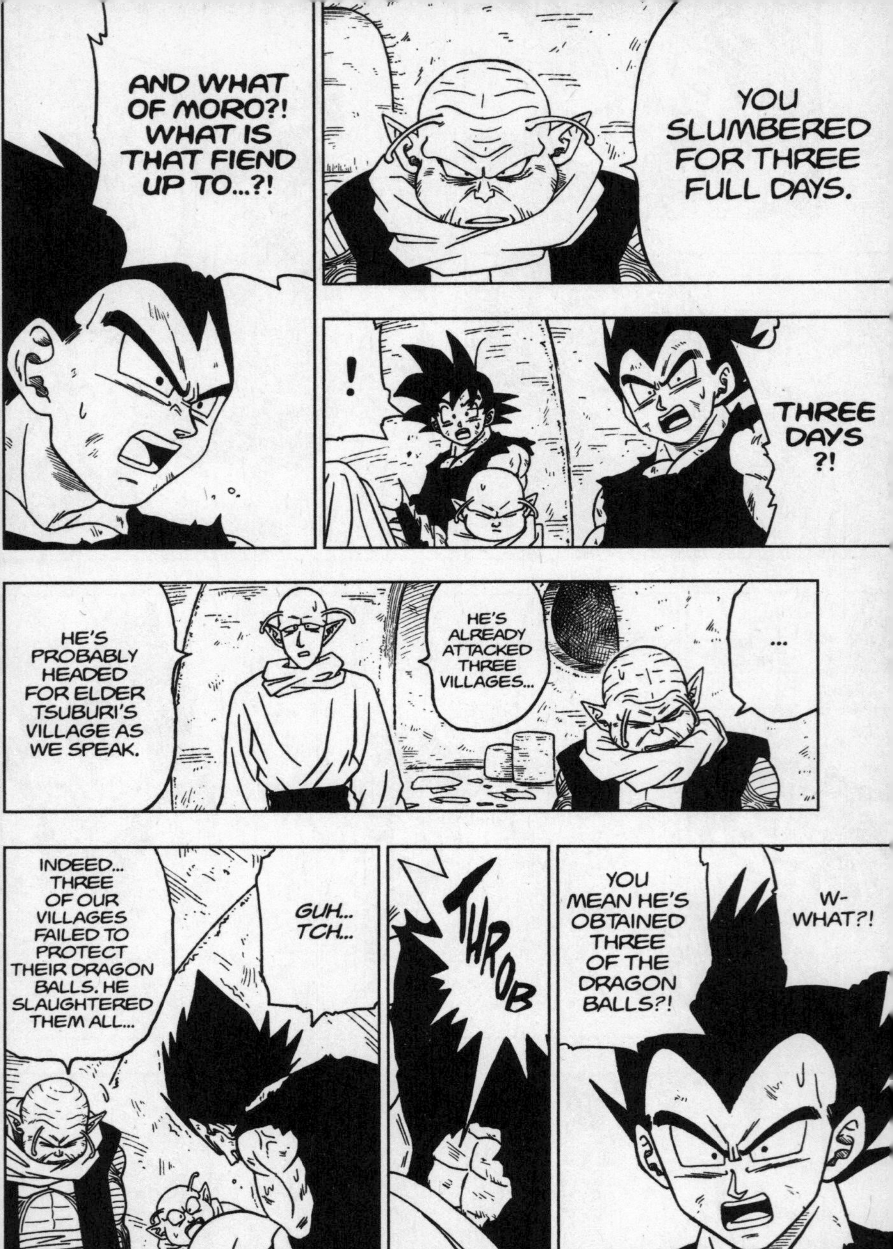
YOU SLUMBERED FOR THREE FULL DAYS.
THREE DAYS ?!
!
AND WHAT OF MORO?! WHAT IS THAT FIEND UP TO...?!
...
HE'S ALREADY ATTACKED THREE VILLAGES...
HE'S PROBABLY HEADED FOR ELDER TSUBURI'S VILLAGE AS WE SPEAK.
W- WHAT?!
YOU MEAN HE'S OBTAINED THREE OF THE DRAGON BALLS?!
THROB
GUH... TCH...
INDEED... THREE OF OUR VILLAGES FAILED TO PROTECT THEIR DRAGON BALLS. HE SLAUGHTERED THEM ALL...

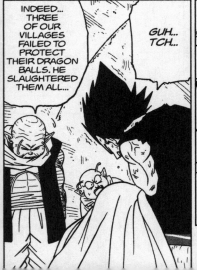

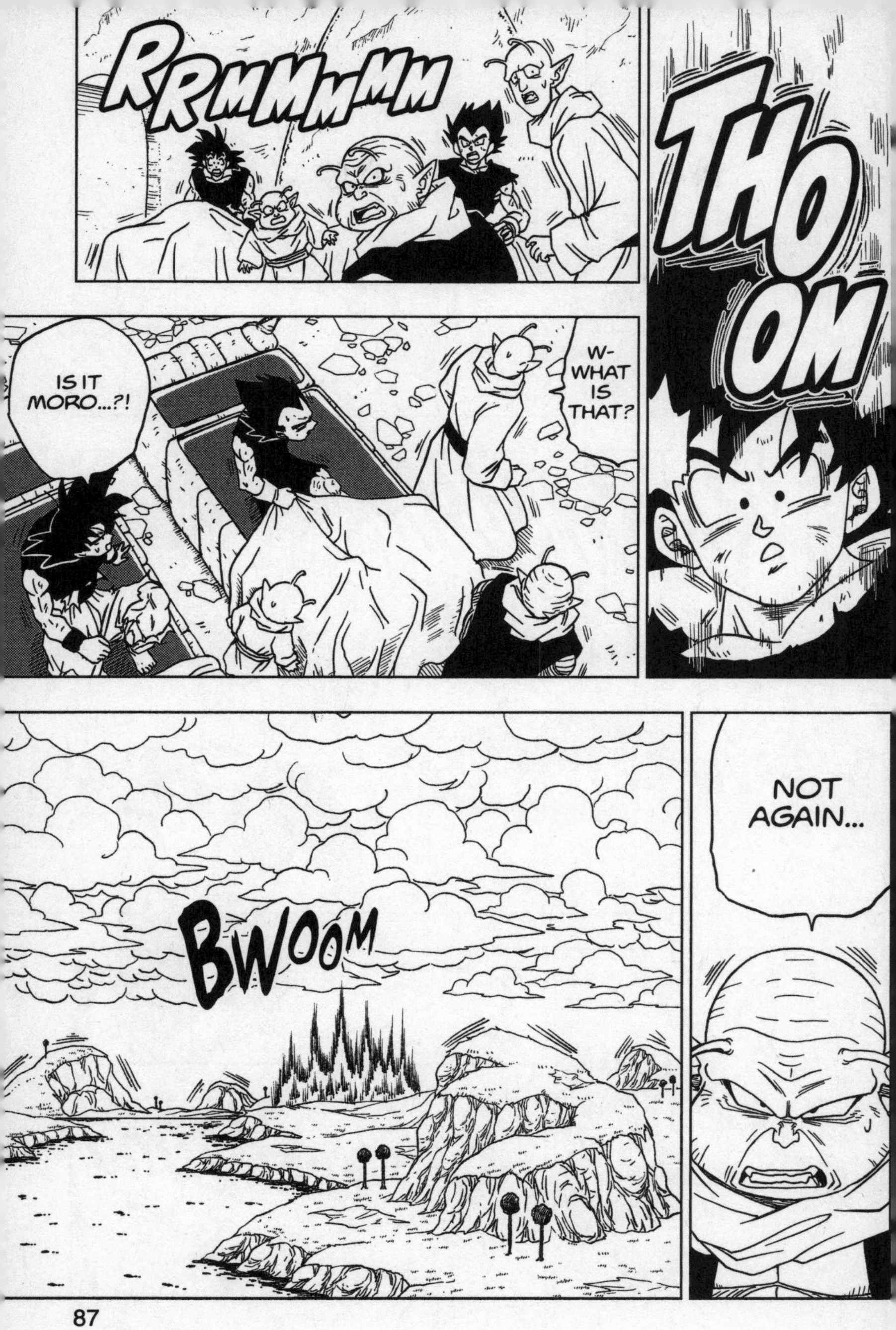
THOOM
RRMMMMMM
W-WHAT IS THAT?
IS IT MORO...?!
NOT AGAIN...
BWOOM

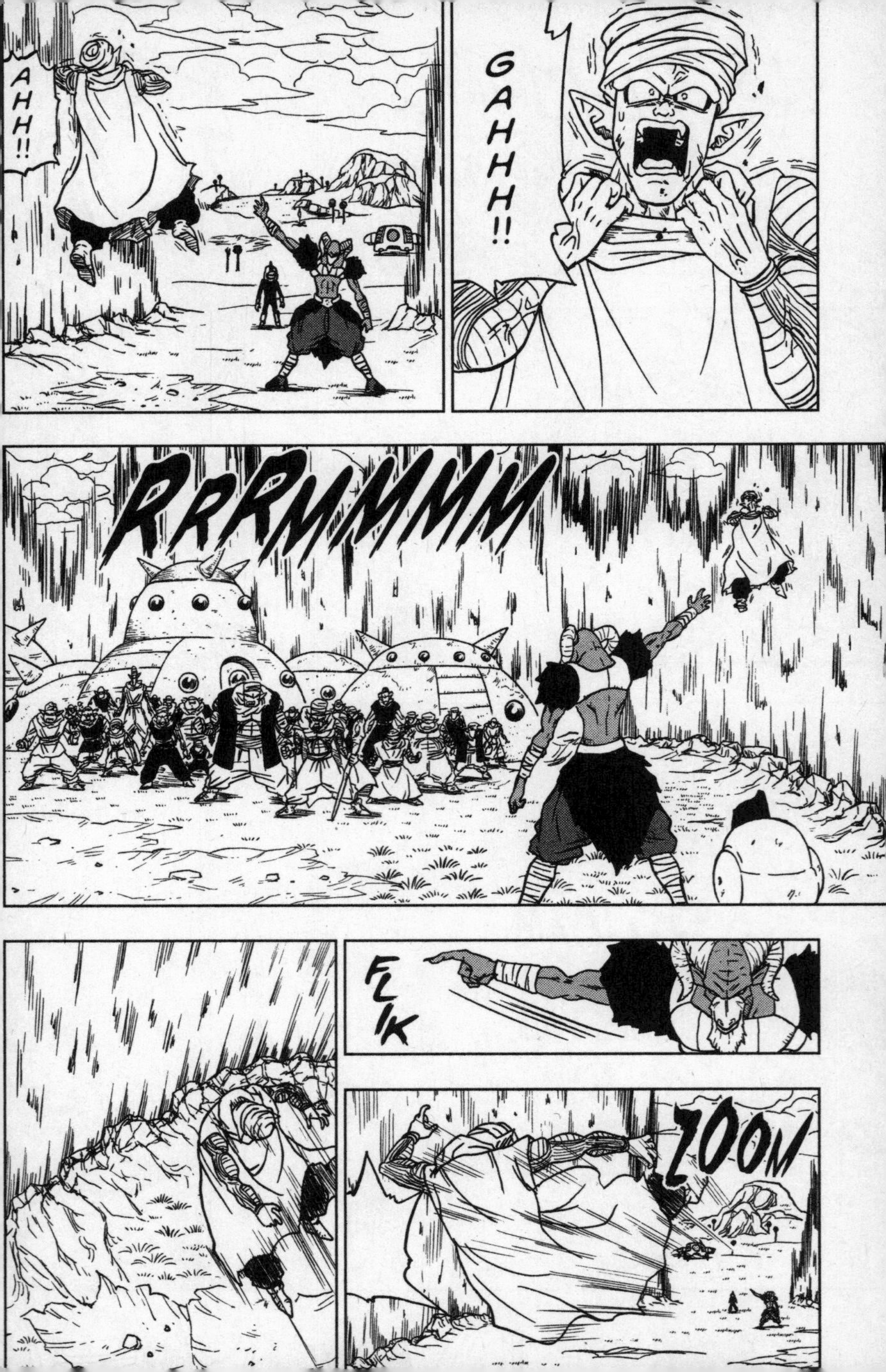
GAHHH!!
AHHH!!
RRRMMMMM
FLIK
ZOOM

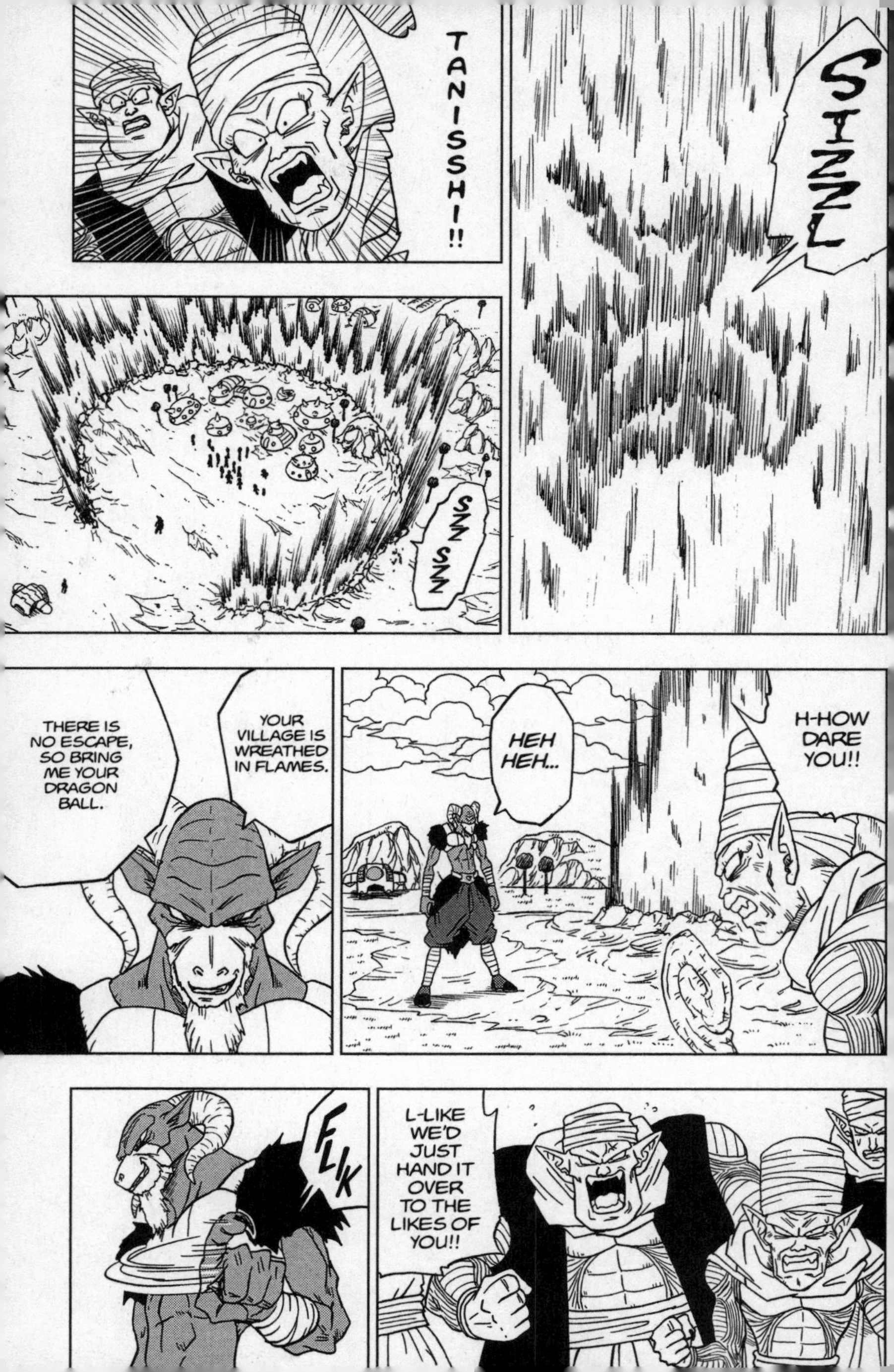
STIZZL
TANISSHI!!
SZZ SZZ
H-HOW DARE YOU!!
HEH HEH...
YOUR VILLAGE IS WREATHED IN FLAMES.
THERE IS NO ESCAPE, SO BRING ME YOUR DRAGON BALL.
L-LIKE WE'D JUST HAND IT OVER TO THE LIKES OF YOU!!
FLIK

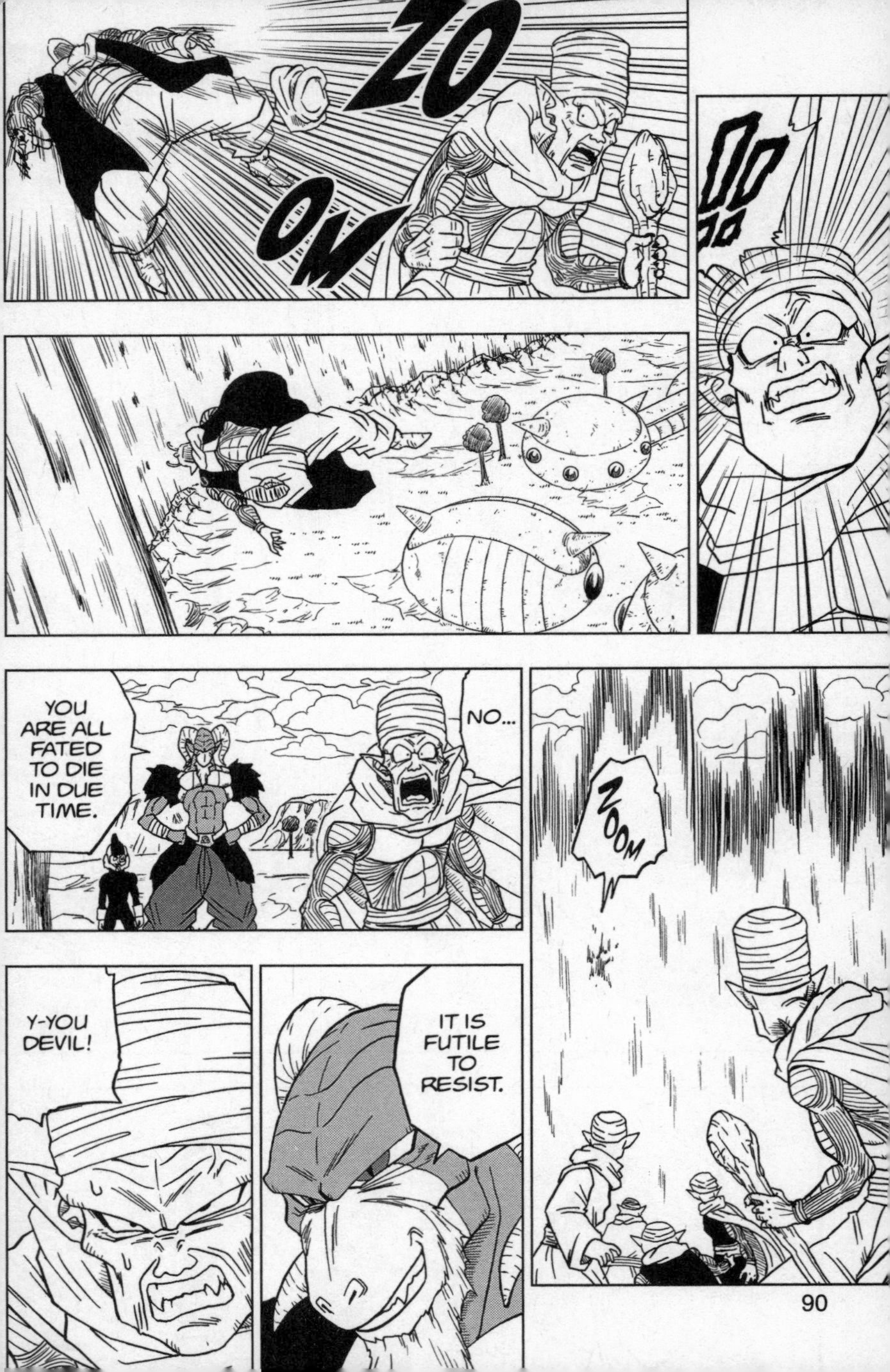
ZOOM
ZOOM
NO...
YOU ARE ALL FATED TO DIE IN DUE TIME.
IT IS FUTILE TO RESIST.
Y-YOU DEVIL!

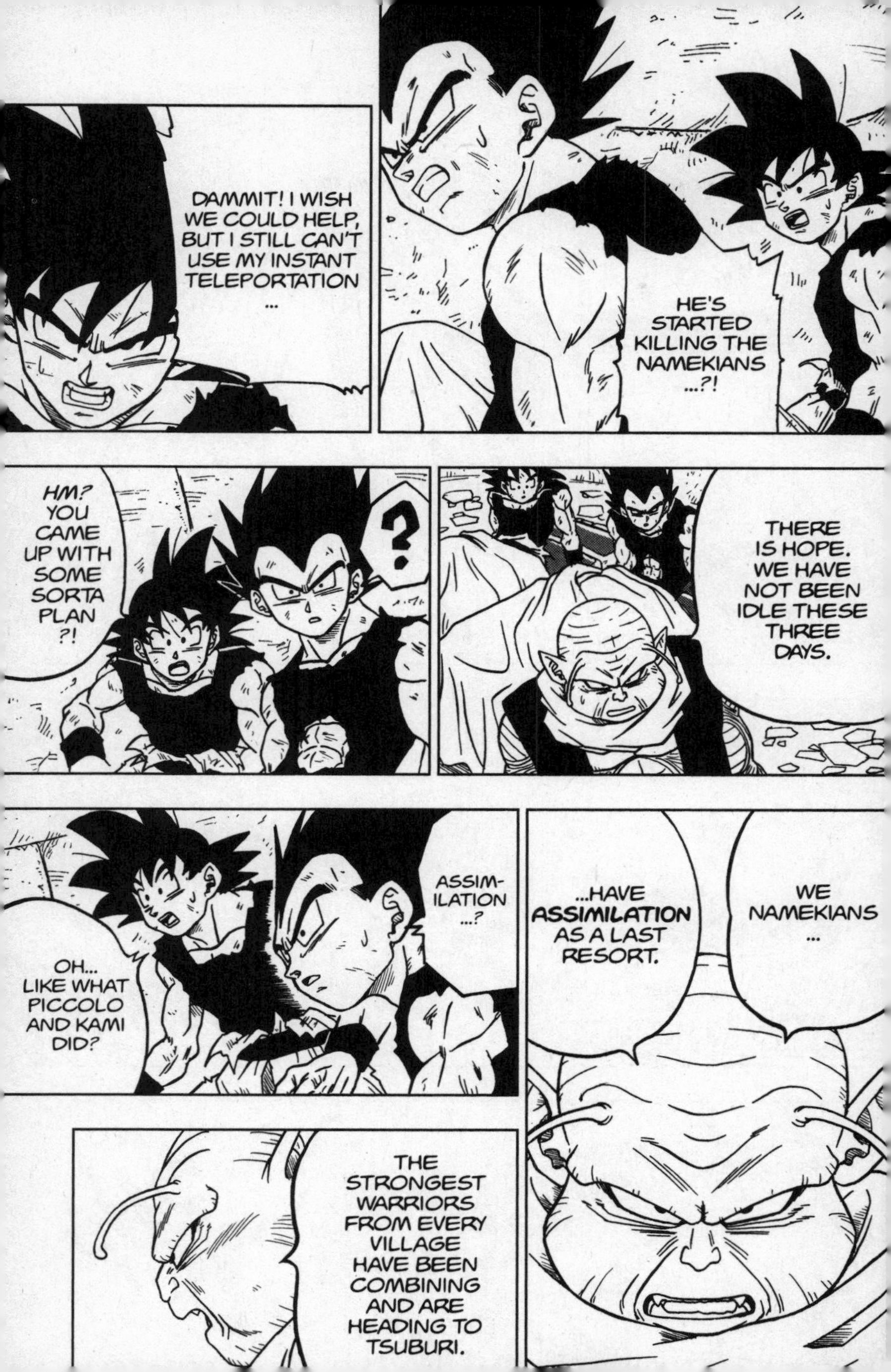
HE'S STARTED KILLING THE NAMEKIANS ...?!
DAMMIT! I WISH WE COULD HELP, BUT I STILL CAN'T USE MY INSTANT TELEPORTATION ...
THERE IS HOPE. WE HAVE NOT BEEN IDLE THESE THREE DAYS.
?
HM? YOU CAME UP WITH SOME SORTA PLAN ?!
WE NAMEKIANS ...
...HAVE **ASSIMILATION** AS A LAST RESORT.
ASSIM-ILATION ...?
OH... LIKE WHAT PICCOLO AND KAMI DID?
THE STRONGEST WARRIORS FROM EVERY VILLAGE HAVE BEEN COMBINING AND ARE HEADING TO TSUBURI.

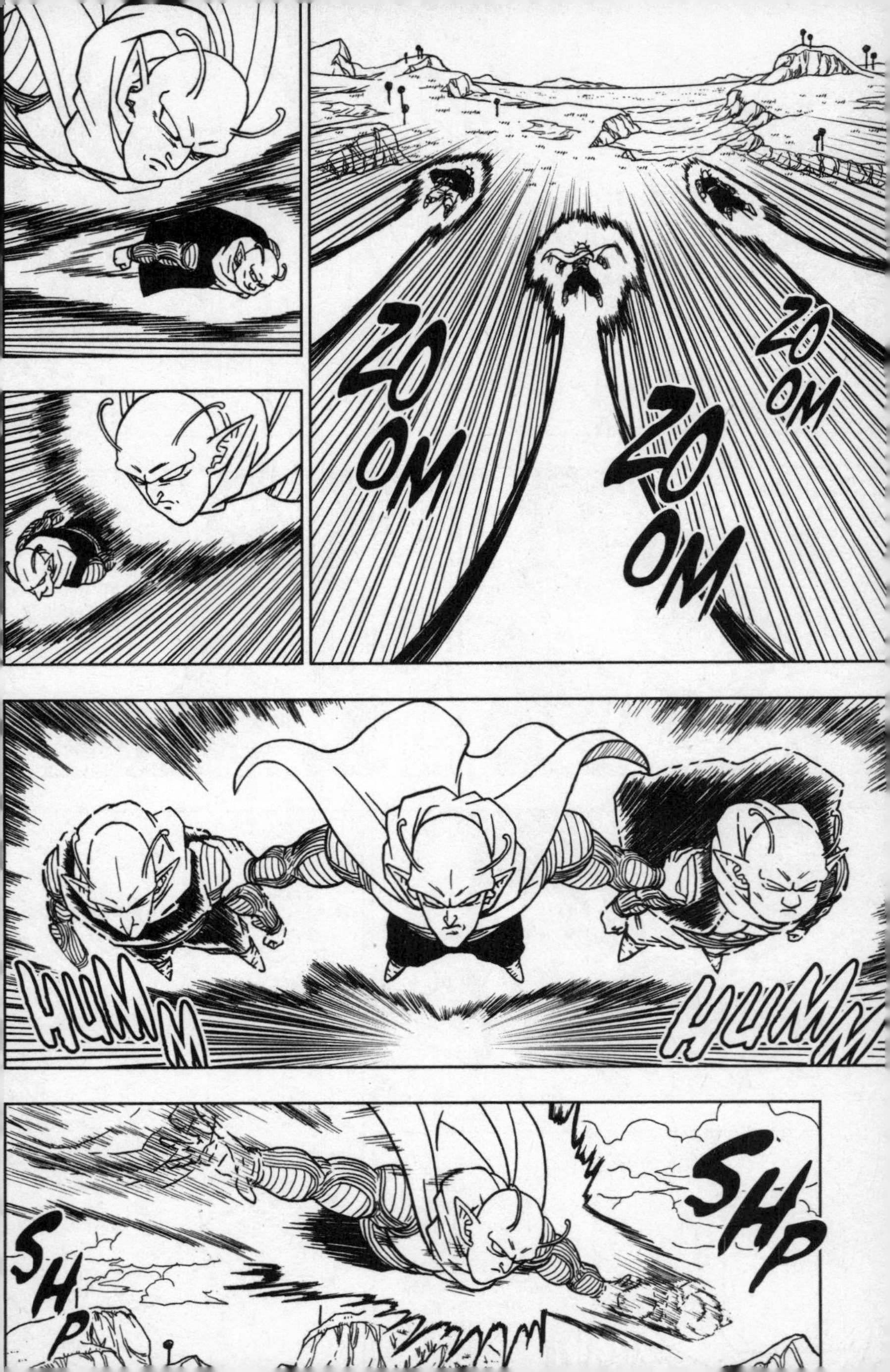
ZOOM
ZOOM
ZOOM
HUMMM
HUMMM
SHP
SHP

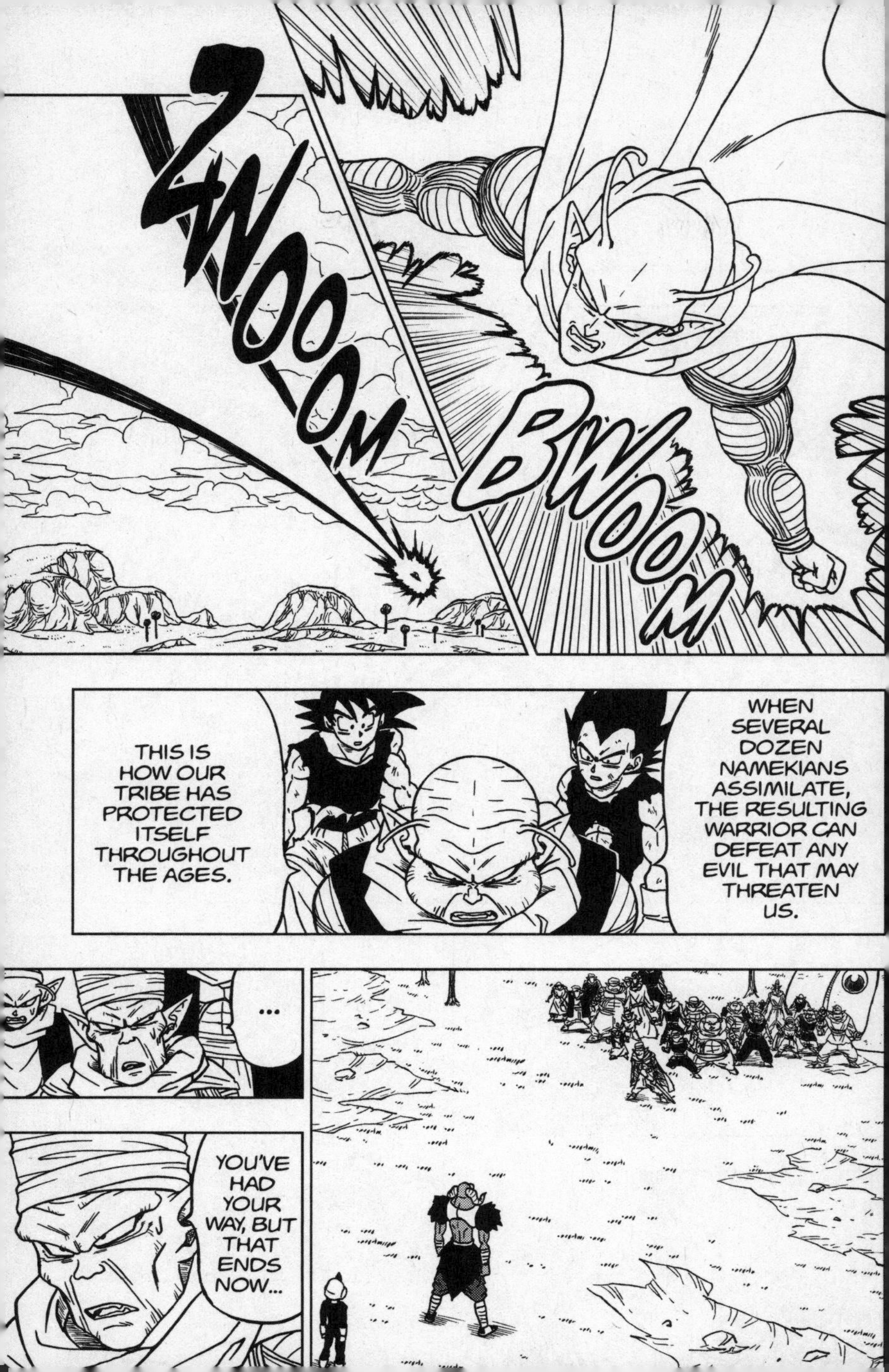

BWOOOM
ZWOOOM
WHEN SEVERAL DOZEN NAMEKIANS ASSIMILATE, THE RESULTING WARRIOR CAN DEFEAT ANY EVIL THAT MAY THREATEN US.
THIS IS HOW OUR TRIBE HAS PROTECTED ITSELF THROUGHOUT THE AGES.
...
YOU'VE HAD YOUR WAY, BUT THAT ENDS NOW...

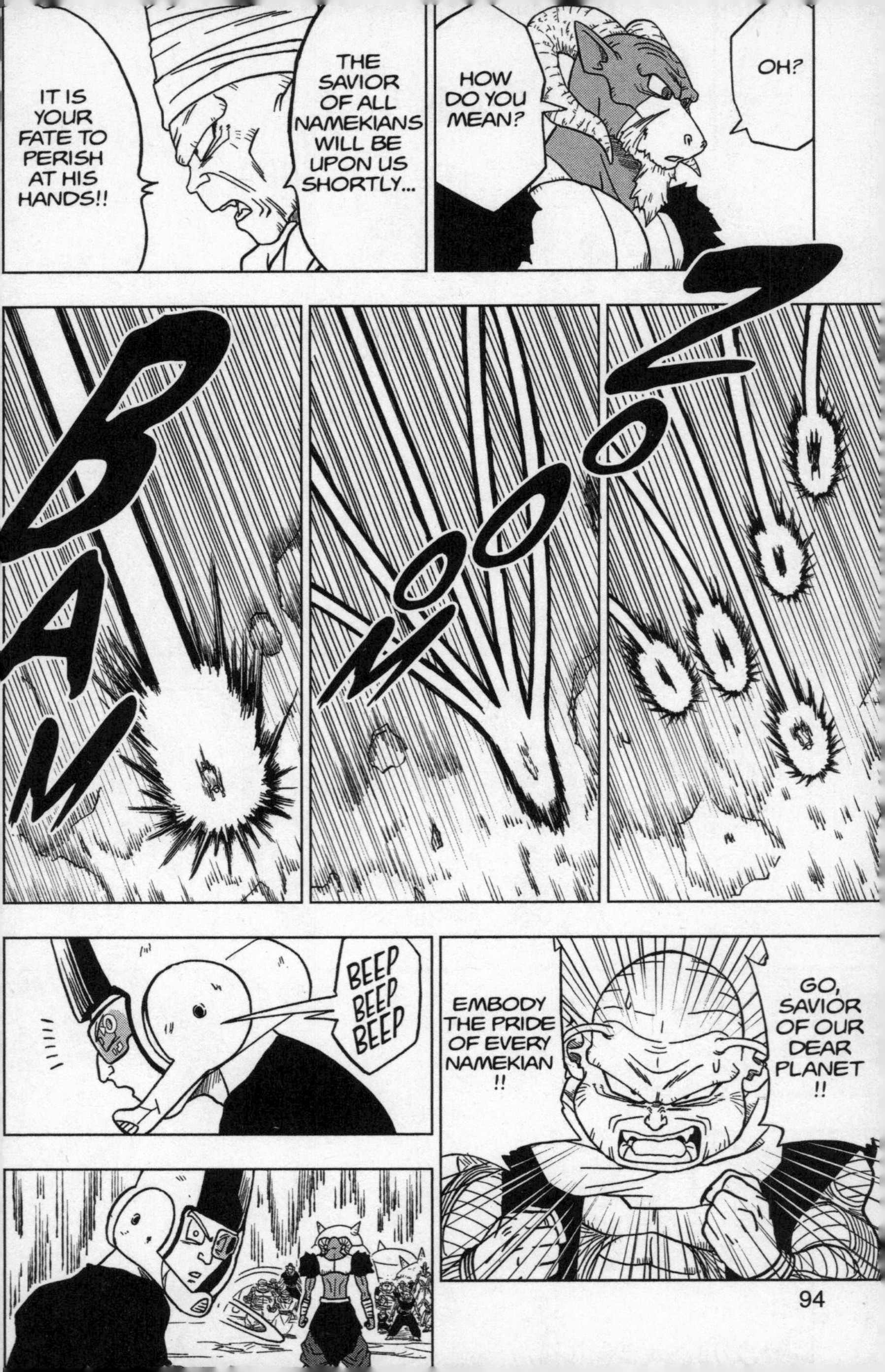
OH?
HOW DO YOU MEAN?
THE SAVIOR OF ALL NAMEKIANS WILL BE UPON US SHORTLY...
IT IS YOUR FATE TO PERISH AT HIS HANDS!!
ZOOOOOM
BAM
GO, SAVIOR OF OUR DEAR PLANET!!
EMBODY THE PRIDE OF EVERY NAMEKIAN!!
BEEP BEEP BEEP

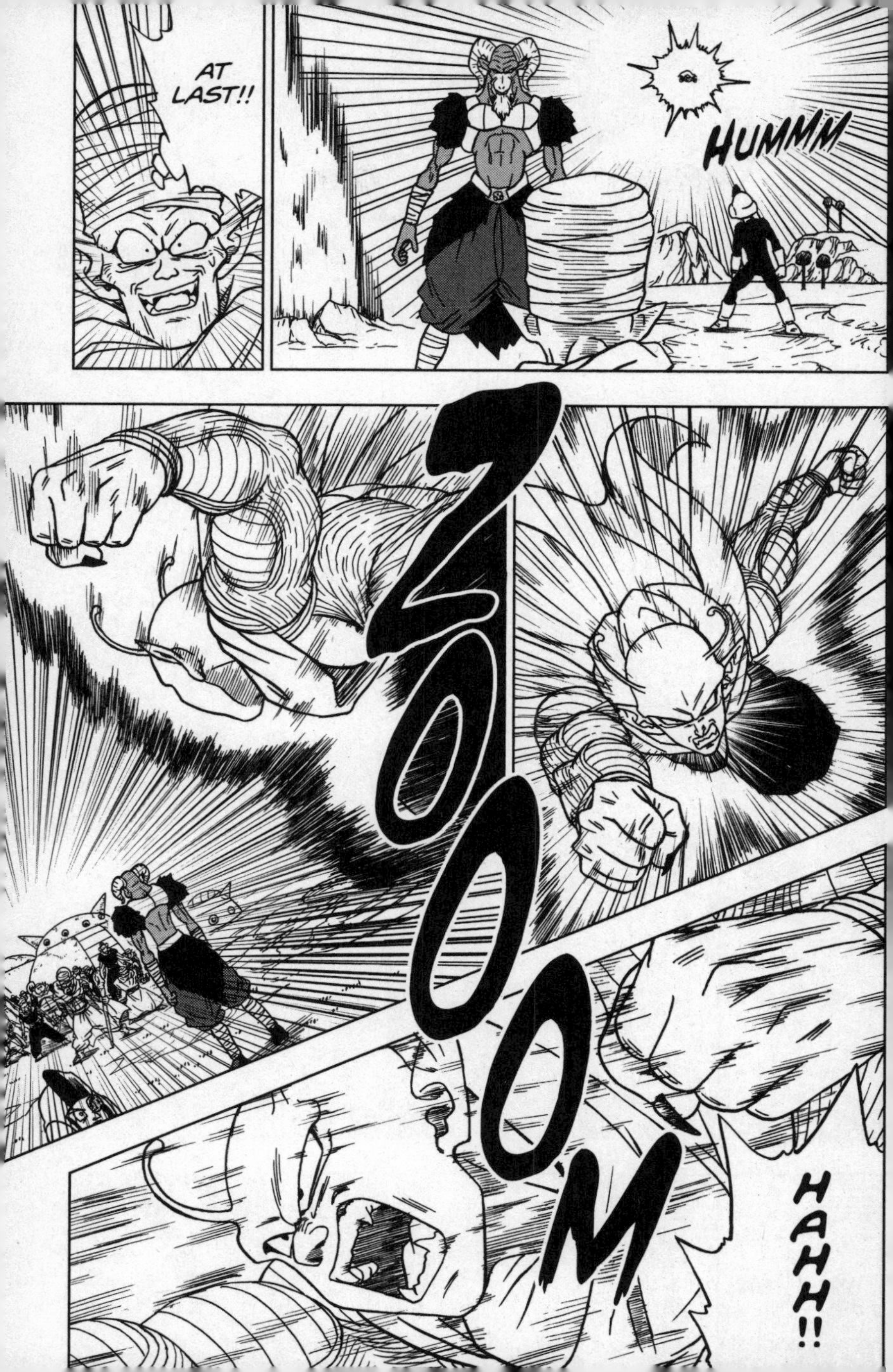
HUMMM
AT LAST!!
ZOOOOM
HAHH!!

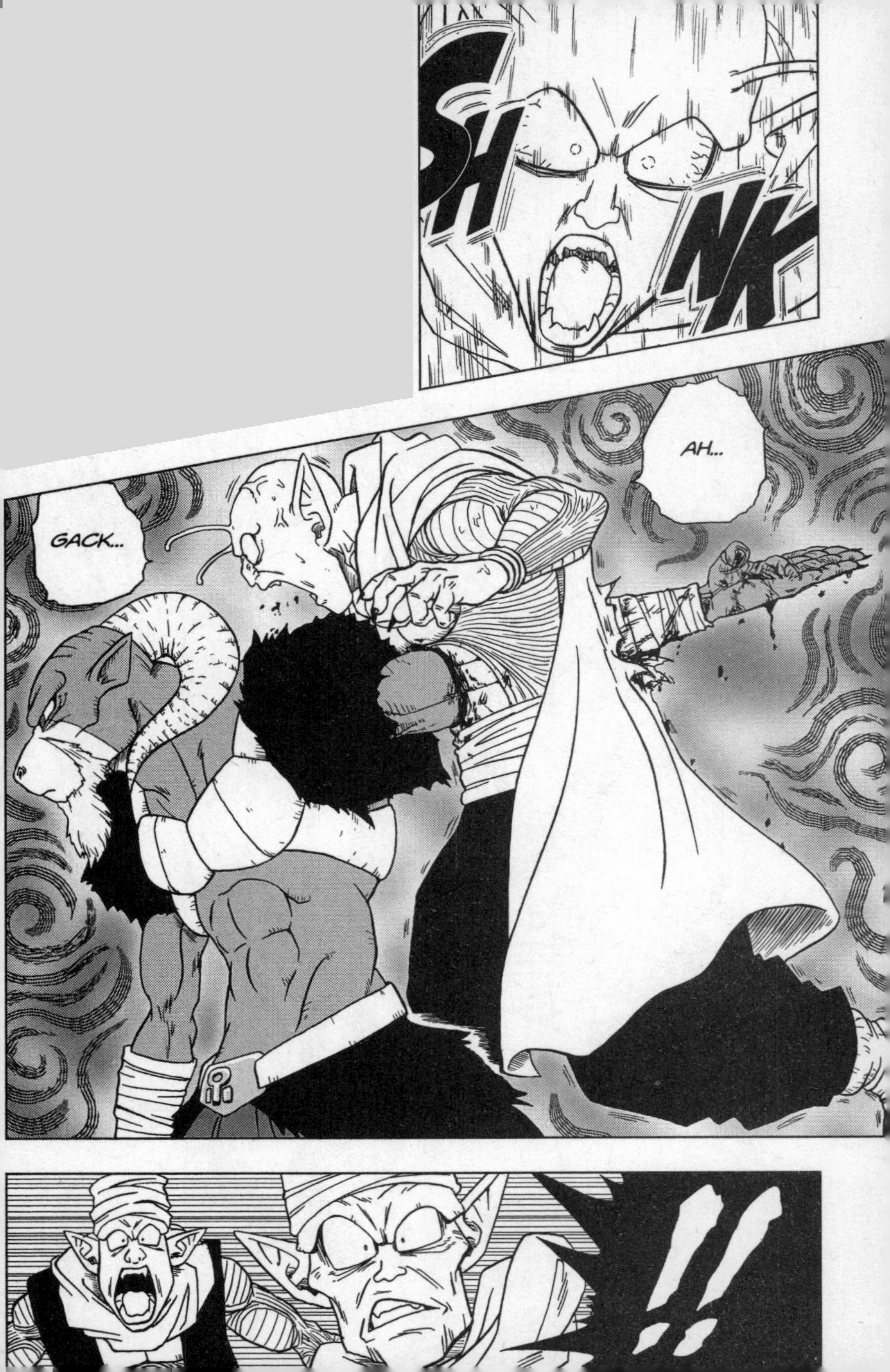
SHNK
AH...
GACK...
!!

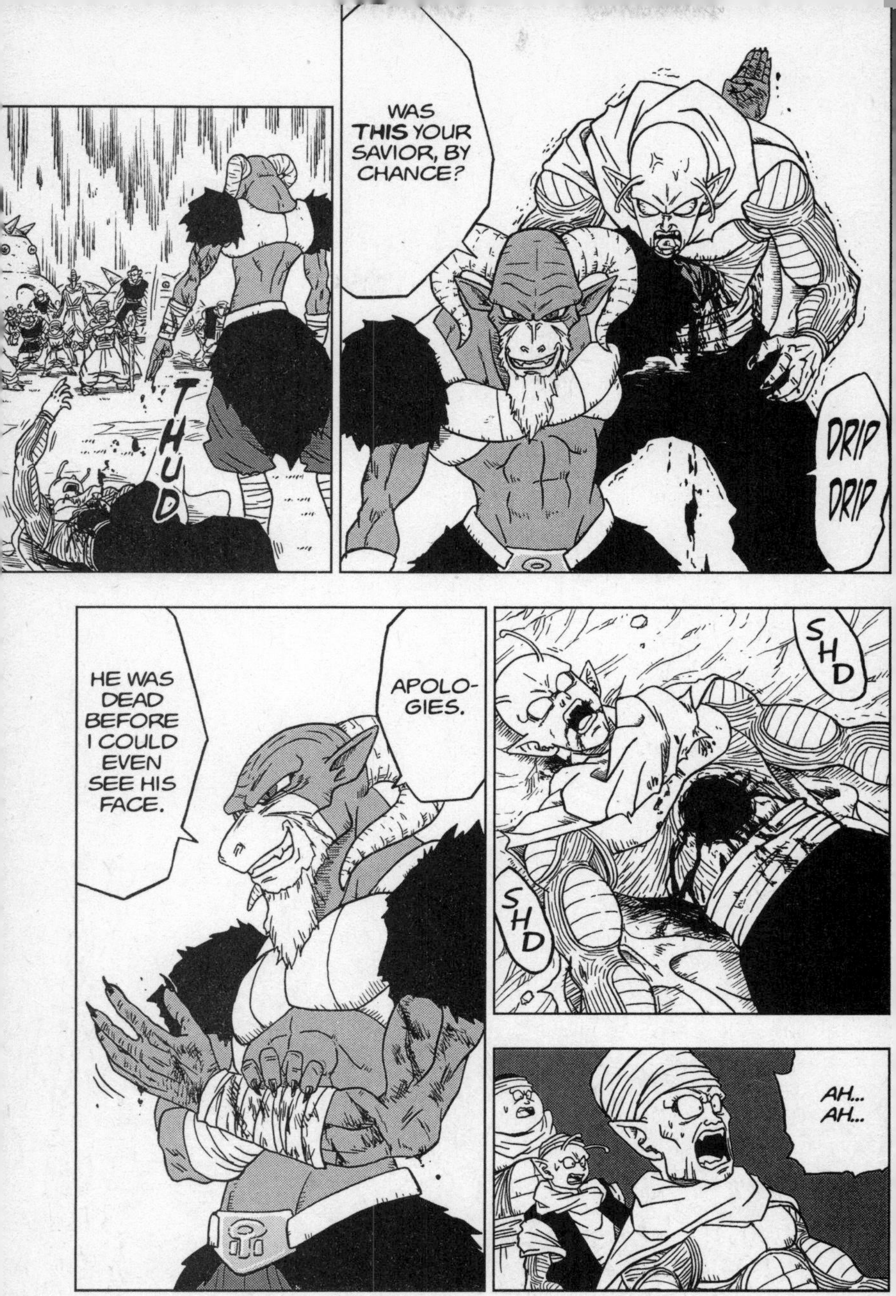
WAS THIS YOUR SAVIOR, BY CHANCE?
DRIP DRIP
THUD
SHD
SHD
AH... AH...
APOLO-GIES.
HE WAS DEAD BEFORE I COULD EVEN SEE HIS FACE.

DRAGON BALL SUPER

CHAPTER 47: STOLEN DRAGON BALLS

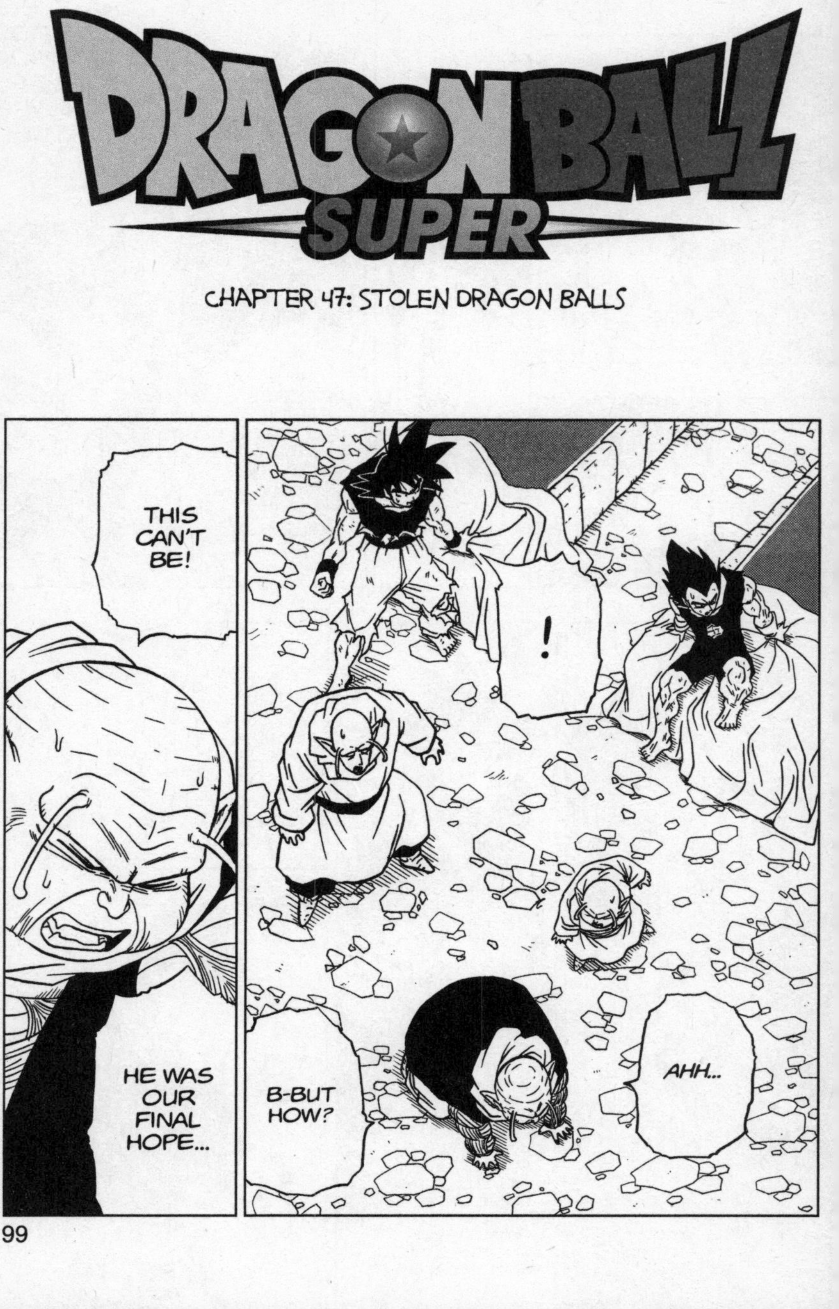
!
AHH...
B-BUT HOW?
THIS CAN'T BE!
HE WAS OUR FINAL HOPE...

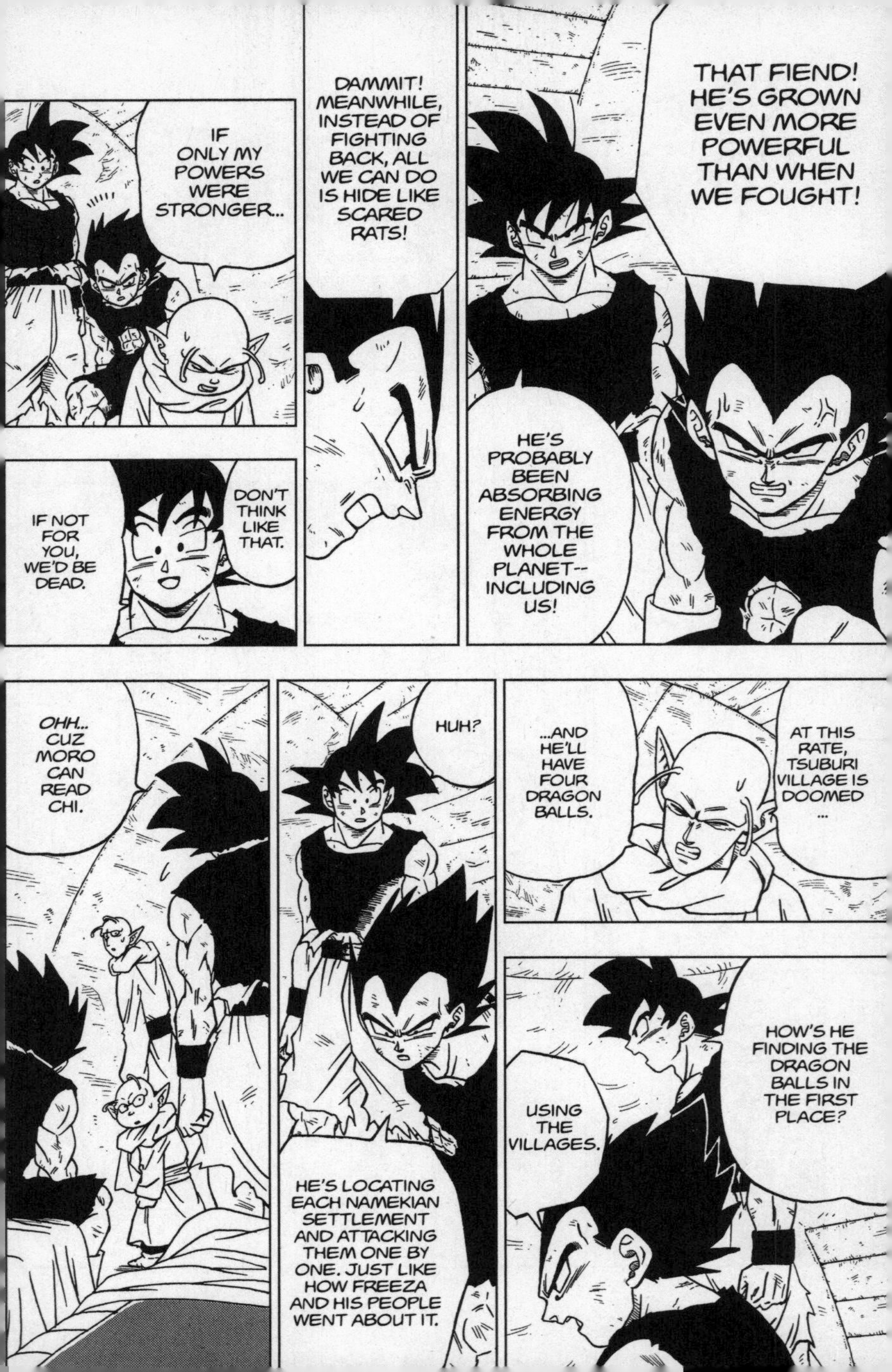
THAT FIEND! HE'S GROWN EVEN MORE POWERFUL THAN WHEN WE FOUGHT!
HE'S PROBABLY BEEN ABSORBING ENERGY FROM THE WHOLE PLANET-- INCLUDING US!
DAMMIT! MEANWHILE, INSTEAD OF FIGHTING BACK, ALL WE CAN DO IS HIDE LIKE SCARED RATS!
IF ONLY MY POWERS WERE STRONGER...
DON'T THINK LIKE THAT.
IF NOT FOR YOU, WE'D BE DEAD.
AT THIS RATE, TSUBURI VILLAGE IS DOOMED...
...AND HE'LL HAVE FOUR DRAGON BALLS.
HOW'S HE FINDING THE DRAGON BALLS IN THE FIRST PLACE?
USING THE VILLAGES.
HUH?
HE'S LOCATING EACH NAMEKIAN SETTLEMENT AND ATTACKING THEM ONE BY ONE. JUST LIKE HOW FREEZA AND HIS PEOPLE WENT ABOUT IT.
OHH... CUZ MORO CAN READ CHI.

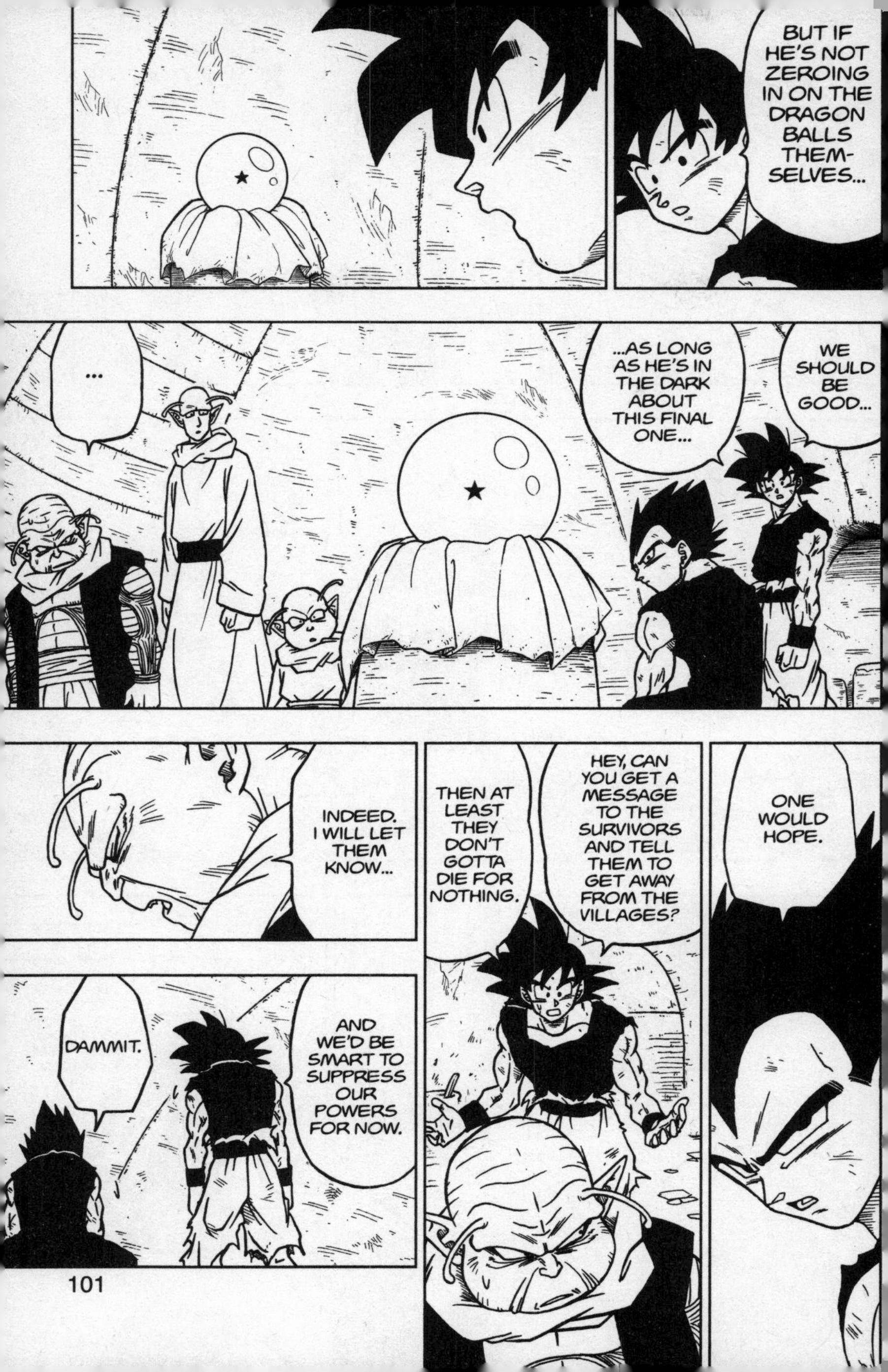
BUT IF HE'S NOT ZEROING IN ON THE DRAGON BALLS THEMSELVES...
WE SHOULD BE GOOD...
...AS LONG AS HE'S IN THE DARK ABOUT THIS FINAL ONE...
...
ONE WOULD HOPE.
HEY, CAN YOU GET A MESSAGE TO THE SURVIVORS AND TELL THEM TO GET AWAY FROM THE VILLAGES?
THEN AT LEAST THEY DON'T GOTTA DIE FOR NOTHING.
INDEED. I WILL LET THEM KNOW...
AND WE'D BE SMART TO SUPPRESS OUR POWERS FOR NOW.
DAMMIT.

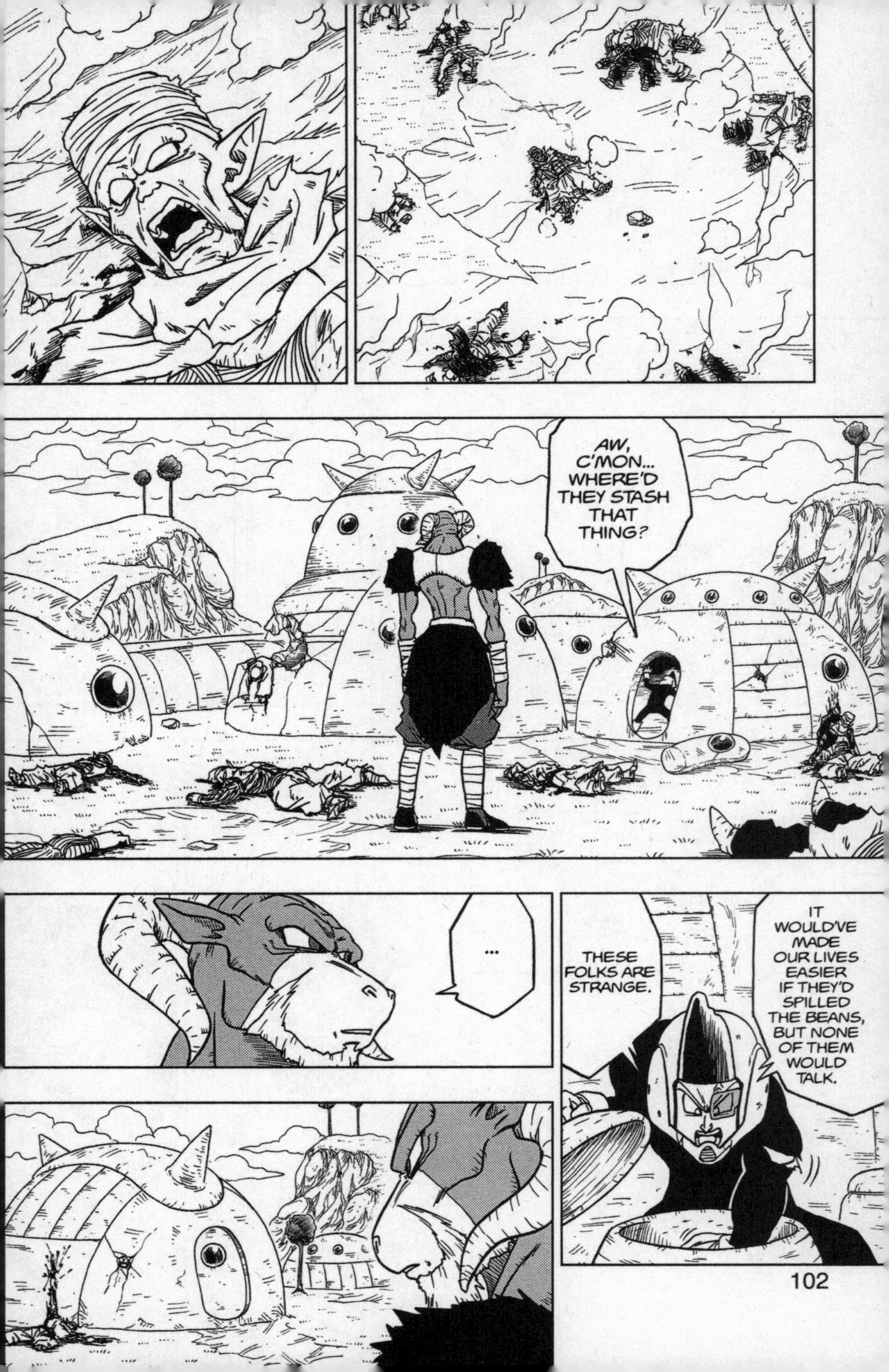
AW, C'MON... WHERE'D THEY STASH THAT THING?
IT WOULD'VE MADE OUR LIVES EASIER IF THEY'D SPILLED THE BEANS, BUT NONE OF THEM WOULD TALK.
THESE FOLKS ARE STRANGE.
...

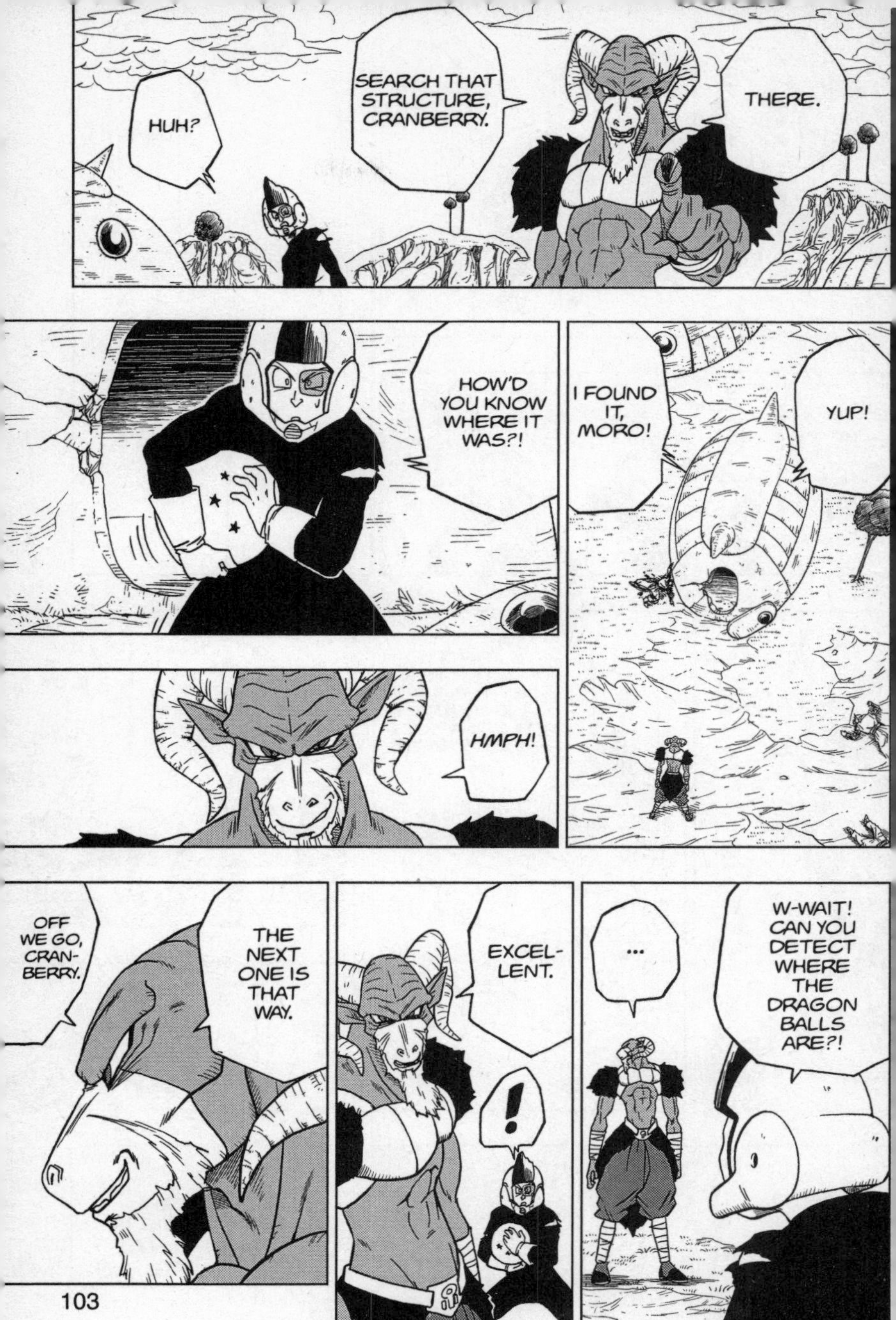
THERE.
SEARCH THAT STRUCTURE, CRANBERRY.
HUH?
I FOUND IT, MORO!
YUP!
HOW'D YOU KNOW WHERE IT WAS?!
HMPH!
W-WAIT! CAN YOU DETECT WHERE THE DRAGON BALLS ARE?!
...
EXCEL-LENT.
!
THE NEXT ONE IS THAT WAY.
OFF WE GO, CRAN-BERRY.

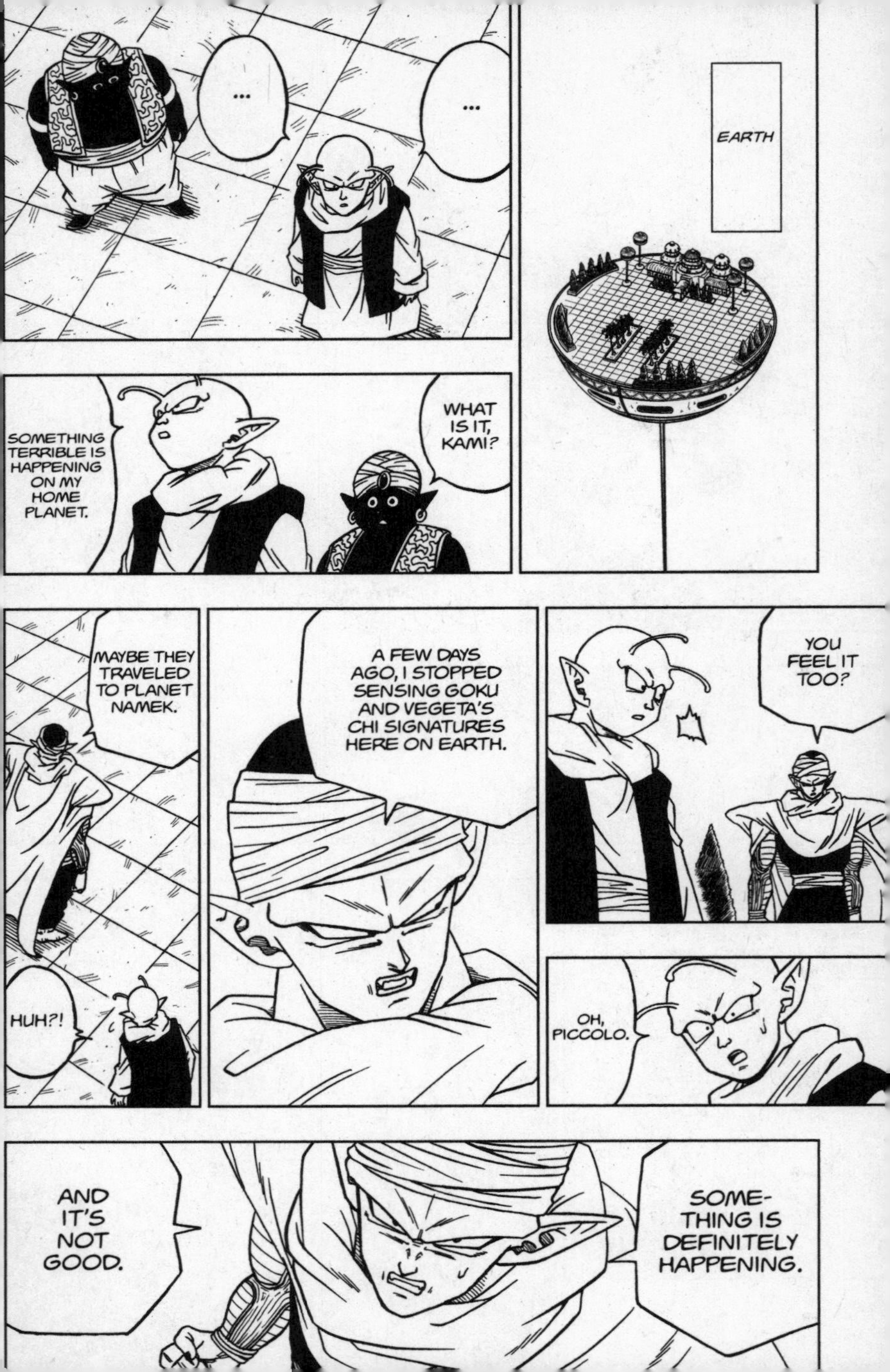
EARTH
...
...
WHAT IS IT, KAMI?
SOMETHING TERRIBLE IS HAPPENING ON MY HOME PLANET.
YOU FEEL IT TOO?
OH, PICCOLO.
A FEW DAYS AGO, I STOPPED SENSING GOKU AND VEGETA'S CHI SIGNATURES HERE ON EARTH.
MAYBE THEY TRAVELED TO PLANET NAMEK.
HUH?!
SOME-THING IS DEFINITELY HAPPENING.
AND IT'S NOT GOOD.

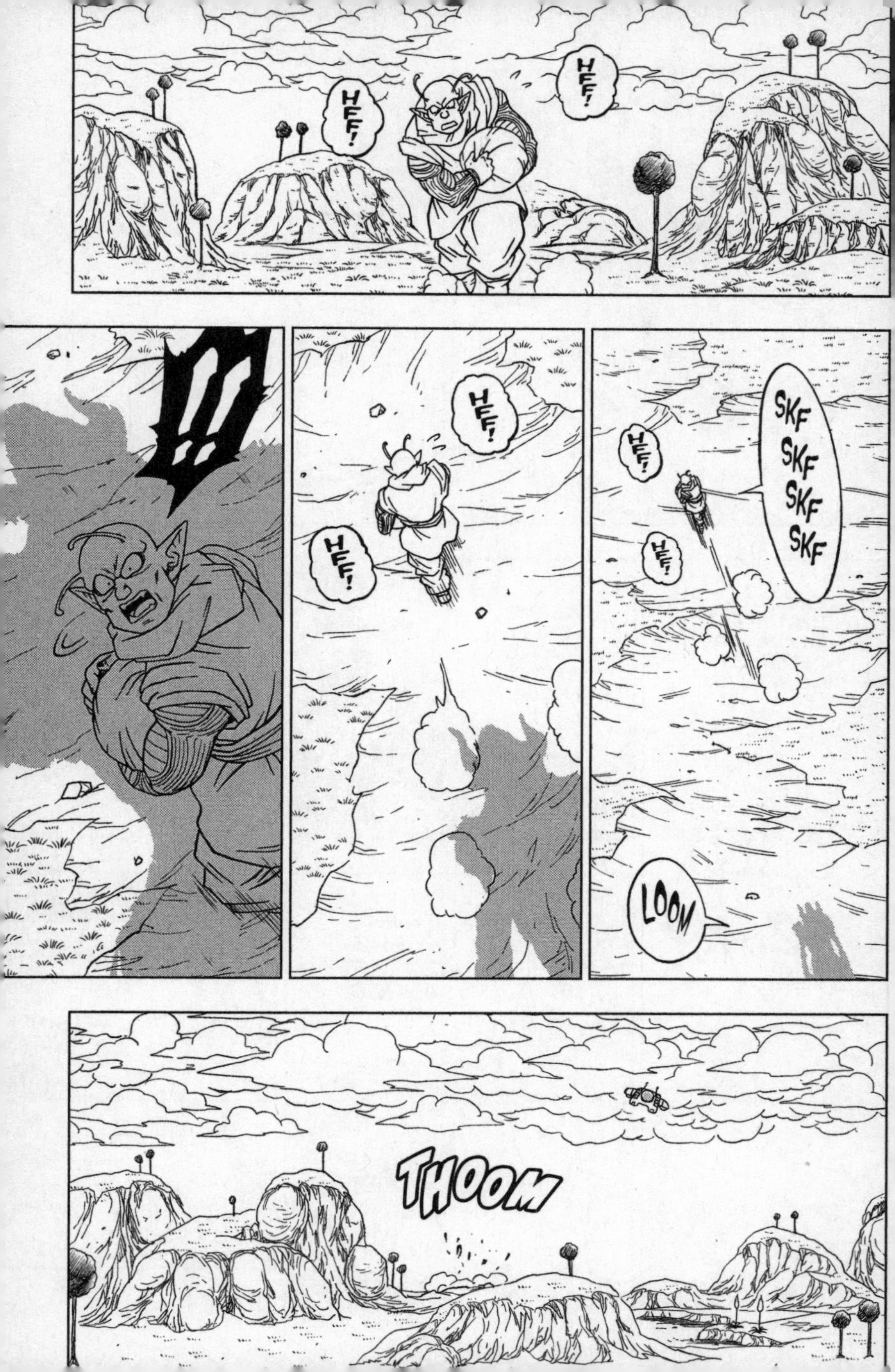
HEF!
HEF!
SKF SKF SKF SKF
HEF!
HEF!
LOON
HEF!
HEF!
!!
THOOM

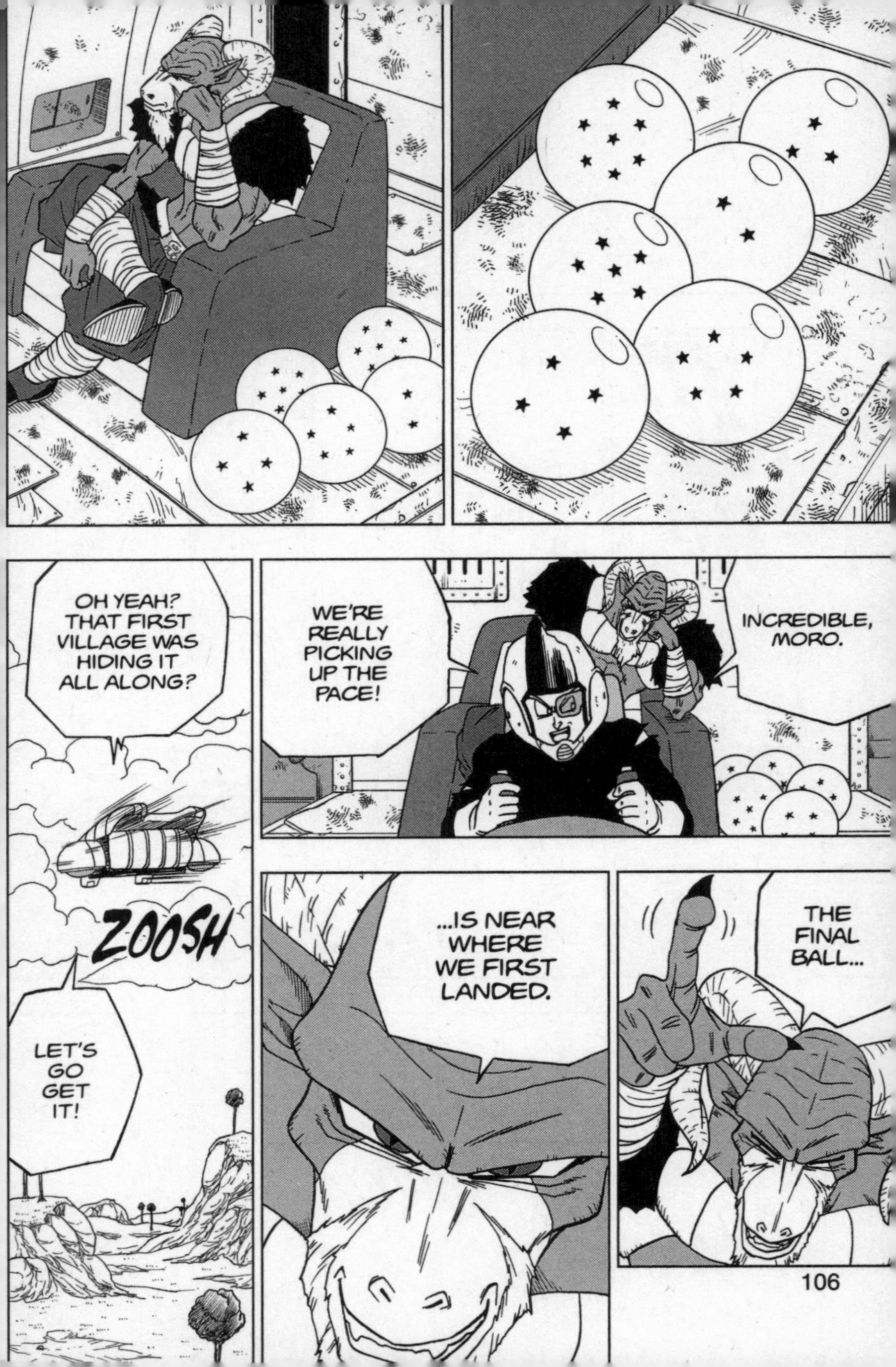
INCREDIBLE, MORO.
WE'RE REALLY PICKING UP THE PACE!
THE FINAL BALL...
...IS NEAR WHERE WE FIRST LANDED.
OH YEAH? THAT FIRST VILLAGE WAS HIDING IT ALL ALONG?
ZOOSH
LET'S GO GET IT!

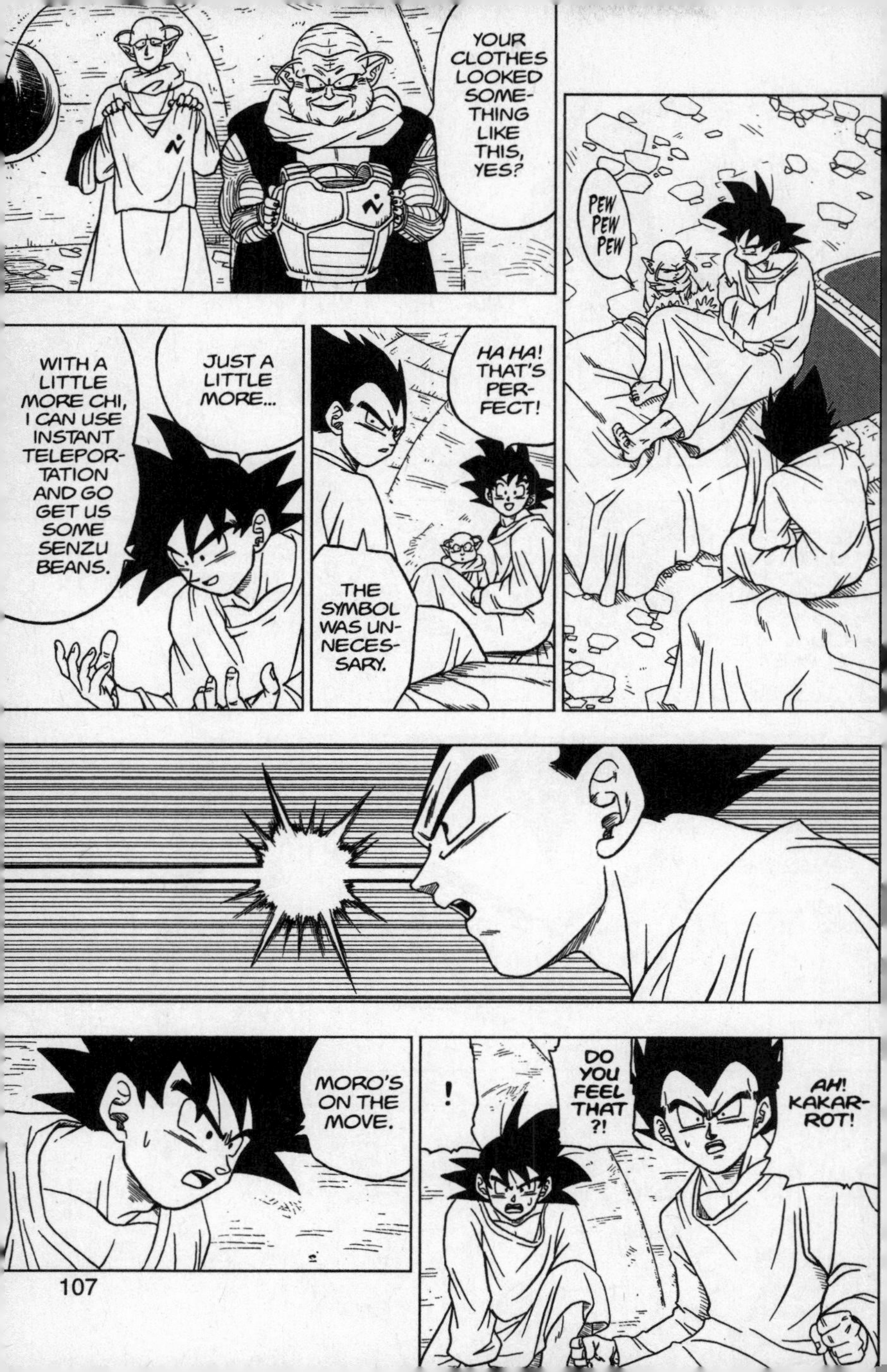
PEW PEW PEW
YOUR CLOTHES LOOKED SOME-THING LIKE THIS, YES?
HA HA! THAT'S PER-FECT!
THE SYMBOL WAS UN-NECES-SARY.
JUST A LITTLE MORE...
WITH A LITTLE MORE CHI, I CAN USE INSTANT TELEPOR-TATION AND GO GET US SOME SENZU BEANS.
AH! KAKAR-ROT!
DO YOU FEEL THAT?!
!
MORO'S ON THE MOVE.

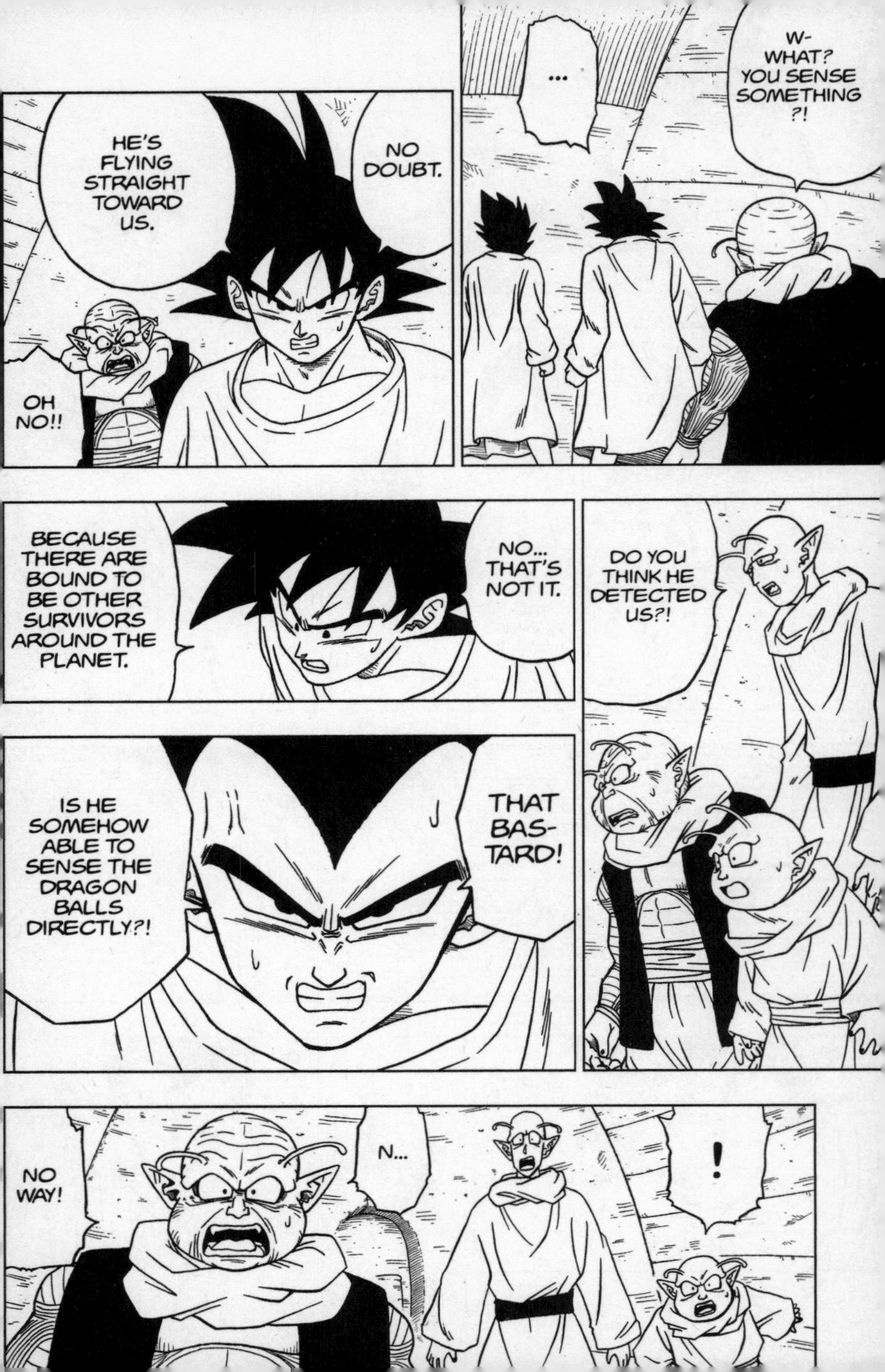
W- WHAT? YOU SENSE SOMETHING ?!
...
NO DOUBT.
HE'S FLYING STRAIGHT TOWARD US.
OH NO!!
DO YOU THINK HE DETECTED US?!
NO... THAT'S NOT IT.
BECAUSE THERE ARE BOUND TO BE OTHER SURVIVORS AROUND THE PLANET.
THAT BAS-TARD!
IS HE SOMEHOW ABLE TO SENSE THE DRAGON BALLS DIRECTLY?!
!
N...
NO WAY!

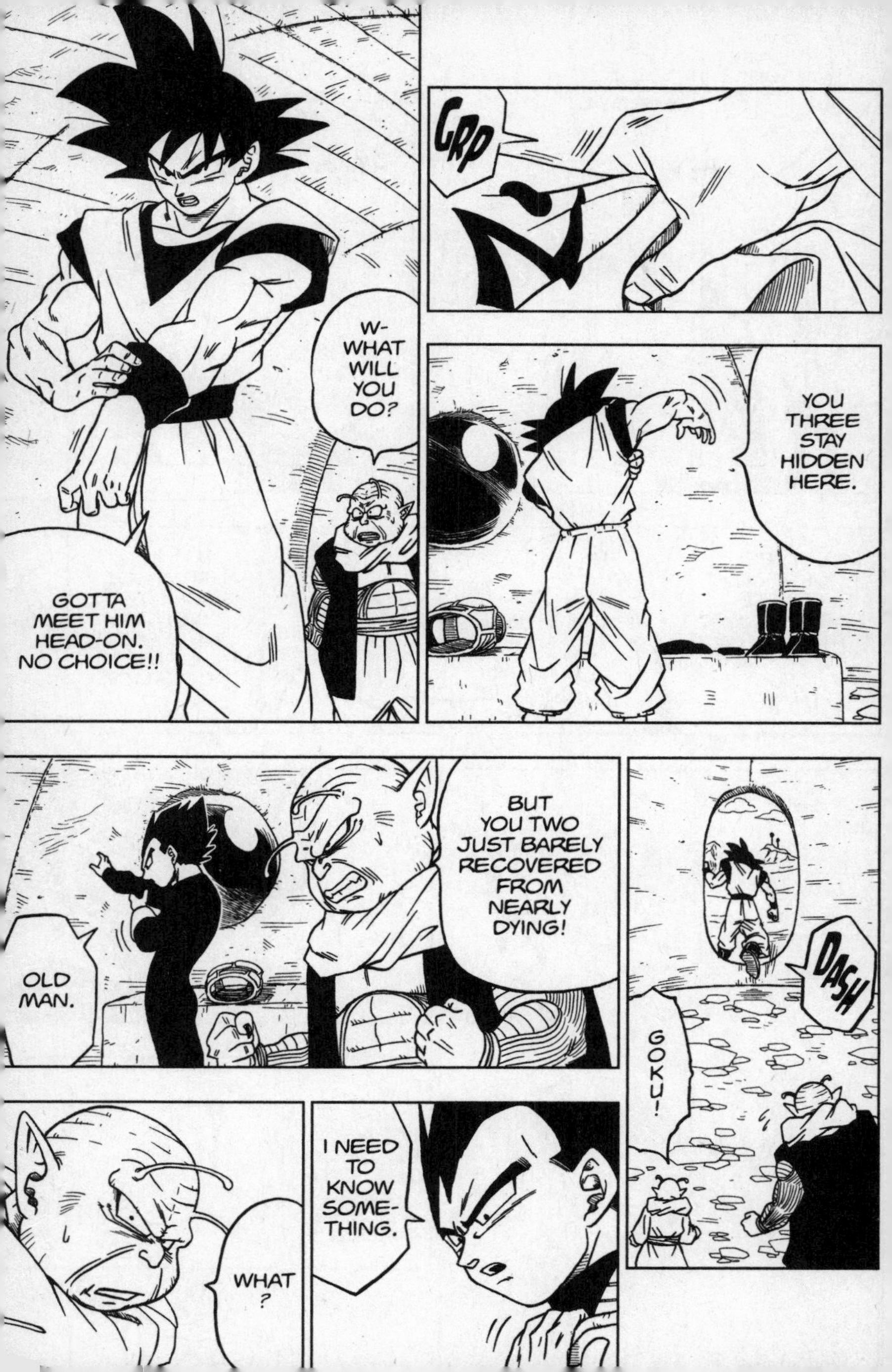
GRP
YOU THREE STAY HIDDEN HERE.
W-WHAT WILL YOU DO?
GOTTA MEET HIM HEAD-ON. NO CHOICE!!
DASH
GOKU!
BUT YOU TWO JUST BARELY RECOVERED FROM NEARLY DYING!
OLD MAN.
I NEED TO KNOW SOMETHING.
WHAT?

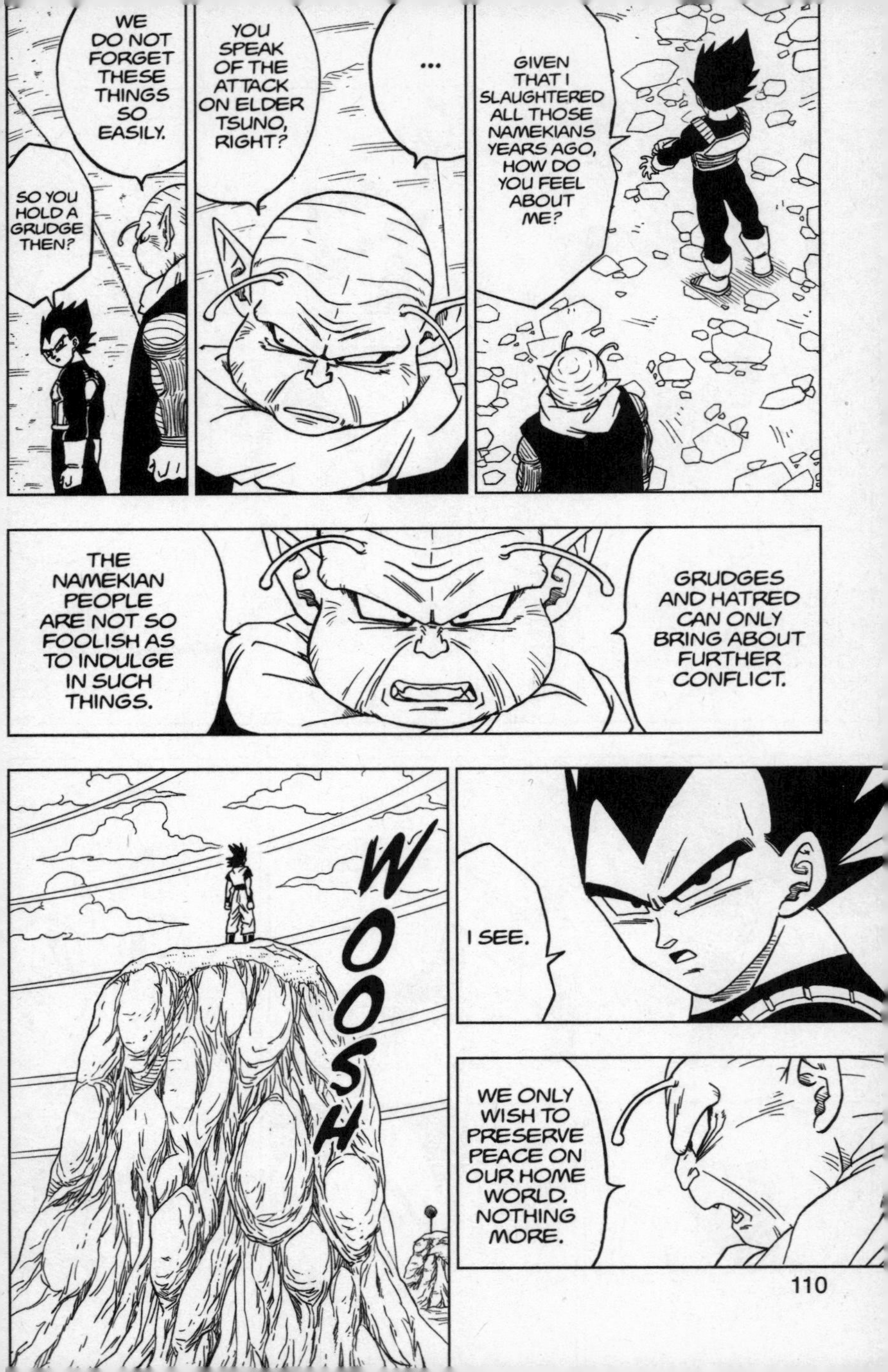
GIVEN THAT I SLAUGHTERED ALL THOSE NAMEKIANS YEARS AGO, HOW DO YOU FEEL ABOUT ME?
...
YOU SPEAK OF THE ATTACK ON ELDER TSUNO, RIGHT?
WE DO NOT FORGET THESE THINGS SO EASILY.
SO YOU HOLD A GRUDGE THEN?
GRUDGES AND HATRED CAN ONLY BRING ABOUT FURTHER CONFLICT.
THE NAMEKIAN PEOPLE ARE NOT SO FOOLISH AS TO INDULGE IN SUCH THINGS.
I SEE.
WE ONLY WISH TO PRESERVE PEACE ON OUR HOME WORLD. NOTHING MORE.
WOOSH

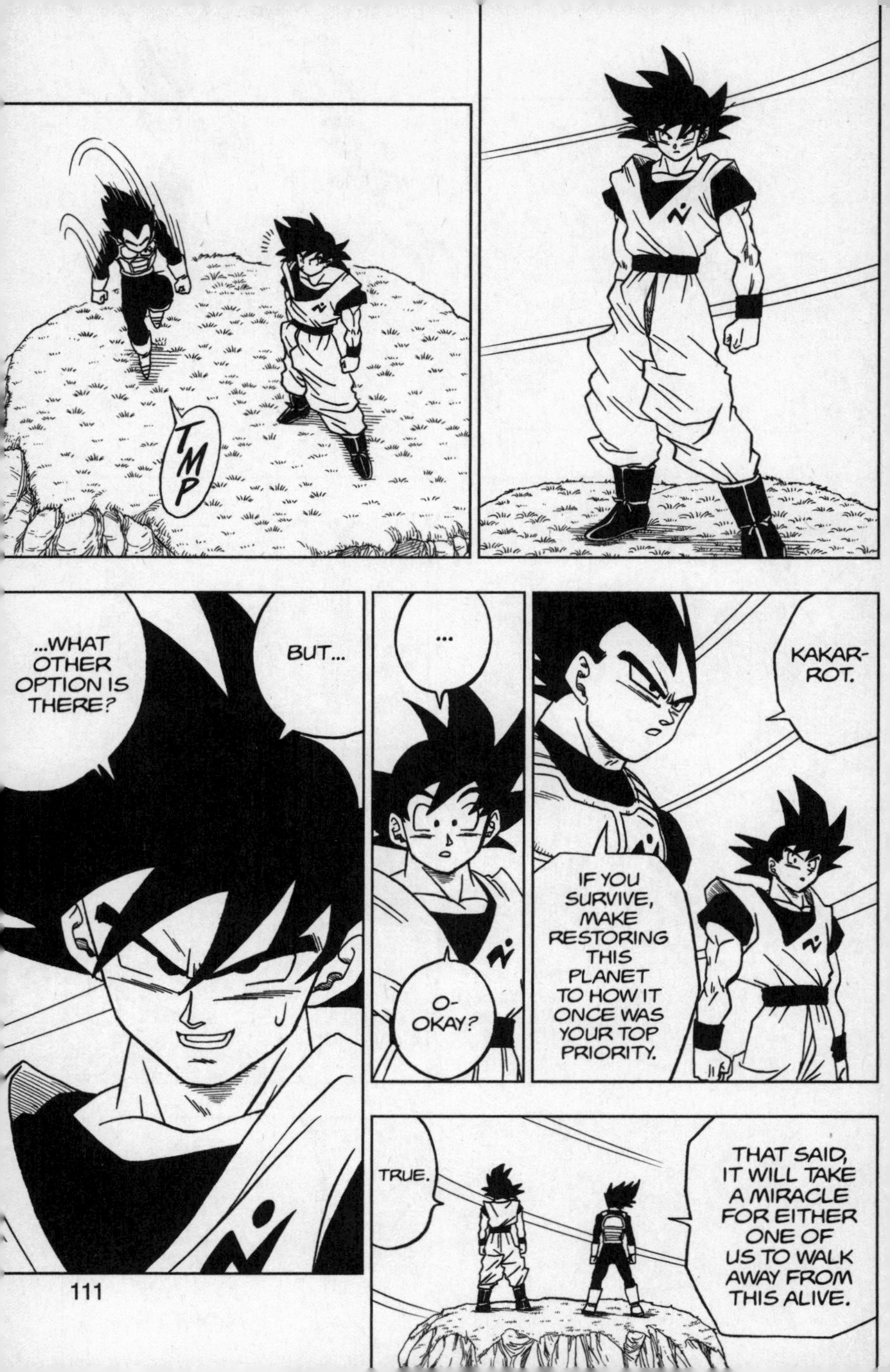
TMP
KAKAR-ROT.
IF YOU SURVIVE, MAKE RESTORING THIS PLANET TO HOW IT ONCE WAS YOUR TOP PRIORITY.
...
O-OKAY?
THAT SAID, IT WILL TAKE A MIRACLE FOR EITHER ONE OF US TO WALK AWAY FROM THIS ALIVE.
TRUE.
BUT...
...WHAT OTHER OPTION IS THERE?

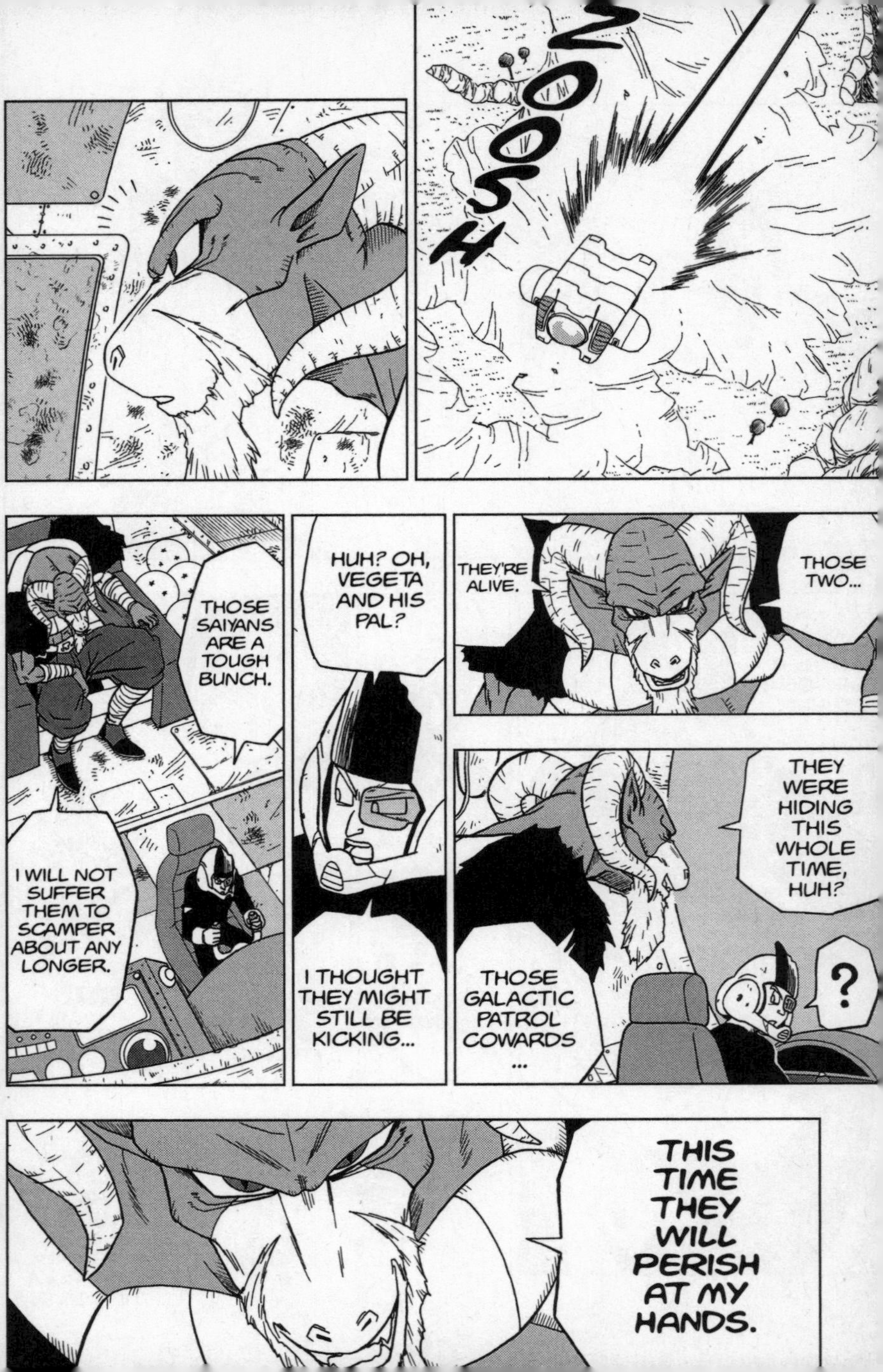
ZOOOSH
THOSE TWO...
THEY'RE ALIVE.
THEY WERE HIDING THIS WHOLE TIME, HUH?
?
THOSE GALACTIC PATROL COWARDS ...
HUH? OH, VEGETA AND HIS PAL?
I THOUGHT THEY MIGHT STILL BE KICKING...
THOSE SAIYANS ARE A TOUGH BUNCH.
I WILL NOT SUFFER THEM TO SCAMPER ABOUT ANY LONGER.
THIS TIME THEY WILL PERISH AT MY HANDS.

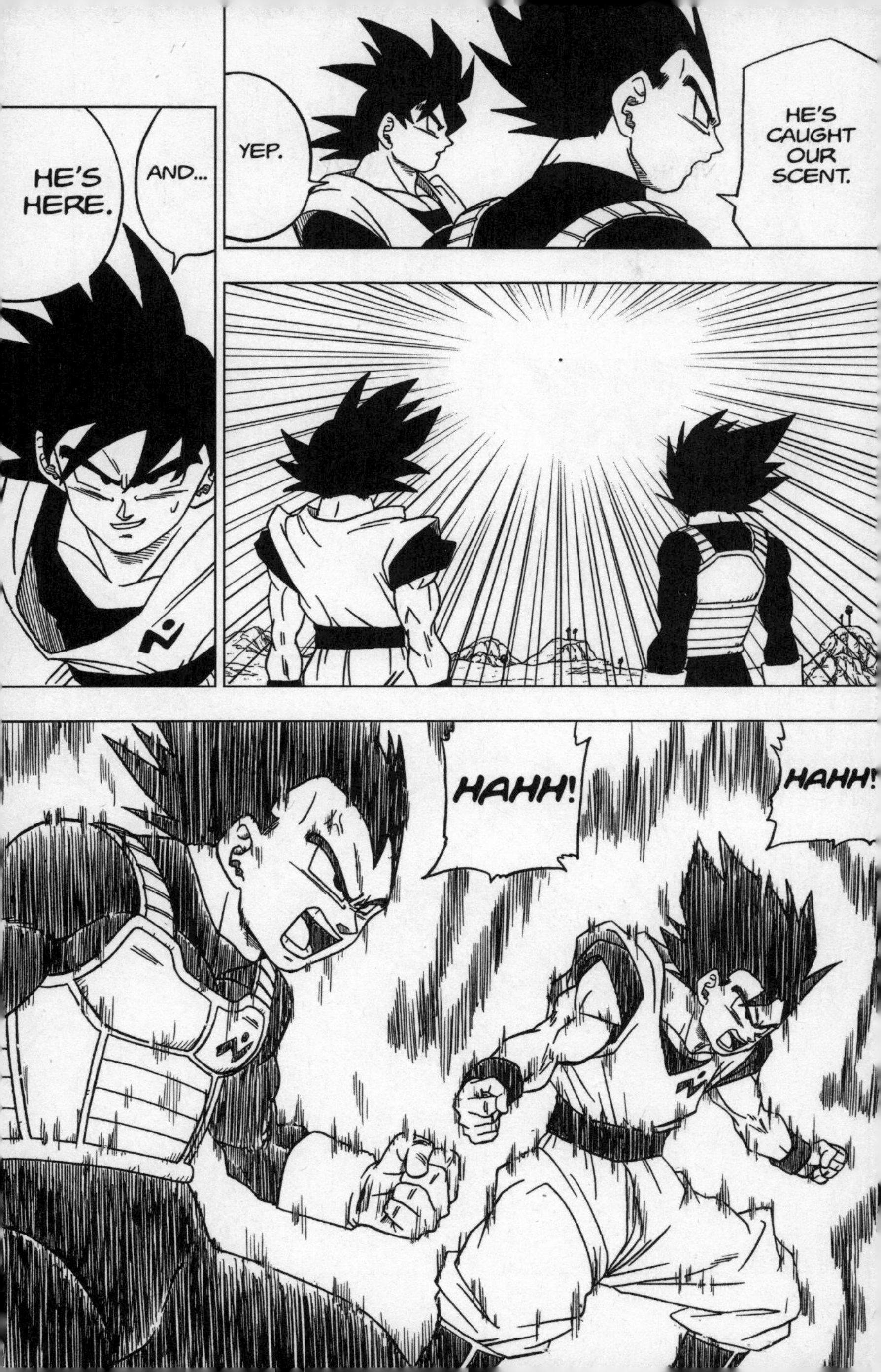
HE'S CAUGHT OUR SCENT.
YEP.
AND...
HE'S HERE.
HAHH!
HAHH!

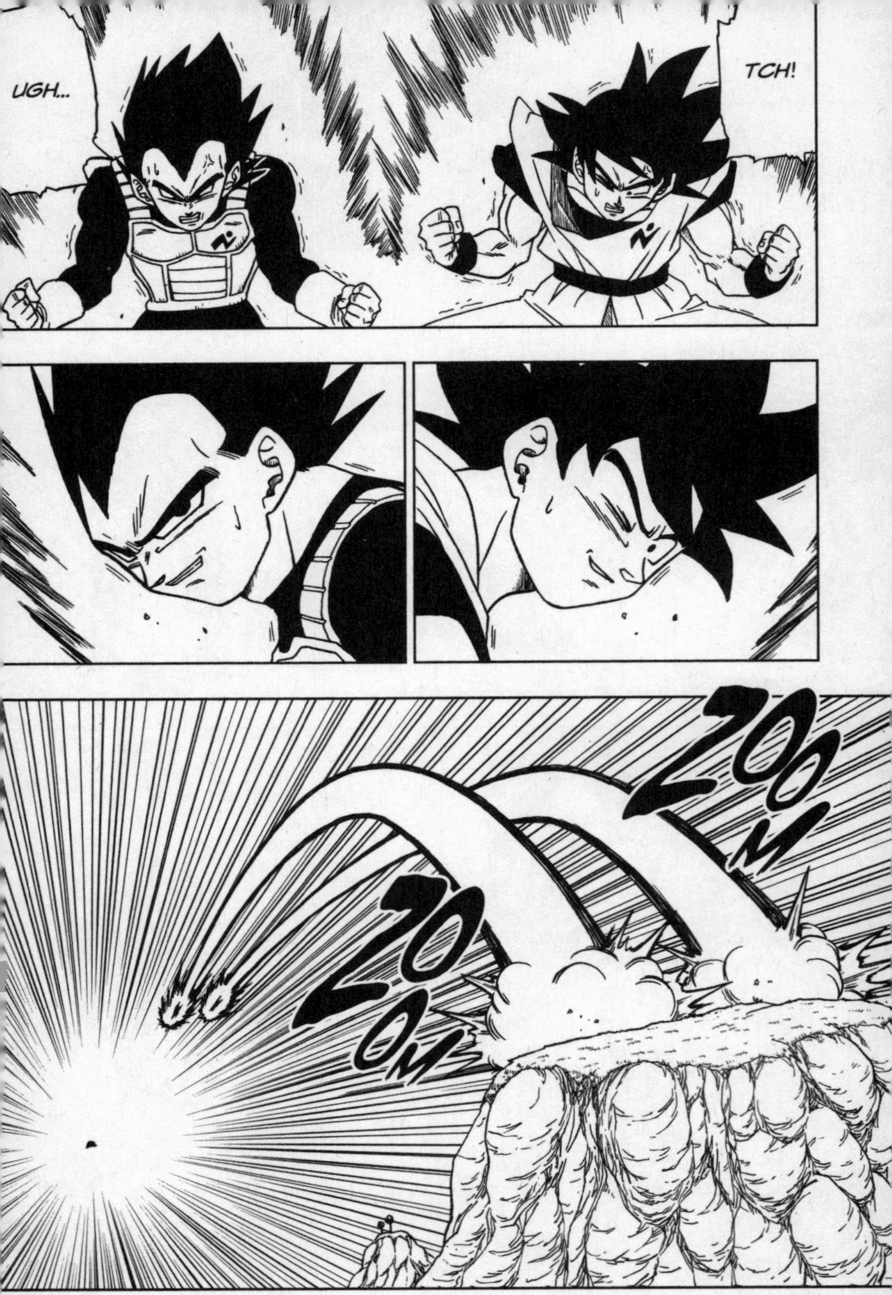
TCH!
UGH...
ZOOM
ZOOM

THEY'RE COMING!

BWOOM

ZOOM

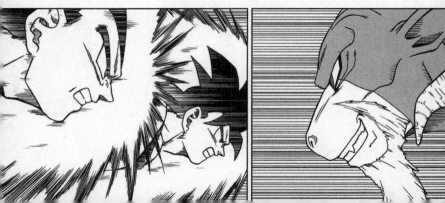

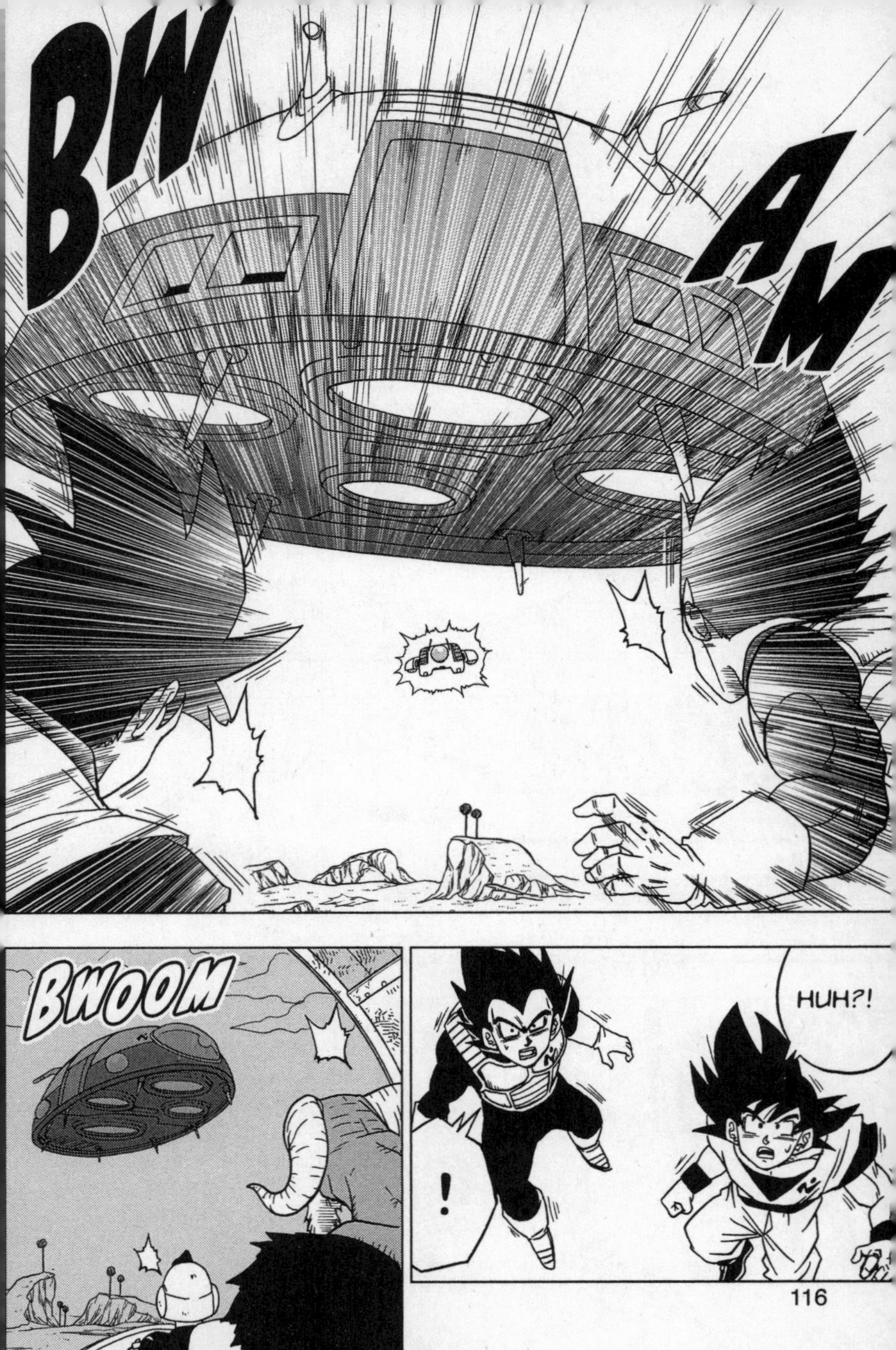
BWAM
HUH?!
!
BWOOM

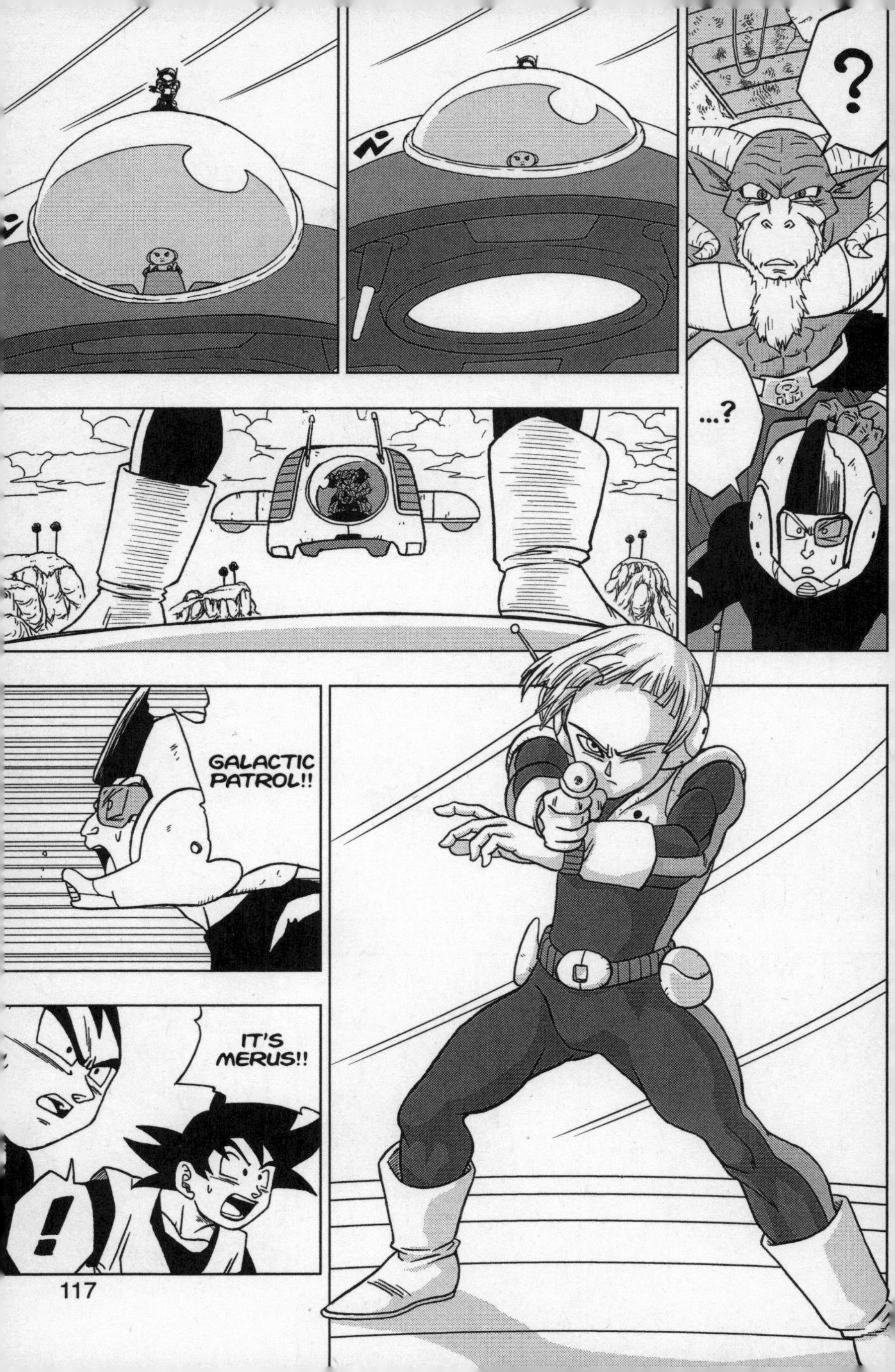
?
...?
GALACTIC PATROL!!
IT'S MERUS!!

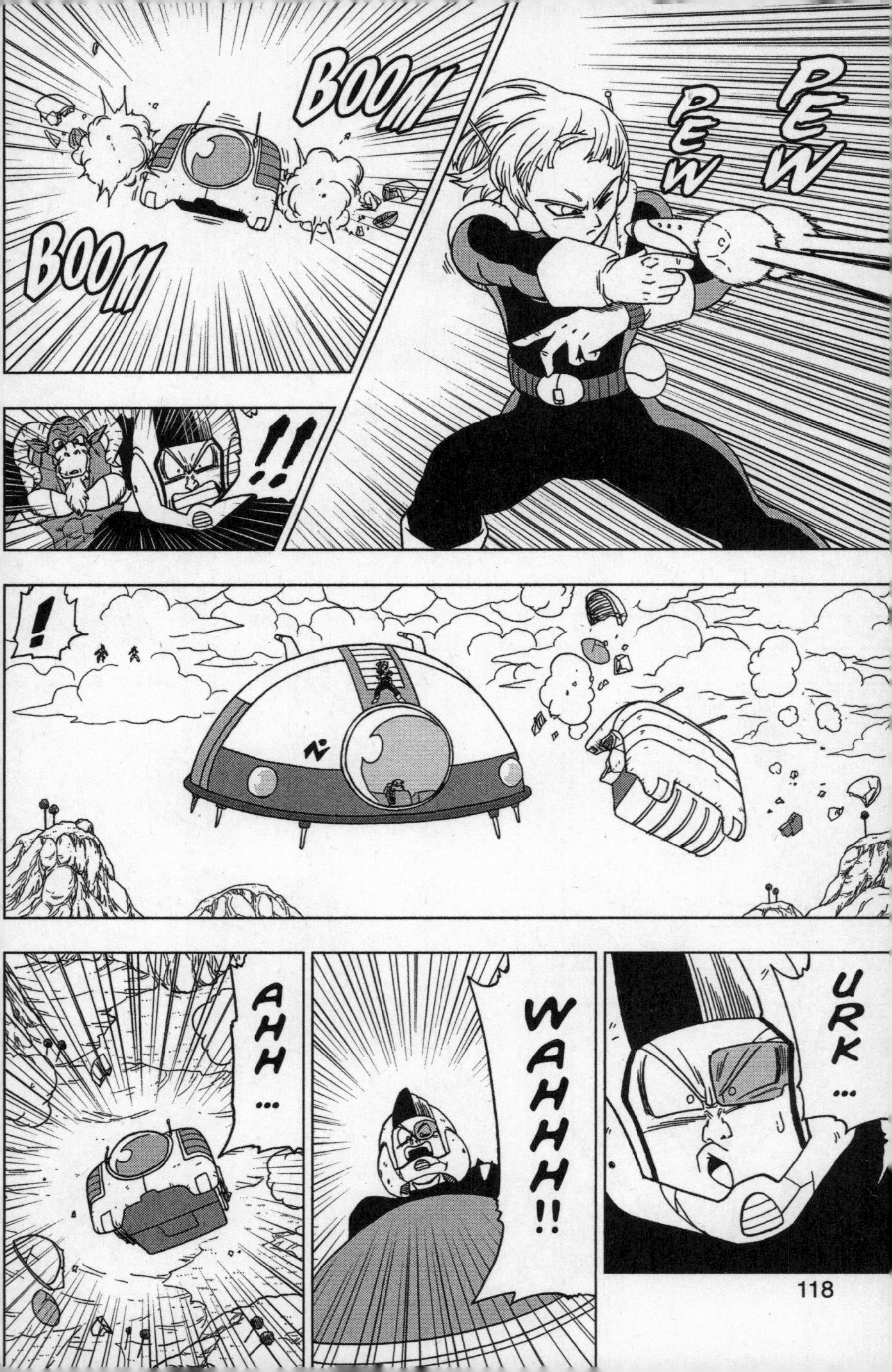
PEW
PEW
BOOM
BOOM
!!
!
URK...
WAHHHH!!
AHH...

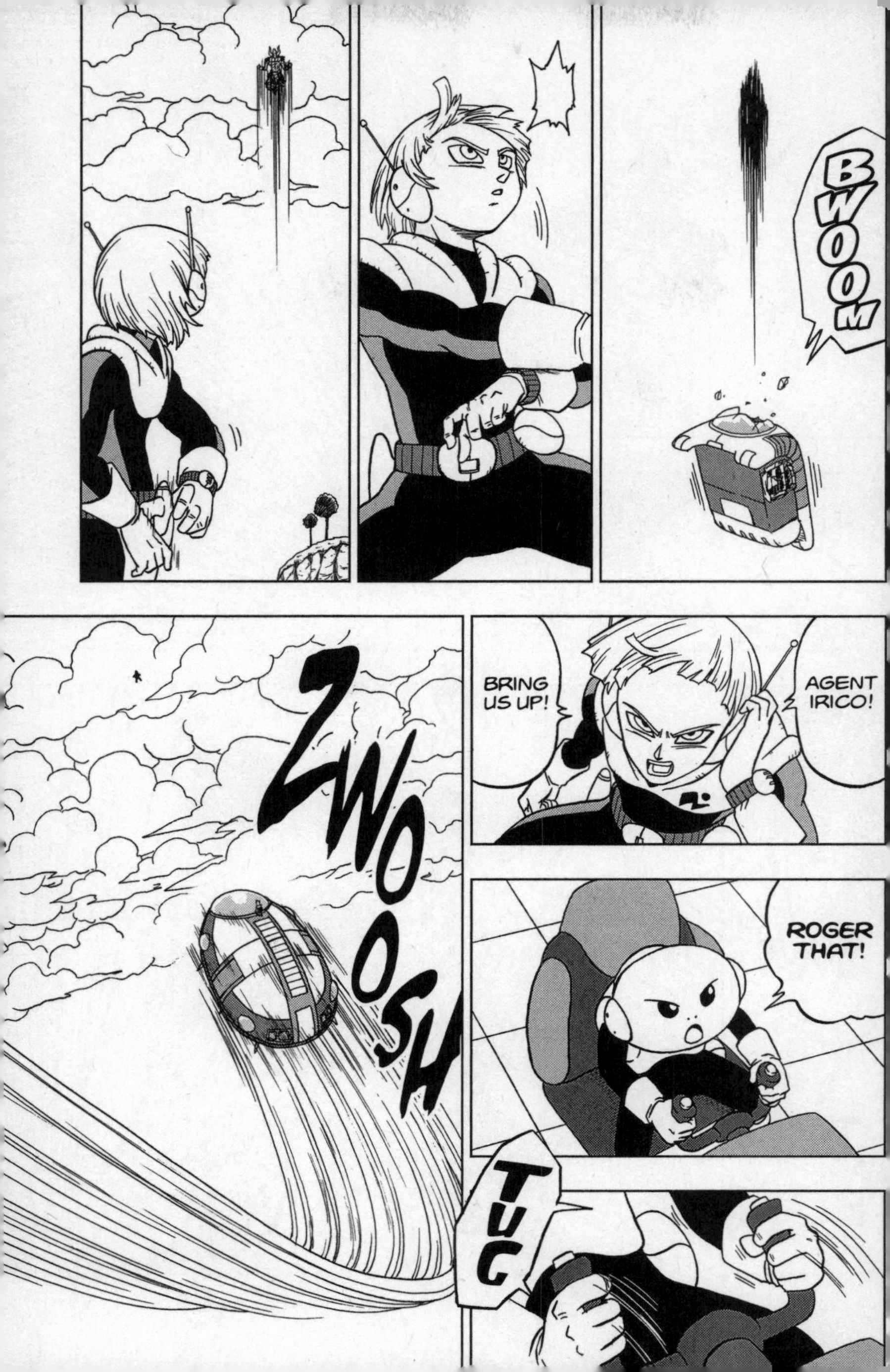
BWOOOM
AGENT IRICO!
BRING US UP!
ROGER THAT!
TUG
ZWOOSH

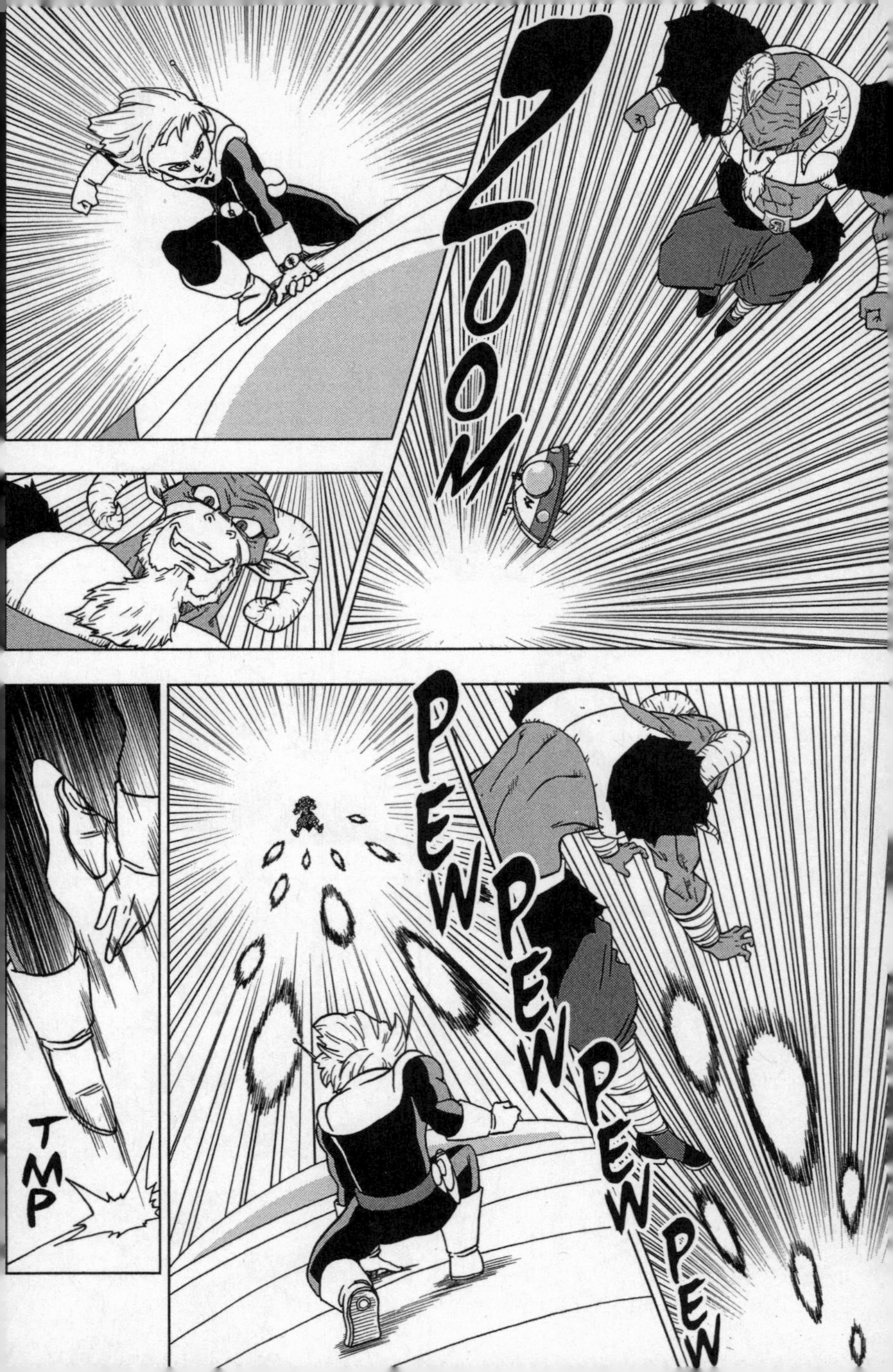
ZOOM
PEW PEW PEW PEW PEW
TMP

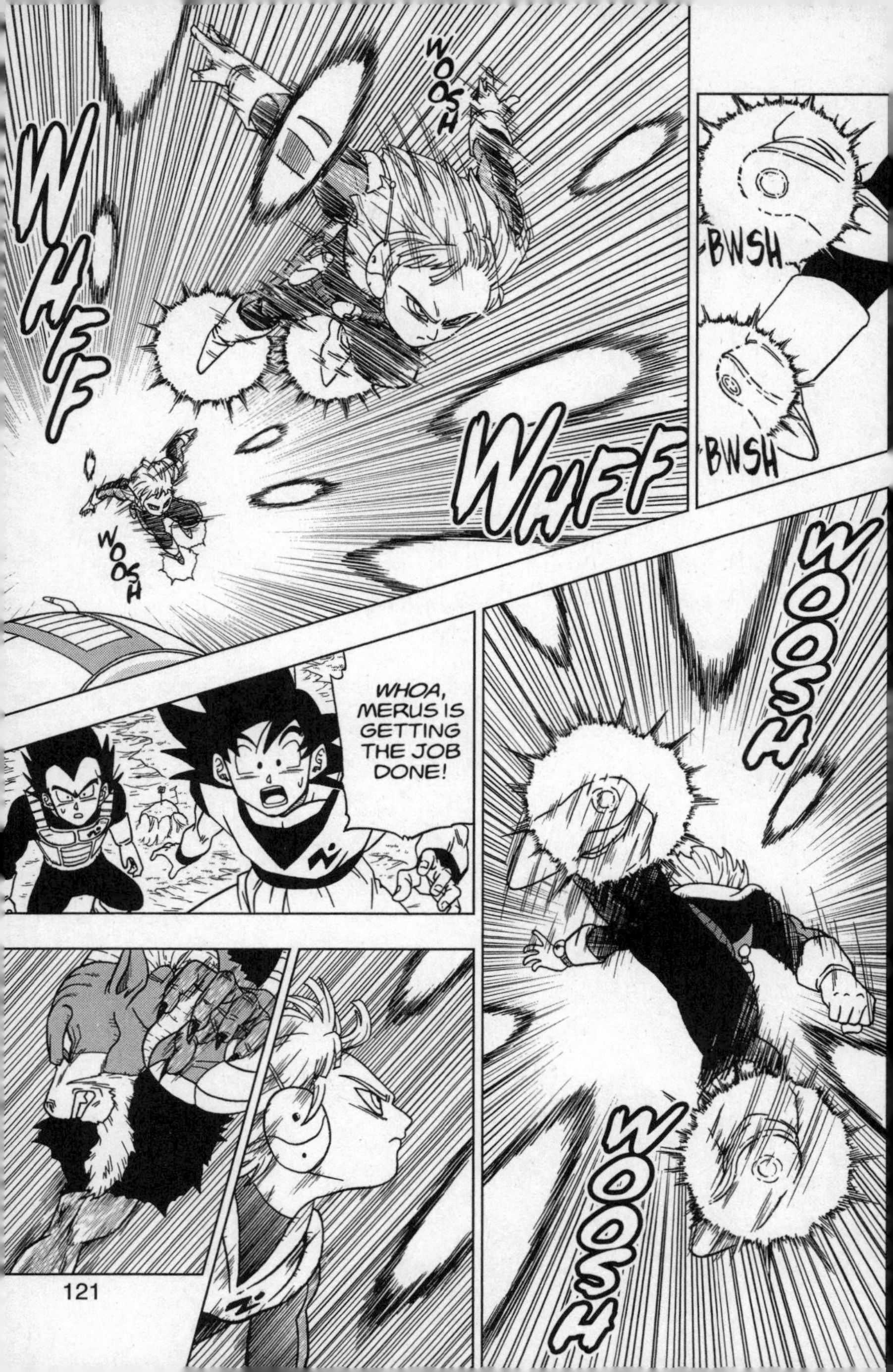
BWSH
BWSH
WOOSH
WHFF
WHFF
WOOSH
WOOSH
WOOSH
WHOA, MERUS IS GETTING THE JOB DONE!

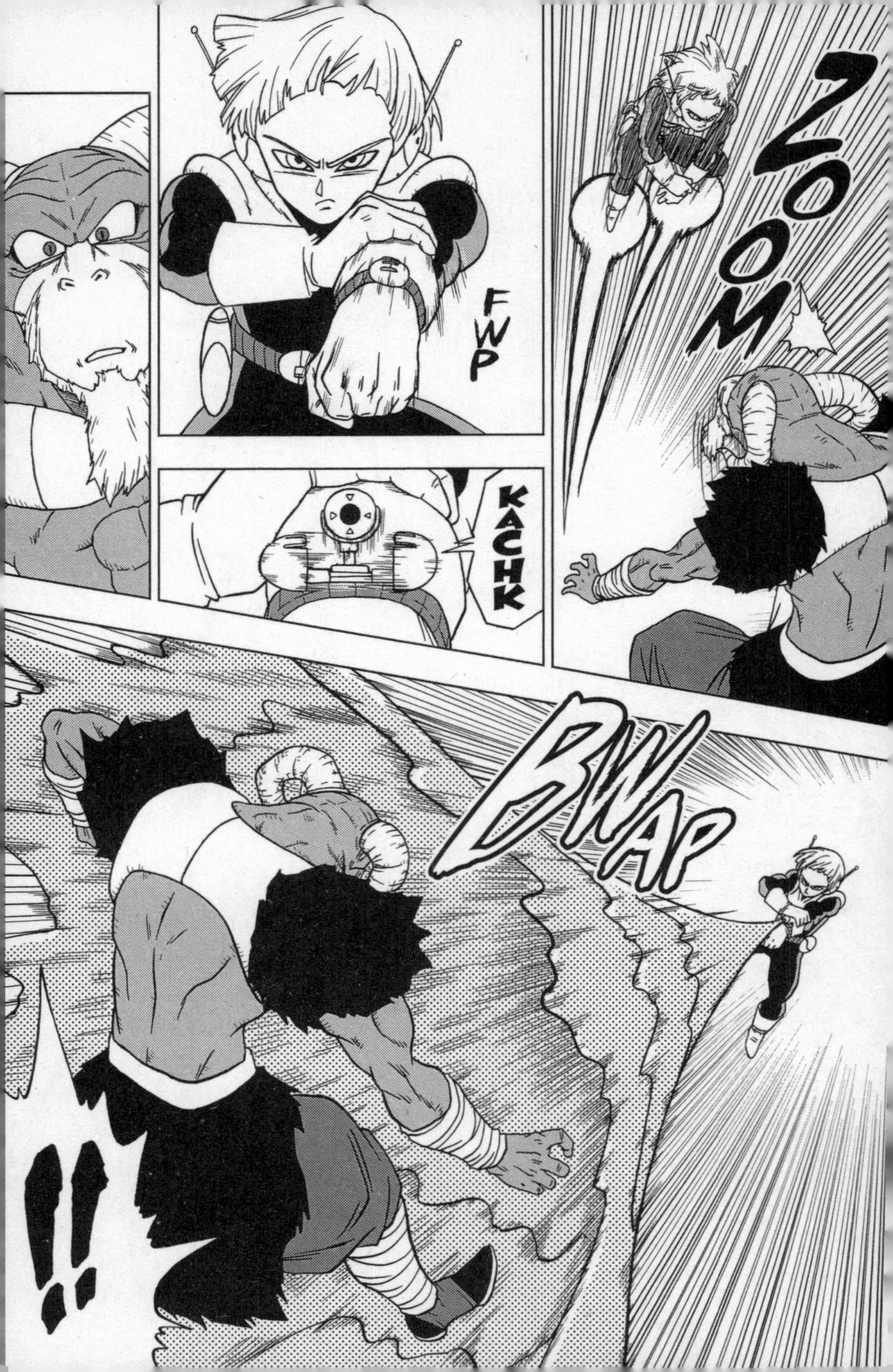
ZOOM
FWP
KACHK
BWAP
!!

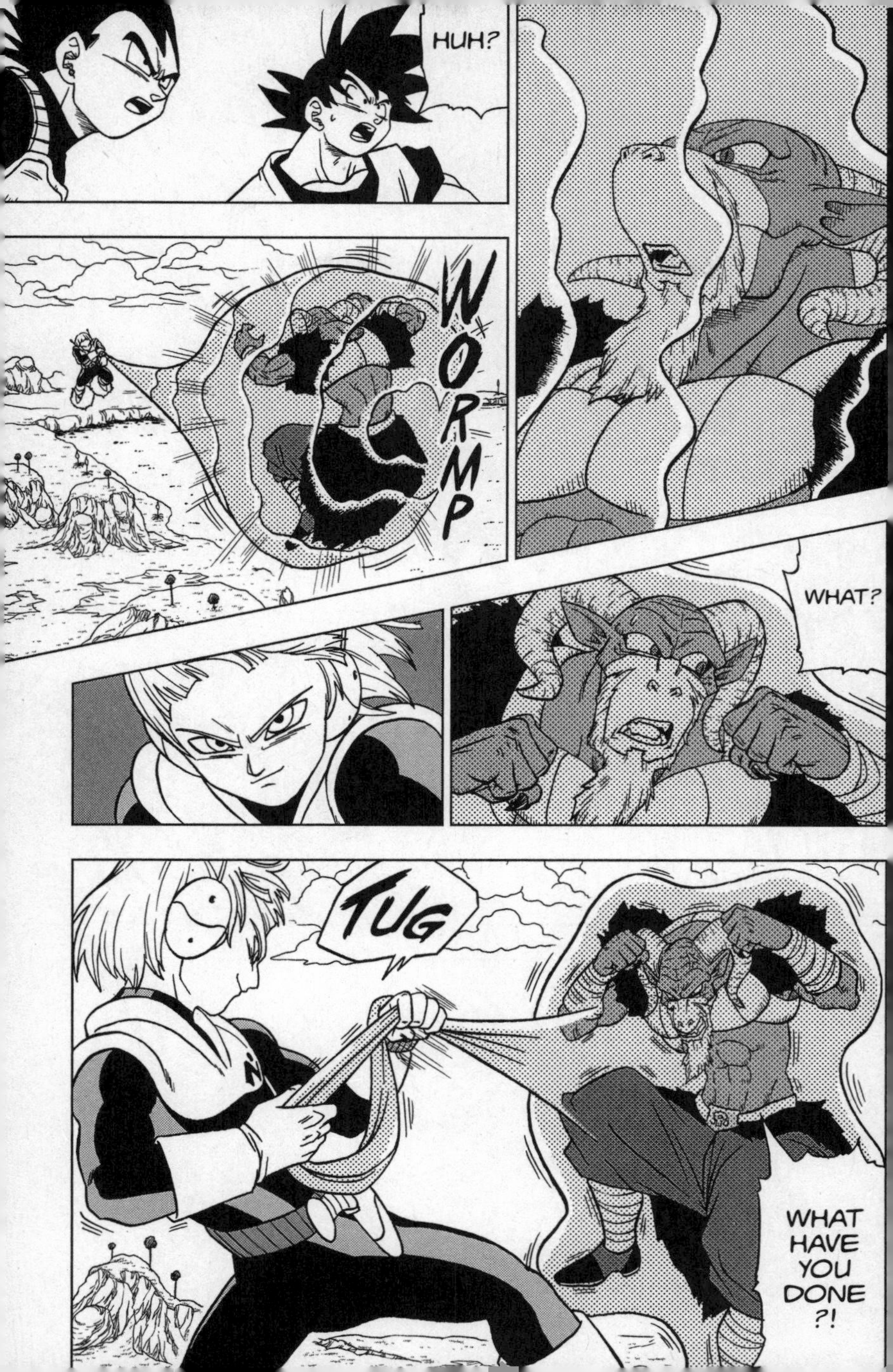
HUH?
WORMP
WHAT?
TUG
WHAT HAVE YOU DONE?!

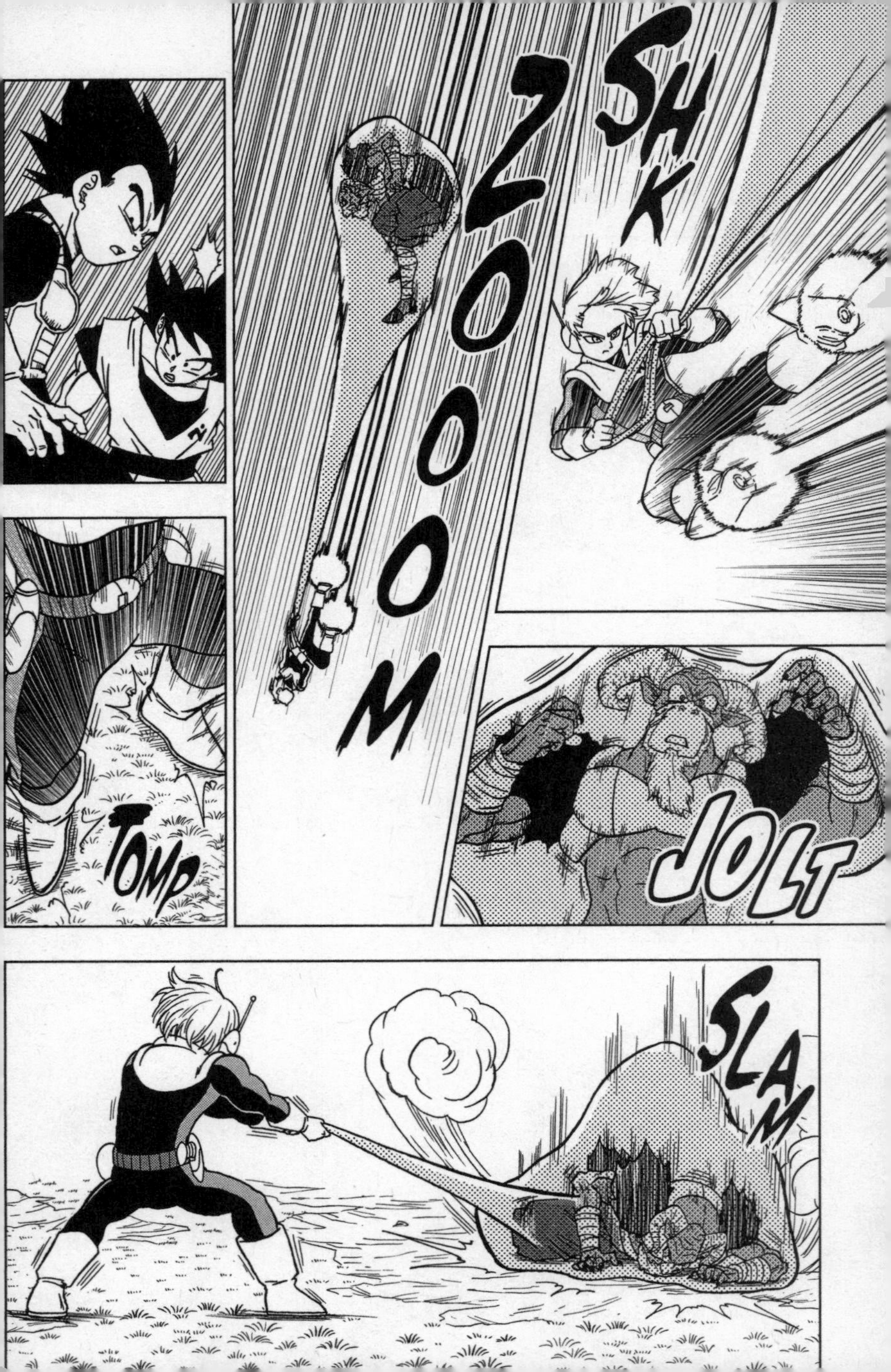
SHK
JOLT
ZOOOOM
TOMP
SLAM

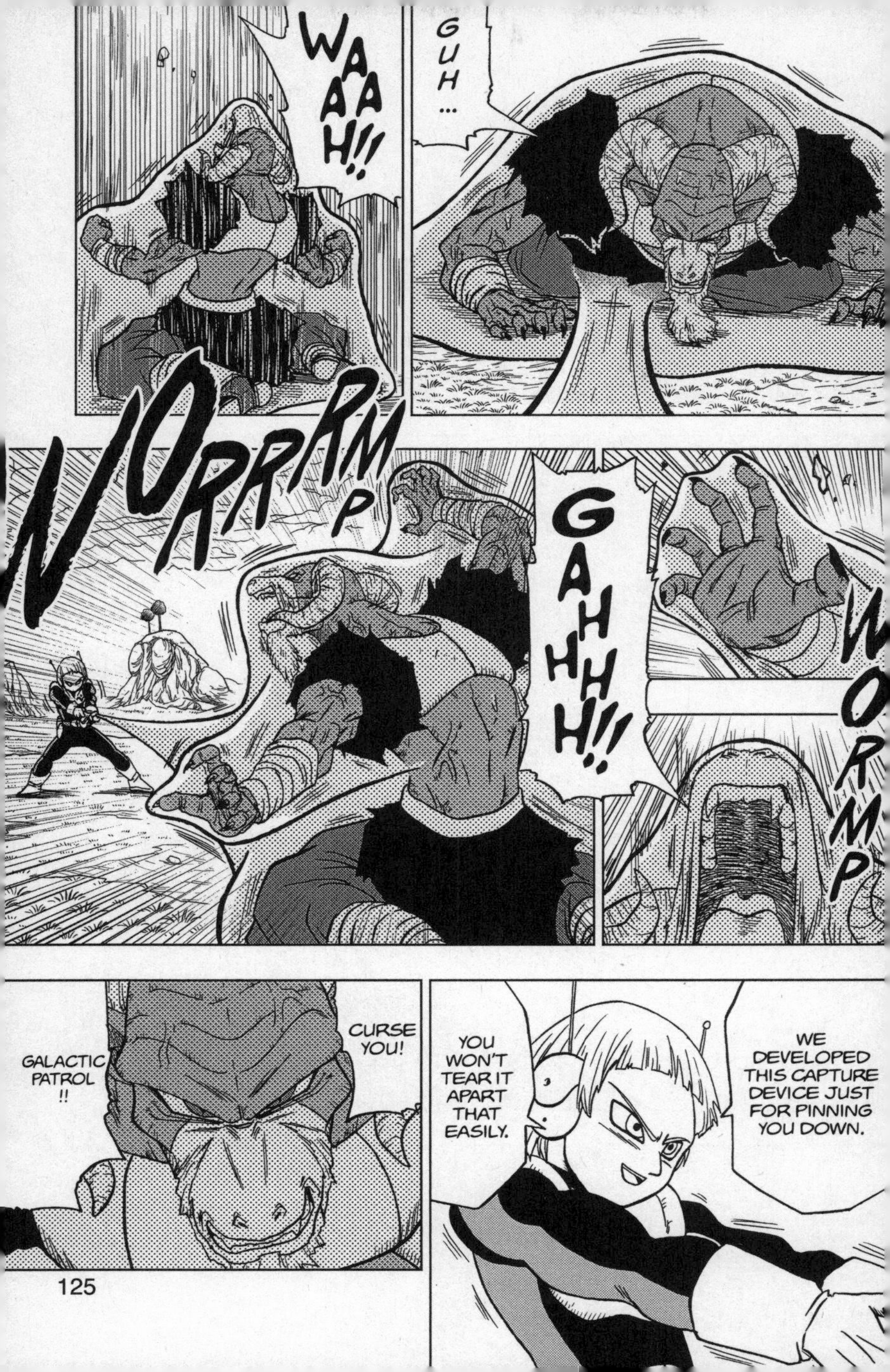
GUH...
WAAAH!!
WORMP
GAHHHH!!
NORRRMP
WE DEVELOPED THIS CAPTURE DEVICE JUST FOR PINNING YOU DOWN.
YOU WON'T TEAR IT APART THAT EASILY.
CURSE YOU!
GALACTIC PATROL !!

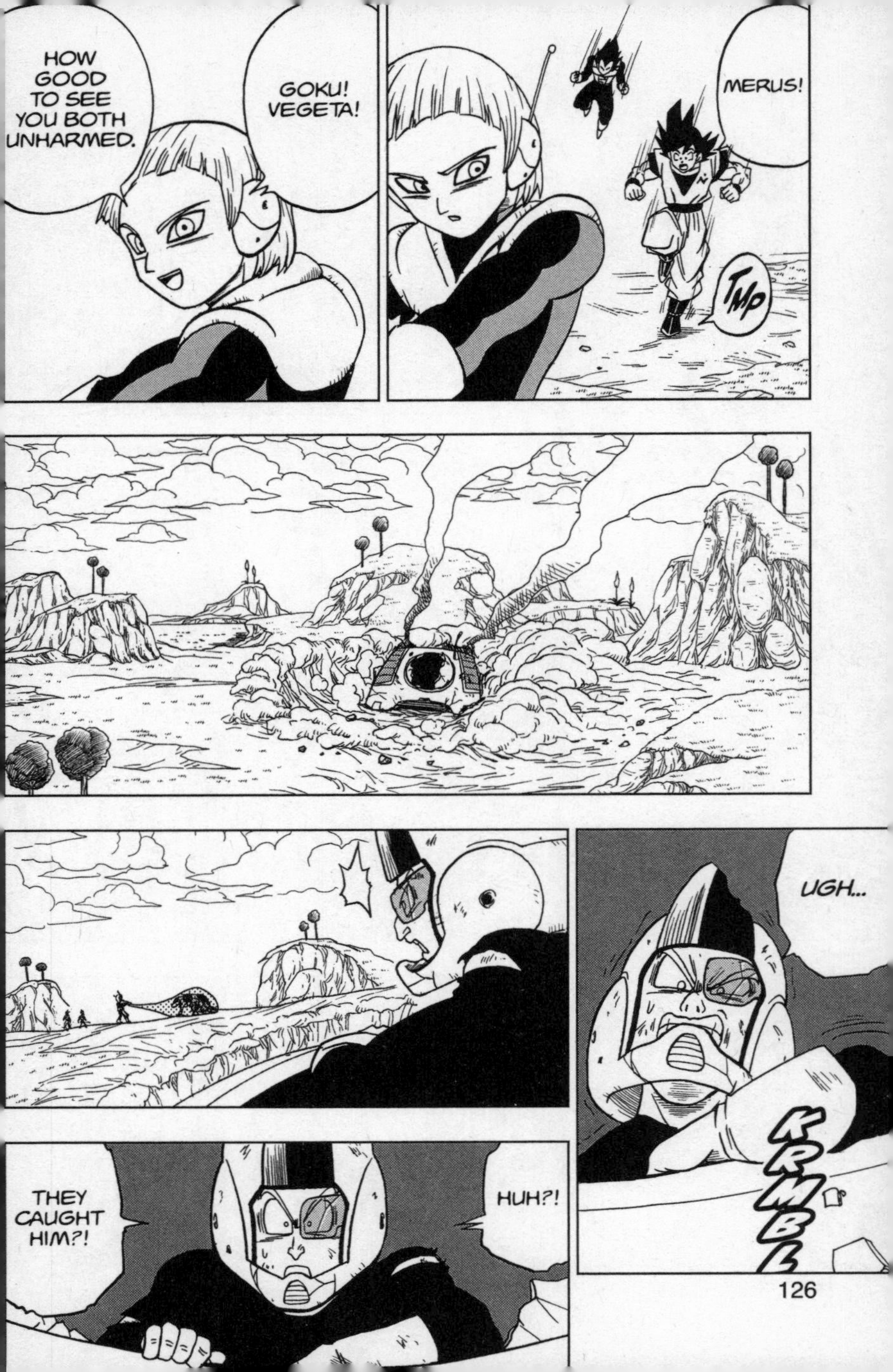
MERUS!
TMP
GOKU! VEGETA!
HOW GOOD TO SEE YOU BOTH UNHARMED.
UGH...
KRMBL
HUH?!
THEY CAUGHT HIM?!

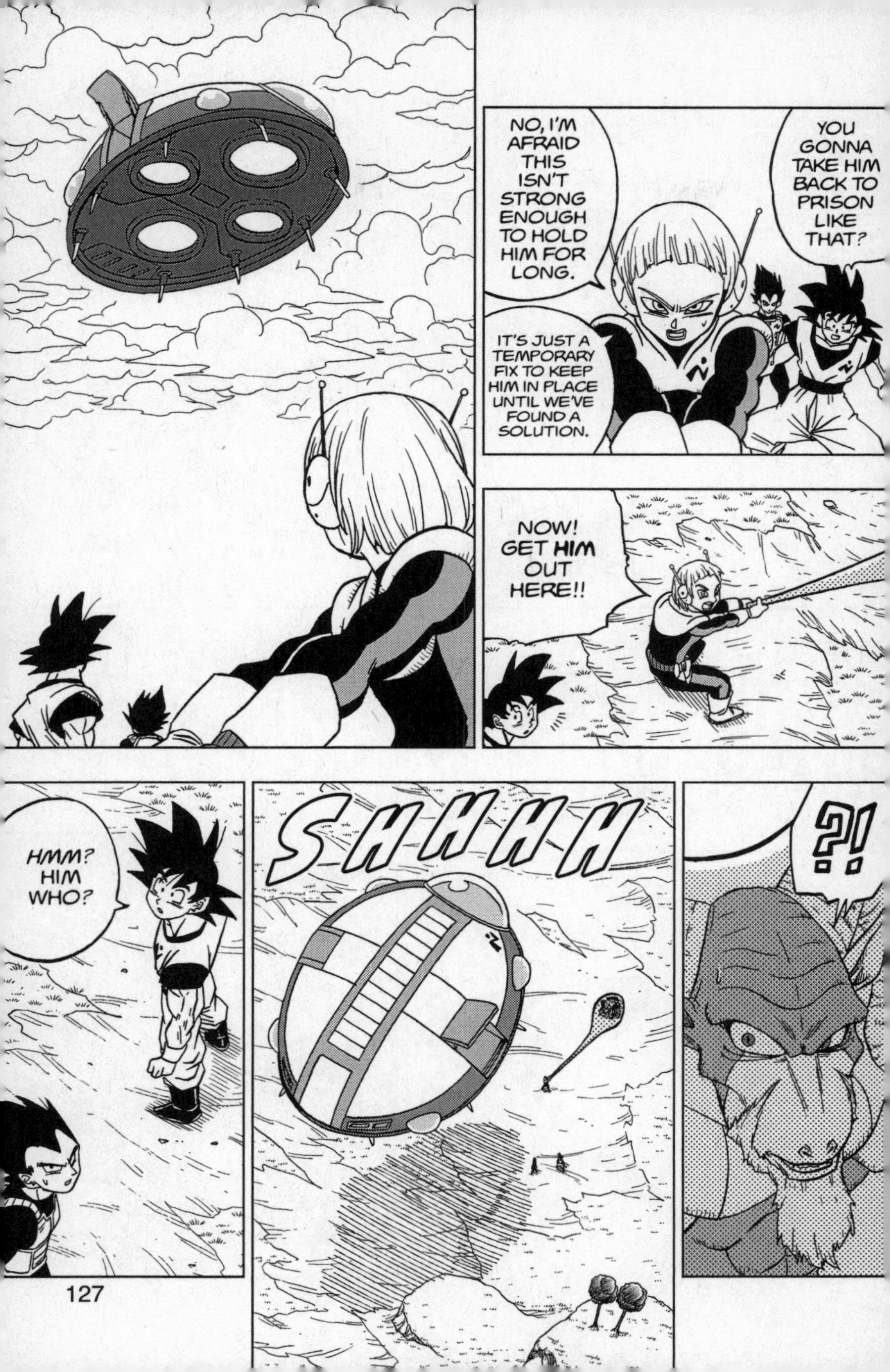
YOU GONNA TAKE HIM BACK TO PRISON LIKE THAT?
NO, I'M AFRAID THIS ISN'T STRONG ENOUGH TO HOLD HIM FOR LONG.
IT'S JUST A TEMPORARY FIX TO KEEP HIM IN PLACE UNTIL WE'VE FOUND A SOLUTION.
NOW! GET **HIM** OUT HERE!!
?!
SHHHHH
HMM? HIM WHO?

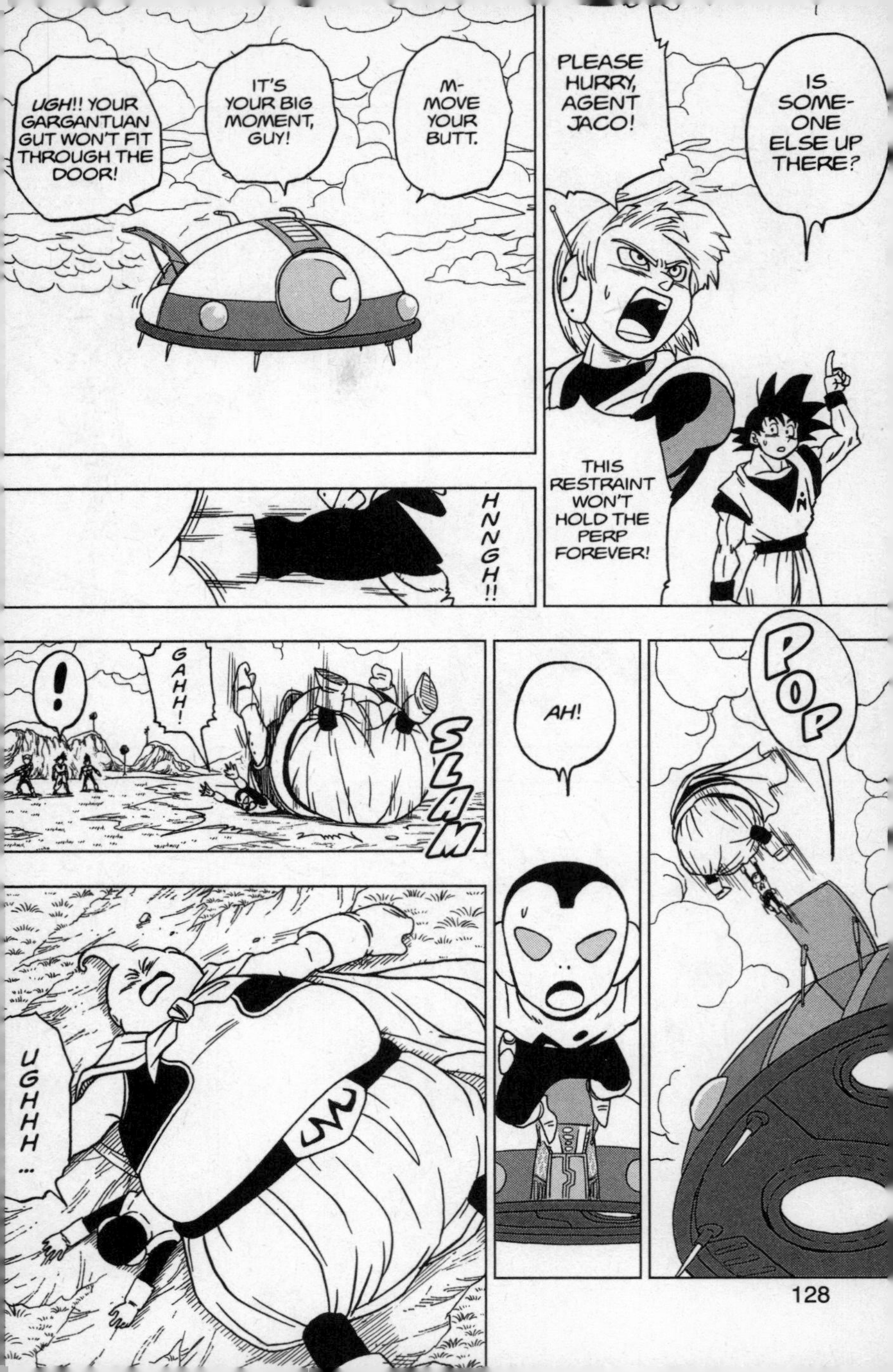

IS SOME-ONE ELSE UP THERE?
PLEASE HURRY, AGENT JACO!
THIS RESTRAINT WON'T HOLD THE PERP FOREVER!
M-MOVE YOUR BUTT.
IT'S YOUR BIG MOMENT, GUY!
UGH!! YOUR GARGANTUAN GUT WON'T FIT THROUGH THE DOOR!
HNNGH!!
POP
AH!
SLAM
GAHH!
!
UGHHH...

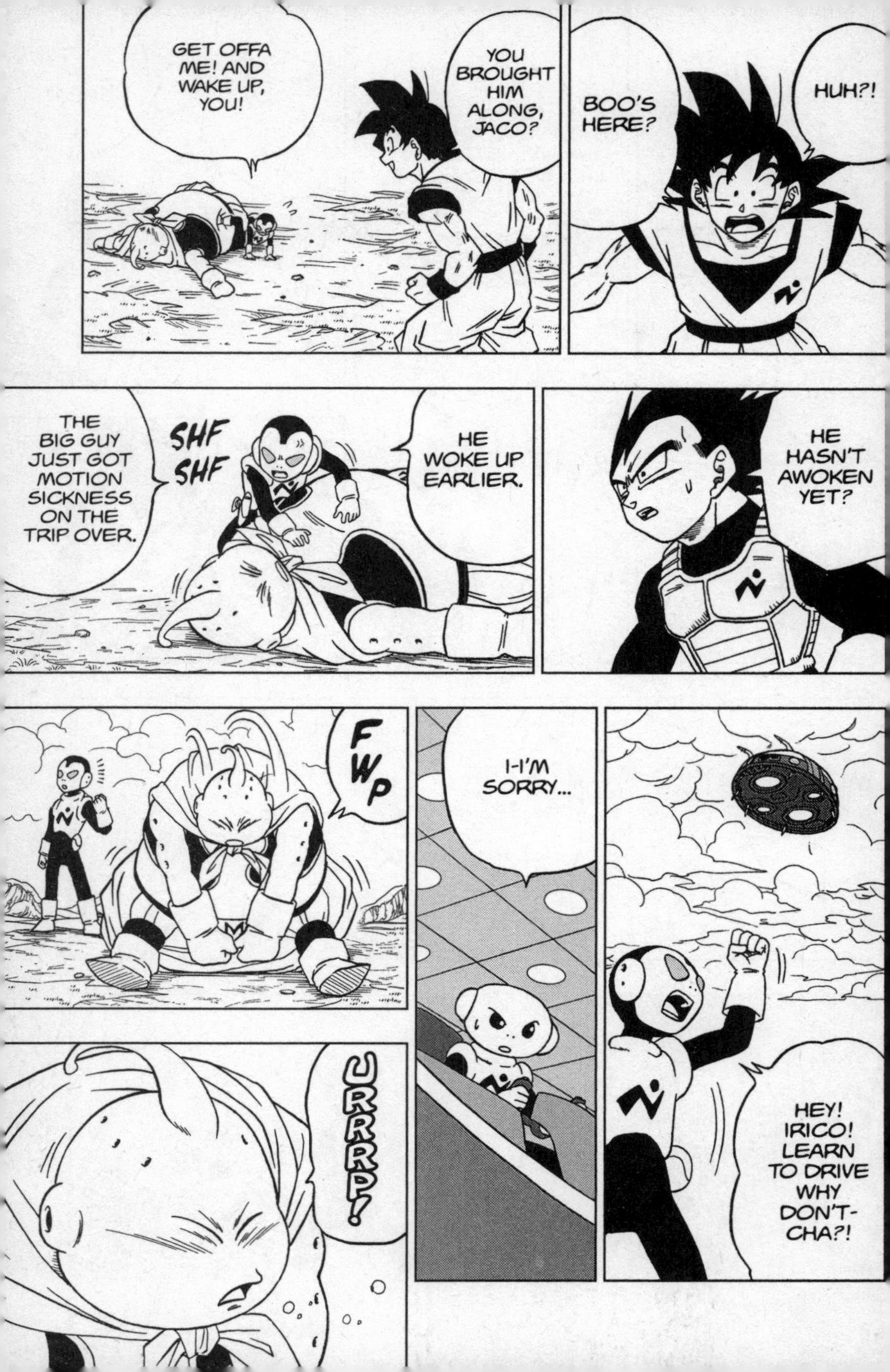
HUH?!
BOO'S HERE?
YOU BROUGHT HIM ALONG, JACO?
GET OFFA ME! AND WAKE UP, YOU!
HE HASN'T AWOKEN YET?
HE WOKE UP EARLIER.
SHF SHF
THE BIG GUY JUST GOT MOTION SICKNESS ON THE TRIP OVER.
HEY! IRICO! LEARN TO DRIVE WHY DON'T-CHA?!
I-I'M SORRY...
FWP
URRRP!

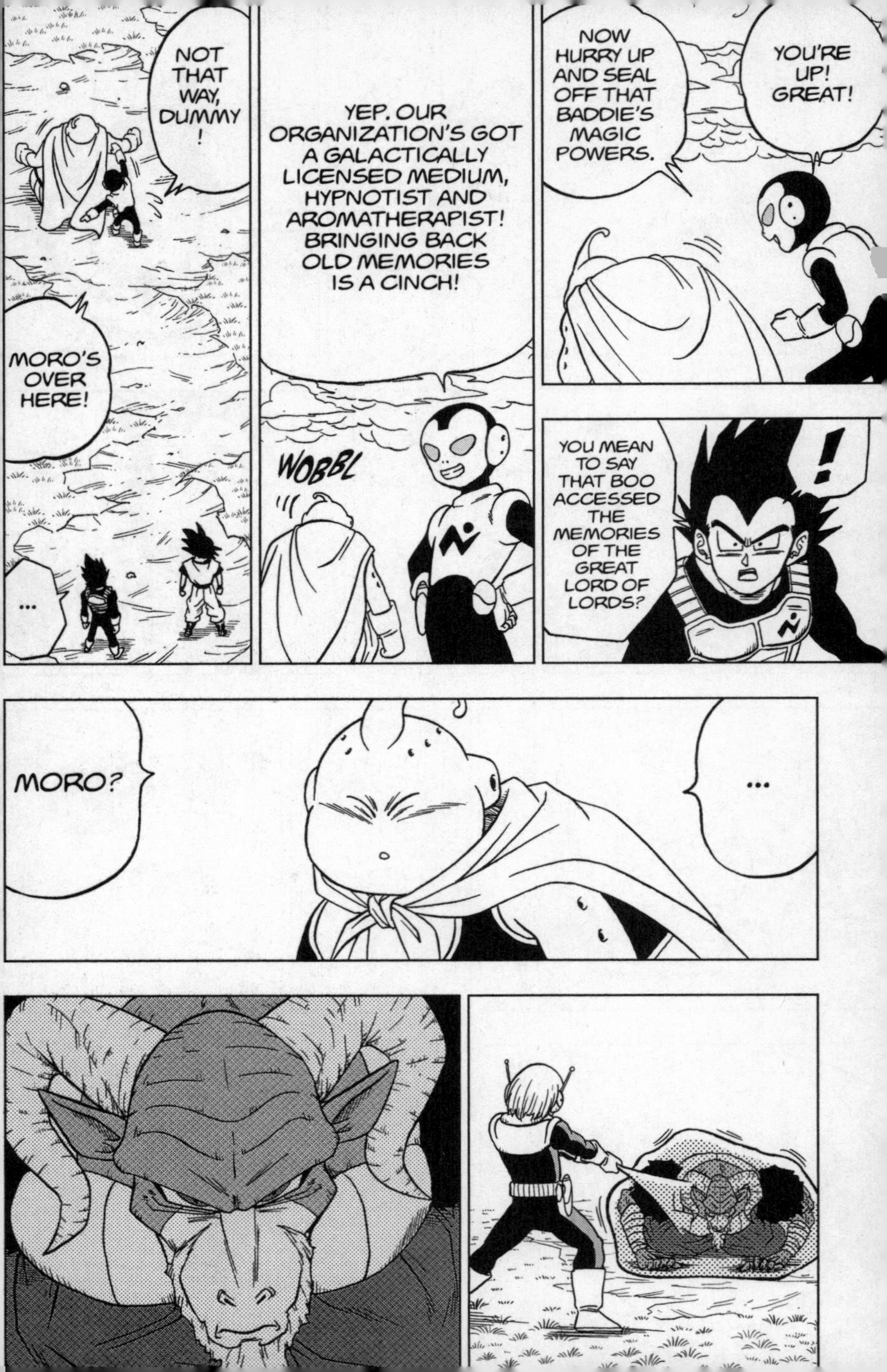
YOU'RE UP! GREAT!
NOW HURRY UP AND SEAL OFF THAT BADDIE'S MAGIC POWERS.
!
YOU MEAN TO SAY THAT BOO ACCESSED THE MEMORIES OF THE GREAT LORD OF LORDS?
YEP. OUR ORGANIZATION'S GOT A GALACTICALLY LICENSED MEDIUM, HYPNOTIST AND AROMATHERAPIST! BRINGING BACK OLD MEMORIES IS A CINCH!
WOBBL
NOT THAT WAY, DUMMY!
MORO'S OVER HERE!
...
...
MORO?

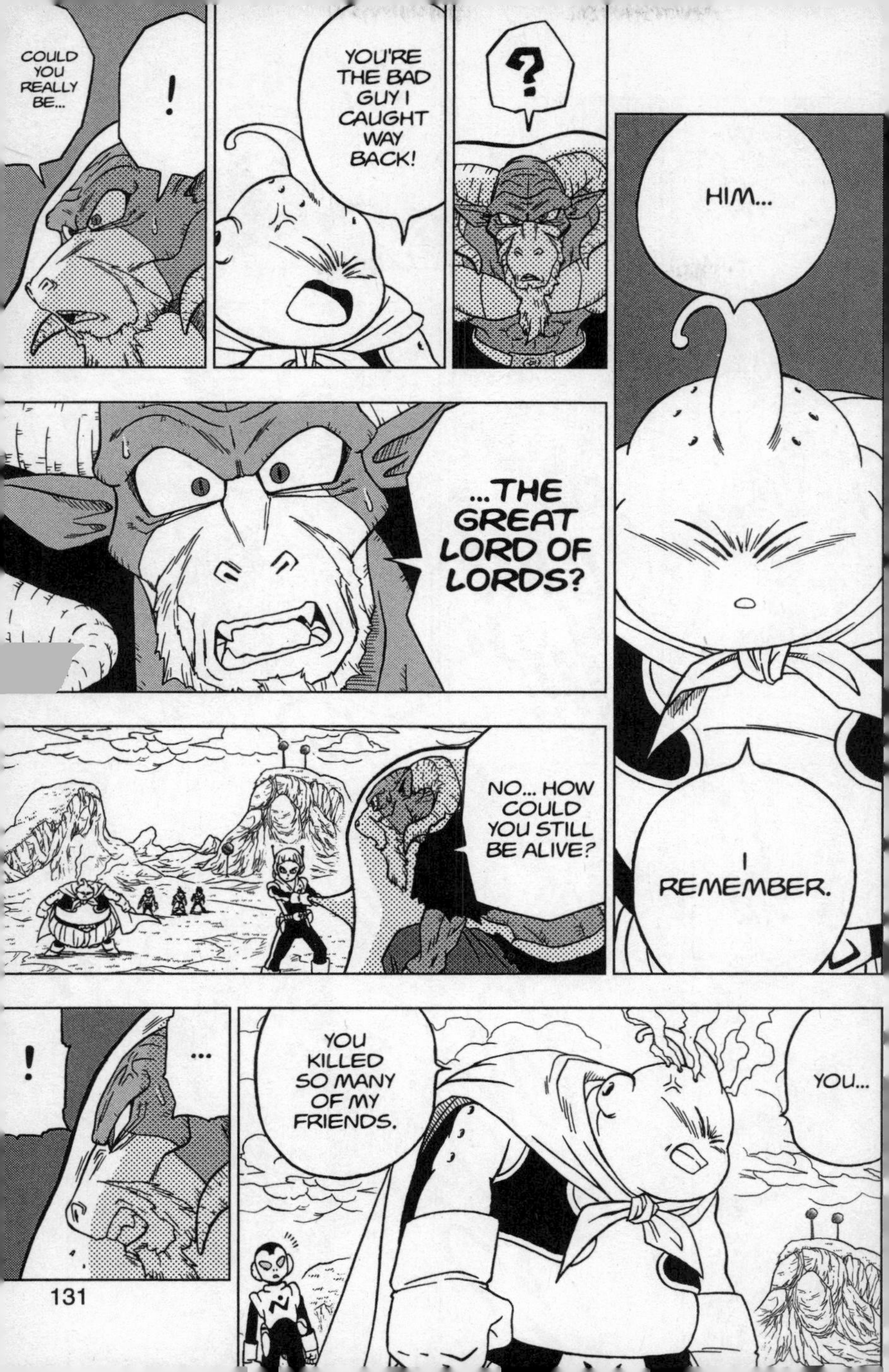
HIM...
I REMEMBER.
?
YOU'RE THE BAD GUY I CAUGHT WAY BACK!
!
COULD YOU REALLY BE...
...THE GREAT LORD OF LORDS?
NO... HOW COULD YOU STILL BE ALIVE?
YOU...
YOU KILLED SO MANY OF MY FRIENDS.
...
!

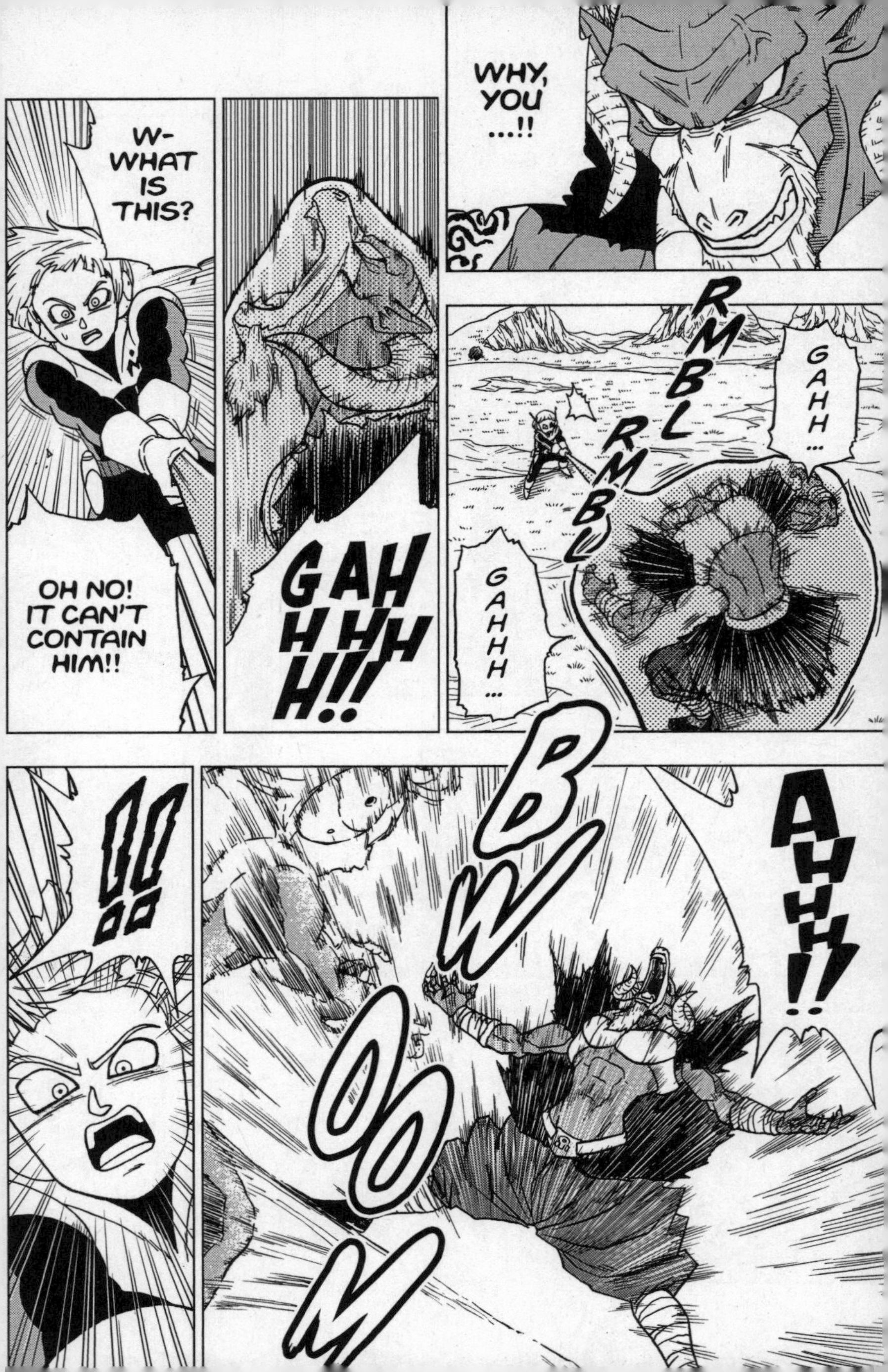
WHY, YOU ...!!
RMBL RMBL
GAHH...
GAHHH...
GAHHHHH!!
W-WHAT IS THIS?
OH NO! IT CAN'T CONTAIN HIM!!
AHHH!!
BWOOOM
!!

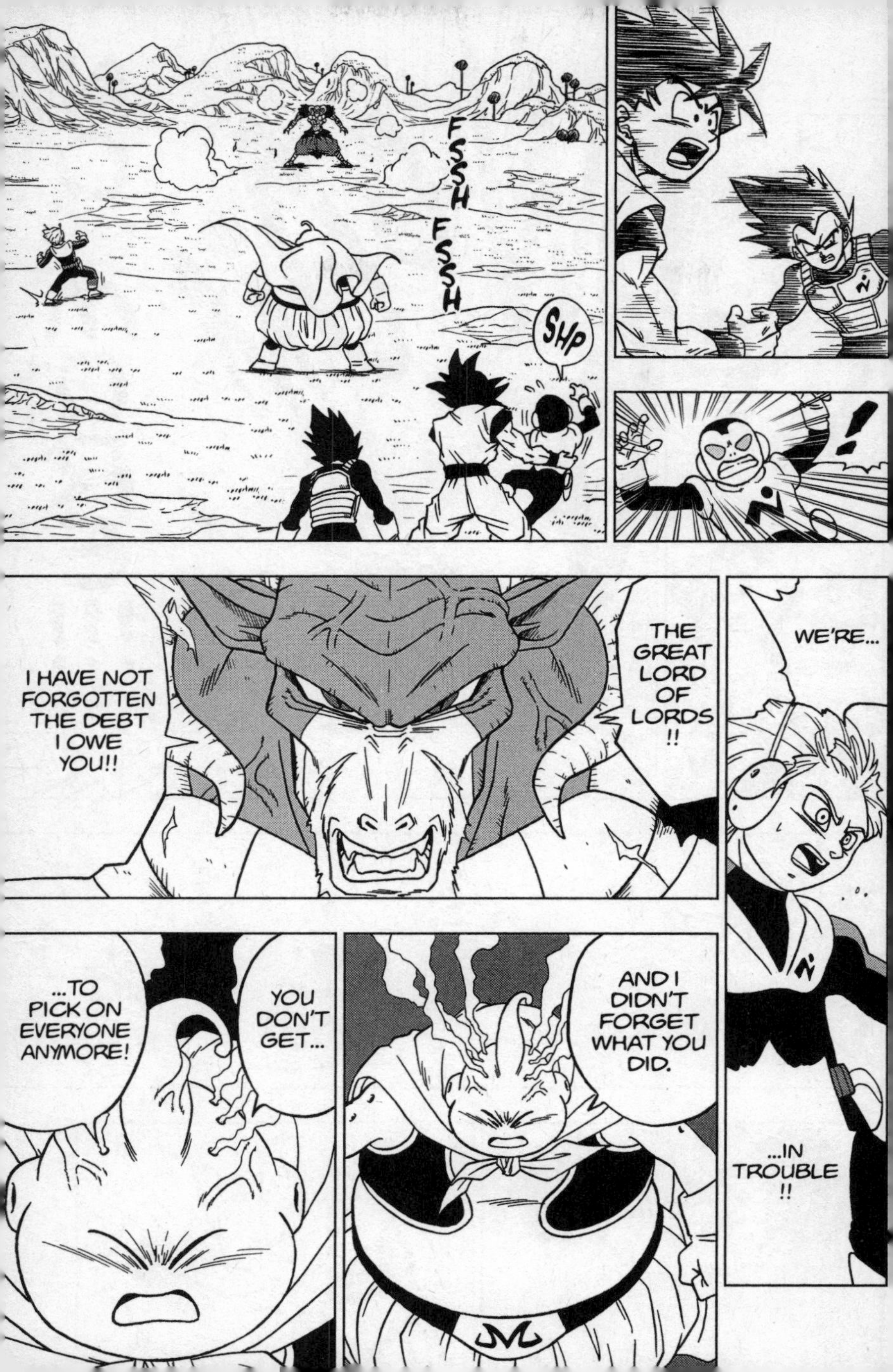
!
FSSH
FSSH
SHP
WE'RE...
...IN TROUBLE !!
THE GREAT LORD OF LORDS !!
I HAVE NOT FORGOTTEN THE DEBT I OWE YOU!!
AND I DIDN'T FORGET WHAT YOU DID.
YOU DON'T GET...
...TO PICK ON EVERYONE ANYMORE!

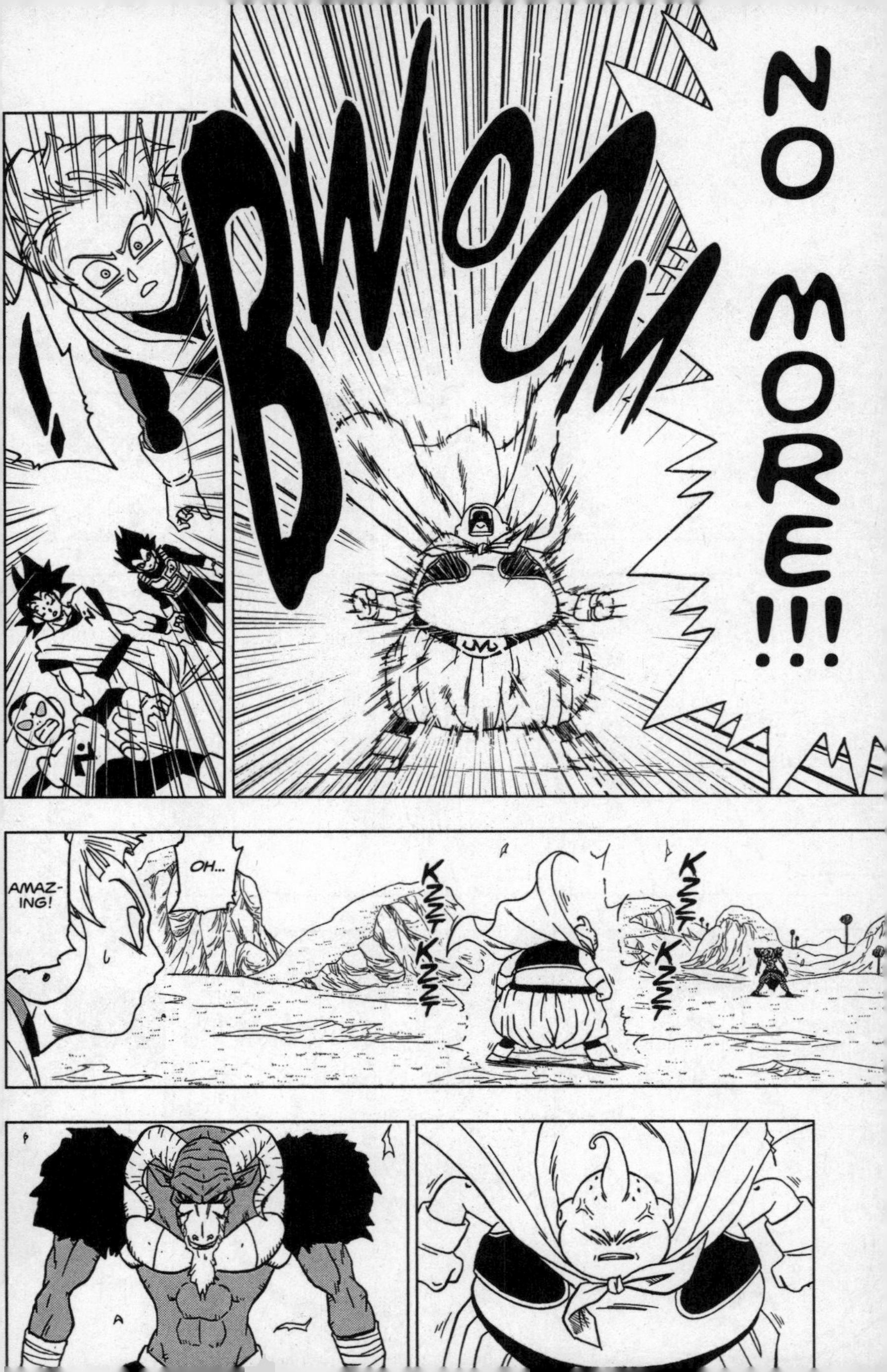
NO MORE!!!
BWOOM
!
KZZT KZZT
KZZT KZZT
OH...
AMAZING!

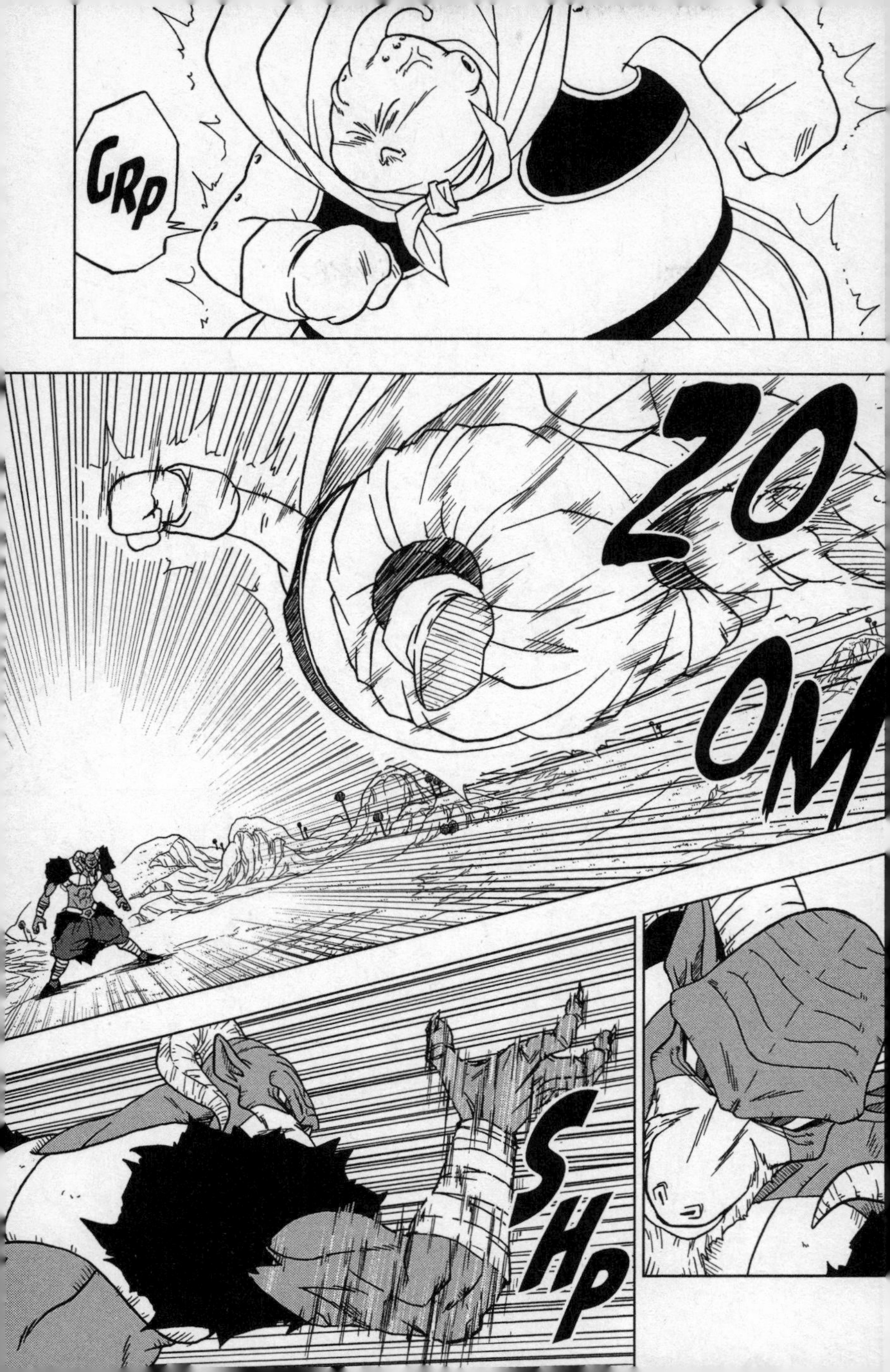
GRP
ZOOM
SHP

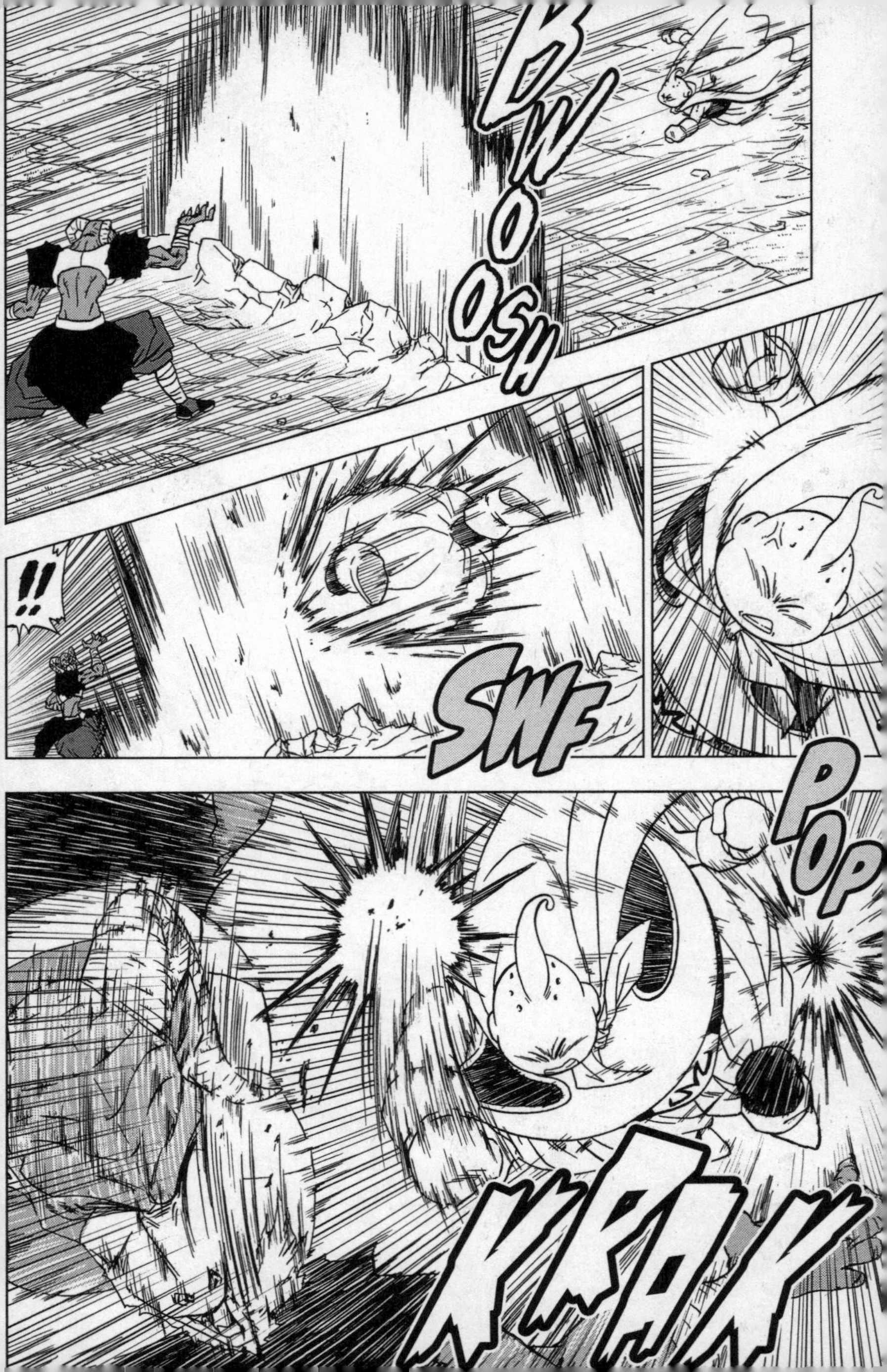
BWOOSH
SWF
!!
POP
KRAK

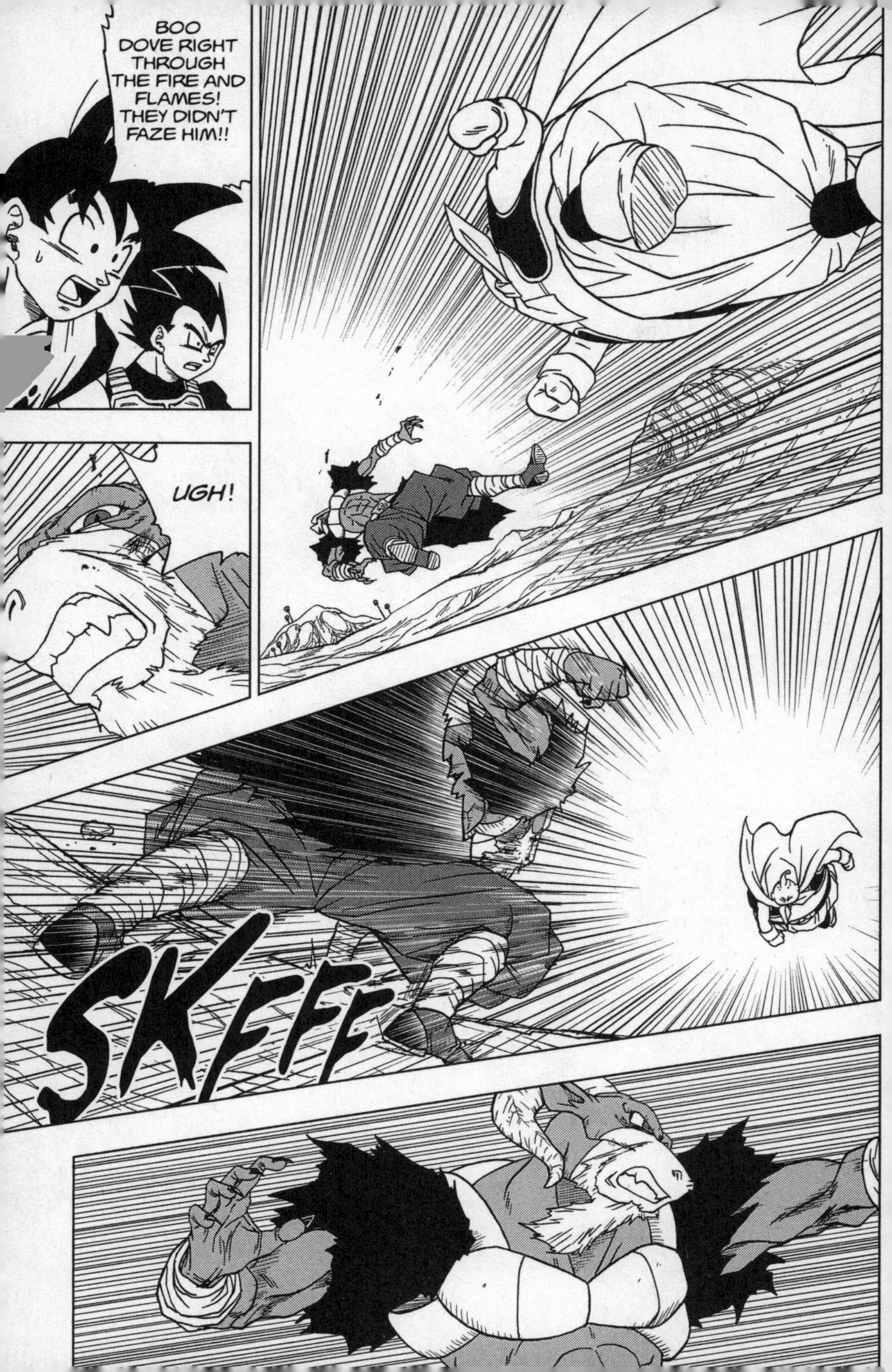
BOO DOVE RIGHT THROUGH THE FIRE AND FLAMES! THEY DIDN'T FAZE HIM!!
UGH!
SKFFF

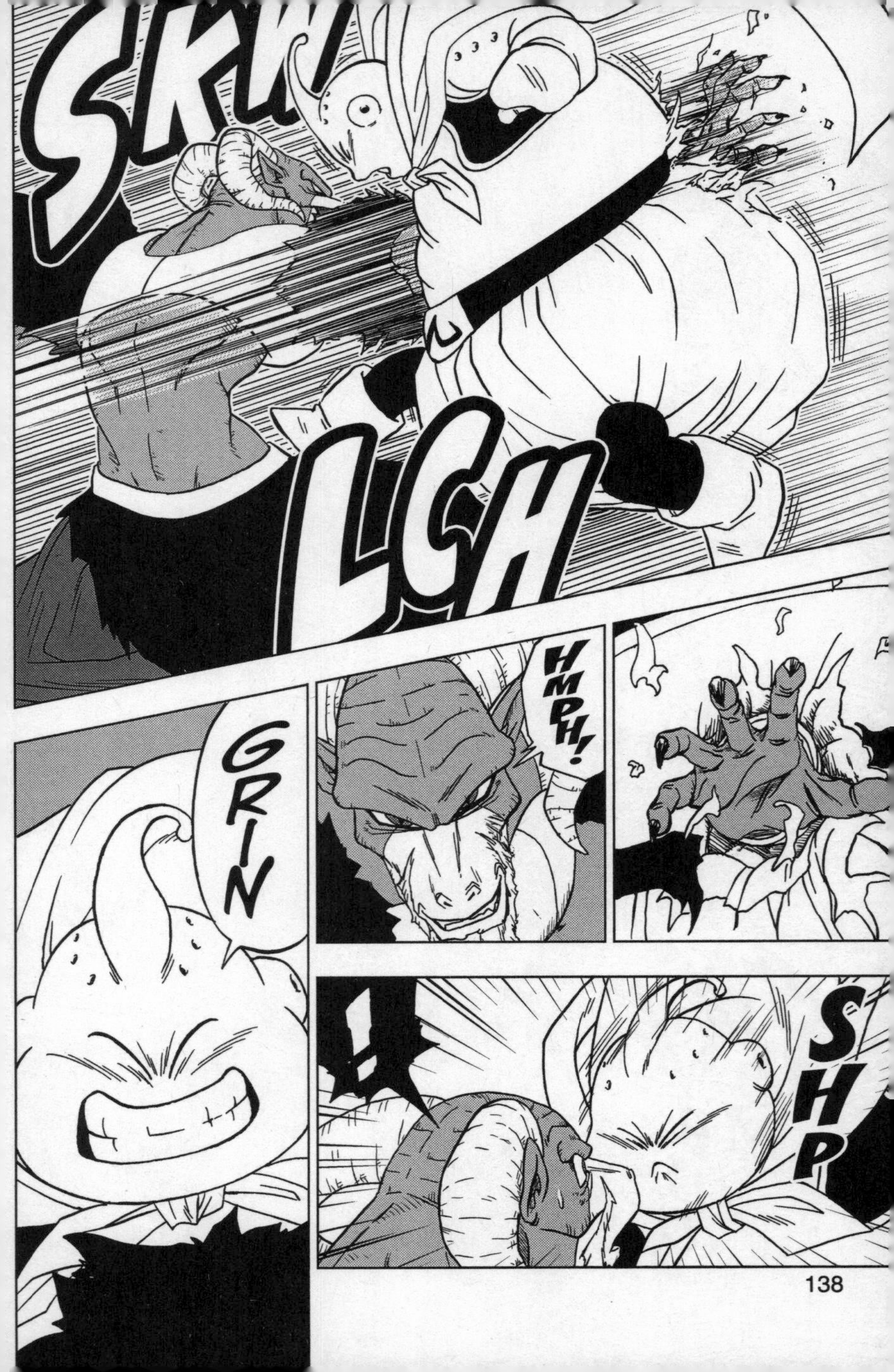
SKWLCH
HMPH!
SHP
!
GRIN

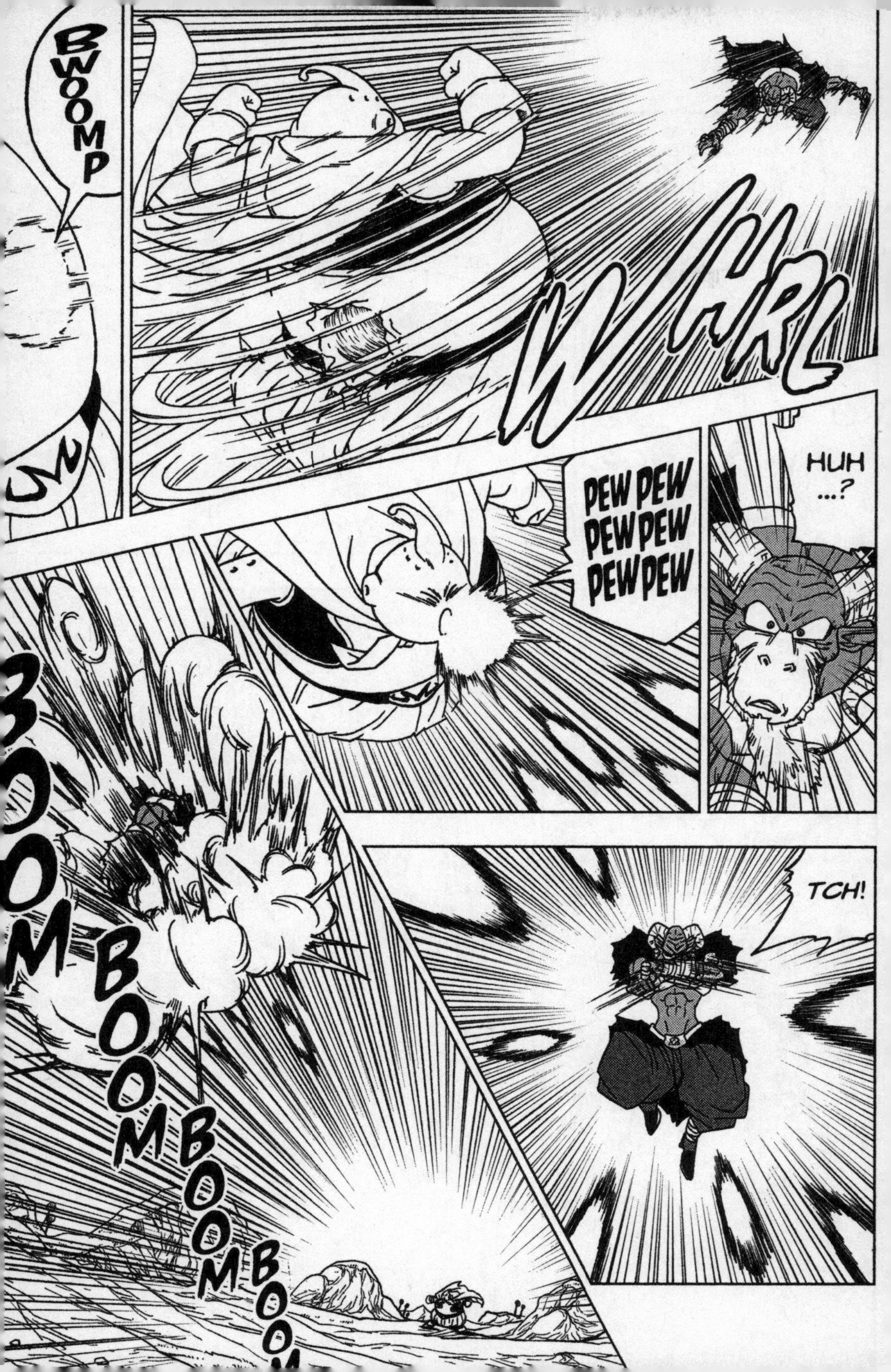
WHRL
BWOOMP
HUH ...?
PEW PEW PEW PEW PEW PEW
TCH!
BOOM BOOM BOOM BOOM

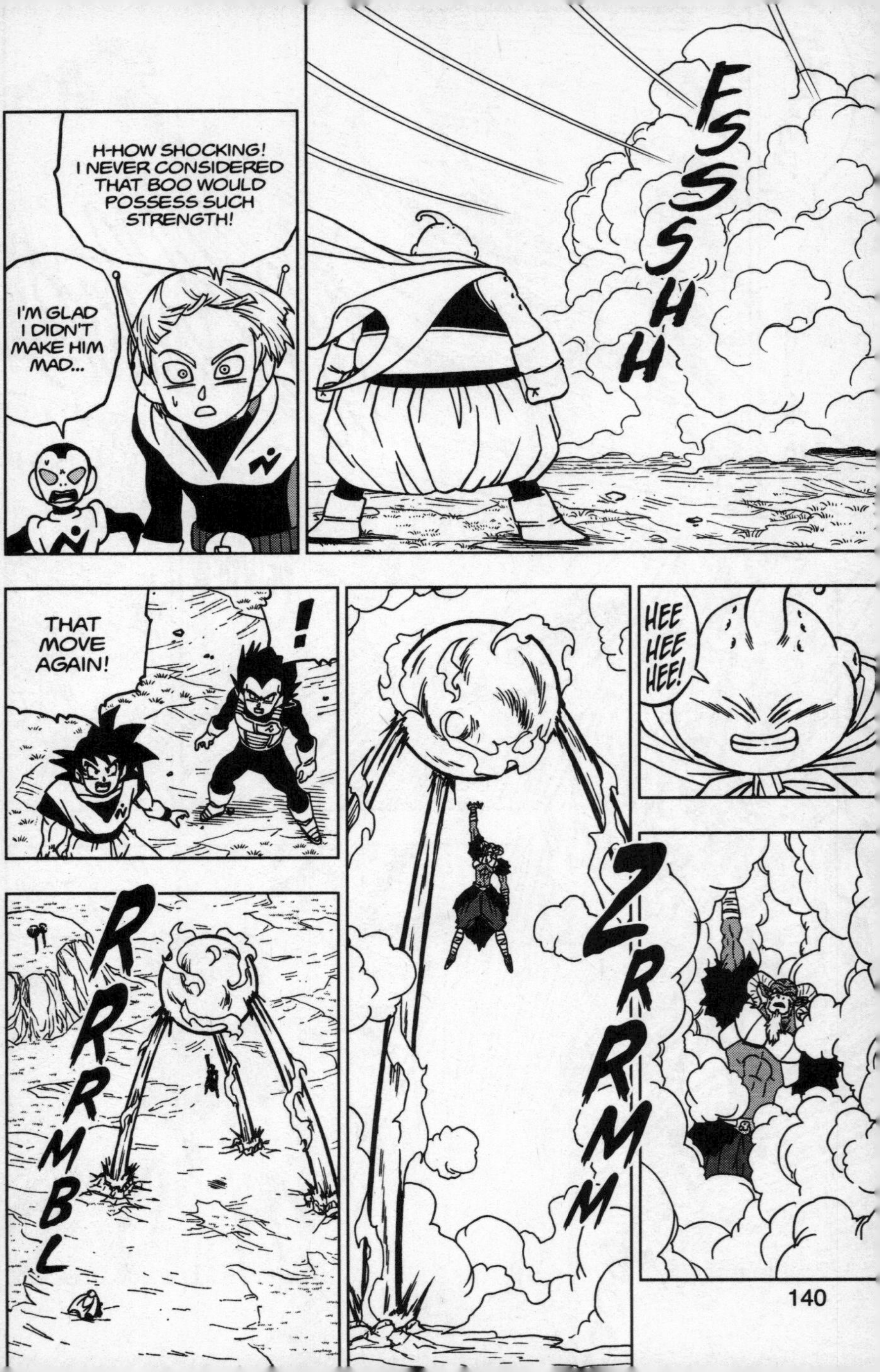
FSSSHH
H-HOW SHOCKING! I NEVER CONSIDERED THAT BOO WOULD POSSESS SUCH STRENGTH!
I'M GLAD I DIDN'T MAKE HIM MAD...
HEE HEE HEE!
ZRRMM
!
THAT MOVE AGAIN!
RRRMBL

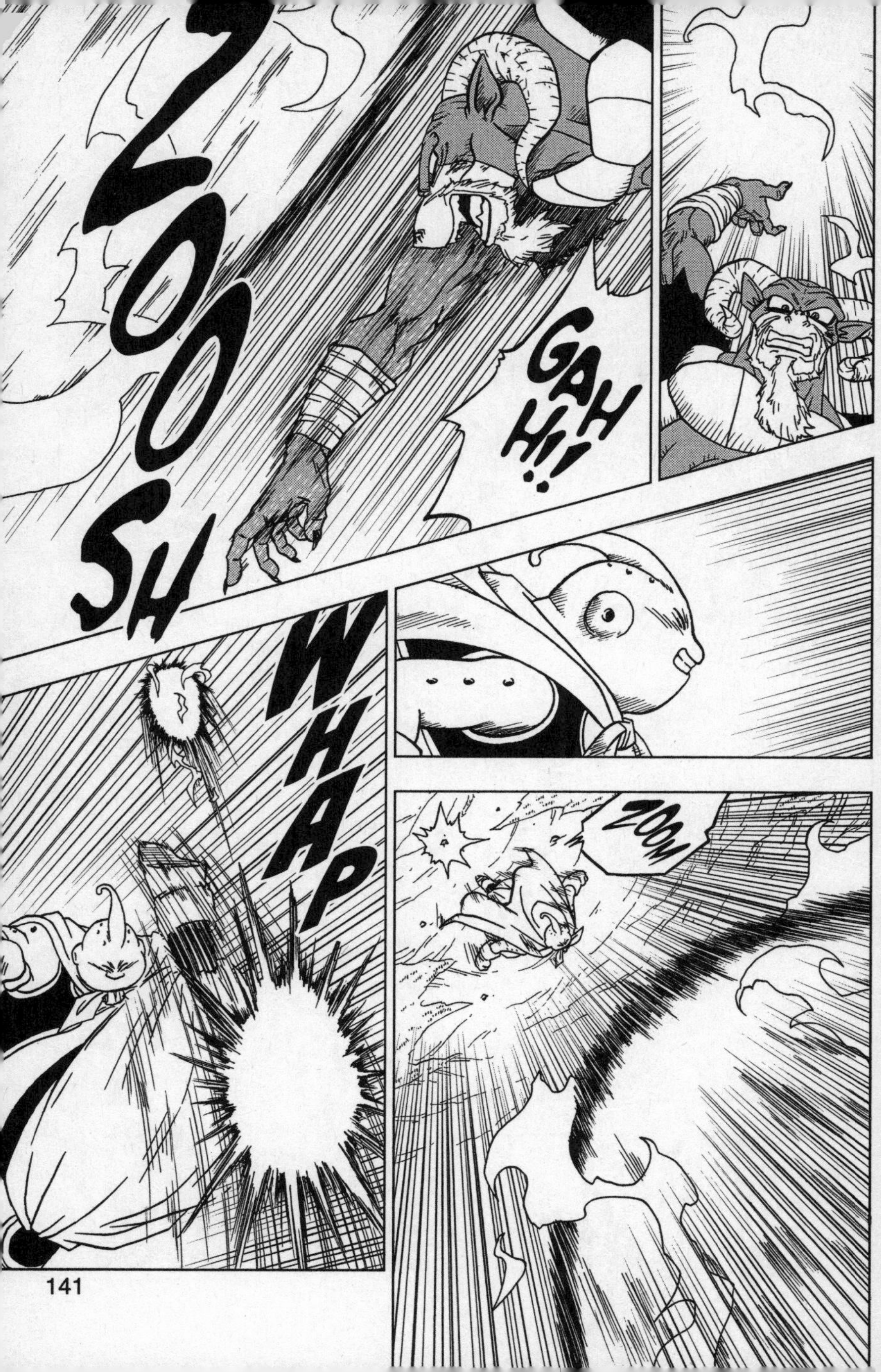
ZOOOSH
GAHH!!
WHAP
ZOOM

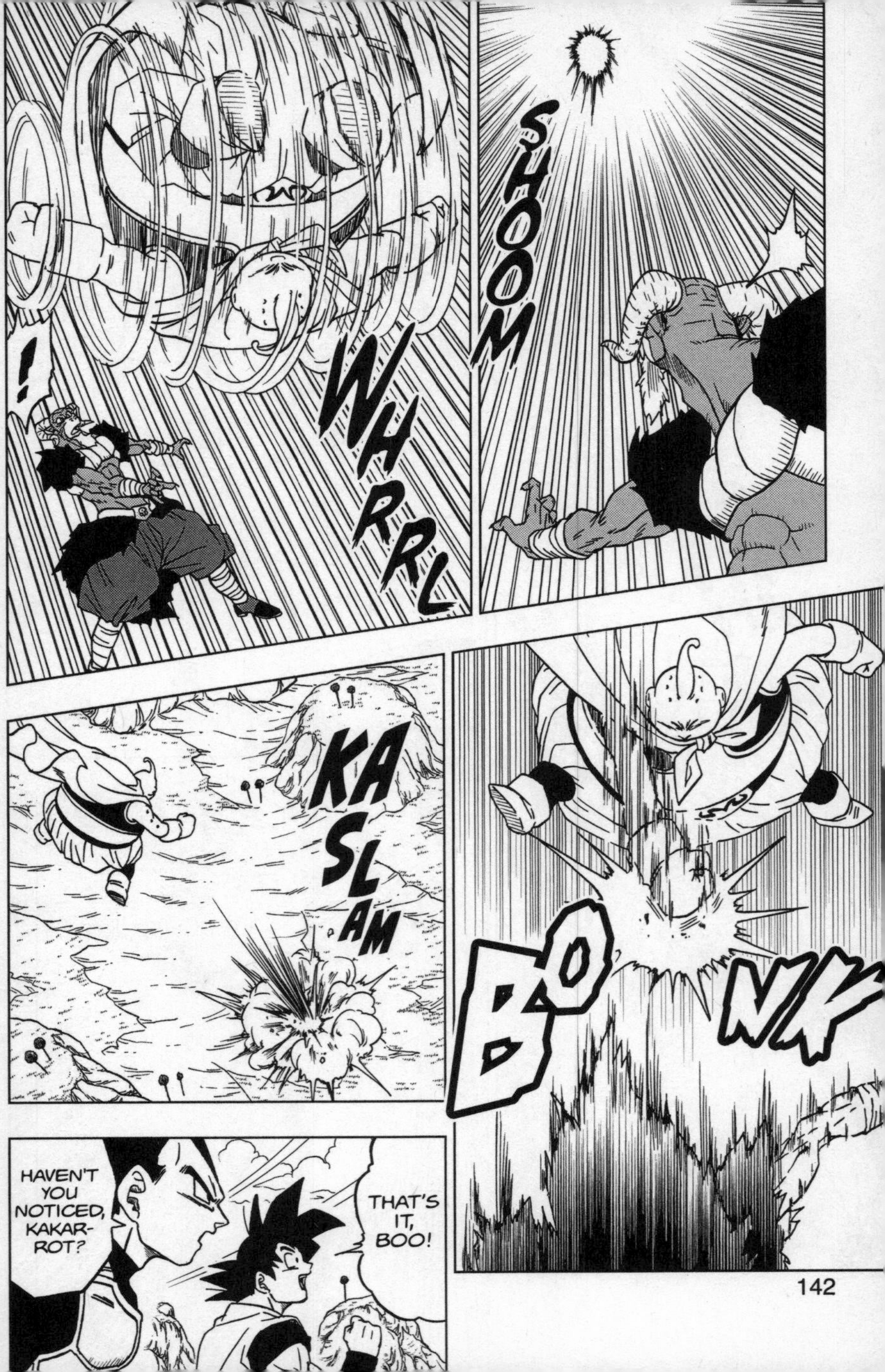
SHOOOM
WHRRRL
!
BONK
KASLAM
THAT'S IT, BOO!
HAVEN'T YOU NOTICED, KAKARROT?

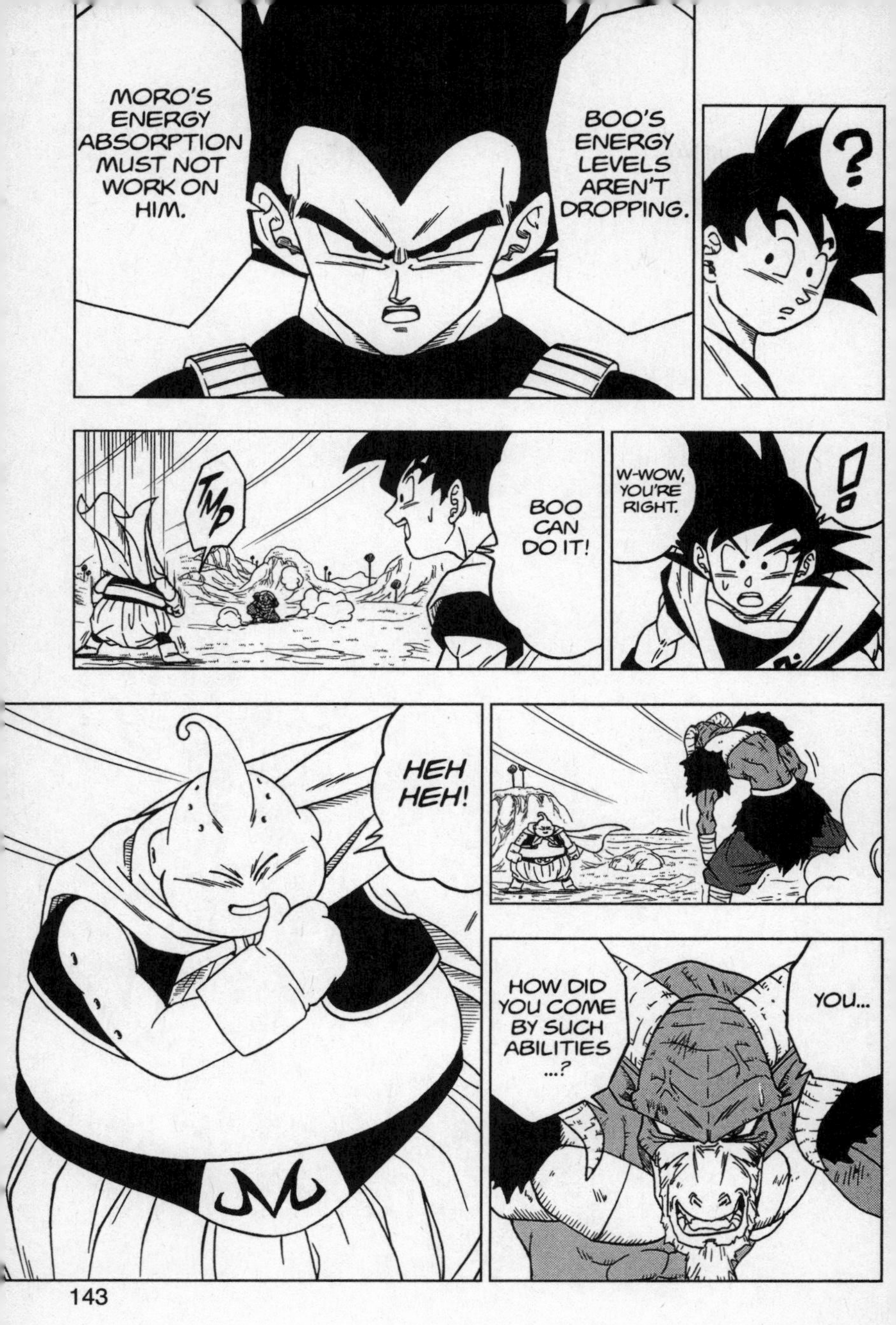
?
BOO'S ENERGY LEVELS AREN'T DROPPING.
MORO'S ENERGY ABSORPTION MUST NOT WORK ON HIM.
!
W-WOW, YOU'RE RIGHT.
BOO CAN DO IT!
TMP
YOU...
HOW DID YOU COME BY SUCH ABILITIES ...?
HEH HEH!

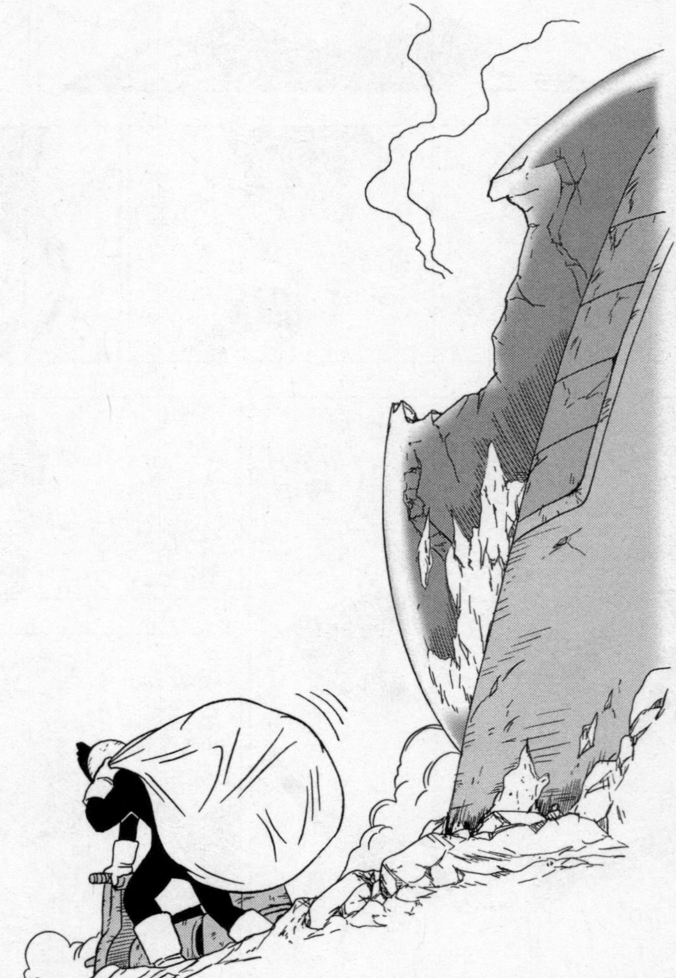

DRAGON BALL SUPER

CHAPTER 48: MORO'S WISH

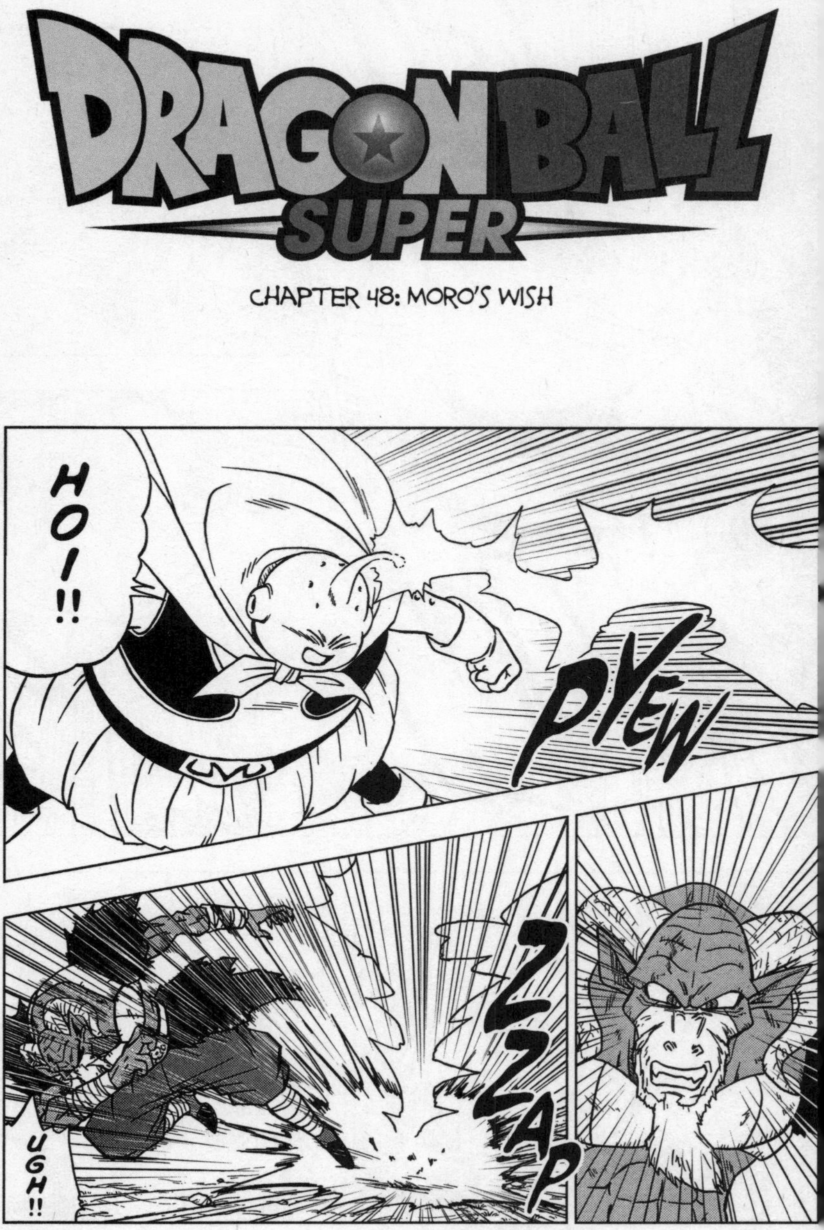
HOI!!
PYEW
ZZAP
UGH!!

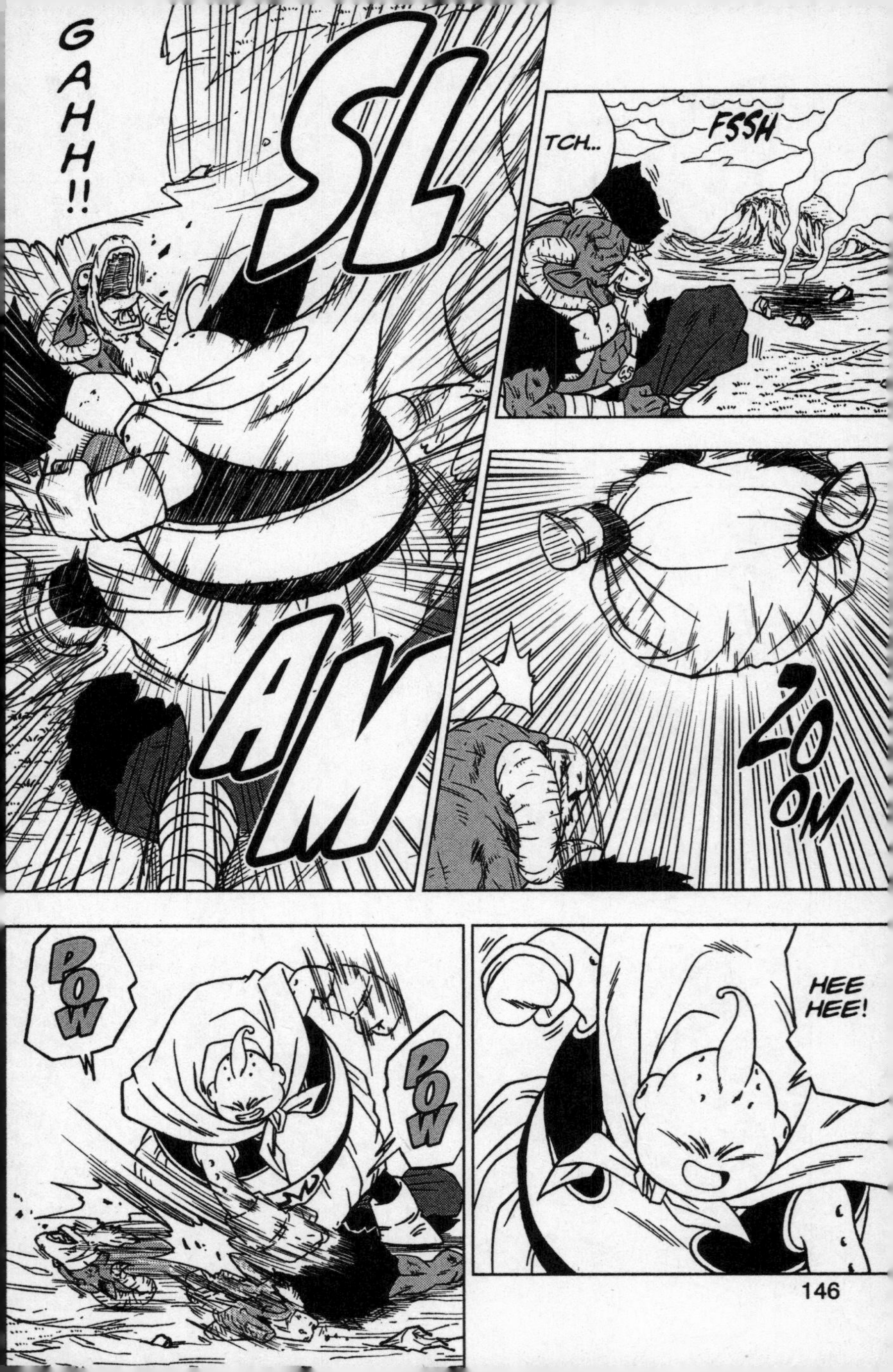
TCH...
FSSH
ZOOM
GAHHH!!
SLAM
HEE HEE!
POW
POW

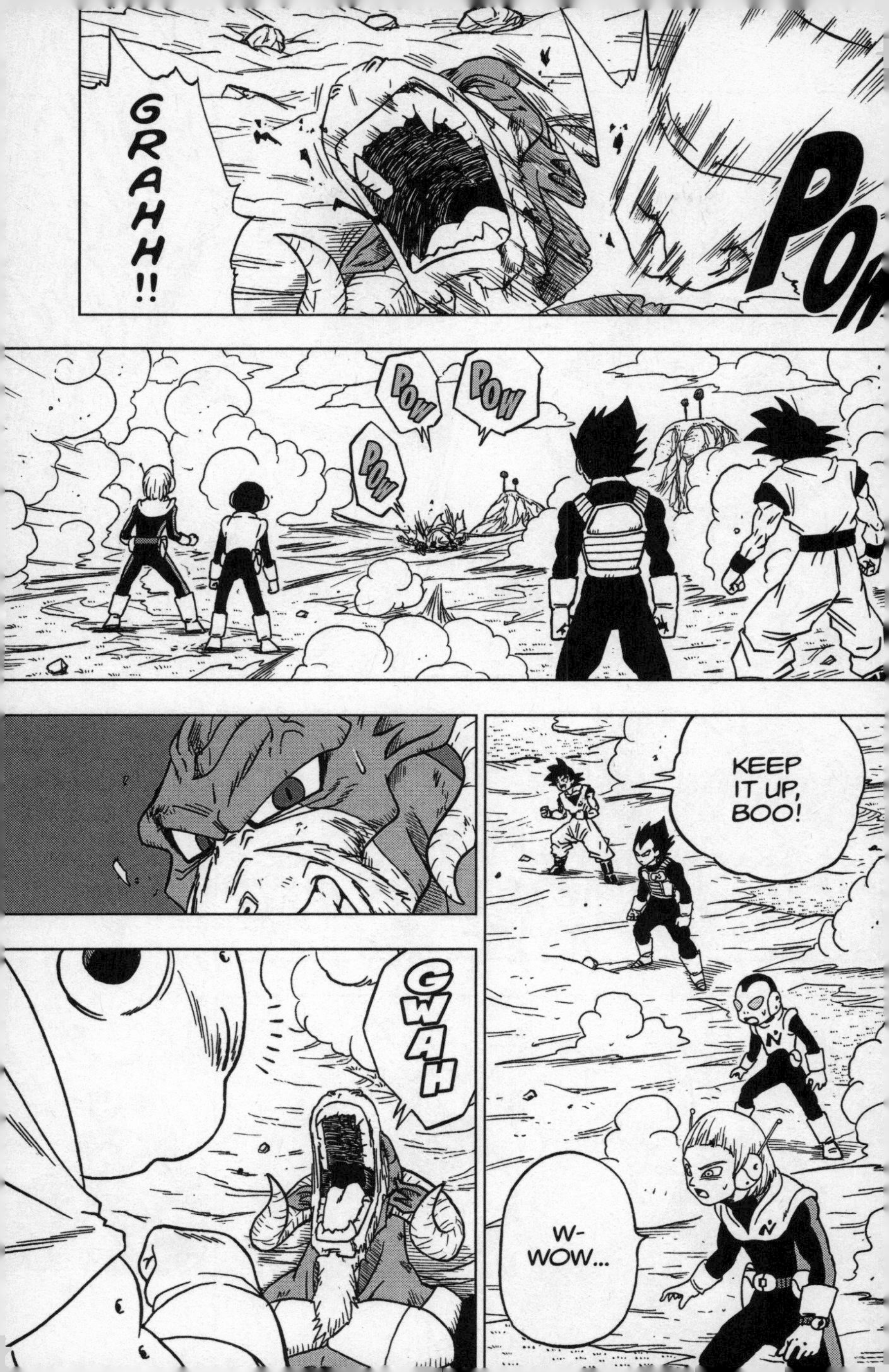
POW
GRAHH!!
POW
POW
POW
KEEP IT UP, BOO!
W-WOW...
GWAH

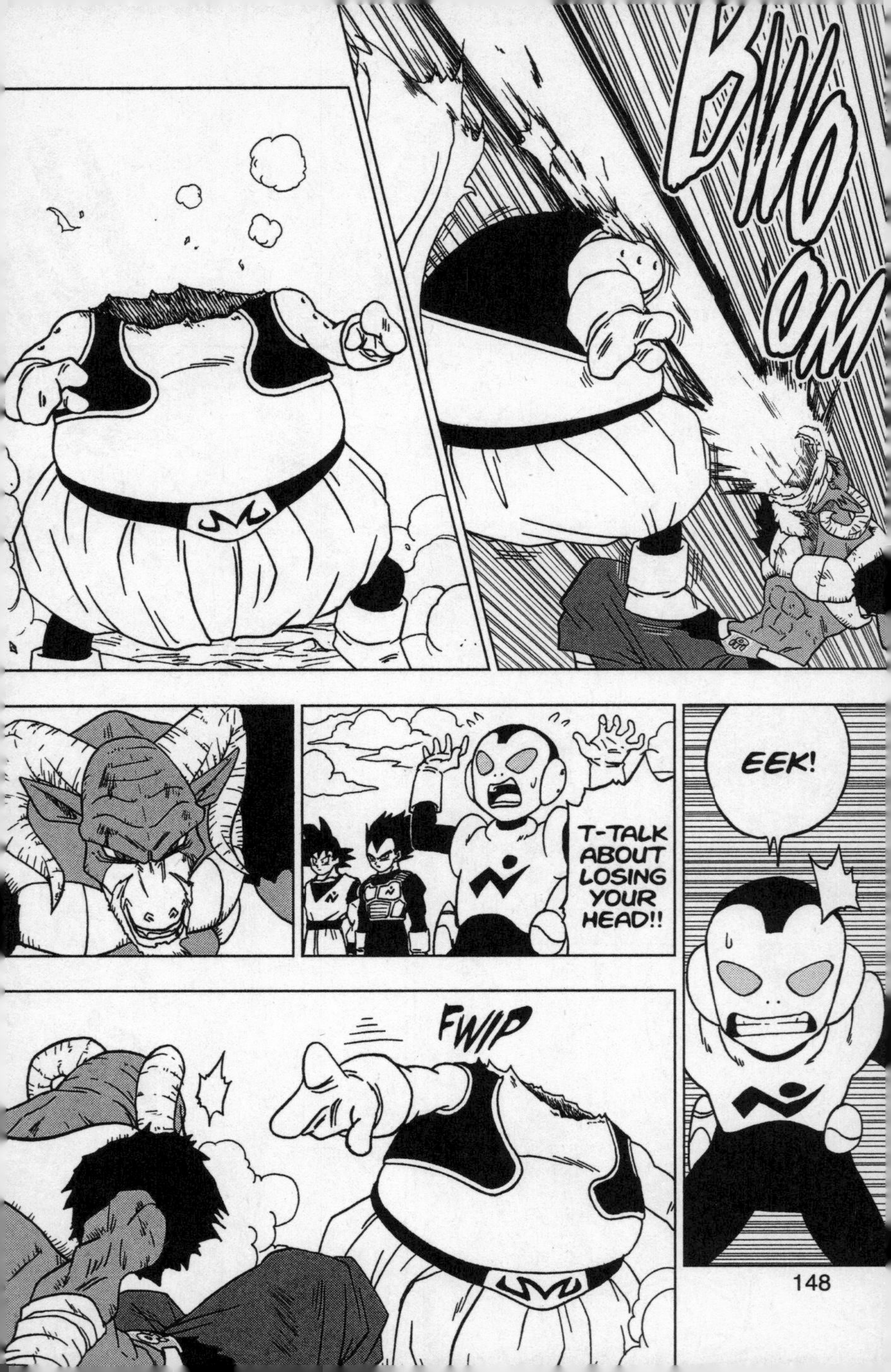
BWOOM
EEK!
T-TALK ABOUT LOSING YOUR HEAD!!
FWIP

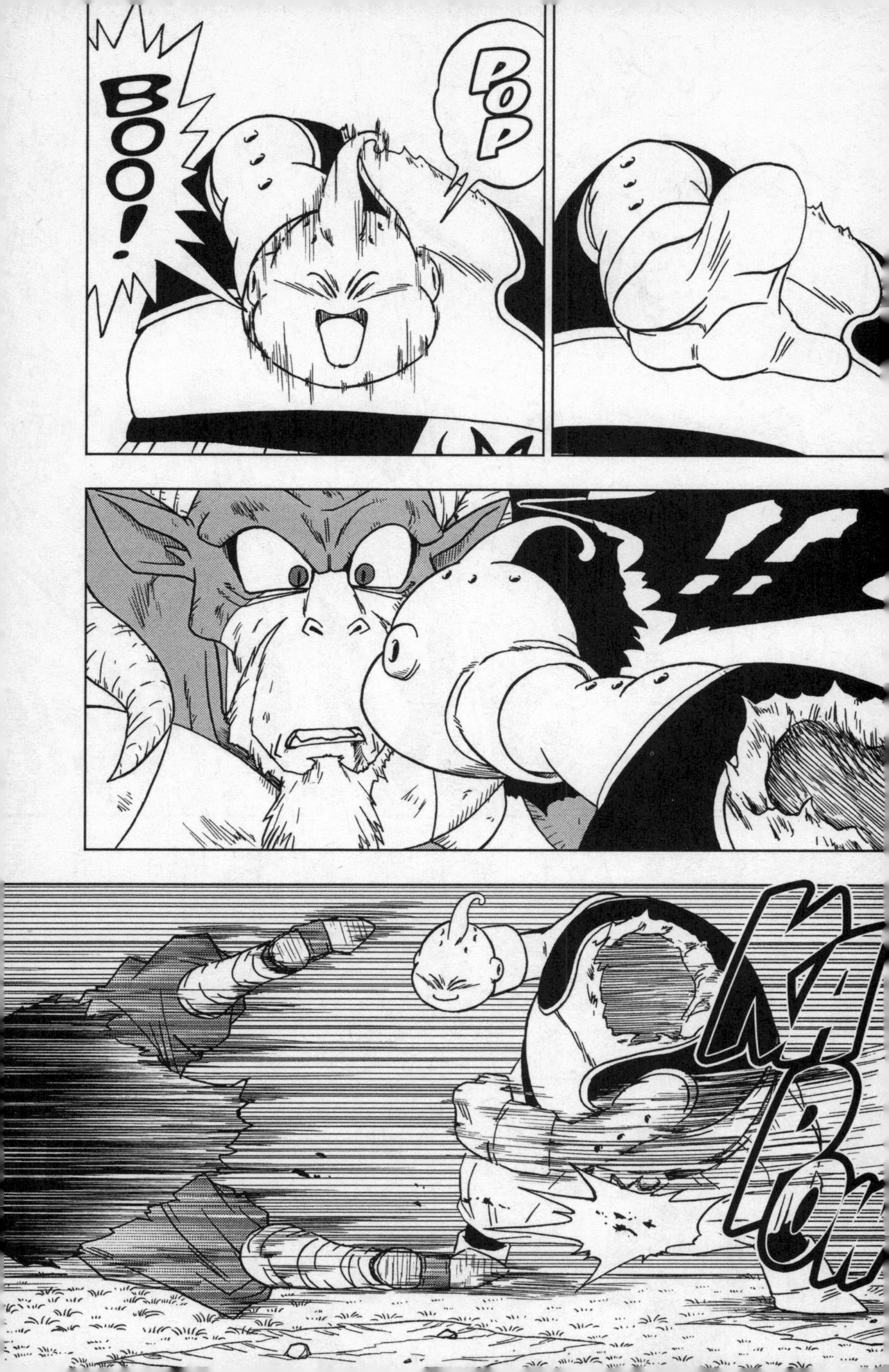
POP
BOO!

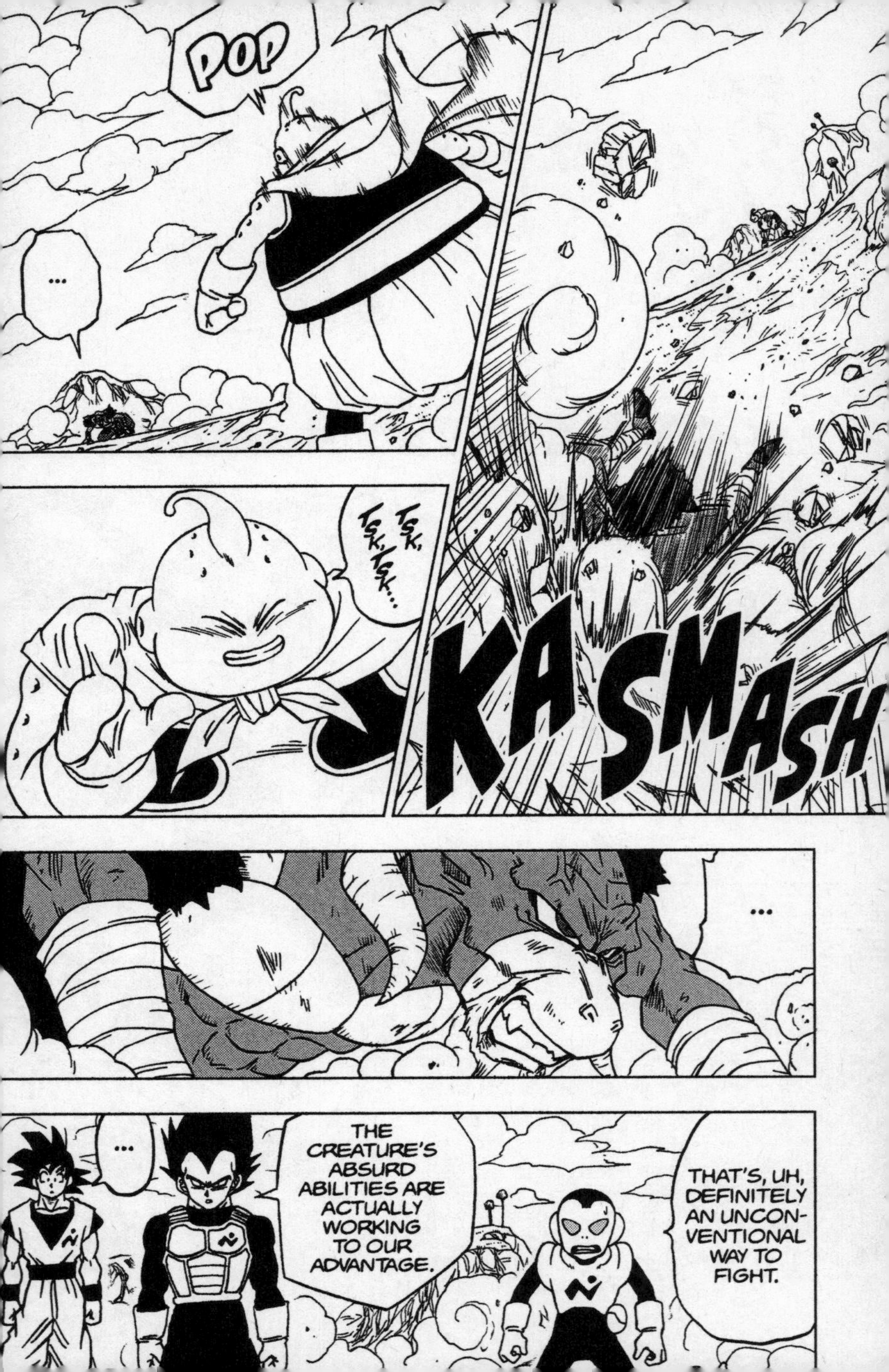
KASMASH
POP
...
TSK, TSK, TSK...
...
THAT'S, UH, DEFINITELY AN UNCONVENTIONAL WAY TO FIGHT.
THE CREATURE'S ABSURD ABILITIES ARE ACTUALLY WORKING TO OUR ADVANTAGE.
...

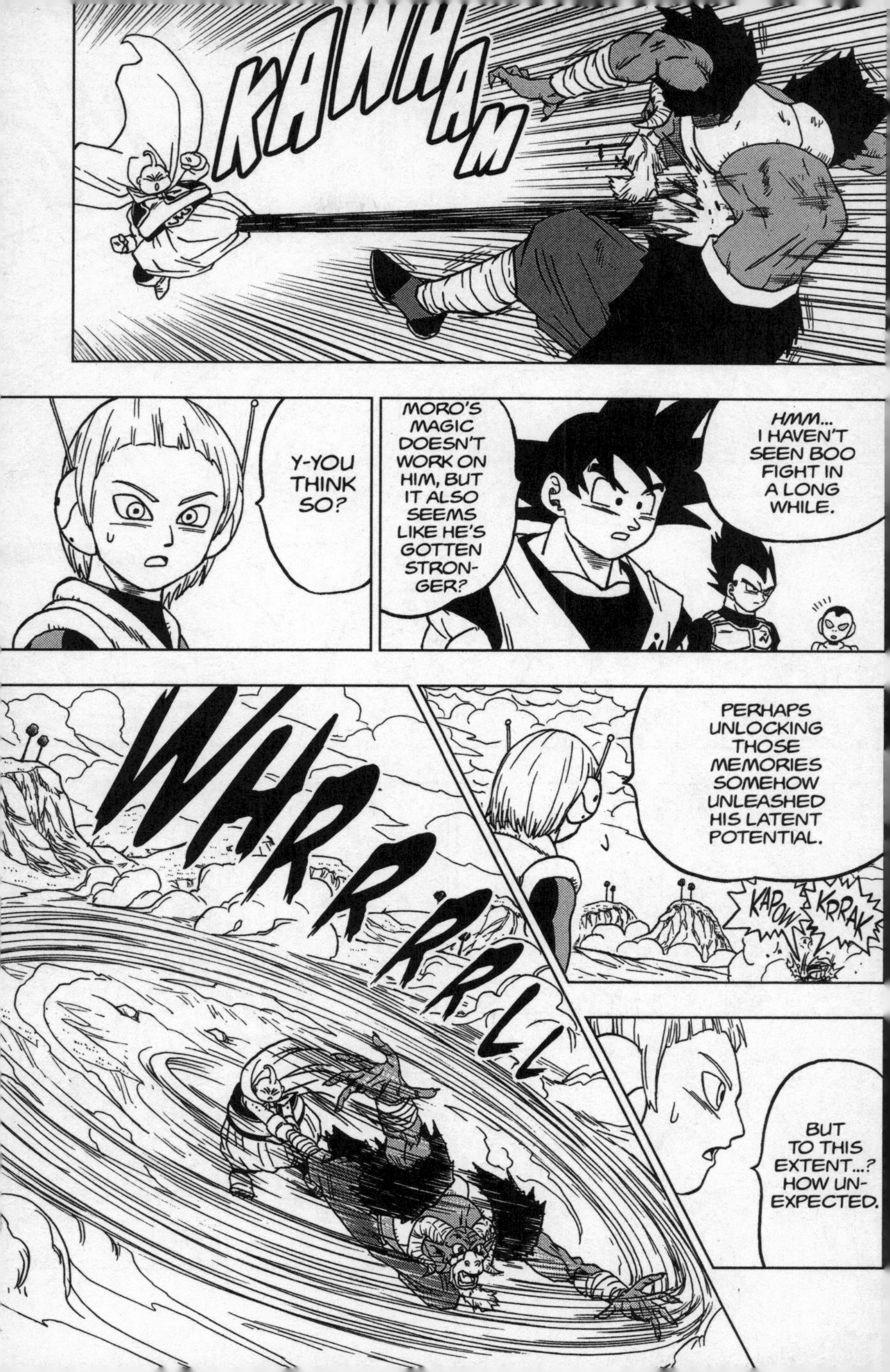
KAWHAM
HMM... I HAVEN'T SEEN BOO FIGHT IN A LONG WHILE.
MORO'S MAGIC DOESN'T WORK ON HIM, BUT IT ALSO SEEMS LIKE HE'S GOTTEN STRONGER?
Y-YOU THINK SO?
PERHAPS UNLOCKING THOSE MEMORIES SOMEHOW UNLEASHED HIS LATENT POTENTIAL.
KRRAK
KAPOW
BUT TO THIS EXTENT...? HOW UNEXPECTED.
WARRRRLL

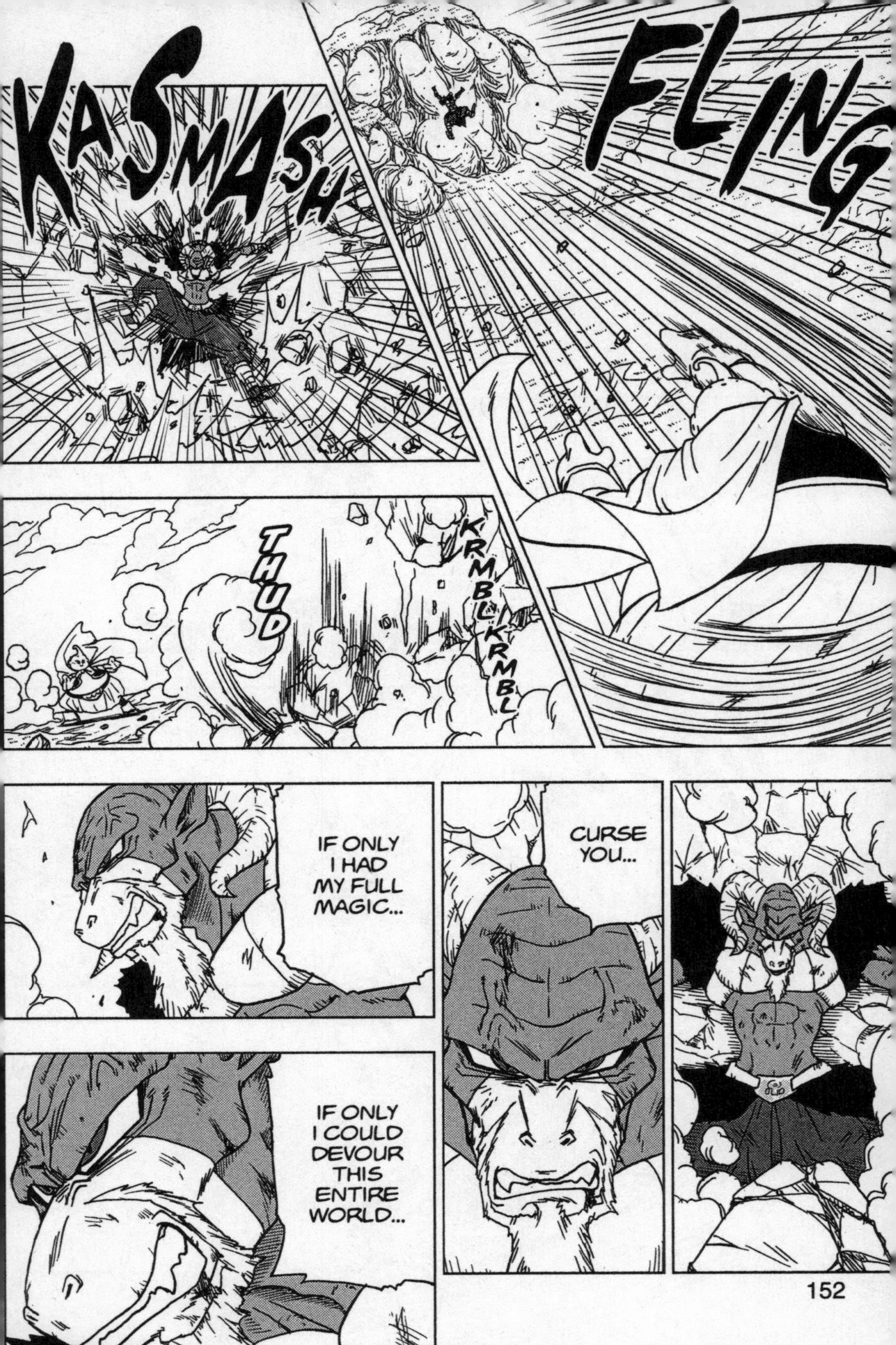
FLING
KASMASH
THUD
KRMBL KRMBL
CURSE YOU...
IF ONLY I HAD MY FULL MAGIC...
IF ONLY I COULD DEVOUR THIS ENTIRE WORLD...

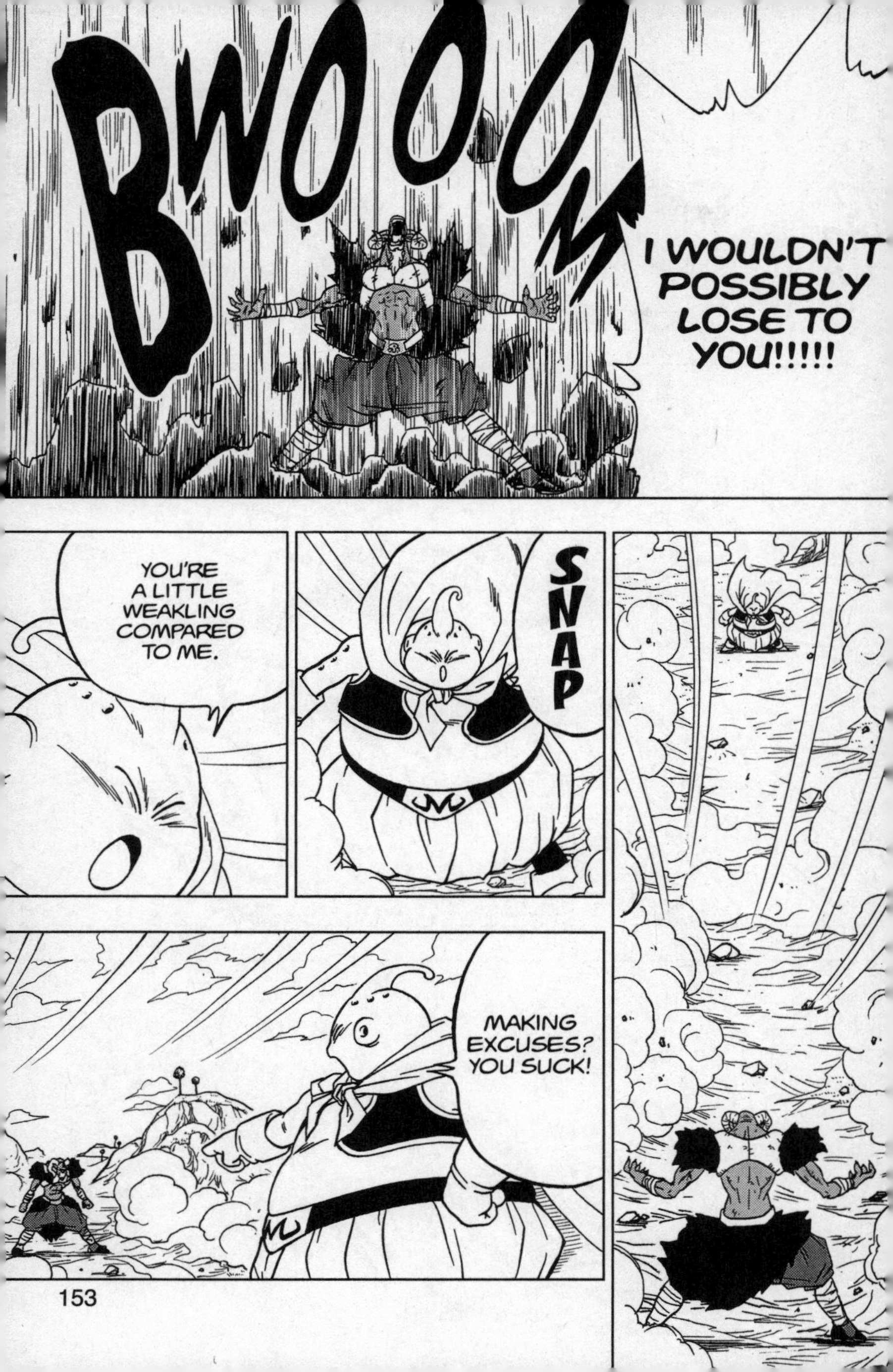
BWOOOM
I WOULDN'T POSSIBLY LOSE TO YOU!!!!!
SNAP
YOU'RE A LITTLE WEAKLING COMPARED TO ME.
MAKING EXCUSES? YOU SUCK!

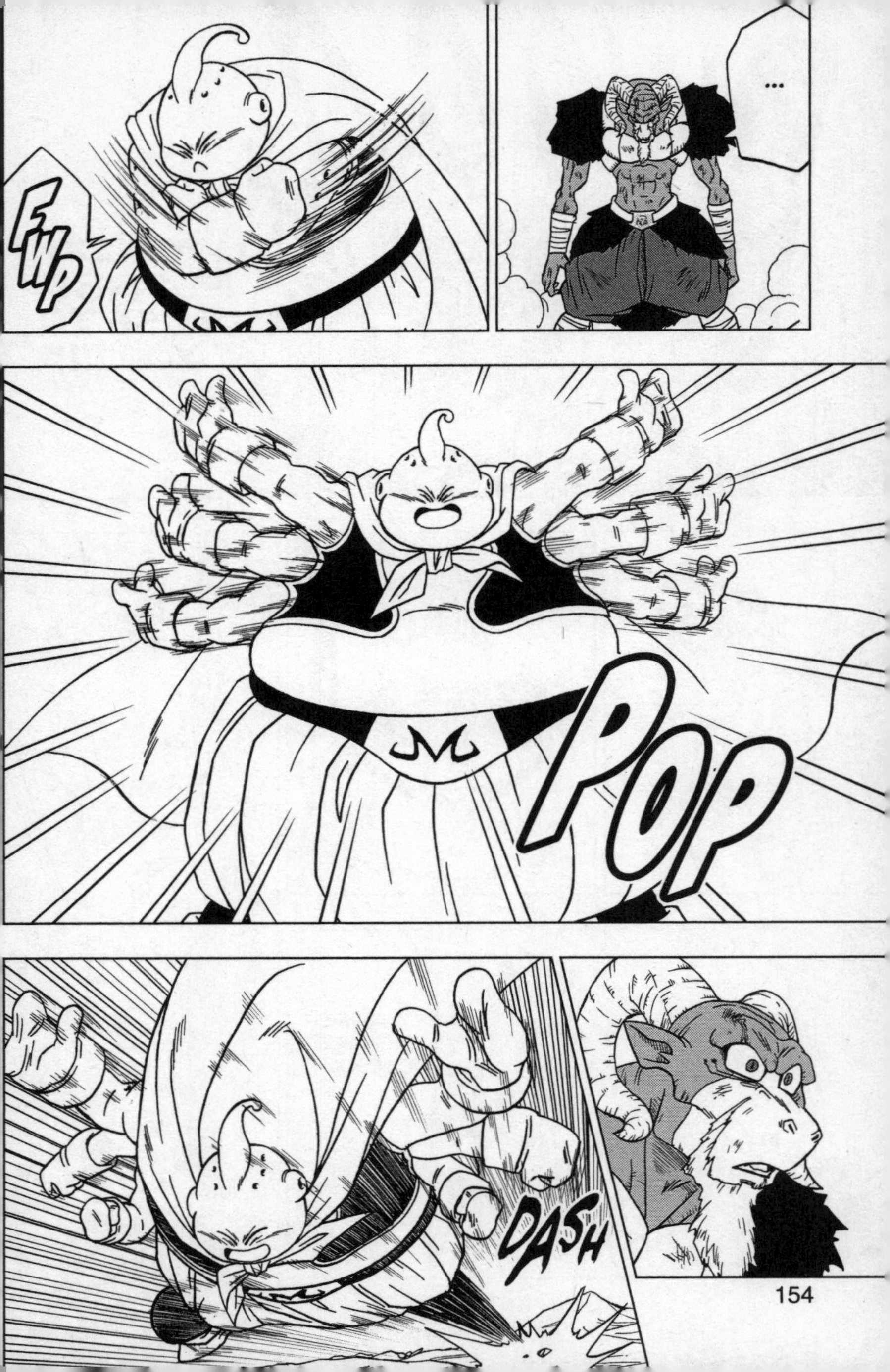
...
FWP
POP
DASH

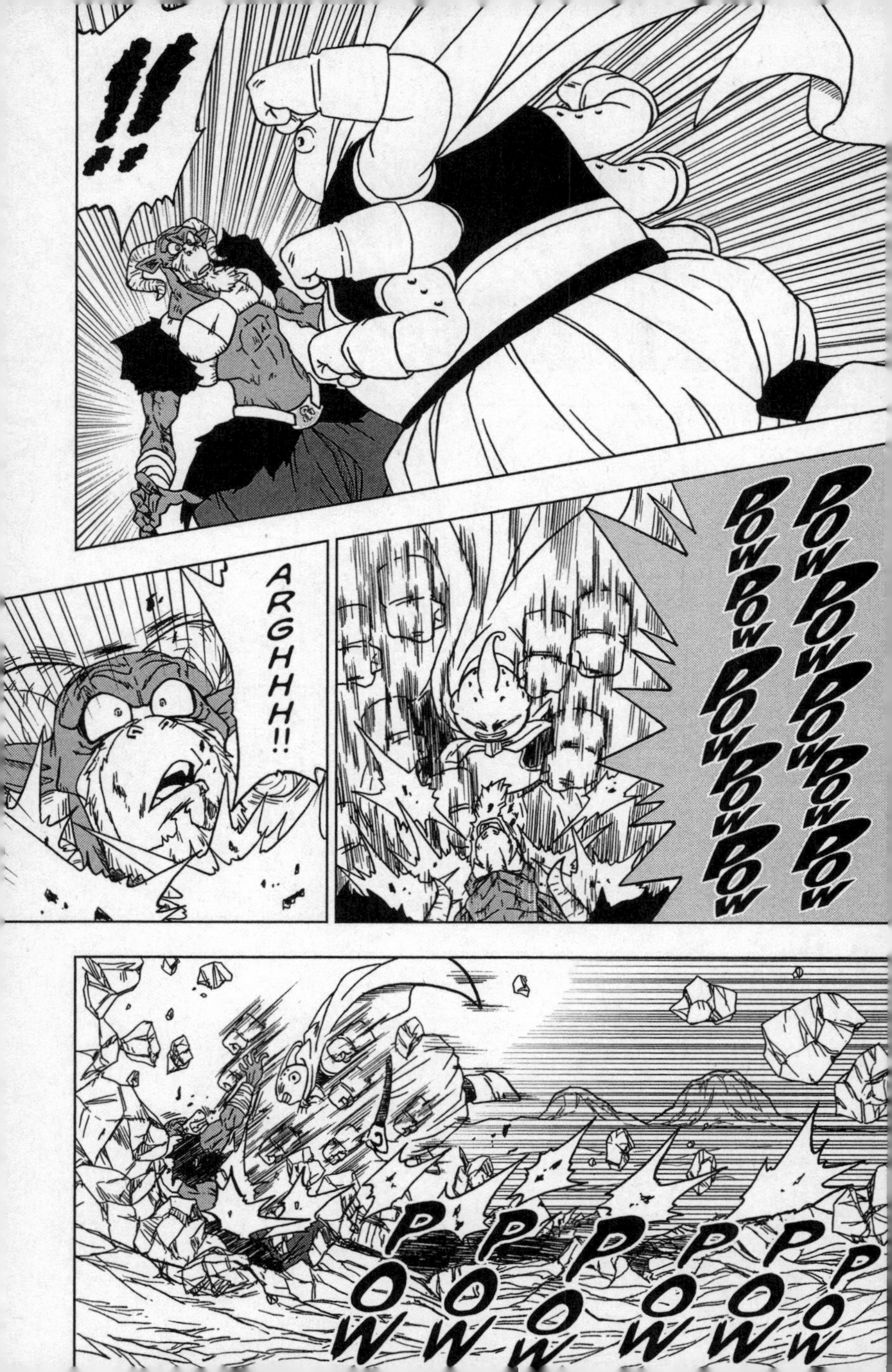
!!
POWPOWPOWPOWPOW
POWPOWPOWPOWPOW
ARGHHH!!
POW POW POW POW POW POW

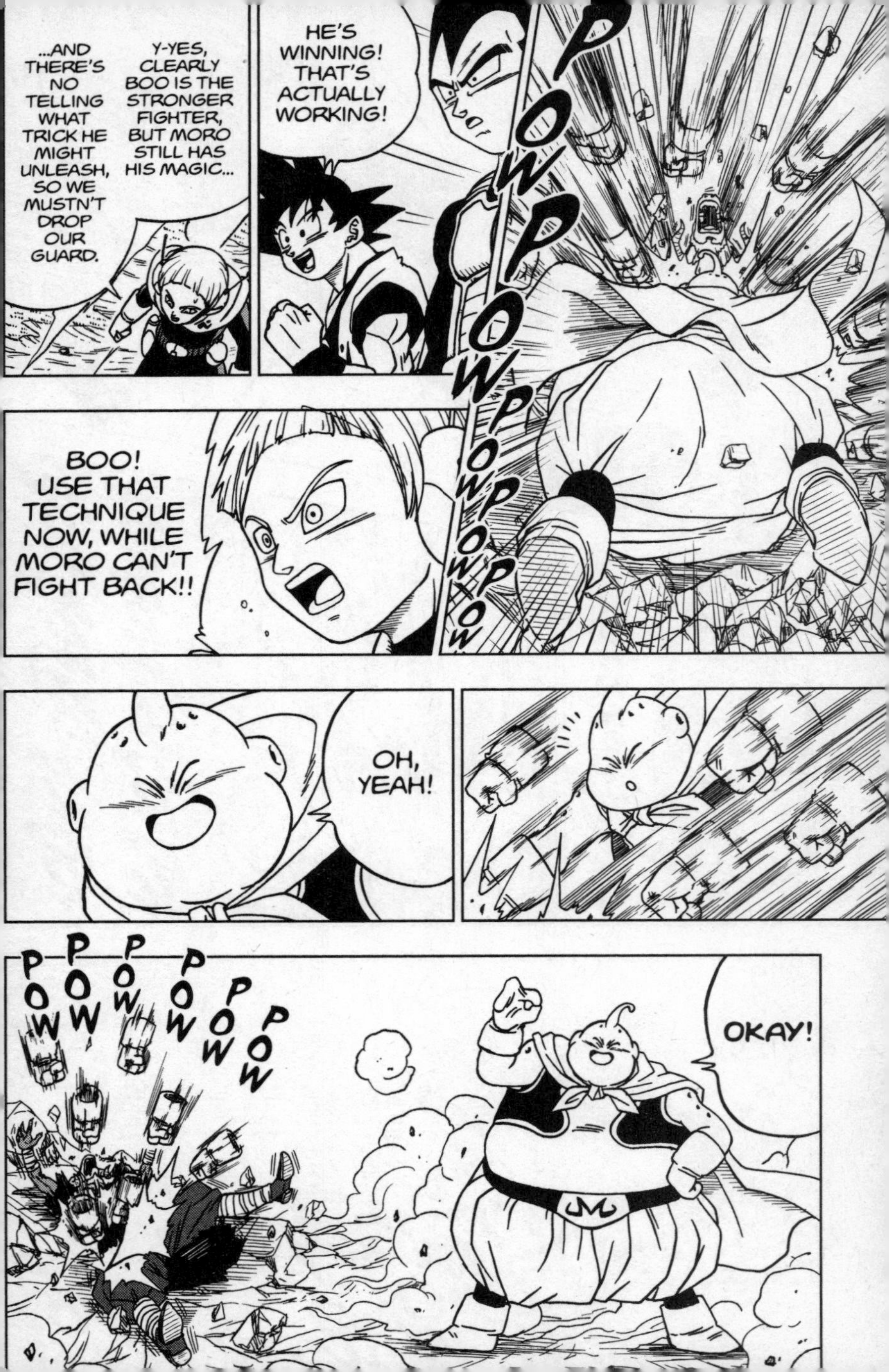
POWPOWPOWPOWPOWPOW
HE'S WINNING! THAT'S ACTUALLY WORKING!
Y-YES, CLEARLY BOO IS THE STRONGER FIGHTER, BUT MORO STILL HAS HIS MAGIC...
...AND THERE'S NO TELLING WHAT TRICK HE MIGHT UNLEASH, SO WE MUSTN'T DROP OUR GUARD.
BOO! USE THAT TECHNIQUE NOW, WHILE MORO CAN'T FIGHT BACK!!
OH, YEAH!
OKAY!
POW
POW
POW
POW
POW
POW
POW

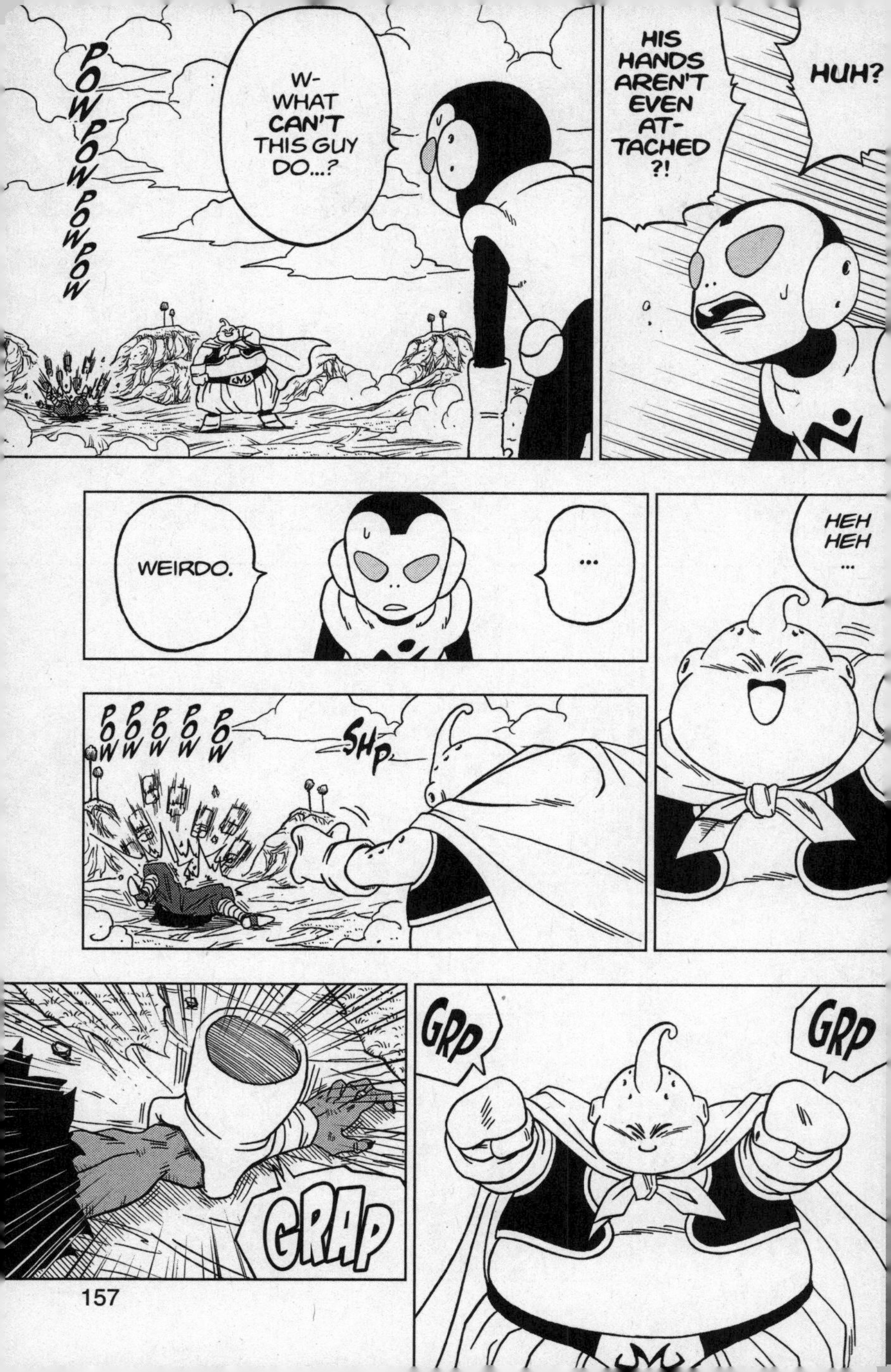

HUH?
HIS HANDS AREN'T EVEN AT-TACHED?!
W-WHAT CAN'T THIS GUY DO...?
POW POW POW POW
HEH HEH...
...
WEIRDO.
SHP
POW POW POW POW POW
GRP
GRP
GRAP

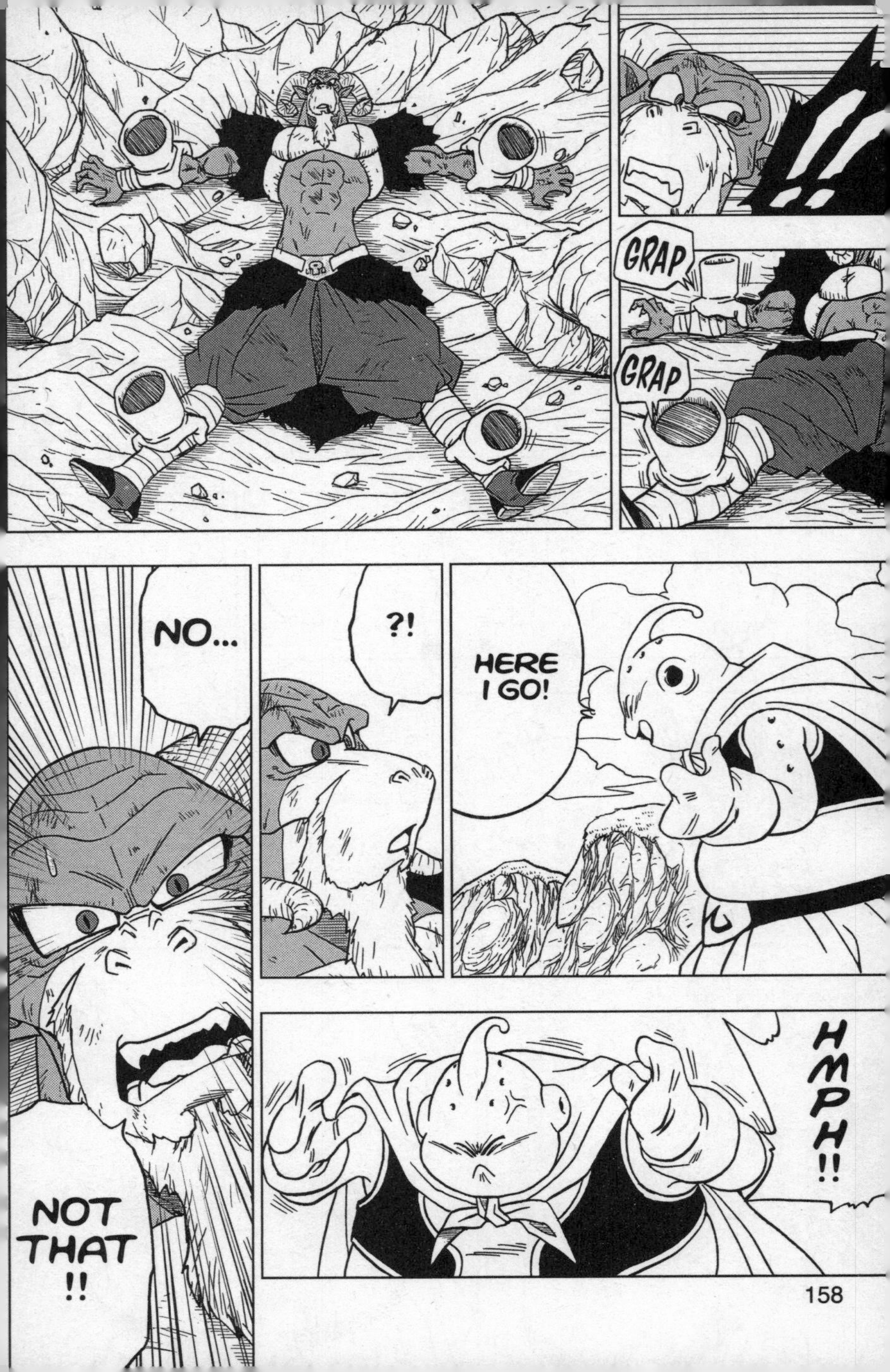
!!
GRAP
GRAP
HERE I GO!
?!
HMPH!!
NO...
NOT THAT !!

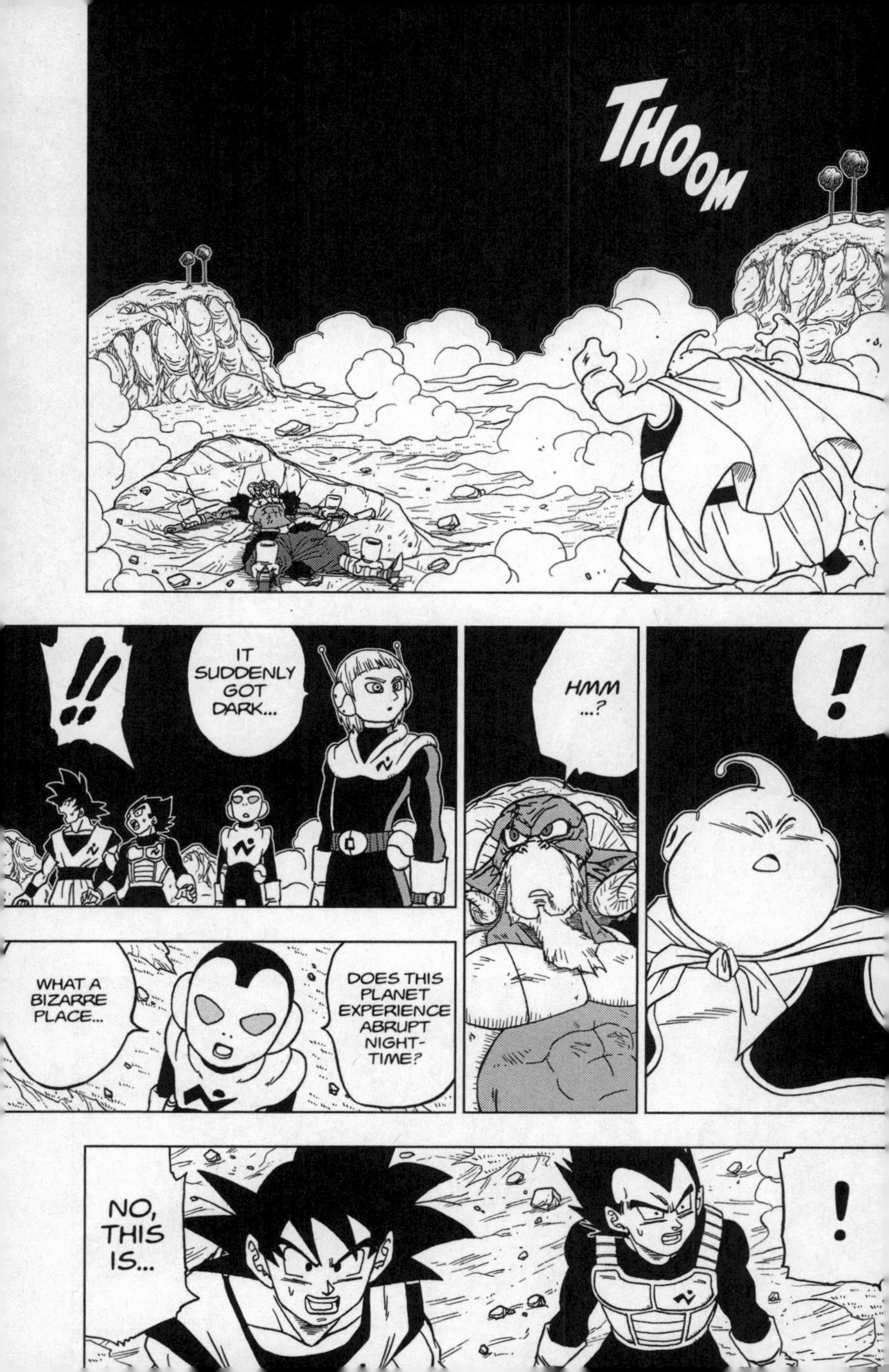
THOOM
!
HMM ...?
IT SUDDENLY GOT DARK...
!!
DOES THIS PLANET EXPERIENCE ABRUPT NIGHT-TIME?
WHAT A BIZARRE PLACE...
!
NO, THIS IS...

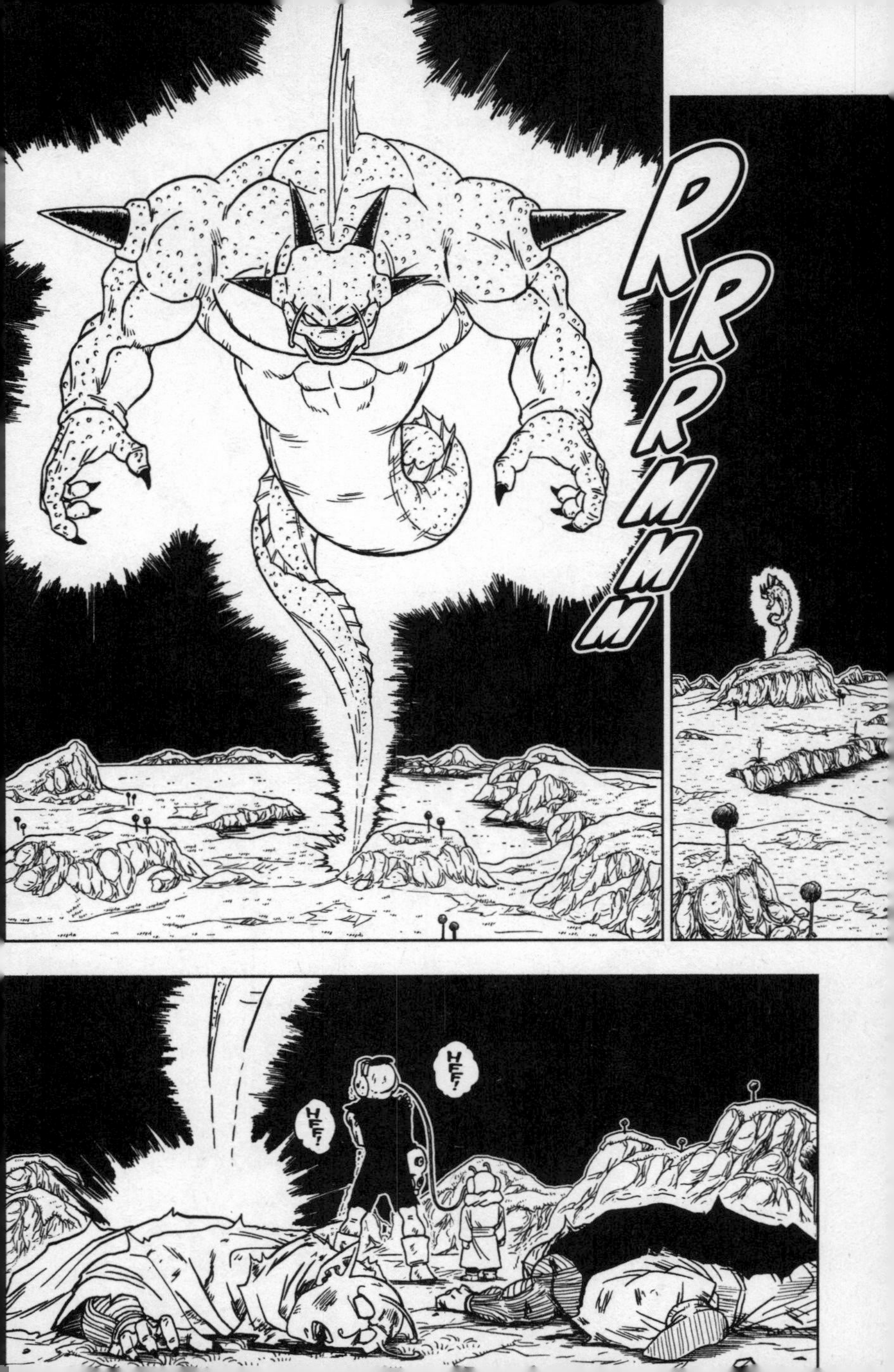
RRRMMMM
HEF!
HEF!

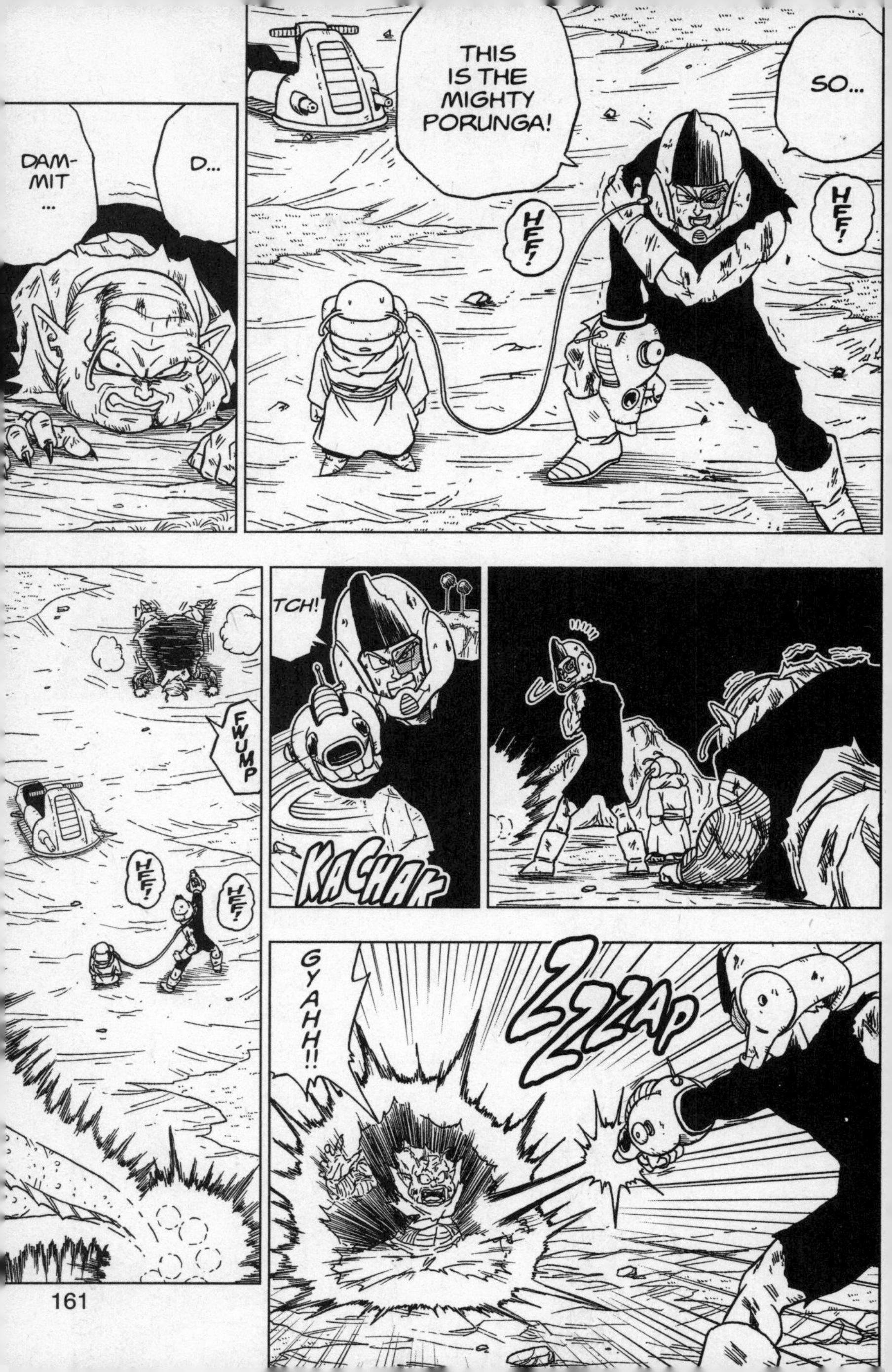
SO...
HEF!
THIS IS THE MIGHTY PORUNGA!
HEF!
D...
DAMMIT...
TCH!
KACHAK
ZZZAP
GYAHH!!
FWUMP
HEF!
HEF!

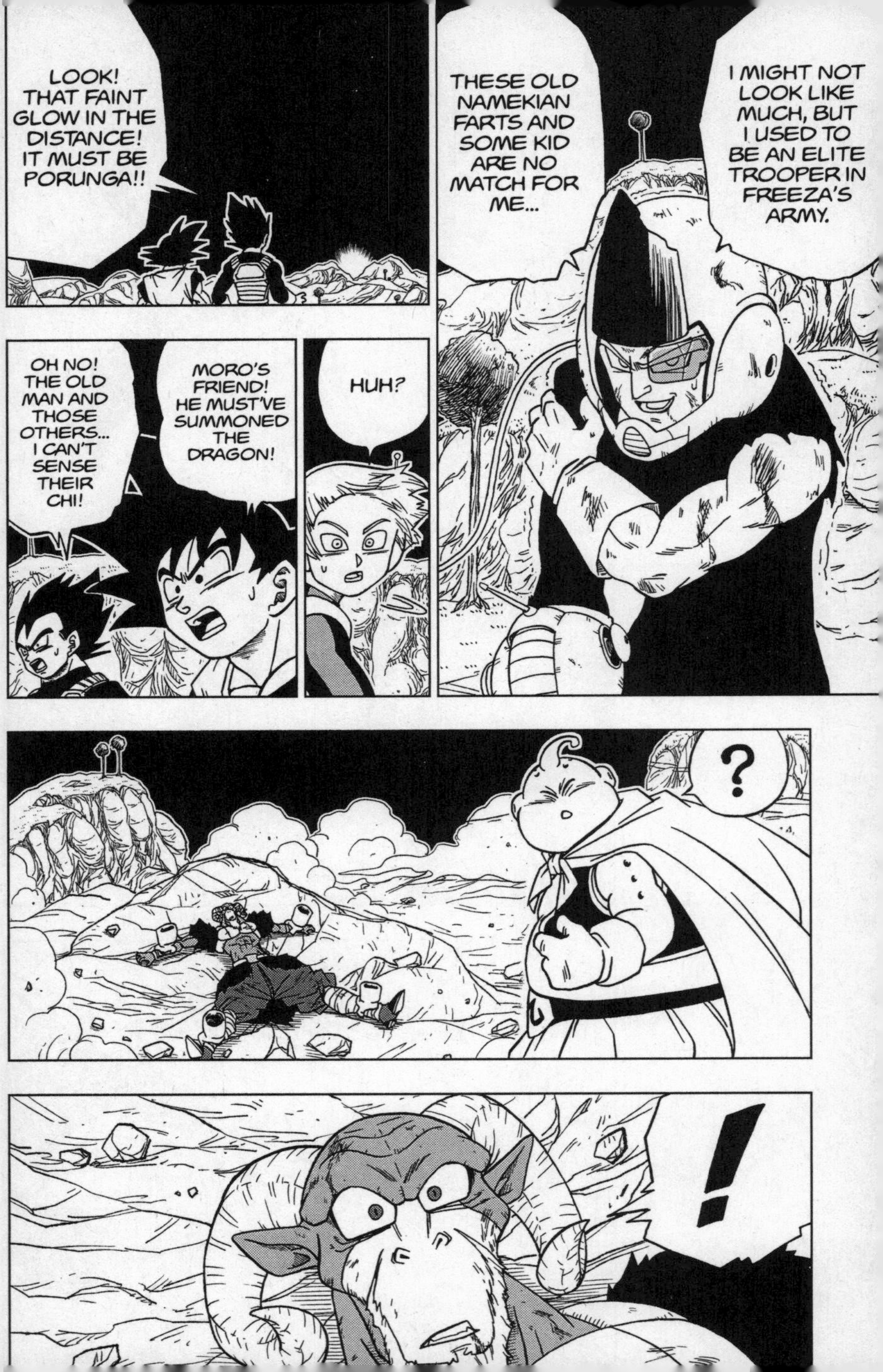
I MIGHT NOT LOOK LIKE MUCH, BUT I USED TO BE AN ELITE TROOPER IN FREEZA'S ARMY.
THESE OLD NAMEKIAN FARTS AND SOME KID ARE NO MATCH FOR ME...
LOOK! THAT FAINT GLOW IN THE DISTANCE! IT MUST BE PORUNGA!!
HUH?
MORO'S FRIEND! HE MUST'VE SUMMONED THE DRAGON!
OH NO! THE OLD MAN AND THOSE OTHERS... I CAN'T SENSE THEIR CHI!
?
!

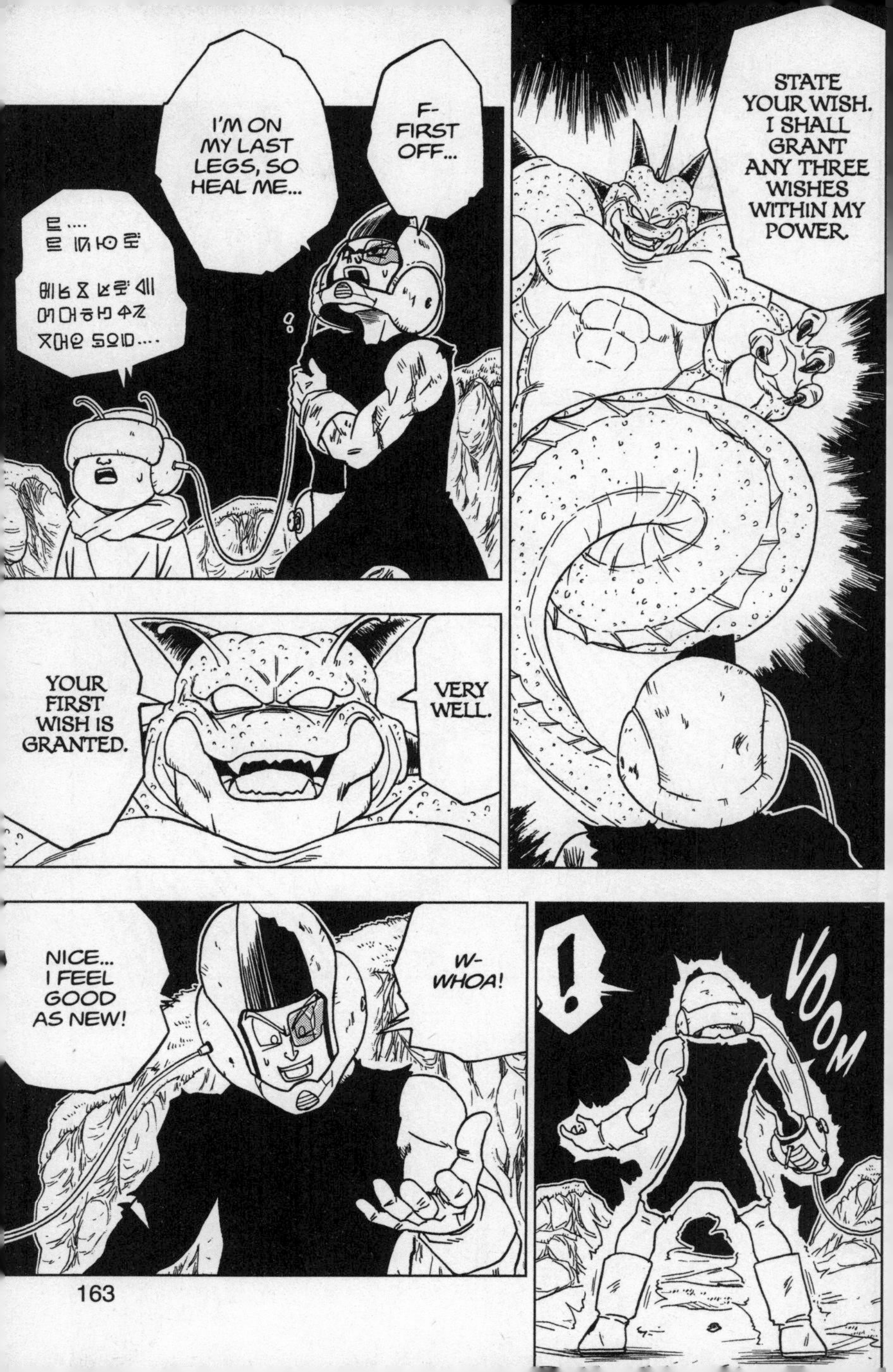
STATE YOUR WISH. I SHALL GRANT ANY THREE WISHES WITHIN MY POWER.
F- FIRST OFF...
I'M ON MY LAST LEGS, SO HEAL ME...
VERY WELL.
YOUR FIRST WISH IS GRANTED.
!
VOOM
W- WHOA!
NICE... I FEEL GOOD AS NEW!

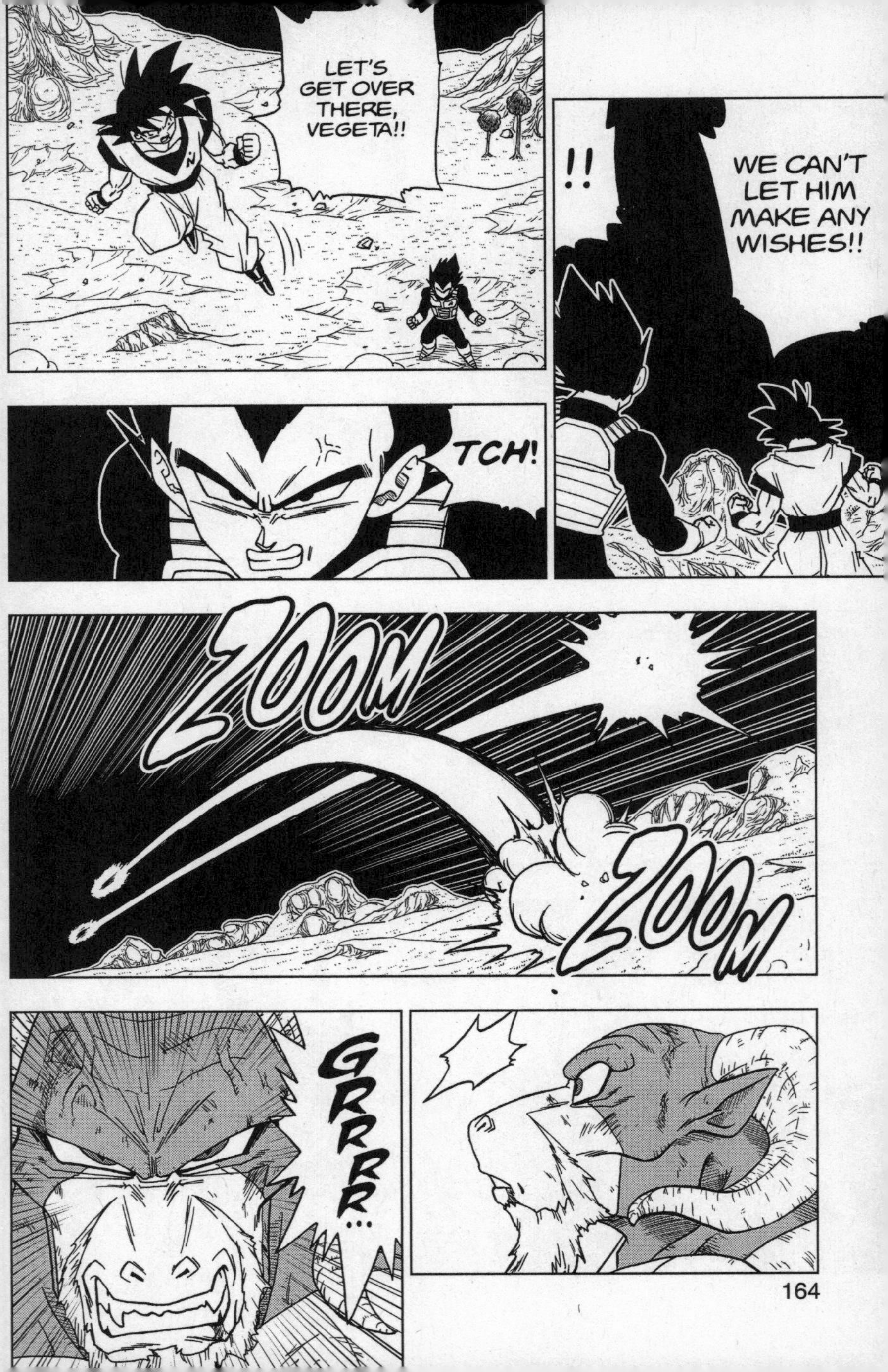
WE CAN'T LET HIM MAKE ANY WISHES!!
!!
LET'S GET OVER THERE, VEGETA!!
TCH!
ZOOM
ZOOM
GRRRR...

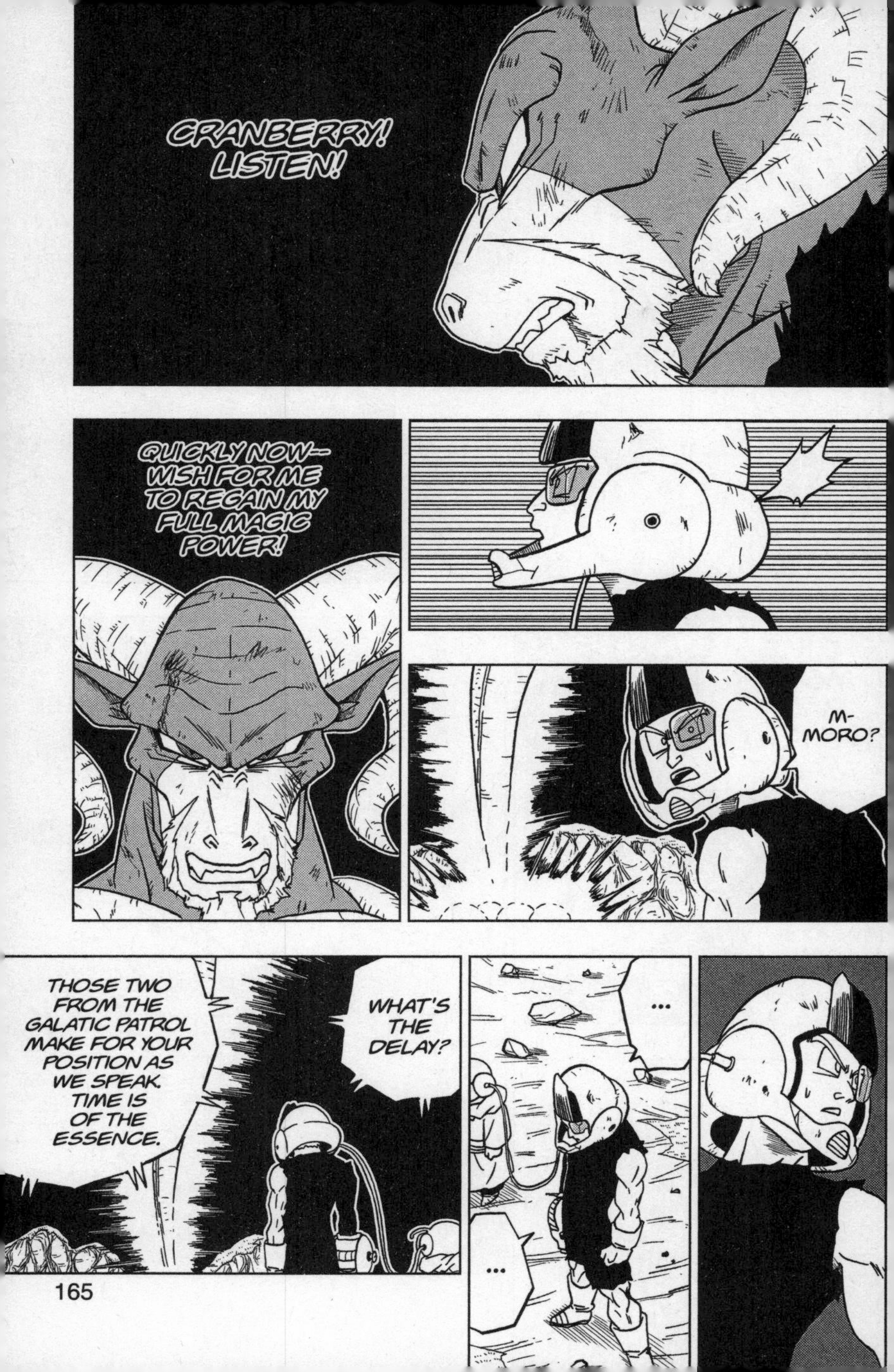
CRANBERRY! LISTEN!
M-MORO?
QUICKLY NOW-- WISH FOR ME TO REGAIN MY FULL MAGIC POWER!
...
...
WHAT'S THE DELAY?
THOSE TWO FROM THE GALATIC PATROL MAKE FOR YOUR POSITION AS WE SPEAK. TIME IS OF THE ESSENCE.

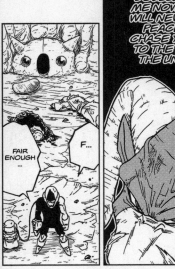

W-WHAT ABOUT MY WISH TO ESCAPE TO SOME OUTLYING PLANET...?
THE THIRD WISH IS YOURS TO USE AS YOU SEE FIT AFTER MINE ARE GRANTED!
KNOW THIS... DOUBLE-CROSS ME NOW AND YOU WILL NEVER KNOW PEACE. I WILL CHASE YOU DOWN TO THE ENDS OF THE UNIVERSE.
F...
FAIR ENOUGH...
STATE YOUR SECOND WISH.
GIVE MORO BACK HIS FULL MAGIC POWER.
VERY WELL.
YOUR SECOND WISH IS GRANTED.

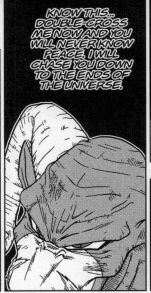

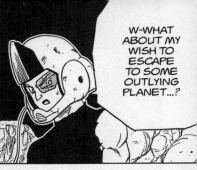

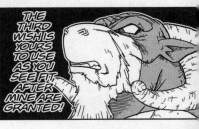

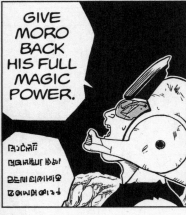

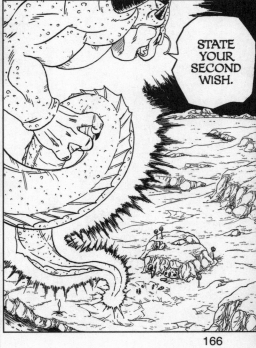

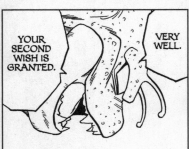

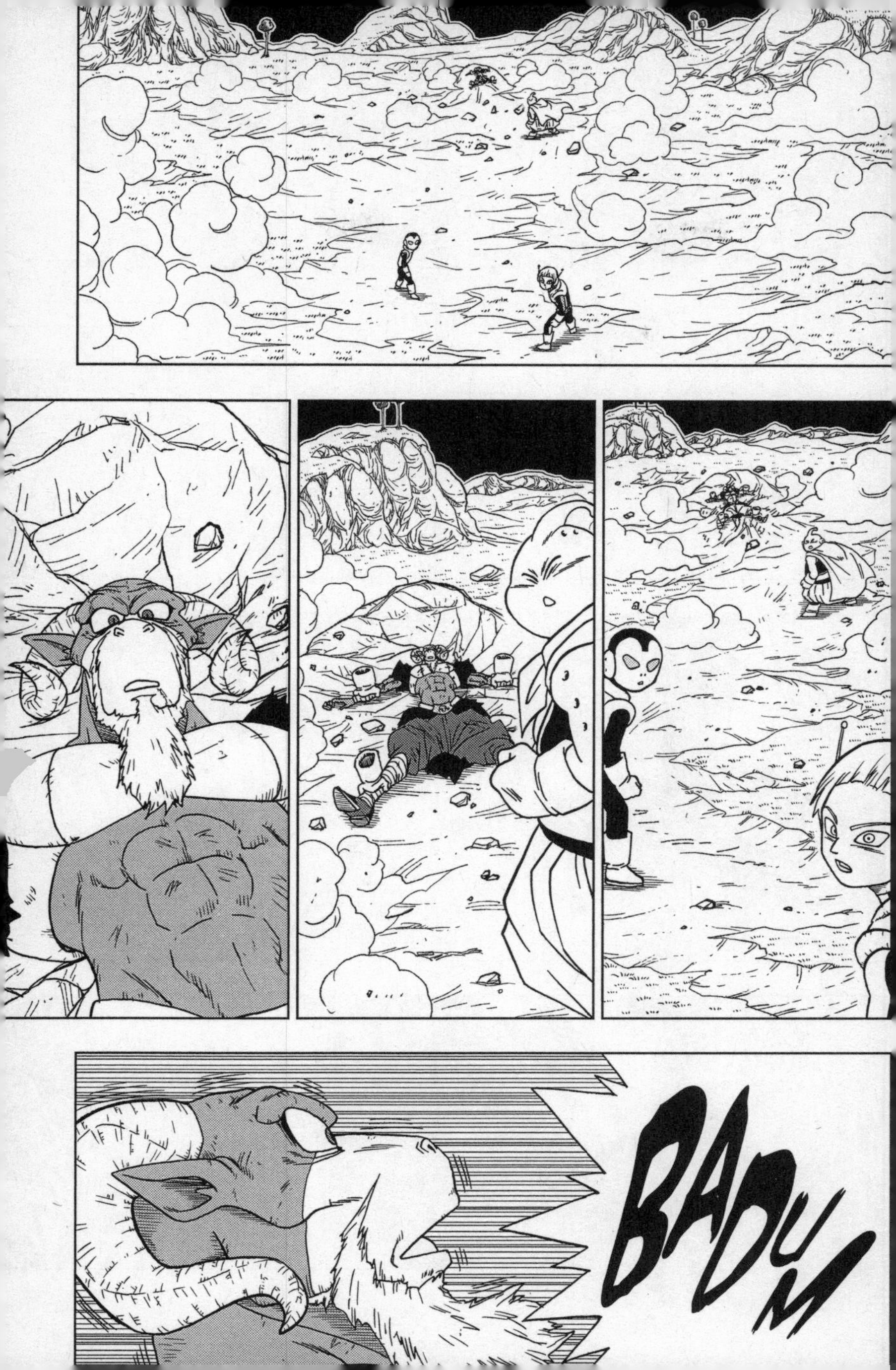
BADUM

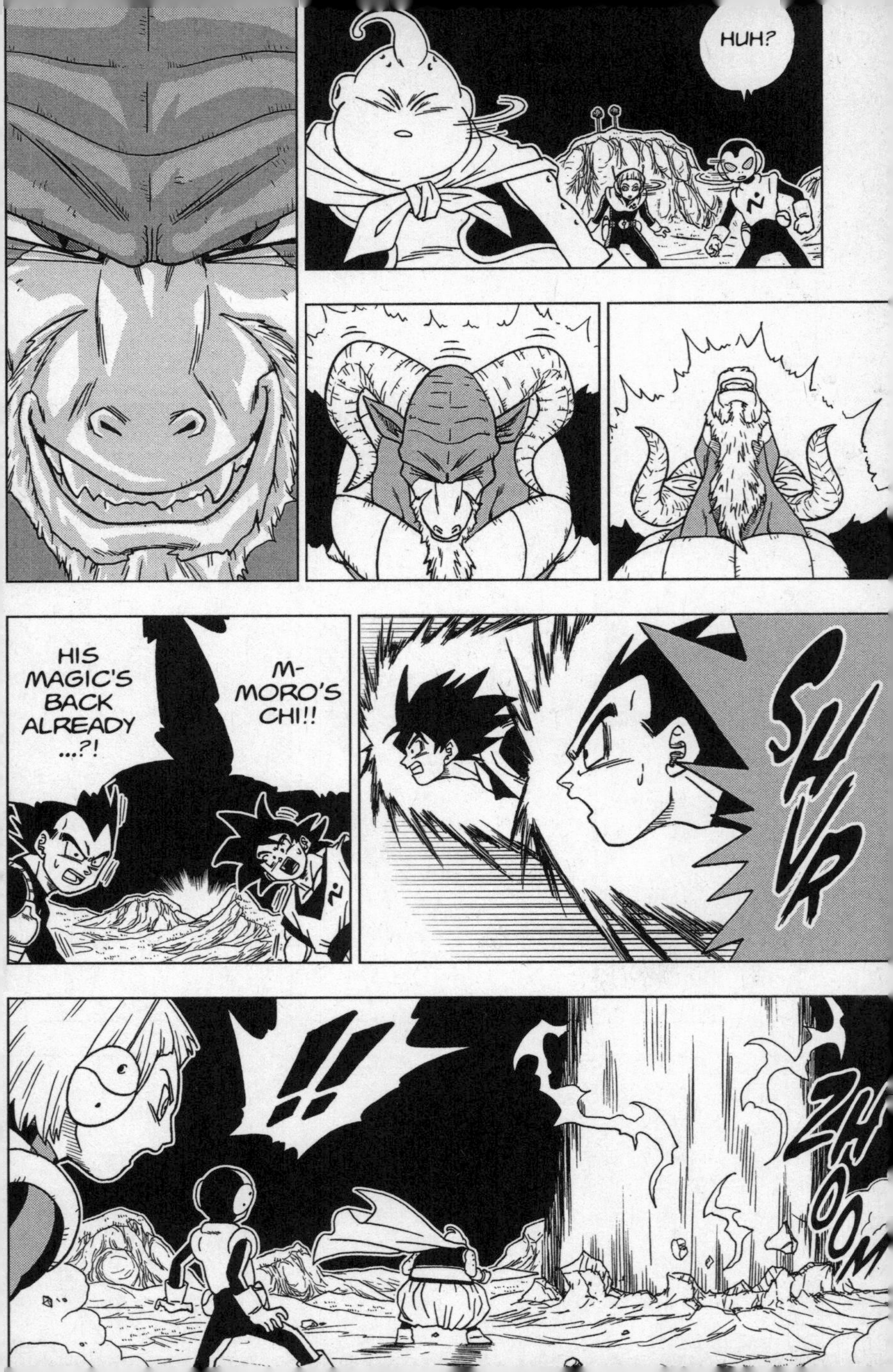
HUH?
SHVR
M-MORO'S CHI!!
HIS MAGIC'S BACK ALREADY ...?!
ZHOOOM
!!

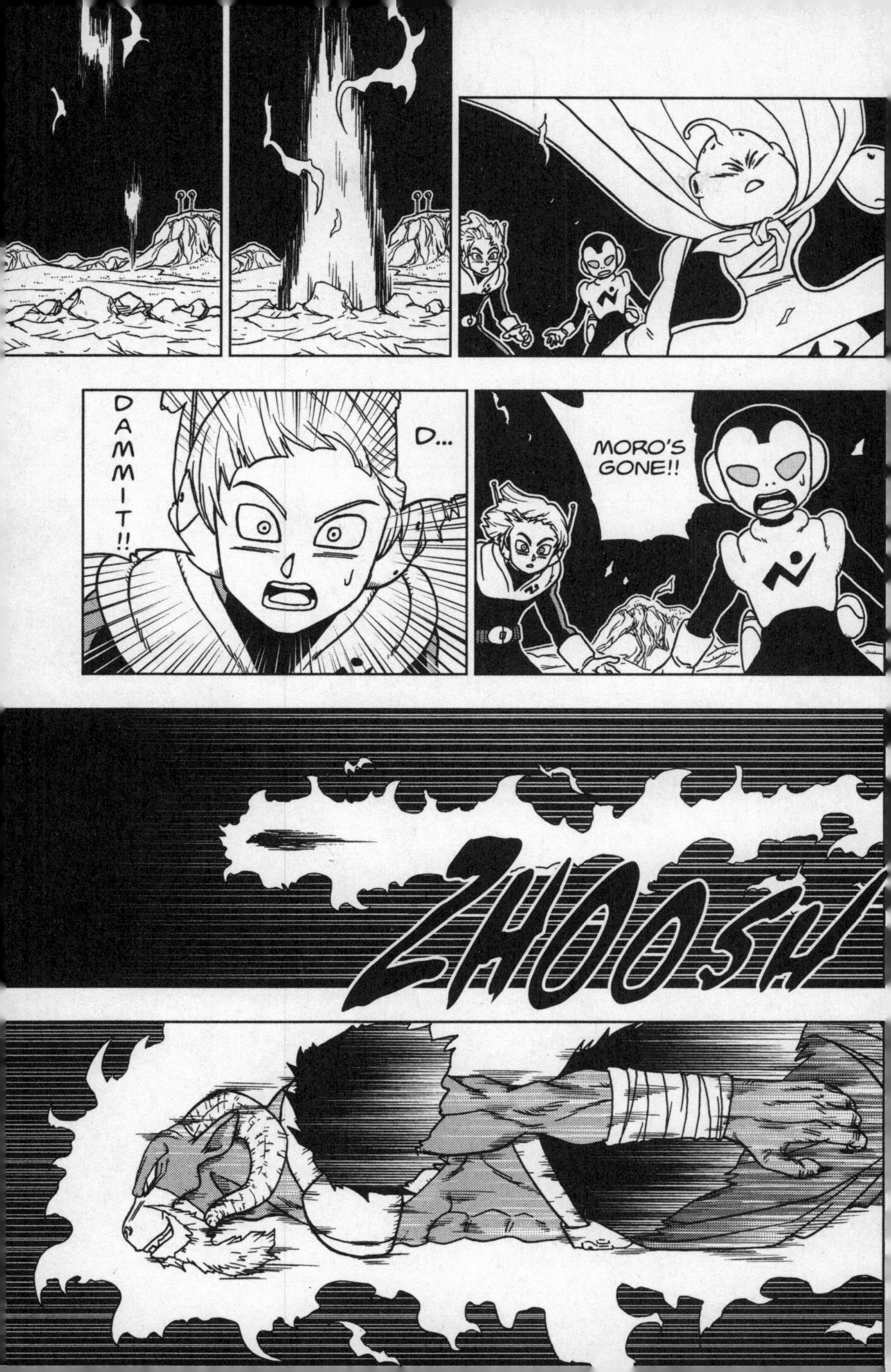
MORO'S GONE!!
D...
DAMMIT!!
ZHOOSH

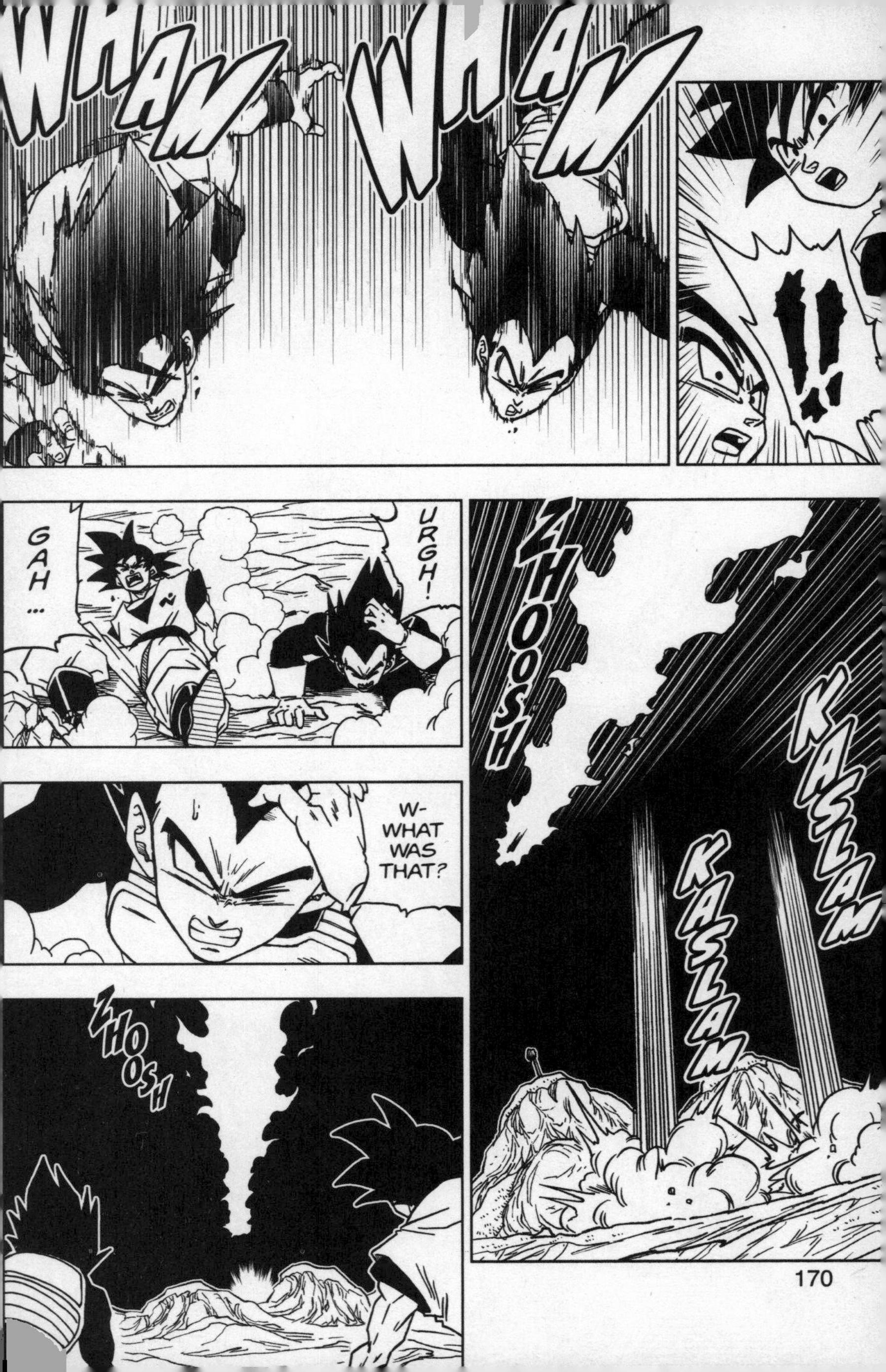
!!
WHAM
WHAM
KASLAM
KASLAM
ZHOOOSH
URGH!
GAH...
W-WHAT WAS THAT?
ZHOSH

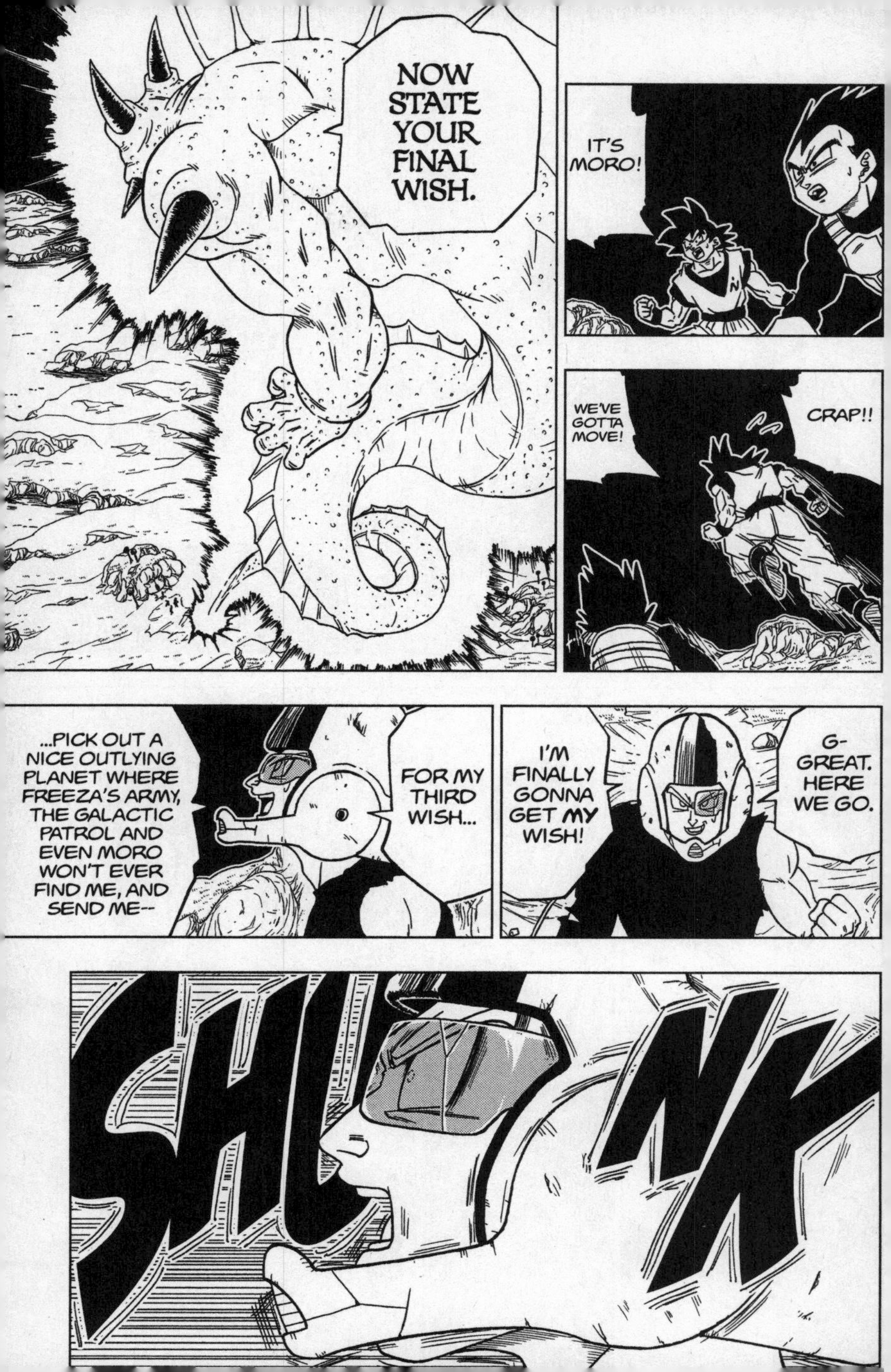
IT'S MORO!
CRAP!!
WE'VE GOTTA MOVE!
NOW STATE YOUR FINAL WISH.
G-GREAT. HERE WE GO.
I'M FINALLY GONNA GET MY WISH!
FOR MY THIRD WISH...
...PICK OUT A NICE OUTLYING PLANET WHERE FREEZA'S ARMY, THE GALACTIC PATROL AND EVEN MORO WON'T EVER FIND ME, AND SEND ME--
SHUNK

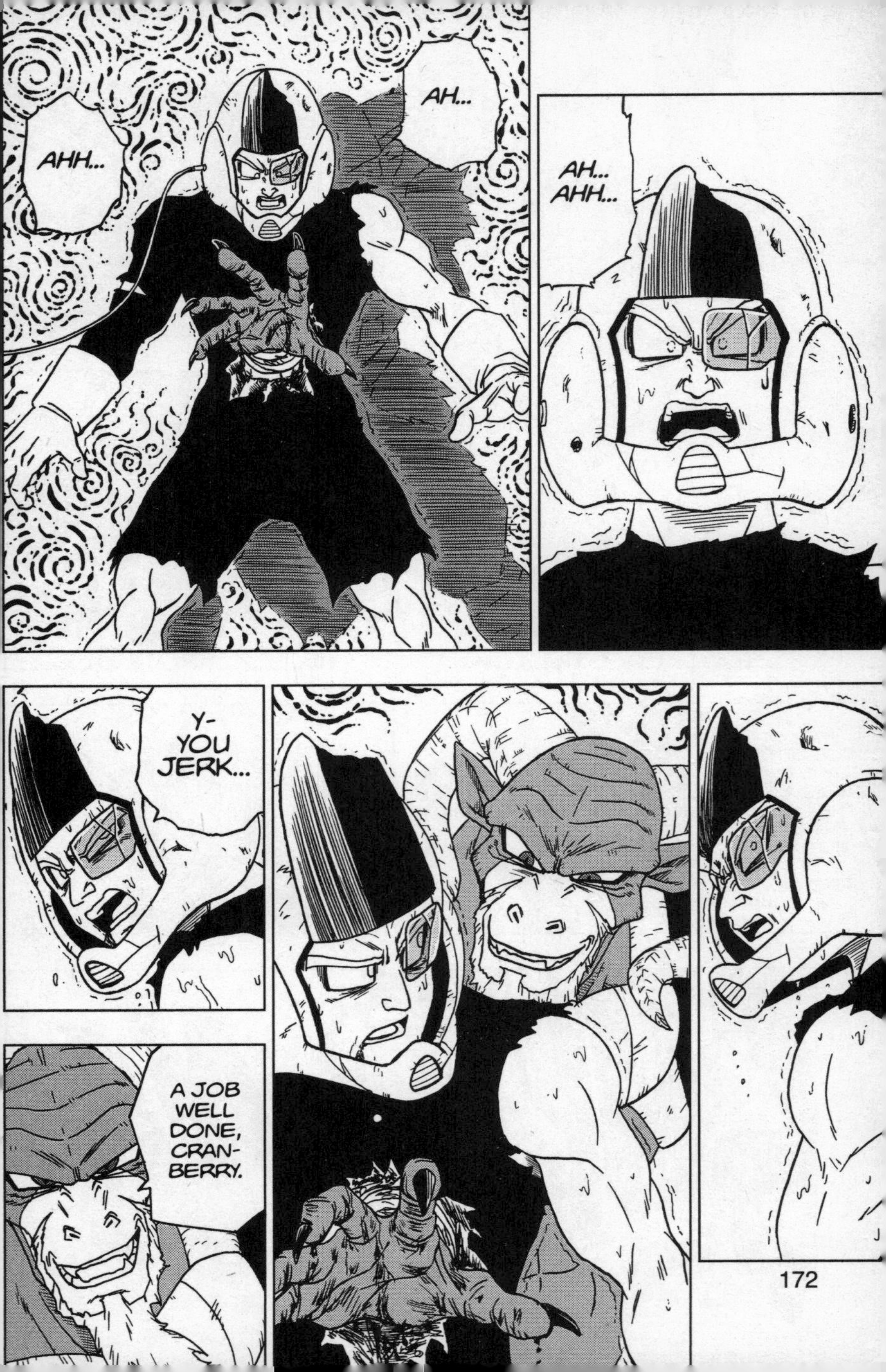
AH... AHH...
AH...
AHH...
Y- YOU JERK...
A JOB WELL DONE, CRAN-BERRY.

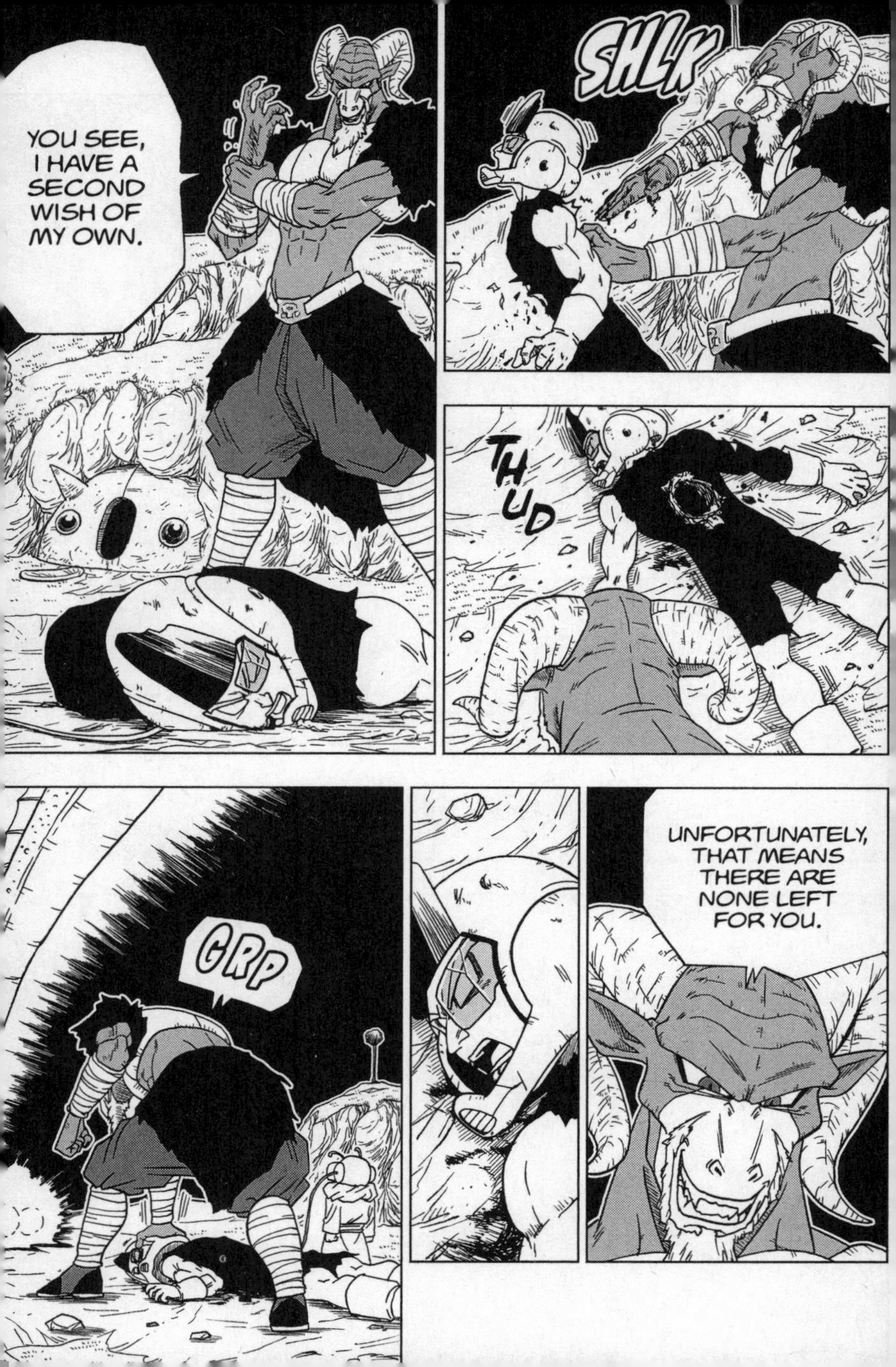
SHLK
THUD
YOU SEE, I HAVE A SECOND WISH OF MY OWN.
UNFORTUNATELY, THAT MEANS THERE ARE NONE LEFT FOR YOU.
GRP

PORUNGA, WAS IT? THERE IS STILL ONE WISH REMAINING, YES?
YES, I AWAIT THE FINAL WISH. STATE IT NOW.
GOOD.
GRIN
I WONDER IF YOU CAN GRANT **THIS** ONE...

GET IN. I'M TRACKING MORO'S LIFE SIGNATURE!

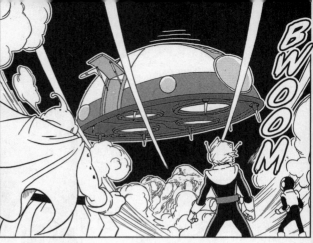

BWOOM

ZOOSH

LET'S HURRY, FRIENDS.

TMP

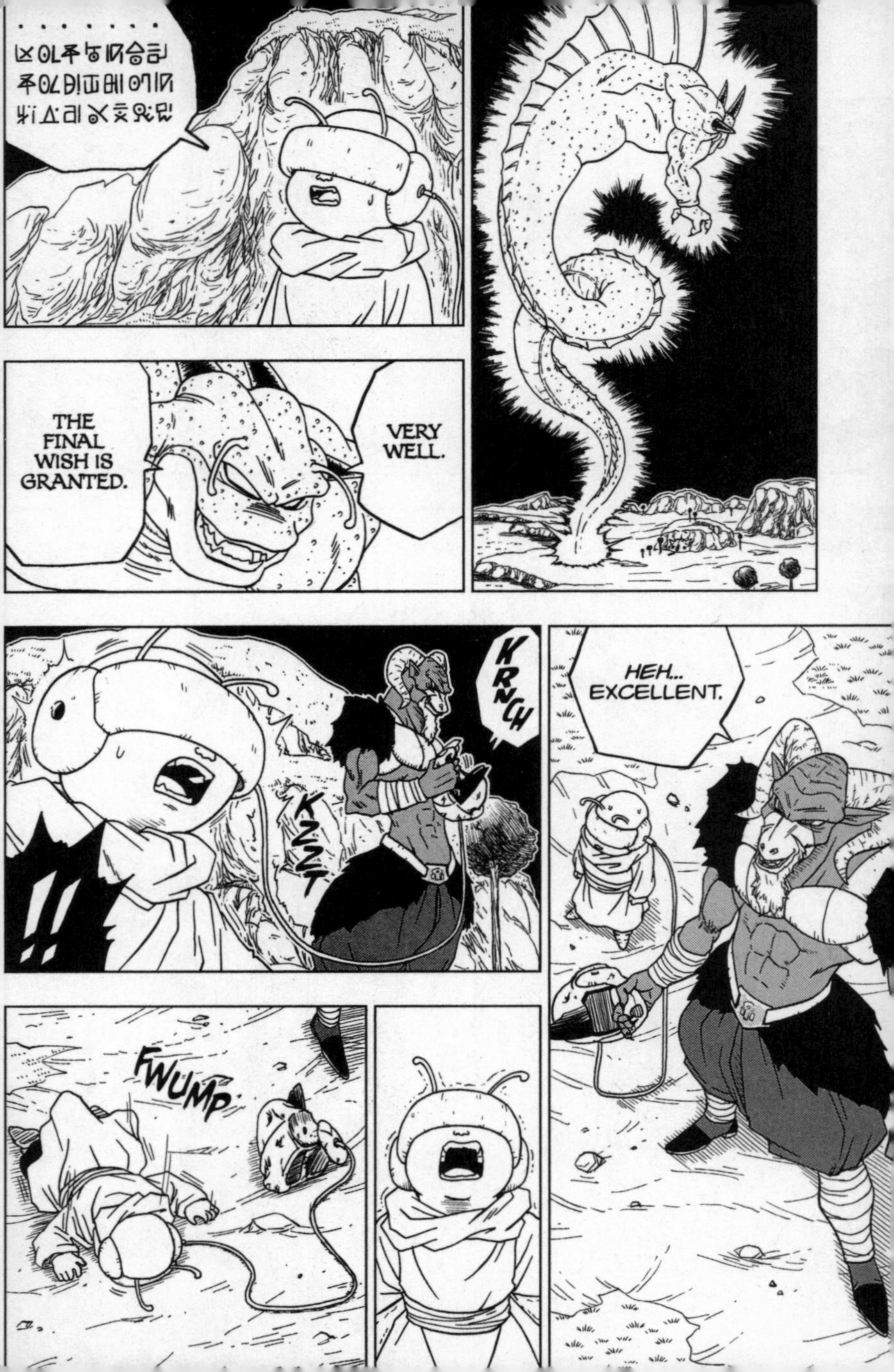

....
VERY WELL.
THE FINAL WISH IS GRANTED.
HEH... EXCELLENT.
KRNCH
KZZT
!!
FWUMP

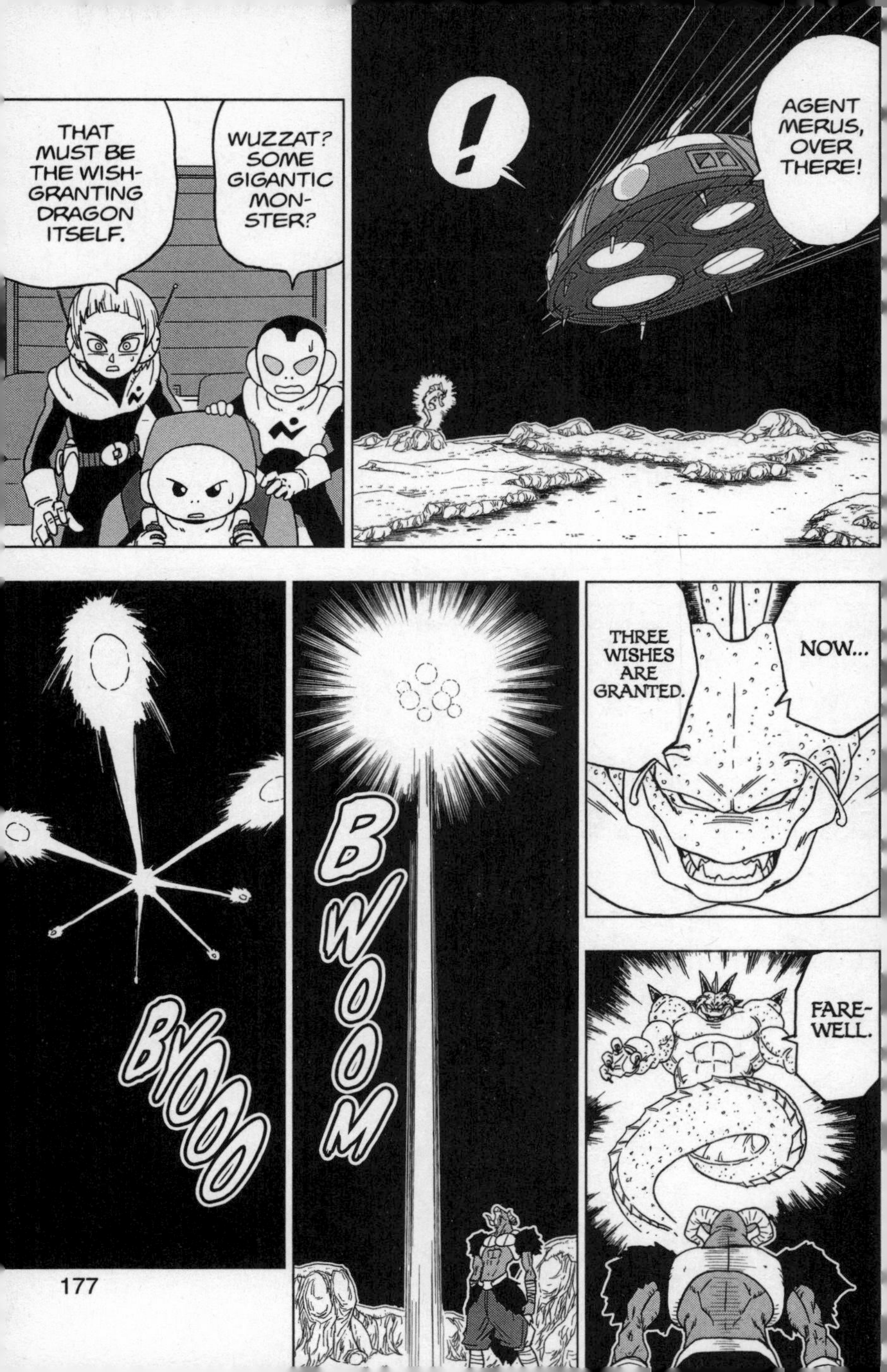
AGENT MERUS, OVER THERE!
!
WUZZAT? SOME GIGANTIC MON-STER?
THAT MUST BE THE WISH-GRANTING DRAGON ITSELF.
NOW...
THREE WISHES ARE GRANTED.
FARE-WELL.
BWOOM
BYOOO

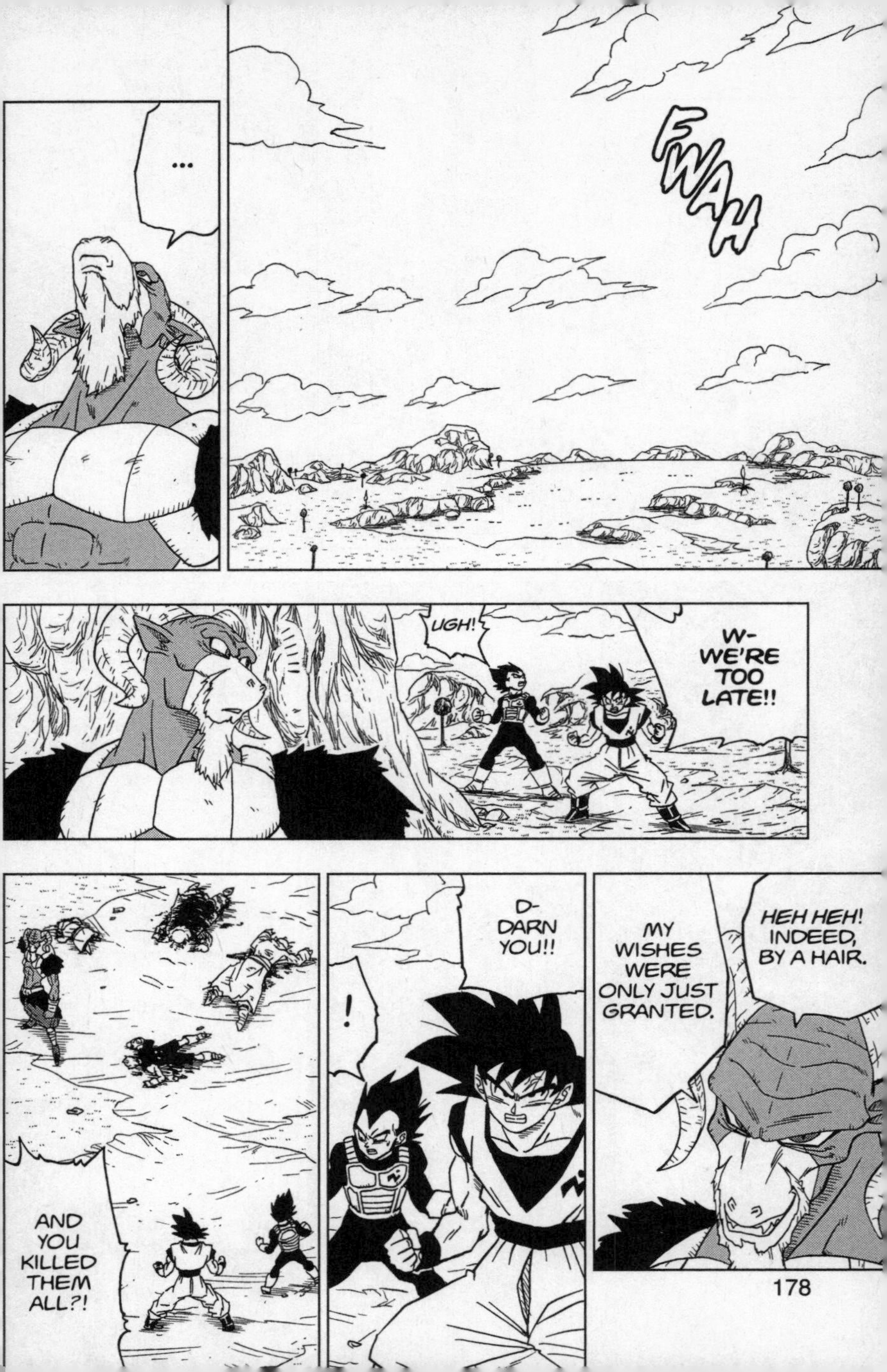
FWAH
...
W-WE'RE TOO LATE!!
UGH!
HEH HEH! INDEED, BY A HAIR.
MY WISHES WERE ONLY JUST GRANTED.
D-DARN YOU!!
!
AND YOU KILLED THEM ALL?!

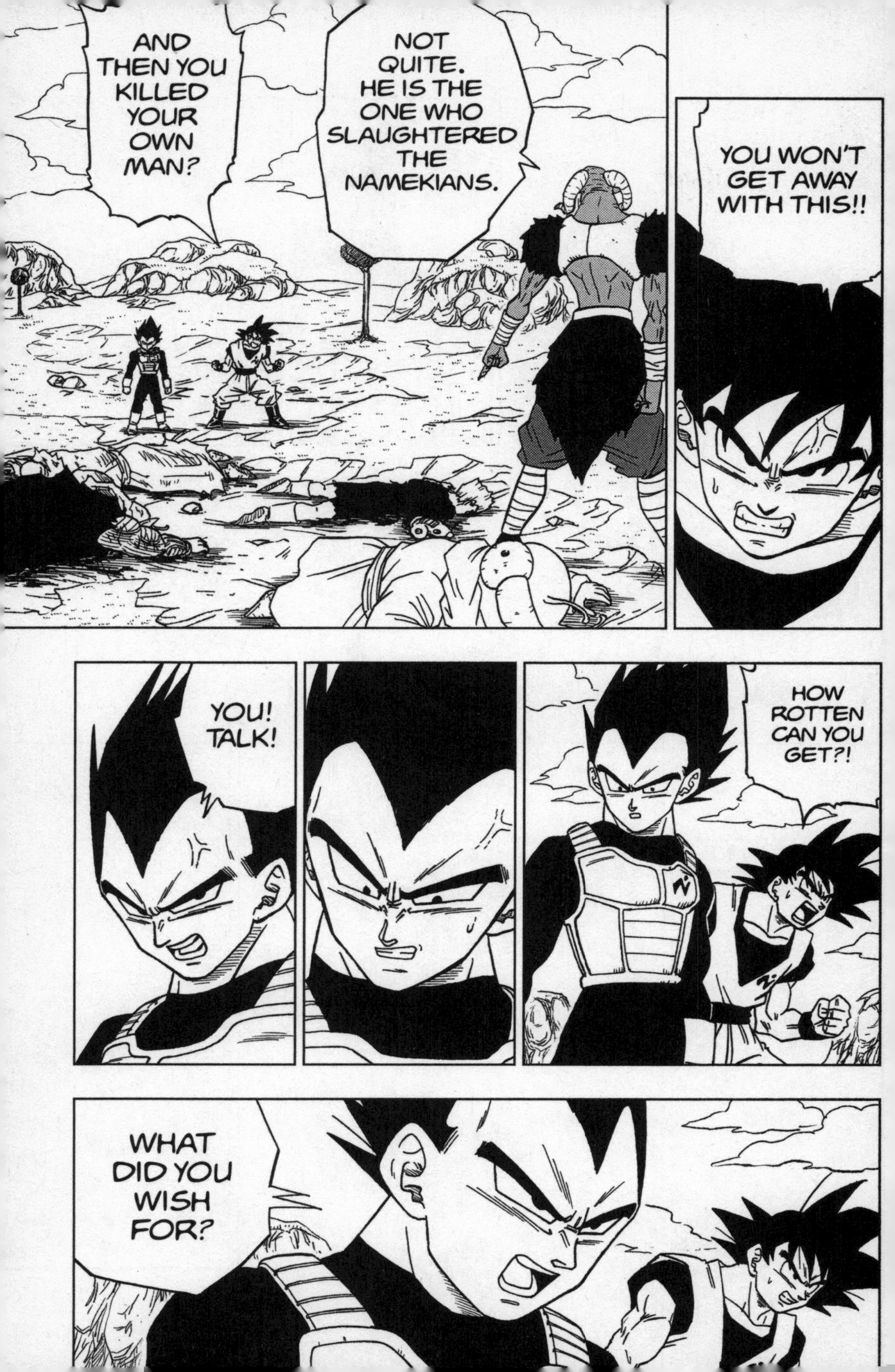
YOU WON'T GET AWAY WITH THIS!!
NOT QUITE. HE IS THE ONE WHO SLAUGHTERED THE NAMEKIANS.
AND THEN YOU KILLED YOUR OWN MAN?
HOW ROTTEN CAN YOU GET?!
YOU! TALK!
WHAT DID YOU WISH FOR?

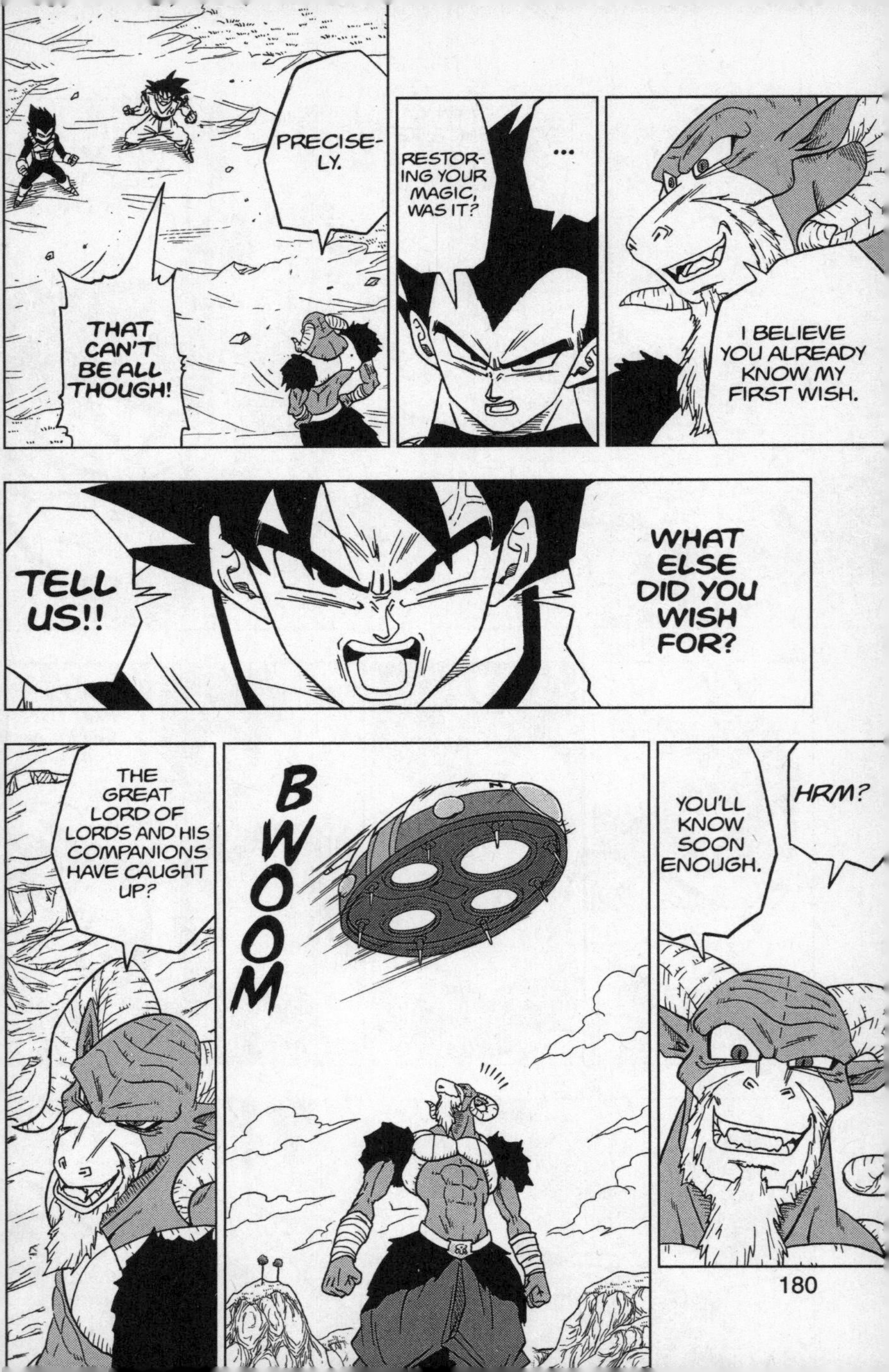
I BELIEVE YOU ALREADY KNOW MY FIRST WISH.
...
RESTORING YOUR MAGIC, WAS IT?
PRECISELY.
THAT CAN'T BE ALL THOUGH!
WHAT ELSE DID YOU WISH FOR?
TELL US!!
HRM?
YOU'LL KNOW SOON ENOUGH.
BWOOM
THE GREAT LORD OF LORDS AND HIS COMPANIONS HAVE CAUGHT UP?

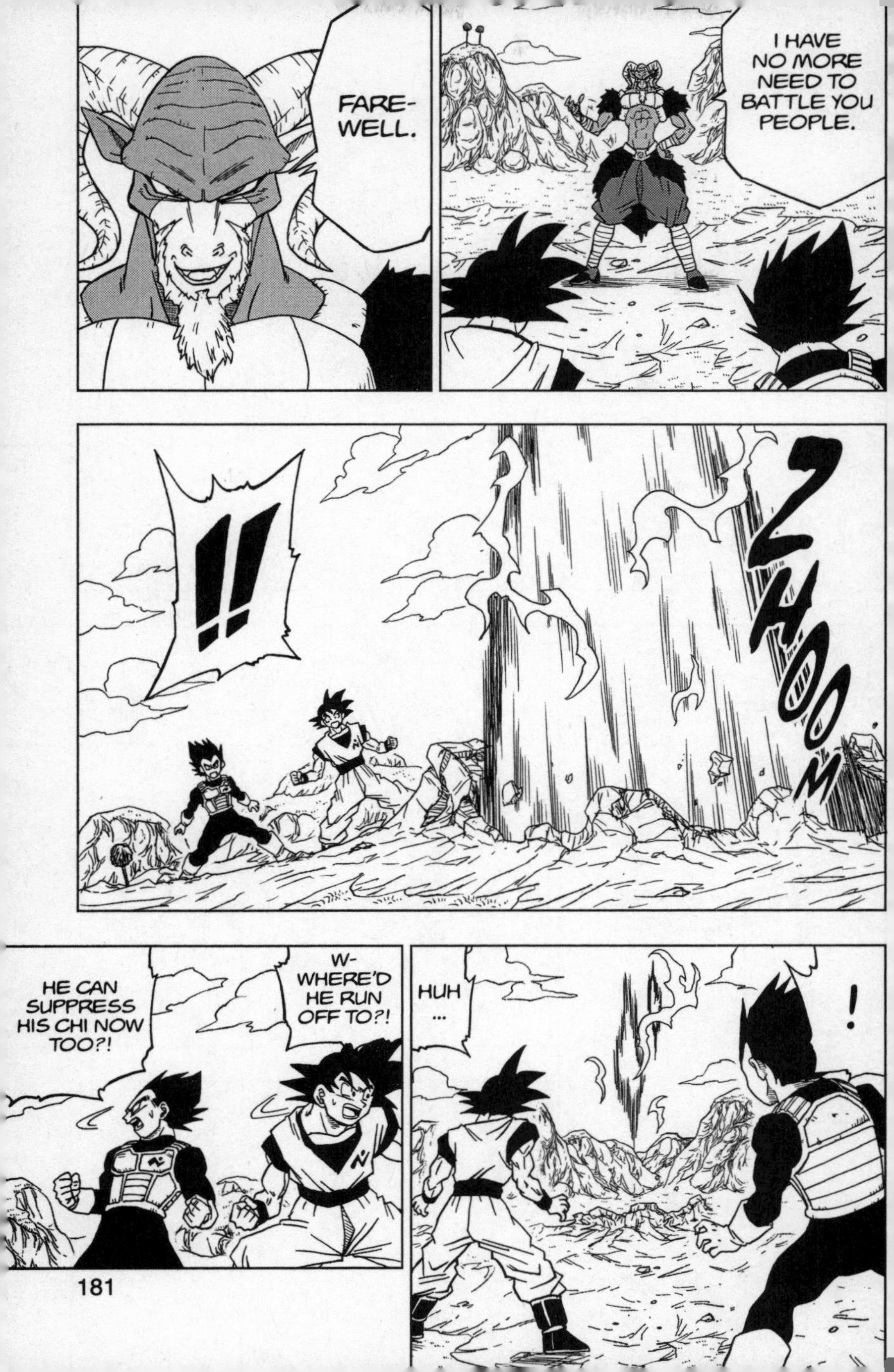
I HAVE NO MORE NEED TO BATTLE YOU PEOPLE.
FARE-WELL.
ZHOOOM
!!
!
HUH ...
W-WHERE'D HE RUN OFF TO?!
HE CAN SUPPRESS HIS CHI NOW TOO?!

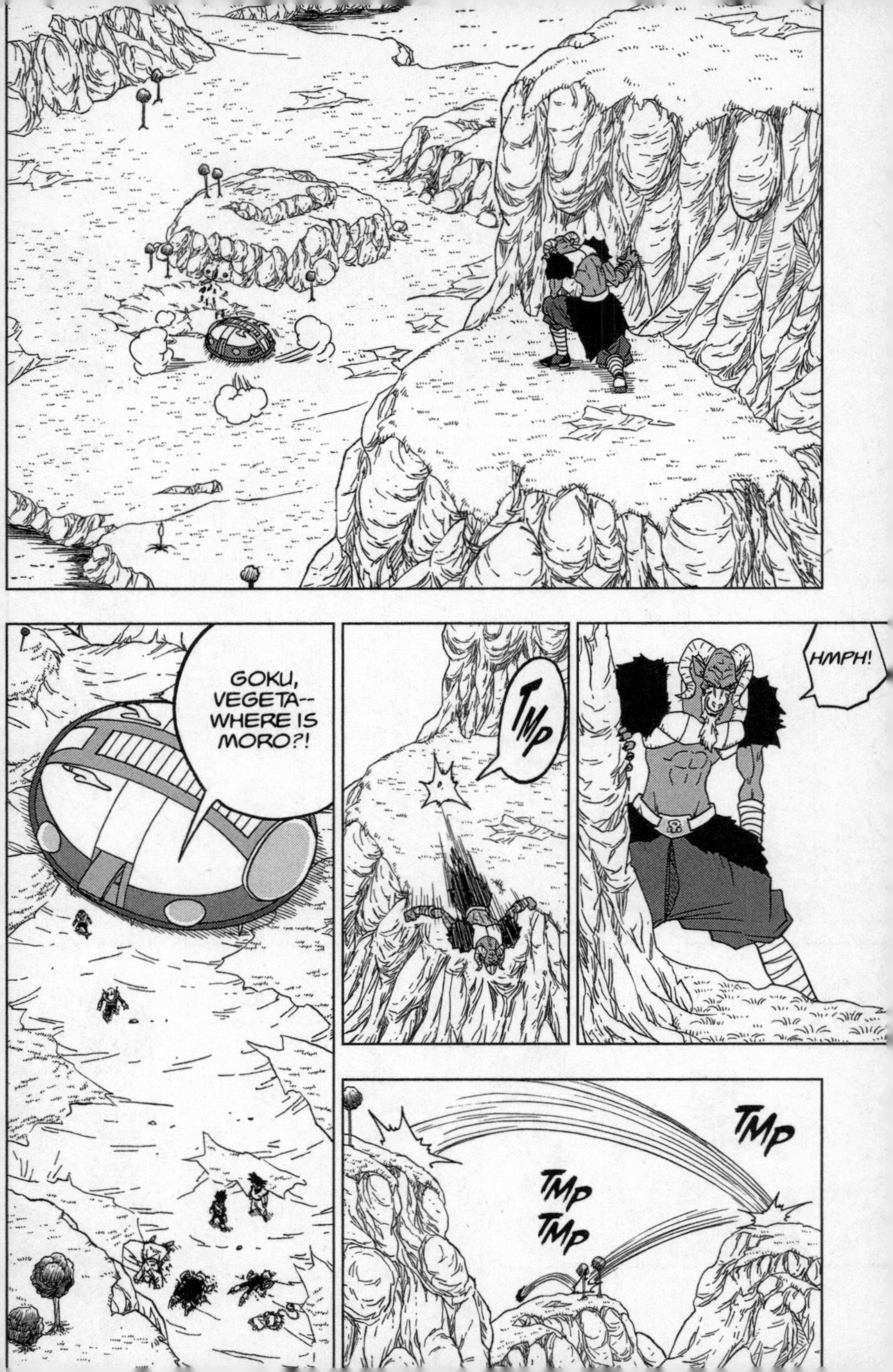
HMPH!
TMP
TMP
TMP
TMP
GOKU, VEGETA-- WHERE IS MORO?!

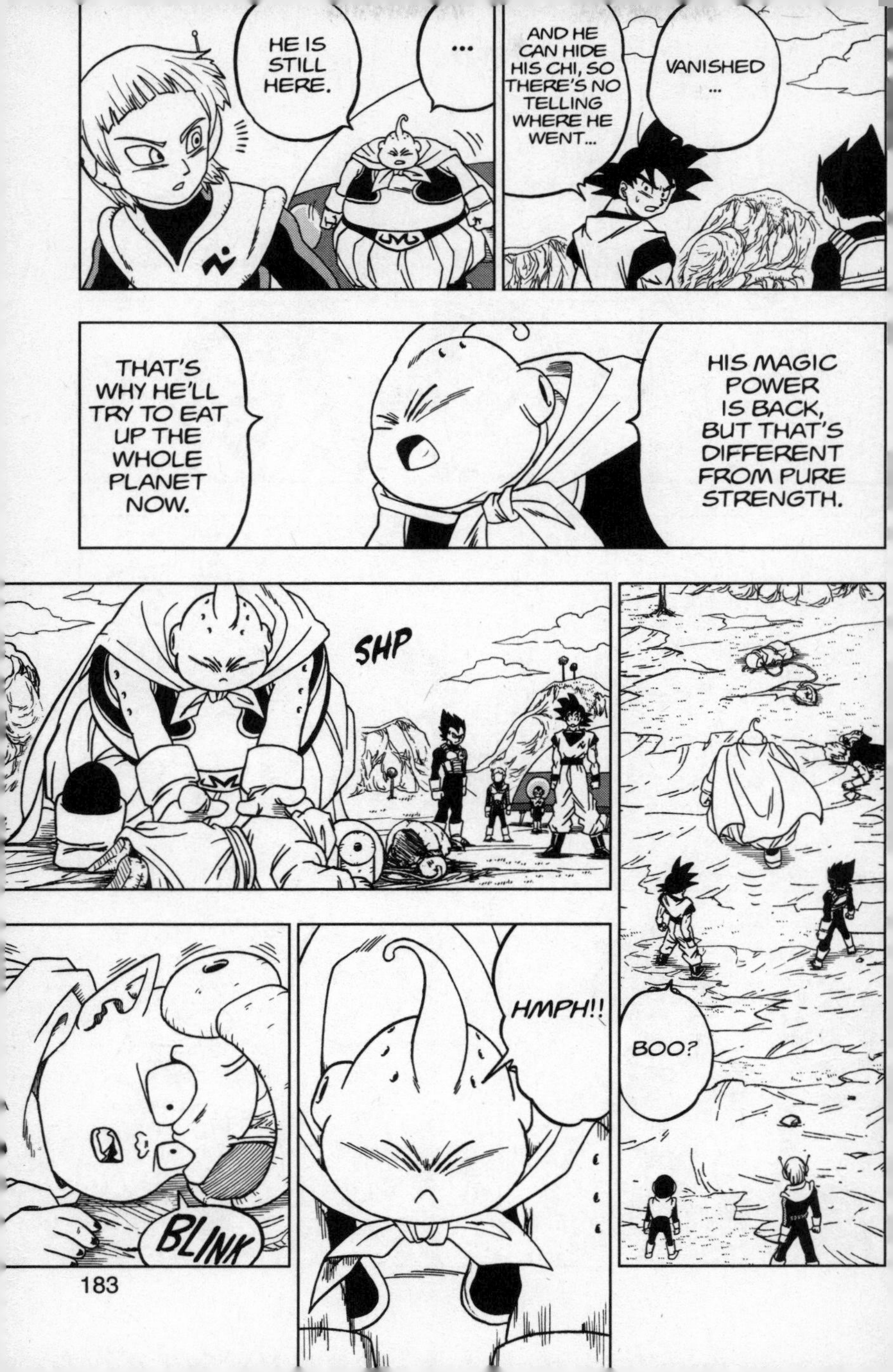

VANISHED ...
AND HE CAN HIDE HIS CHI, SO THERE'S NO TELLING WHERE HE WENT...
...
HE IS STILL HERE.
HIS MAGIC POWER IS BACK, BUT THAT'S DIFFERENT FROM PURE STRENGTH.
THAT'S WHY HE'LL TRY TO EAT UP THE WHOLE PLANET NOW.
BOO?
SHP
HMPH!!
BLINK

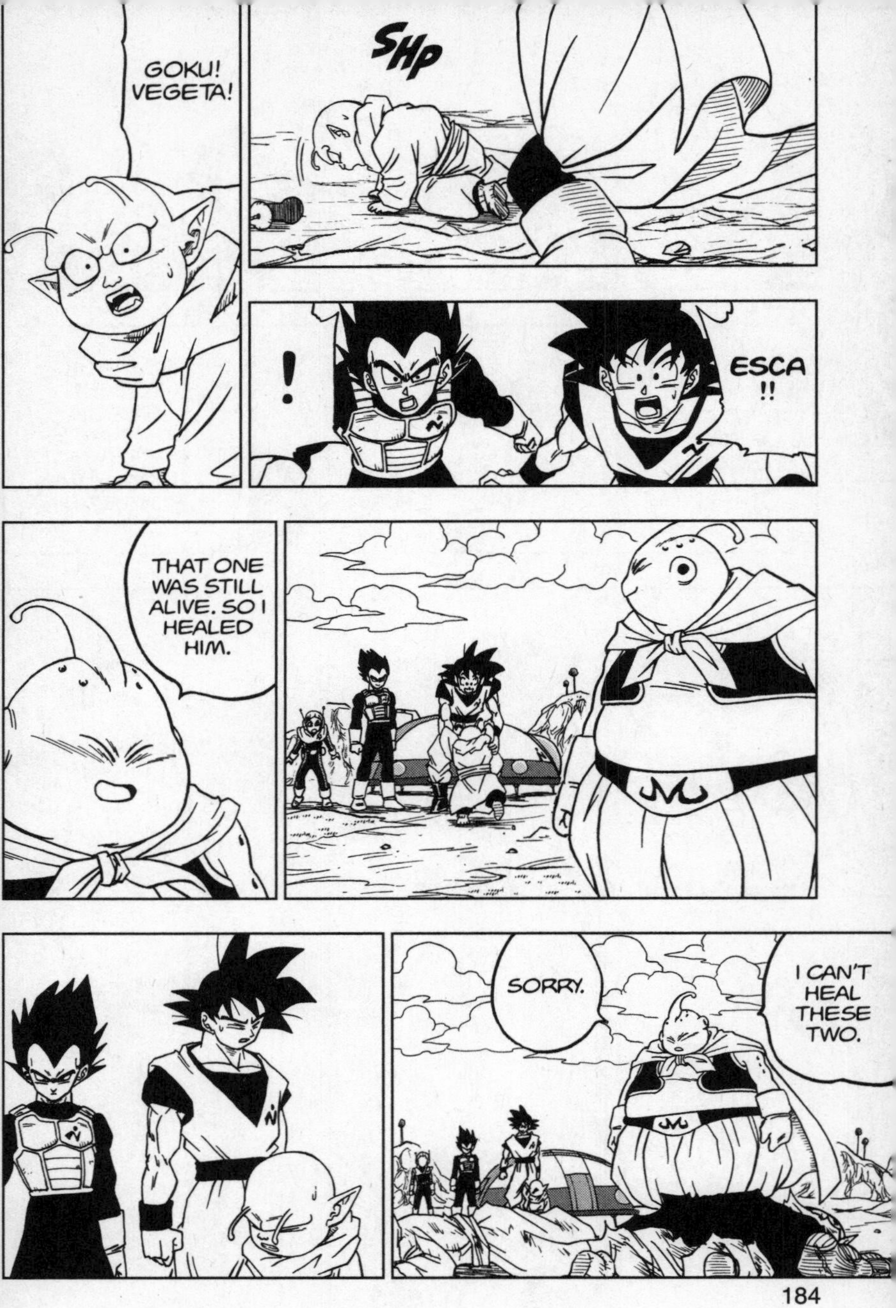
SHP
ESCA
!!
!
GOKU! VEGETA!
THAT ONE WAS STILL ALIVE. SO I HEALED HIM.
I CAN'T HEAL THESE TWO.
SORRY.

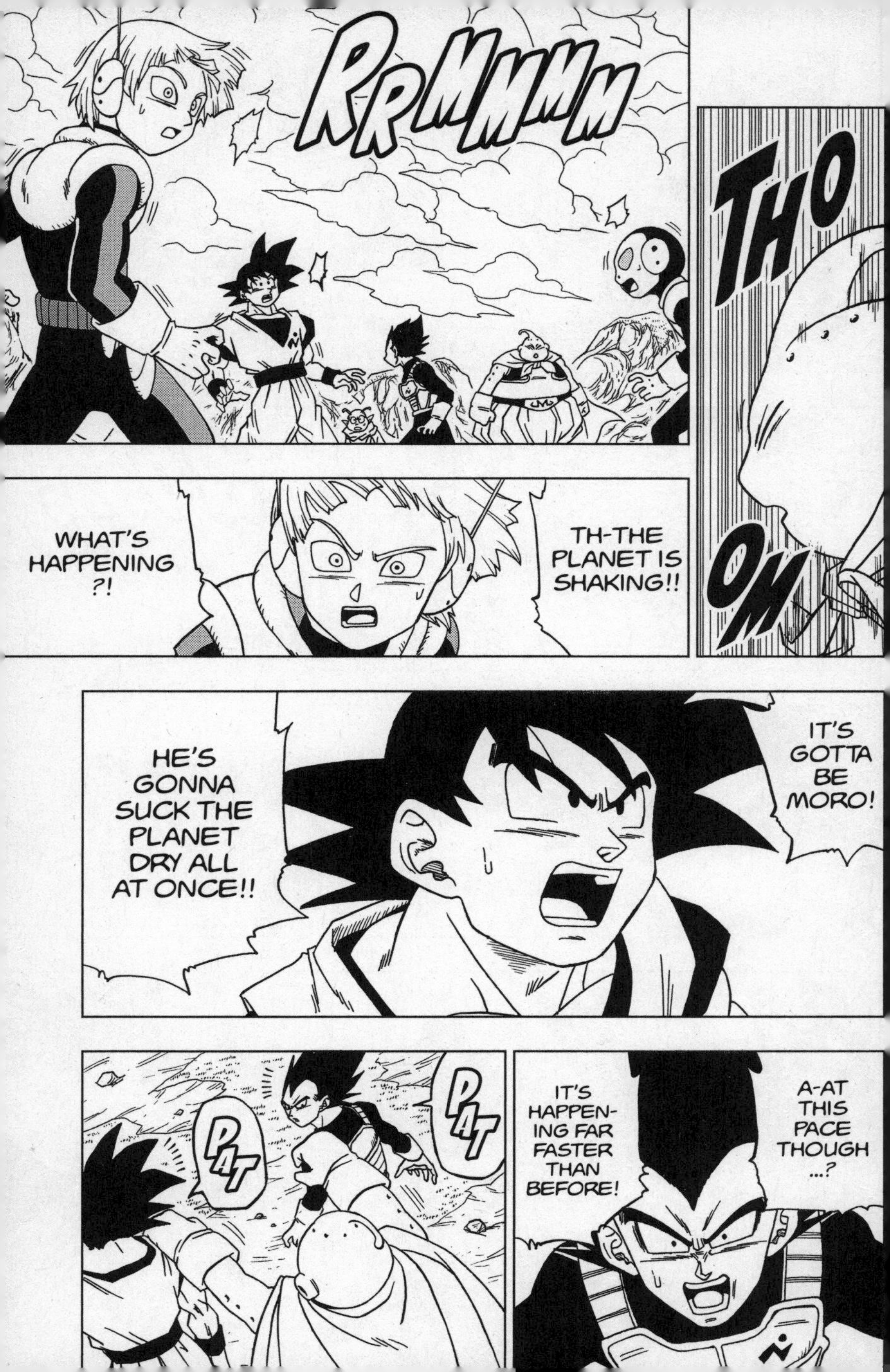
THOOM
RRMMMMM
TH-THE PLANET IS SHAKING!!
WHAT'S HAPPENING ?!
IT'S GOTTA BE MORO!
HE'S GONNA SUCK THE PLANET DRY ALL AT ONCE!!
A-AT THIS PACE THOUGH ...?
IT'S HAPPENING FAR FASTER THAN BEFORE!
PAT
PAT

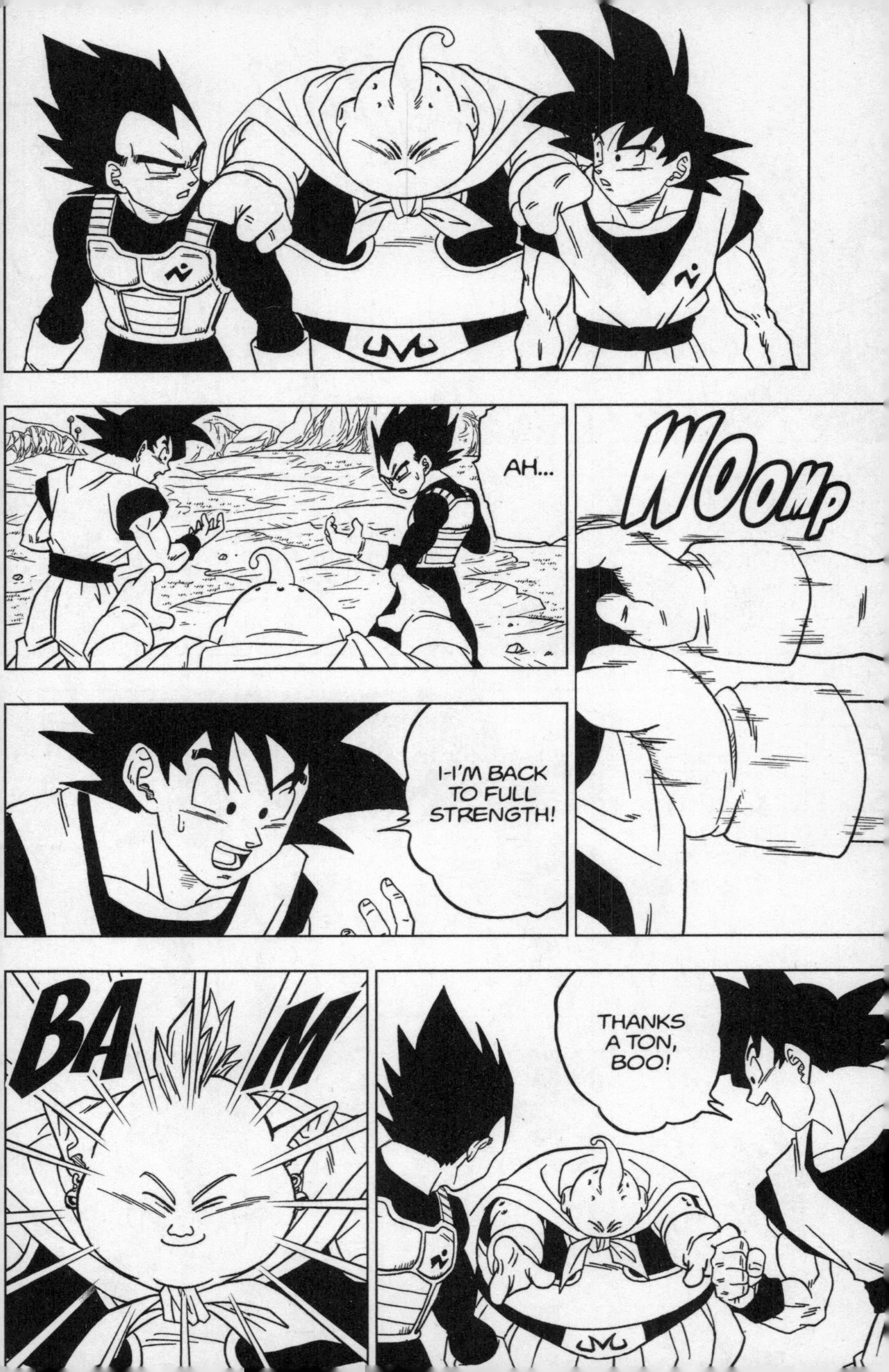
WOOMP
AH...
I-I'M BACK TO FULL STRENGTH!
THANKS A TON, BOO!
BAM

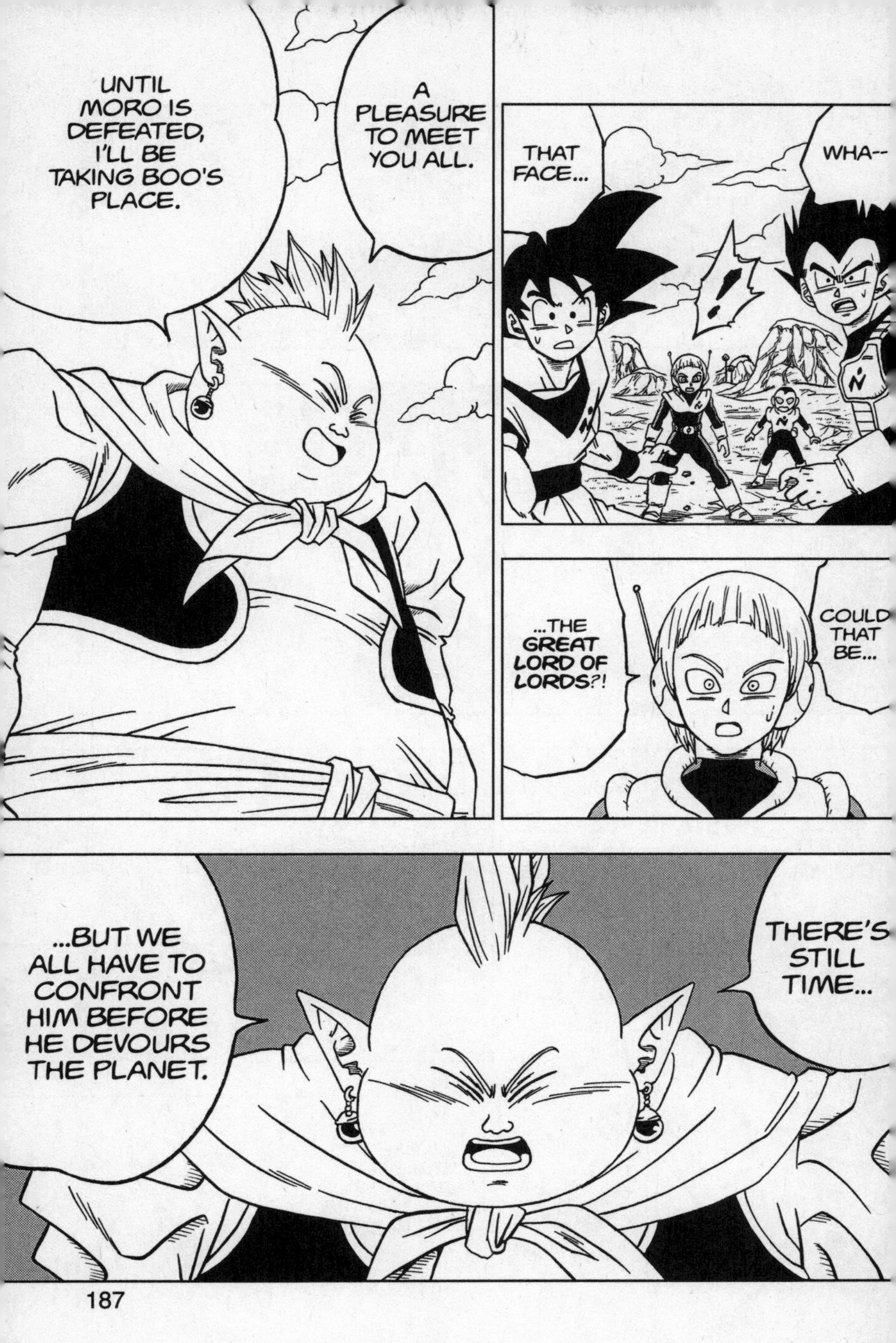
WHA--
THAT FACE...
COULD THAT BE...
...THE GREAT LORD OF LORDS?!
A PLEASURE TO MEET YOU ALL.
UNTIL MORO IS DEFEATED, I'LL BE TAKING BOO'S PLACE.
THERE'S STILL TIME...
...BUT WE ALL HAVE TO CONFRONT HIM BEFORE HE DEVOURS THE PLANET.

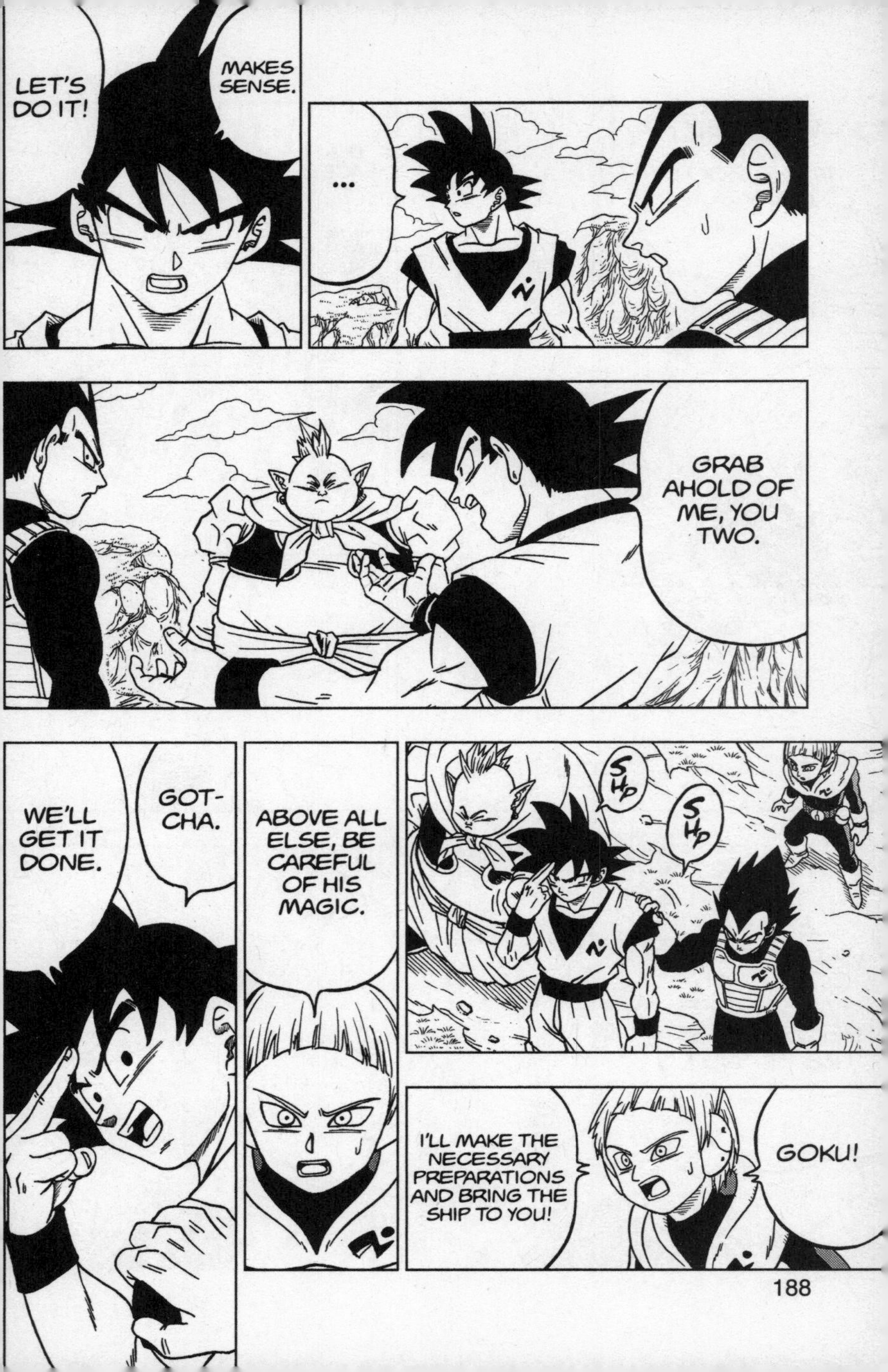
...
MAKES SENSE.
LET'S DO IT!
GRAB AHOLD OF ME, YOU TWO.
SHP
SHP
GOKU!
I'LL MAKE THE NECESSARY PREPARATIONS AND BRING THE SHIP TO YOU!
ABOVE ALL ELSE, BE CAREFUL OF HIS MAGIC.
GOT-CHA.
WE'LL GET IT DONE.

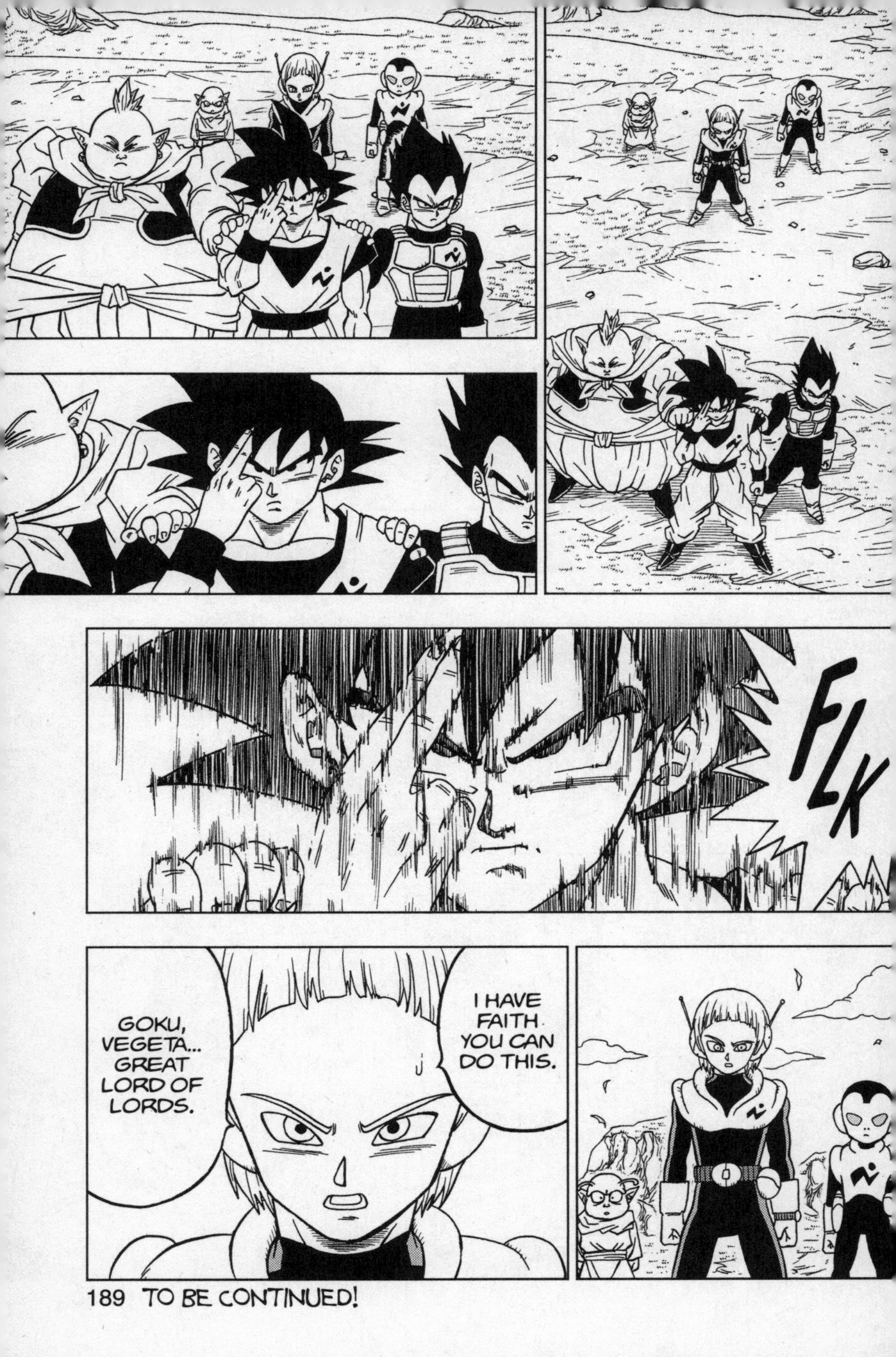
FLK
I HAVE FAITH YOU CAN DO THIS.
GOKU, VEGETA... GREAT LORD OF LORDS.

 TO BE CONTINUED!

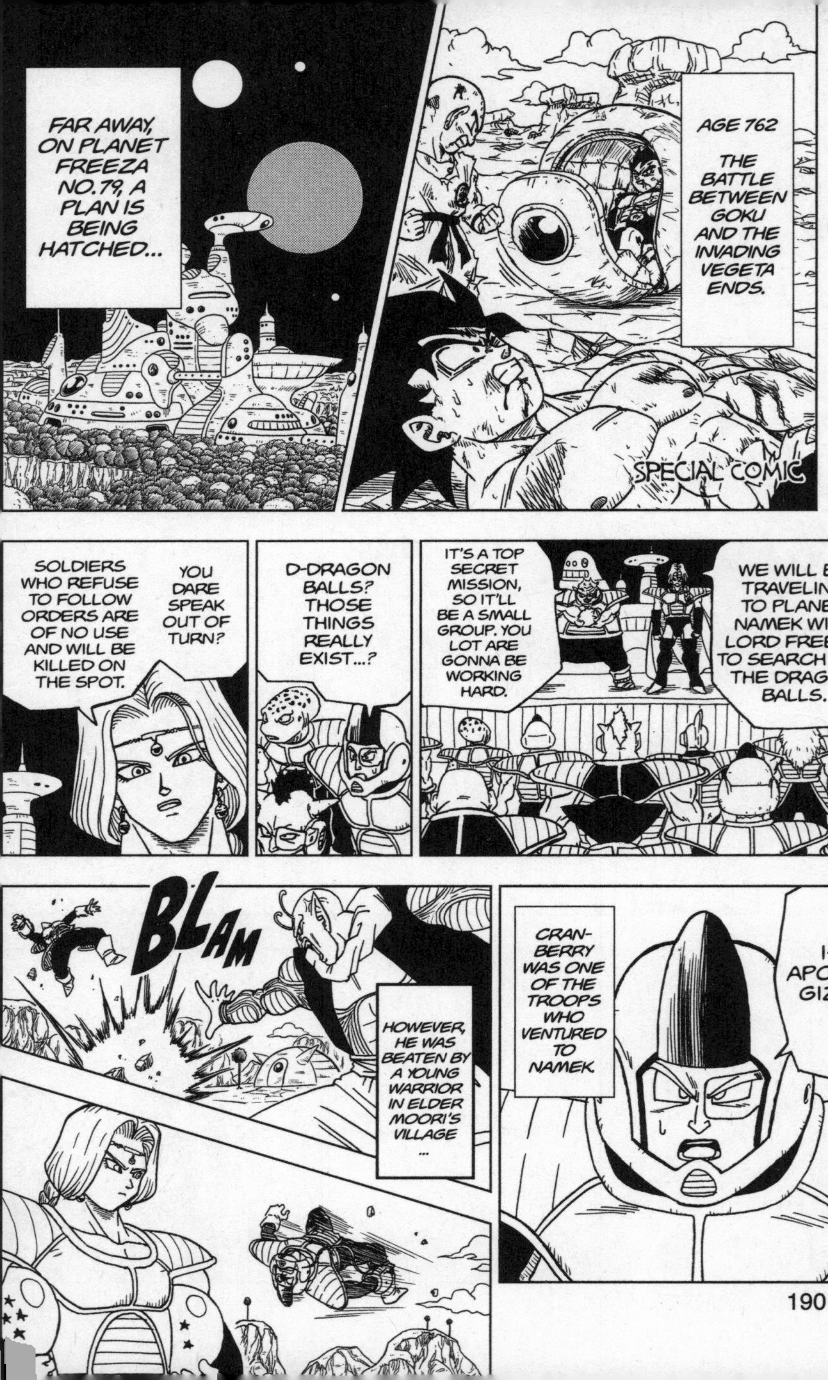
AGE 762
THE BATTLE BETWEEN GOKU AND THE INVADING VEGETA ENDS.
SPECIAL COMIC
FAR AWAY, ON PLANET FREEZA NO.79, A PLAN IS BEING HATCHED...
WE WILL BE TRAVELING TO PLANET NAMEK WITH LORD FREEZA TO SEARCH FOR THE DRAGON BALLS.
IT'S A TOP SECRET MISSION, SO IT'LL BE A SMALL GROUP. YOU LOT ARE GONNA BE WORKING HARD.
D-DRAGON BALLS? THOSE THINGS REALLY EXIST...?
YOU DARE SPEAK OUT OF TURN?
SOLDIERS WHO REFUSE TO FOLLOW ORDERS ARE OF NO USE AND WILL BE KILLED ON THE SPOT.
I-I APOLOGIZE!
CRANBERRY WAS ONE OF THE TROOPS WHO VENTURED TO NAMEK.
BLAM
HOWEVER, HE WAS BEATEN BY A YOUNG WARRIOR IN ELDER MOORI'S VILLAGE ...

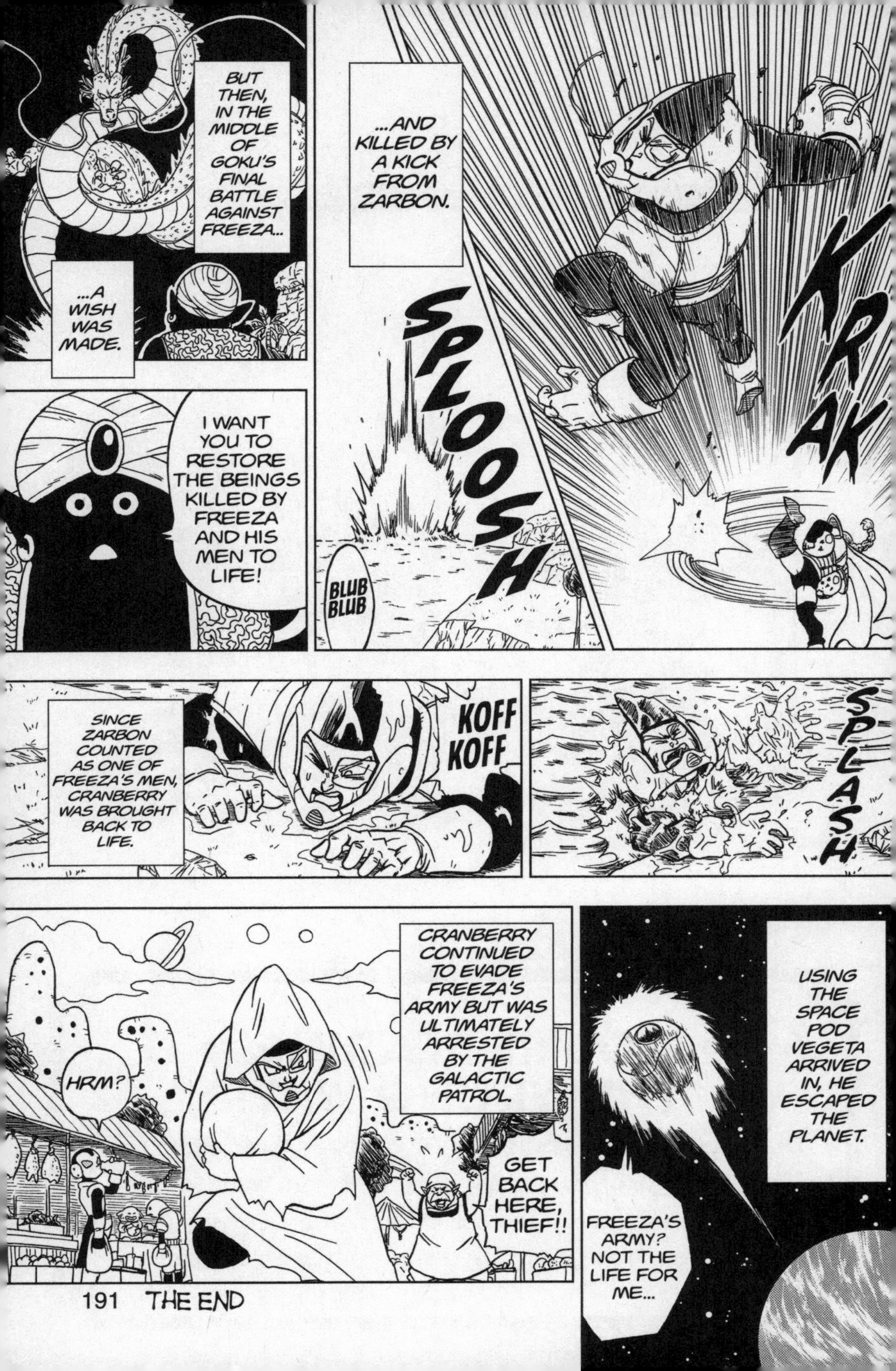
...AND KILLED BY A KICK FROM ZARBON.
KRAK
SPLOOSH
BLUB BLUB
BUT THEN, IN THE MIDDLE OF GOKU'S FINAL BATTLE AGAINST FREEZA...
...A WISH WAS MADE.
I WANT YOU TO RESTORE THE BEINGS KILLED BY FREEZA AND HIS MEN TO LIFE!
SPLASH
KOFF KOFF
SINCE ZARBON COUNTED AS ONE OF FREEZA'S MEN, CRANBERRY WAS BROUGHT BACK TO LIFE.
USING THE SPACE POD VEGETA ARRIVED IN, HE ESCAPED THE PLANET.
FREEZA'S ARMY? NOT THE LIFE FOR ME...
CRANBERRY CONTINUED TO EVADE FREEZA'S ARMY BUT WAS ULTIMATELY ARRESTED BY THE GALACTIC PATROL.
GET BACK HERE, THIEF!!
HRM?

THE END

YOU'RE READING
THE WRONG WAY!

Dragon Ball Super reads from right to left, starting in the upper-right corner. Japanese is read from right to left, meaning that action, sound effects, and word-balloon order are completely reversed from English order.